A Regional
Economic History
of Thailand

A Regional
Economic History
of Thailand

Porphant Ouyyanont

CHULALONGKORN UNIVERSITY PRESS

 YUSOF ISHAK
INSTITUTE

First published in Thai language by Chulalongkorn University Press under the title ประวัติศาสตร์เศรษฐกิจ 5 ภูมิภาคของไทย by พอพันธ์ อุยยานนท์ in 2015. Translated with the kind permission of Chulalongkorn University Press

The responsibility for facts and opinions in this publication rests exclusively with the author and his interpretation does not necessarily reflect the views or the policy of the publishers or their supporters.

ISEAS Library Cataloguing-in-Publication Data

Porphant Ouyyanont.
A Regional Economic History of Thailand.
  1. Economic history.
  2. Thailand—Economic conditions.
  HC445 P832   2017

ISBN 978-981-4786-12-6 (soft cover)
ISBN 978-981-4786-13-3 (E-book PDF)

Typeset by International Typesetters Pte Ltd
Printed in Singapore by Markono Print Media Pte Ltd

CONTENTS

PREFACE

A regional economic history of Thailand is important for a broad picture of the economic changes in the country for a number of reasons. First, most existing studies focus to a large extent on Bangkok and the economic progress of this city and the central areas. This is understandable. Bangkok itself, since its inception as Thailand's capital in 1782, has always been the most significant urban centre in Thailand — indeed, the only city of considerable size in the country until the very recent period. Thus, Bangkok has been the centre of court and government, manufacturing production, consumption, finance and foreign trade, and a host of other economic activities. This has naturally induced historians to look mainly at Bangkok for significant changes in the Thai economy, and to ignore what is happening in the rest of the country.

Again, there is a cultural dimension to Bangkok's centrality in the story of Thailand's economic development. Bangkok has traditionally been seen as the focus of social changes, and regional developments have been obscured by such an emphasis on the capital. Equally, many of the existing sources, whether records of government departments, newspapers, or descriptions by foreign travellers, all tend to pay attention primarily to Bangkok.

Of course, Bangkok is a major part of the story of Thai economic development, and in this study Bangkok is given a prime place as one of the important regions of Thailand. But we also emphasize changes in the other regions, give importance to the ways in which Bangkok had an impact on the other regions, as well as how changes in the other regions affected Bangkok.

Another reason for a regional approach to Thai development is that for much of the nineteenth and well into the twentieth century, the realities of communications and transport in Thailand meant the existence of quite separate regional economies. Certainly river transport linked many parts of the country, but away from the main river arteries, road transport was often non-existent and local specialization and regional commercial hubs were prevalent. Such regional economies often fall below the radar of studies whose focus is national rather than regional. We may reflect, for example, that until the close of the nineteenth century, links between the northern cities of Chiang Mai and Lampang were often more developed with Burma (through overland trade) than they were with Siam proper. In the South, the mining industries were linked with Penang and Singapore rather than with Bangkok.

Regional diversity in raw materials, climate and soil, topography, access to the coasts or river communications, all encourage distinct regional economies to appear. Such distinct regional economies follow to some extent the major administrative regions which form the basis of much statistical material. Thus, Bangkok, the Central Region, the North, the Northeast, and the South, all to some extent display the main economic patterns which are our concern here.

Of course, administrative divisions can only be a rough guide to economic realities, and although we shall use the main administrative divisions (inevitable since so much official material is based on these divisions), we will also note the occasions where different regional classifications seem appropriate.

Any regional economic history of Thailand must place great weight on population patterns and agricultural systems. The broad distinctions between the "sticky rice" subsisting communities in the North and Northeast, and "*suay* rice" communities of other regions are fundamental to regional economic patterns as they developed. Thus, the subsistence crops affected work systems (such as communal methods of agriculture), the existence of export crops (sticky rice was never produced as a significant commercial crop), and the regional patterns of income distribution.

Indeed, one of the main purposes of this study is to explore the origins of the regional inequalities in wealth and income that we see in the present day. It is a contention of this study that such patterns can be traced back to the nineteenth century and beyond.

Finally, a theme of this study is to explore how the various regional economies were gradually drawn into a national economy. This involves looking at the evolution of administrative structures, the development of a national transportation network, and the necessary financial and other infrastructures that enabled a national economy to develop.

Various major sources of the study come from the following:

(1) Ministry Records from Bangkok National Archives

The most important materials for a study of the book are from the National Archives in Bangkok. Of those following sources of documents were often quoted: the Ministry of Finance, the Ministry of the Capital, the Ministry of Public Works, the Ministry of Agriculture, Office of the Prime Minister, and the Ministry of Communications. There still exist thousands of documents in the Thai language written of the economic basis of Bangkok since the second half of the nineteenth century. However, it was very difficult to read them all in a limited length of time of my research. Possibly, it would take several years. Therefore, an attempt was made to limit the task to an identification of all documents necessary for writing of this book. So many of the useful unpublished data remained unexplored and need to be analysed. Of the most important sources from the Bangkok National Archives cover a number of aspects of this study.

Files from the Ministry of the Capital contain the following information: the population census, house and shop tax, the revenue which was collected by the Ministry of the Capital, the administration of Bangkok, especially the improvement of conditions of sanitation in Bangkok, report on the Chinese affairs in Bangkok and the provinces, the record of price of land in Bangkok, etc.

Files from the Ministry of Agriculture contain the following: canal construction in the Central Plain, rural labour markets in the provincial areas, such as source of labour supply in rice cultivation, the methods of payment for hired farm labourers, wage rates for unskilled and skilled labourers, etc.

Files from the British Consular Report contain information on regional production and exported trade from various *monthons*, the conditions of work and income of migrant labourers, for example, *Khamu* workers in teak industry, shipping lines called at Bangkok Port, etc.

Files from Office of the Prime Minister contain information on national highways construction programme and the inspection of ministers in the provinces.

(2) Official Publications

Besides the archival sources, important information were obtained from the Thai Government including Department of Post and Telegraph, Central Service of Statistics, Ministry of Commerce and Communications, Ministry of Interior, Ministry of Agriculture and Cooperatives, Office of National Economic and Social Development Board, and National Statistical Office.

Department of Post and Telegraph's publication on the 1883 Bangkok Postal Census (*sarabanchi*) recorded the names of the residents (household heads) and their occupations and/or economic activities, social relation of masters and their corvee labour, ethnicity, type of houses, owner or renter status, and addresses classified by roads, ditch and irrigation canals, and clustered villages and river, the departments to which household heads were attached, the title and/or rank of household heads. The source is significant for understanding the economy and society of Bangkok in the latter half of the nineteenth century.

Zimmerman's survey, *Siam: Rural Economic Survey, 1930–31*, was published by the Ministry of Commerce and Communications. The first nationwide rural economic survey provides invaluable information on various aspects of rural households including incomes, expenditures, farm costs, marketing, regional problems, etc.

Data from the Ministry of Agriculture and Cooperatives on the 1953 Thailand Economic Farm Survey and Agricultural Statistics of Thailand provide information on household income and expenditures, cash and income in kind, agricultural production, etc.

Data from Office of the National Economic and Social Development Board on Gross Domestic Product, Gross Regional and Provincial Product, and Income Distribution and Poverty Study provide information on national, regional and provincial economic development.

Data from the National Statistical Office on the Population and Housing Census, the Labor Force Survey, Business Trade and Services Survey, Industrial Census, Agricultural Census, the Household Socio-Economic Survey, *Statistical Yearbook of Thailand* provide information on the structural changes in demographic situations, and the working conditions and changing economic conditions in Bangkok and the provinces, especially in the countryside.

(3) Newspapers, Research and Theses

Last but not least, other sources were consulted, including newspapers, such as *The Bangkok Times Weekly Mail* (in the early twentieth century), research and theses, especially in the field of provincial and regional history.

ACKNOWLEDGEMENTS

I am indebted to a number of individuals and organizations for their assistance with this study. I cannot mention all who have helped, but I particularly wish to acknowledge my debt to Professor Malcolm Falkus, Professor Emeritus, University of New England, Australia. He was not only my first teacher in the field of economic history, but also supported, encouraged and directed assistance in the preparation of this book.

I also owe special thanks to Professor Chatthip Nartsupha, Professor Emeritus, Chulalongkorn University, who has provided constant encouragement in the preparation of this book. I would also like to thank Professor Kevin Hewison, Dr Francois Molle and Dr Thippawal Srijantr who provided me with data and materials.

Thanks, too, are due to Professors Pasuk Phongpaichit, Michael Herzfeld, Thongchai Winichkul, Nicola Tannenbaum, Junko Koizumi, and Fumiharu Mieno who helped with sources, comments, ideas and encouragement.

This book aims to bring together my various published and unpublished academic works, pursued for some 20 years, and such works are included here in the bibliography. In the course of writing this book, I had the opportunity to visit various academic institutes. In Japan, I undertook research at Kyoto University Graduate School of Asian and African Area Studies in June 1998–May 2000, and at Kyoto University Centre for Southeast Asian Studies (CSEAS) in December 2003–May 2004. I am most grateful to these institutions and to Professor Yoshihiro

Tsubouchi and Professor Yukio Hayashi for inviting me. Special thanks are due to Professor Kaoru Sugihara (formerly at CSEAS), head of the project on Labour-Intensive Industrialization in Southeast Asia conducted under the Core University Program Kyoto–National Research Council of Thailand (NRCT), who invited me to contribute a paper and attend workshops on a number of occasions. I am also indebted to Professor Kazuhiko Sugimaru of Fukui Prefectural University and to Professor Tadasu Tsumura of Kinki University who invited me to present papers for the international conference on Moral Economy of Africa from a comparative perspective.

In Singapore, I was invited as a Visiting Senior Fellow attached to the ISEAS – Yusof Ishak Institute (formerly the Institute of Southeast Asian Studies) between August 2014 and January 2016. Here I had the opportunity to revise my manuscript and undertake additional research. I am particularly grateful to Mr Tan Chin Tiong, Director of the Institute, and to Dr Michael Montesano and Dr Terence Chong, coordinators of the Thai Studies Programme, for inviting me.

In Thailand, I am indebted to several institutes for their assistance with research material while preparing this book: Bangkok National Archives; Bangkok National Library; Library of the Siam Society; and the Central Library of Thammasat University. The library staff were a constant source of help, and I would mention especially Khun Gritchya Rattanaprateep of the Central Library, Thammasat University.

My thanks go, too, to Sukhothai Thammathirat Open University which granted me sabbatical leave in 2011–12 during which most of this book was written.

The book was first published in 2015 in the Thai language by Chulalongkorn University Press. I am indebted to the Press' reader whose insightful comments and suggestions were of great help in revising the manuscript for publication.

The English version of the book could not be possible without the generosity of the ISEAS – Yusof Ishak Institute which gave financial assistance for the translation. I owe special thanks to Mr Tan Chin Tiong with the assistance of Dr Cassey Lee, who provided support and inspiration. I am most grateful to the helpful staff of the ISEAS

Publications Unit, especially Ng Kok Kiong, Catherine Ang Lay Kee, and Sheryl Sin Bing Peng. Last but not least, my thanks go to the staff at Chulalongkorn University Chalermprakiat Center of Translation and Interpretation who helped with this translation.

Sole responsibility for the views expressed in the book, of course, rests with the author.

Porphant Ouyyanont
Bangkok
October 2017

GLOSSARY

Amphoe	District, administrative subdivision of province
Chao Phraya	The highest rank of the Thai ancient civil nobility
Changwat or *Changwad*	Province
Chanot thidin	Land deed denoting full title
Chao	Lord, ruler
Hab	A measure of weight equal to 60 kg
Isan	Northeast-region of Thailand
Khlong	Canal
Krasuang	Ministry
Krom	Government department
Kwien	A Thai capacity measure equal to 1,000 kg
Luang	Conferred rank, higher than "Khun", below "Phra"
Monthon	Unit of provincial administration, one *monthon* contains a set of *changwats*
Mueang	City, town

Nakhonban	City administration
Nai Roi	Caravan trader or labour broker
NS5, NS3, NS3K, NS3khor	Land deed denoting occupancy rate
SPK 4-01/NK/STK/KSN	Land deed denoting right of utilization
Phra	Conferred rank, higher than "Luang", below "Phraya"
Phraya	Conferred rank, higher than "Phra", below "Chaophraya"
Picul	One picul equal to 133.5 lb or 60 kg
Rai	Unit of land; 1 *rai* = 0.16 hectare = 1,600 square metres
R&R	Rest and Recuperation
Suai	Tax, especially tax in kind
Tanon	Road
Tical	European word for Thai baht
Tumbon or *Tambon*	Group of villages, official administrative subdivision under *amphoe*
Wat	Buddhist Monastery

ABBREVIATIONS

ACMECS	=	Ayeyawady–Chao Phraya–Mekong Economic Cooperation Strategy
AEC	=	ASEAN Economic Community
BCR	=	British Consular Report
BTWM	=	*Bangkok Times Weekly Mail*
DORAS	=	Development Oriented Research on Agrarian Systems
ESCAP	=	The United Nations Economic and Social Commission for Asia and the Pacific
EWEC	=	East–West Economic Corridor
GDP	=	Gross Domestic Product
GMS	=	Greater Mekong Subregion
GPP	=	Gross Provincial Product
GRP	=	Gross Regional Product
ILO	=	International Labor Organization
kg	=	kilogram
km	=	kilometre
N.A.	=	National Archives, Bangkok

NESDB	=	Office of National Economic and Social Development Board
NSEC	=	North–South Economic Corridor
NSO	=	National Statistical Office
PRO	=	Public Record Office
TDRI	=	Thailand Development Research Institute
USOM	=	United States Operation Mission

SIAMESE MONEY AND WEIGHT

A. Money:

800 bia	= 1 fueang
2 fueang	= 1 salueng
4 salueng	= 1 baht
1 satang	= 1/100 baht
4 baht	= 1 tumlueng
20 tumlueng	= 1 chang

B. Expressed as decimals of baht:

1 bia	= .00015625
1 fueang	= .125
1 salueng	= .25
1 baht	= 1.0
1 tumlueng	= 4.0
1 chang	= 80.0

REIGNS OF THE KINGS OF THE CHAKRI DYNASTY

Rama I	Phra Phulthayotfa	1782–1809
Rama II	Phra Phutthaloetla	1809–1824
Rama III	Phra Nangklao	1824–1851
Rama IV	Mongkut	1851–1868
Rama V	Chulalongkorn	1868–1910
Rama VI	Vajiravudh	1910–1925
Rama VII	Prajadhiphok	1925–1935
Rama VIII	Ananda Mahidol	1935–1946
Rama IX	Bhumibol Adulyadej	1946–2016
Rama X	Maha Vajiralongkorn	2016–

1

INTRODUCTION

This book, *A Regional Economic History of Thailand*, presents an economic history of Bangkok, the Central Region, the North, the South, and Northeastern Regions from the signing of the Bowring Treaty in 1855 to the present. It takes a regional perspective, which is meant to provide a more accurate picture of the long-term development of the country's infrastructure, economy and society than a Bangkok-centric approach. Although Bangkok has undeniably had a wide-ranging influence on Thai society, studying the economic history of all of the kingdom's regions at the same time yields a more complete picture of the changes in the Thai economy. Four reasons support this argument.

Firstly, past studies of the long-term economic changes in Thailand have focused primarily on Bangkok, its surrounding areas and the central delta region. This is because Bangkok is the capital city and centre of government, finance, commerce, industry, consumption, and international trade. It is the most populous city and exerts tremendous influence over the social, cultural, and economic development of other regions. Furthermore, research resources, such as government documents, newspapers, and foreign records of Thailand's history, most commonly originated from the capital. Most research has, therefore, focused on Bangkok as the centre of change affecting other regions and has neglected other regions that had an influence on Bangkok.

Secondly, the social and economic fundamentals of the five regions are inherently different and are unique to each region. These fundamentals include population (for example, ethnicity); economy; agriculture, industry and service infrastructure; and geography (plains, hills, mountains, seas). It is therefore important to study each region separately. Stark social and economic differences may exist even within the same region, such as in the eastern and western parts of the Central Region, so the distinct characteristics of each should also be explained. In contrast, almost all past studies of long-term economic changes (such as over a 100-year period) have addressed a particular area in isolation instead of examining the five regions together to compare factors such as geography, including an area's distance to a river or sea, and the availability of natural resources and raw materials. All these factors affect a region's economic development. Other important factors include, for example, how "sticky rice" is planted and consumed within the family in the Northeast and parts of the North in comparison to the "paddy rice" economy in other regions; the use of labour and local traditions; productivity; and agricultural technology and income distribution.

Thirdly, the outdated transportation and shipping infrastructure of the nineteenth and early twentieth centuries, namely the lack of roads and the difficulty in river transportation, led to segregated development of a region's economy with no easy linkage. This had an impact on the local production and manufacturing expertise of each region. Up until the end of the nineteenth century, Chiang Mai and Lampang traded more with Burma (through land-based transportation) than with other regions of Thailand such as Bangkok. In the South, the ore mining industry exported more to Penang and Singapore than to Thailand's capital.

Fourthly, during the last three decades, Thailand's regional economy has changed and expanded very rapidly. The growth of cities, industries, services, and tourism, and changes in rural communities and agriculture have altered the population's way of life, types of jobs, employment, income distribution, as well as the environment and natural resources. Studying each region separately makes it possible to understand the development characteristics, economic potential, resources, problems and challenges in each region.

The four objectives of this book are to explain: (1) the factors affecting long-term economic changes in the five economic regions of Thailand, namely population and ethnicity; geography; population settlement and migration; urban growth; agricultural economy; commerce and industry; tourism and services; transportation and other economic development; (2) the merging of these five regional economies into a national economy based in Bangkok as a result of the centralization of transportation and other economic developments; (3) changes in regional economies and societies affecting the growth of Bangkok; (4) the impacts of economic development, particularly in specific areas such as border trade, income distribution, natural resources, the environment and agricultural productivity.

2

BANGKOK

Background

Ever since its designation as capital in 1782, Bangkok has prospered more than any of Thailand's other cities. It is the seat of the monarchy, the country's administrative centre, its centre of wealth, its principal port, home to the largest non-agricultural labour market, as well as the centre of internal and international trade. Bangkok is also the country's most populous city. In 1850, the population of Bangkok was estimated to be between 50,000 and 100,000[1] and since that time it has remained Thailand's primate city.[2]

Bangkok is located favourably in the fertile lower Chao Phraya River delta in the country's Central Plain, an area that has long been the country's rice bowl with transport made easy and relatively inexpensive by a network of canals connecting with the Chao Phraya.

---

[1] Terwiel (1989, p. 232).

[2] Ibid., p. 142; Sternstein (1964, pp. 300–5); Crawfurd estimated that Bangkok's population in 1822 was 50,000; Malloch's estimate was 134,090 in 1828; Tomlin's estimate was 77,300 whereas Dean's estimate was 505,000 in 1835; Malcolm's estimate for 1843 was 100,000; Neil's estimate was 35,000 whereas Bishop Pallegoix's estimate was 404,000 in 1854; Bowring's estimate for 1855 was 300,000 (cited by Skinner 1957, p. 81 and ibid., p. 226).

As the country's capital, Bangkok was the tribute collection centre from various places, as well as a centre for exports and international trade.[3] Even before the signing of the Bowring Treaty with Great Britain in 1855, Bangkok was an important port not just in Thailand but also in the Asian region, receiving goods from India, the Malay Peninsula, and elsewhere for re-exporting to China.[4] Trade was largely monopolized by the royal government, with China as the kingdom's major trading partner. Growth in both internal and international trade led to the expansion of Bangkok's economy.[5] Revenues from international trade were especially important as they constituted one of the major sources of income of the kingdom.[6]

International trade helped to open Siam to western and, through Singapore, Chinese influences. In 1820, Portugal set up a consulate in Bangkok and built a warehouse on the Thonburi side of the Chao Phraya River to store goods shipped from England. Westerners like the Portuguese were mainly employed in shipping,[7] and as the port grew, Bangkok became a major employer of Chinese immigrants involved in shipping-related activities. Increasingly, the Chinese came to play major

---

[3]   Bangkok is situated on the right bank of the Chao Phraya River, about 32 km from the river's mouth. Transportation between Bangkok, the Central Plain and the North was through the Chao Phraya, Ping, Wang, Yom, and Nan Rivers, as well as the Central Plain canal system. Connection to the East and the South was by coastal navigation whereas transportation to the Northeast was by carts and other land routes through Saraburi, and the Dong Phraya Fai Mountain (Dong Phraya Yen), to Khorat.

[4]   Crawfurd recorded in the early 1820s that "[the Bangkok port], far exceeds that of any other Asiatic Port not settled by the Europeans, with the single exception of the port of Canton in China" (Crawfurd 1987, p. 415). Apart from China, which was the most important trading partner, international trade through Bangkok included Malaya, Singapore and Penang, as well as the Cambodian Peninsula and other regions such as Batavia, Saigon, and Bombay (Crawfurd 1987, pp. 414–15). The number of junks called at Bangkok rose from 302 in 1836 to 322 in 1850. The number of Siamese junks called at Singapore was 31 during 1829–30, 28 during 1841–42, and 63 in 1850–51 (Sarasin 1977, p. 209). For more on this issue, see Crawfurd (1987); Sarasin (1977); and Nidhi (2000).

[5]   Skinner (1957).

[6]   Vella (1957).

[7]   Chulalongkorn University (1991, p. 80) and Office of the Prime Minister (1982, p. 21).

roles in various sectors of Bangkok's economy, as skilled and unskilled labour, concessionaires, tax collectors, entrepreneurs, and property owners. They acted as middlemen and merchants forging links between Bangkok and other economic centres in Asia and other parts of the globe. In time, more than half of Bangkok's population were Chinese.[8]

The Chinese were involved in trade, manufacturing, and services in Bangkok at all levels. High wages in the capital attracted large numbers of Chinese migrant workers.[9] In 1821, an ordinary labourer could earn 1.25 *satang* per day, twice Calcutta's wages, and enough to feed 18 people. Carpenters could earn as much as 50 *satang* per day.[10] Daily wages remained high during the reign of King Rama III — 4 *fueang* for an ordinary labourer.[11] Under the traditional *sakdina* feudal system, the expansion of international trade led to capital accumulation among members of the merchant class, many of them Chinese, who enjoyed close relations with high-ranking government officers. Toward the end of King Rama III's reign Chinese merchants were appointed ministers in the Port Department, Left Division (*krom tha sai*) responsible for dealing with countries to the east of the kingdom. For instance, *Phraya* Choduek Ratchasetthi (Thong Chin) was a tax farmer, sugar mill owner, and junk owner who traded with China. Tax farmers like him were very important to the Siamese aristocracy.[12]

Construction in Bangkok was handled in part by the appropriation of materials and labour under the tribute system, whereby resources were

---

[8] See Purcell (1980, p. 95); Skinner (1986, p. 80); Vella (1957); Crawfurd (1967); Terwiel (1989, p. 232) for estimations of the Chinese population in Bangkok prior to 1855.

[9] Although their wages were rather high, Chinese workers were popular among the aristocrats for various construction work, such as working on canals and moats, because they were hardworking. When comparing wages between Thai and Chinese workers, it is apparent that those paid to Chinese migrant workers were low. In 1821 an unskilled Chinese worker could earn 1.25 *satang* per day, amounting to 4.50 baht per year. On the other hand, a Thai worker had to pay an annual fee of 18 baht to avoid being recalled into military service. That is, 18 baht could hire as many as four Chinese workers in one year.

[10] Crawfurd (1915, p. 139); Thompson (1941, p. 607).

[11] Pallegoix (reprinted 2006, p. 15).

[12] Adisorn (1988, pp. 249–69).

moved from rural areas to Bangkok. During the reign of King Rama III, 83 new temples, 72 palaces for the royal family and the aristocracy, as well as 62 km of canals (including *khlong* Saen Saep-Bang Kha Nak) were built.[13] Canals required a particularly high investment of labour and materials. In 1837, the construction of Saen Saep canal, carried out chiefly with hired Chinese labour, cost 96,000 baht. Such projects would not have been possible without tributes from various regions as well as profits from international trade.[14]

BANGKOK FROM 1855–1932

The signing of the Bowring Treaty between Siam and Great Britain in 1855, followed by similar treaties signed with other powers,[15] decidedly changed Bangkok's economy. While the Bowring Treaty removed the Royal Treasury's monopoly on trade, it also led to the growth of private businesses because it created the opportunity for more free trade that, in turn, brought capital, technology, Western entrepreneurs, and Chinese migrant labour into the kingdom. Trading firms and manufacturing enterprises set up by Westerners completely transformed the capital into an outward-looking port city. Nevertheless, the importance of the Bowring Treaty should not be overemphasized since the market economy had begun to develop some time earlier, especially in the 1820s.[16] It was during this time that the Siamese economy came to rely on rice exports, particularly, after the 1860s when Siam became one of the world's leading rice exporters. Prior to 1855, Siam's international trade centred around

---

[13] Chulalongkorn University (1991, pp. 26–68); Hubbard (1977, pp. 28–37).

[14] See Koizumi (1992, pp. 276–360) and Boonrawd (1975).

[15] Major principal economic importances in the Bowring Treaty were that the Thai government must: (1) abolish all monopoly and trade constraints; (2) collect no more than 3 per cent of the value of imports; (3) grant the British the rights to trade and live in Bangkok, and if they would ever be involved in cases or conflicts with a Thai citizen, the Thai government must grant extraterritoriality to the British without having to stand trial in a Thai court. Afterwards, the Thai government had to sign similar treaties with other powers: the United States, France, and Denmark in 1856; Portugal in 1859; the Netherlands in 1860; Germany in 1862; Sweden, Norway, Belgium, and Italy in 1869; Austria–Hungary in 1870; Japan in 1898; and Russia in 1899.

[16] Terwiel (1989, p. 236); Nidhi (2000).

forest and other natural products. In 1850, for instance, the kingdom's total exports amounted to 5.6 million baht, of which more than 50 per cent came from natural products. (Sugar accounted for about 15 per cent and pepper for another 3 per cent. Rice was not included in the list of exports for that year.[17])

Exports were essential to Bangkok's growth. More than 85 per cent of all exports and imports were handled through the Port of Bangkok. Rice accounted for 75 per cent of Siam's total exports before 1932. In the sixty years between 1860 and 1920, rice exports increased from 100,000 tonnes to 400,000 tonnes, and then surged to more than one million tonnes annually in 1925–29.[18] Apart from rice, other exports, in order of value, were: teak, tin, and rubber (after 1922). Combined, rice and teak brought in more than 90 per cent of export revenues at the Port of Bangkok. Most Thai rice exports were shipped to Singapore and Hong Kong, from where they were sent on to other countries. Teak exports increased particularly after the 1880s, when teak began to be transported to Bangkok.[19] In turn, the capital's economy experienced further growth in export and import activities such as shipping, rice milling, warehousing, saw milling, and shipping offices.

Growth of Bangkok as a Port City

The number of ships from various countries calling at the Bangkok Port rapidly increased in step with growth in international trade. British ships accounted for 50–70 per cent of all ships between 1880 and 1899.[20] After 1900, however, the number of British ships decreased, replaced largely by German ships, whose numbers continued to grow throughout

---

[17] Quoted in Ingram (1971, p. 22).
[18] Wilson (1983, pp. 212–14); Suehiro (1996, p. 26).
[19] Wilson (1983, pp. 216–17).
[20] BCR, *Bangkok* (various years); *Bangkok Calendar, Annually* (various years); *Statistical Yearbook of the Kingdom of Siam* (various years).

the early years of the First World War (1914–18). But in 1917, when the Thai government entered the war on the side of the Allies, led by Britain, German ships and other German naval assets were confiscated and became the property of the Thai government.[21] After 1917, the number of Danish, French, and Japanese ships calling at the Port of Bangkok significantly increased. Tonnage also increased correspondingly, from slightly above 100,000 tonnes in 1866 to more than 800,000 tonnes in 1924, and more than one million tonnes in 1932.[22]

Beginning in the late 1880s, steamships replaced junks and sailing ships, and in 1888, the Holt Line of Liverpool opened a shipping line between Bangkok and Singapore. This was followed by Scottish Oriental, which inaugurated a line between Bangkok, Swatow and Hong Kong.[23] Then, in 1897, the North German company Lloyd opened shipping lines between Bangkok and other countries, making British ships less competitive, and by 1914, German vessels accounted for more than half the total number of ships berthed at the Bangkok Port. But after the First World War, Germany's dominance ended, and British shipping lines returned to the forefront. British firms Straits Steamship (Singapore) and China Navigation took control of not only the shipping lines previously run by Lloyd, but also the German company's private docks in Bangkok.

In the years after the conclusion of the First World War, Japanese shipping companies became increasingly prominent at the Bangkok Port. The three Japanese shipping lines plying nearby seas were: (1) Osaka Shosen Kaisha, servicing Java–Singapore–Bangkok as well as Formosa–Hong Kong–Bangkok–Singapore, (2) Yamashita Kaisen Kaisha servicing Hong Kong–Singapore–Bangkok, and (3) Mitsubishi Kaisha servicing Bangkok–Singapore and Bangkok–Hong Kong.[24] A report from the British Consul stated:

---

[21] Photjana (1980, p. 117).

[22] BCR, *Bangkok* (various years) and *Statistical Yearbook of the Kingdom of Siam* (various years).

[23] Swatow was the gathering point for Chinese migrant workers travelling to Thailand.

[24] BCR, *Bangkok* (1919).

At the beginning of 1919 competition among shipping lines at the Bangkok Port intensified especially when the Japanese lines entered the business. The increased numbers of ships at the Bangkok Port exceeded the amount of rice for exports, leading to lower shipping costs due to competition from the Japanese lines.[25]

Since shipping between Bangkok and other countries was controlled by foreigners,[26] both Thai and Chinese businessmen were subjected to unfavourable freight rates set by Westerners that lessened Siam's foreign currency revenue. Moreover, the colonial power, i.e France, repeatedly dispatched gunboats in 1893 (or called "Paknam" incident) to lay siege to the mouth of the Chao Phraya River, further antagonizing local merchants and administrators. Therefore, in the last decade of the nineteenth century, both the government and the private sector began to lay the ground work for Siam's own shipping business.[27]

In 1909, the first Thai private shipping line called The Chino Siam Steam Navigation Co. Ltd. (*borisat rua maelu chin siam thai chamkat*) was established. Owned and operated by a group of Chinese and Thai businessmen with a registered capital of three million baht, the Company provided cargo and passenger services between Bangkok, Singapore, Hong Kong and China, on six ships, with orders for several more to be constructed in Britain and Japan. It remained in business for four years before it, too, was forced to terminate its operations.[28]

---

[25] *Report on the Commercial Situation in Siam in 1919.*

[26] Although shipping lines in Siam had long been in operation, most of them were small with only domestic passenger service. "Chao Phraya" was the first Siamese mail boat that carried passengers, cargo, and mail with regular services between Bangkok and Singapore. This iron boat was built in England and bought in 1858 by *Phra Phasi Sombat Boribun* (*chao sua* Yim). The second and third steamboats servicing Bangkok and Singapore were "Kala Hom" and "Bangkok" bought in 1867 and 1869, respectively (see details in Chai 1979, pp. 306–12).

[27] See Photjana (1980).

[28] N.A. M. of Foreign Affairs 46, no. 3/3 (1908); Suehiro (1996, pp. 55–56). In fact, in 1908 it was the first effort at forming joint ventures with foreign companies: with the Danish through the Siam Steam Navigation Company (*borisat rua thun thai chamkat*) (Suehiro 1996, p. 55). However, this shipping line could not be called a true Thai shipping line.

In 1918, the Thai government established The Siamese Steamship Co. Ltd. (*borisat panit navi sayam thun chamkat*) with registered capital totalling one million baht, 50 per cent of which came from the Privy Purse and the Royal Thai Navy and an additional 26 per cent from the Chotikapuk family, a prominent Chinese clan.[29] The Siamese Steamship owned 21 ships, some of which had been German but were confiscated after the War. The business proved immediately profitable, with almost half a million baht in revenue in the first year. But over the next six years, the Company sustained heavy losses totalling 2.2 million baht due to the declining rice trade and increasing costs,[29] and in 1926, the Company shut down with all debts paid.[30]

Expansion of international trade led to the construction of several canals linking Bangkok and the Central Plain. More than 15 canals were dug around Ayutthaya, Chachoengsao, and areas west of Bangkok which were the major rice growing areas for exports from Bangkok. Among the new canals were *khlongs* Maha Sawat (1861–65), Nakhon Nueang Khet (1876), and Prawet Burirom (1878).[31] As a result, Bangkok spread increasingly away from the centre. The canals proved to be invaluable to the export of rice. Up to the Second World War, more than 80 per cent of all rice was transported via canals and the Chao Phraya River.[32] The rest was transported by rail. The river, canals, and the city's role as an international port, which spurred

---

[29] N.A. Royal Secretariats 20/22 (1917–26); Suehiro (1996, pp. 55–56). W.J.F. Williamson, the advisor to the Ministry of Finance, argued that the reasons for deficits were: (1) the motor was not commercially suitable, only two boats were used for transporting Chinese workers; (2) the boats used too much fuel; (3) a lot of money was wasted on repairs due to the dilapidated condition of the boats; (4) difficulties in linking cargo shipping to domestic trade (N.A. Royal Secretariats 20/22 (1917–26)).

[30] Photchana cited by Suehiro (1996, p. 56).

[31] N.A. R.5. M. of Agriculture (Department of Canal) 34/791 (1910).

[32] N.A. R.7. M. of Commerce 8.1 (1929). In 1929, the Ministry of Commerce recorded that 786,901 *kwien* of rice arrived in Bangkok by water as compared to 121,656 *kwien* by rail (N.A. R.7. M. of Commerce 8.1 (1929)). Even in the 1930s, despite the existence of a railway network amounting to some 6,400 km, more than 80 per cent of exported rice was carried by water from the interior to the rice mills.

construction of company headquarters, warehouses, private piers, rice mills, saw mills, and various consulates along the banks of the Chao Phraya and other major waterways, all contributed to the physical and economic changes occurring in Bangkok.[33]

Bangkok was transformed into a modern business hub, home to western communities comprising businessmen, merchants, consular officials, and various other activities. Although these western communities were small, they were very influential. For instance, the construction of the outer Charoen Krung Road was the result of a European request.[34] Western communities also spurred the development of a public transportation system with, for example, the opening of tram services in Bangkok in 1888, built and operated by the Danes. Later, in 1893, British and Danish merchants collaborated in establishing a private railway to carry passengers between Bangkok and Pak Nam. Indeed, Westerners were instrumental in the administration of the Harbour Department as well as the implementation of improved customs procedures to facilitate the country's advancement. These included better port operations, navigation, naval signage, and the enactment of new shipping laws. John Bush, a British captain, oversaw harbour operations to facilitate merchant ships at the Bangkok Port. He took up his first position as *"chao tha"* (harbour master) in 1859, and after a long career with the Harbour Department, he was granted the royal title *Phraya* Visut Sakhondit.[35] Bush was also the managing director and major shareholder of the Bangkok Dock Company from 1865–99. Bangkok today still has a *soi* Captain Bush, named in his honour.[36]

In the years between 1857 and 1866, Bangkok expanded outside the city walls partly due to the construction of *khlong* Phadung Krung Kasem

---

[33] Sternstein (1982, p. 25).
[34] *Royal Chronicle, King Rama IV*, vol. 2 (1961, pp. 6–7).
[35] Marine Department (1966, pp. 19–20).
[36] *Soi* Captain Bush connects Charoen Krung Road with the Chao Phraya River near the Oriental Hotel. The management of the port under Captain Bush enhanced the role of Bangkok Port in international trade through changes in shipping legislation and the improvement of the port in many ways.

in 1851. At the same time, new businesses and residences were built along both banks of the Chao Phraya. Undoubtedly road construction further contributed to the capital's economic expansion. Bangkok, which had begun life as a "water-based city", became decidedly land-based. Charoen Krung Road, constructed between 1861 and 1863, stimulated the growth of Chinatown (the area around Sampeng, Yaowarat and Bang Rak), which became the centre for retail and wholesale trade, banks, warehouses, and leading hotels until the Second World War.

Between 1890 and 1919, as many as 130 roads were constructed. Major roads built in the 1890s included Lanluang, Samsen, Sukhothai, and eighteen roads in *amphoe* Sampeng. Roads changed settlement patterns away from the riverside and large and small canals, to roadside communities characterized by shophouses, in particular. Trade and investment flourished in tandem with the development of land transportation, both roads and rails (trams and railways).[37] Road construction also stimulated investment in shophouses for rent by the Privy Purse Bureau (*krom phrakhlang khangthi*), an agency in charge of the royal assets and property, officially established as an independent department within the Ministry of Finance (*krasuang phra khlang maha sombat*) in 1890. The Privy Purse was allocated a budget equivalent to 15 per cent of total government revenue, its revenue derived mainly from land and shophouse rents as well as investments in various businesses.[38]

---

[37] Porphant (1999*a*, pp. 463–66).

[38] Ibid., p. 446. The PPB was formally established as an independent department within the Ministry of Finance (*phraklang*) in 1890. Its predecessor was established during the reign of King Rama II under the name *ngoen khang-thi,* which was changed to *phara khlang khang-thi* in the following reign. This organization was the king's personal institution. He was able to allocate money to his own interests. During the reign of King Rama IV, 5 per cent of the total state revenue, around 2,000 *chang* (160,000 baht), was regularly allocated to the PPB, together with the extra revenue from the land tax, another 2,000 *chang* (160,000 baht) (Thaweesilp 1985, pp. 124–28). In 1890, 15 per cent of the total revenue was allocated to the PPB (N.A. R.5. M. of Finance 9.1-1 (1892)).

Land prices also rose as a result of road construction. The Privy Purse Bureau had accumulated large tracts of land, especially in the inner city, through trading, private mortgaging for Chinese merchants and noblemen, and ownership of public land or land belonging to various ministries and vacant palaces. In 1902, the Privy Purse controlled as much as 6,458 *rai* of prime commercial real estate, including 1,831 *rai* in Sampeng, 458 *rai* in Bang Rak, 4,083 *rai* in Dusit, and 86 *rai* within the city walls — around *wat* Chana Songkhram, the Grand Palace, Samran Rat, and Phahurat.[39] By 1907, the Department was the largest landowner in the country, with 22.2 per cent of the land in the capital.[40] When land prices increased, real estate became the major source of income for the Privy Purse and members of the royal family involved in this business, and thus affected capital accumulation among the aristocracy. The Department built hundreds of shophouses and many fresh markets for rent along major thoroughfares, such as Charoen Krung, Chakkrawat, Yaowarat, Ratchawong, Hua Lum Phong, Si Phraya, Samsen, Sang Hi Nok, Duang Duean Nok, and Dao Chang. Shophouses served as accommodation as well as offices, companies, and stores.[41]

A note from the British Consul dated 1892 indicates that many new buildings were springing up each year:

A considerable amount of building has been going on during the year in Bangkok. Most of this has been done by the Government [meaning the PPB], which has seen the advantage of substituting on Government land in and around the city substantial houses, bringing in good rents, for the wretched wooden shanties which used to encumber valuable property. Three large blocks of two-storied houses, suitable for shops in the form of squares, with the fourth side open to the river, have been constructed at a cost of over 40,000*l*. The houses, built substantially of brick, each measure 20 feet by 30 feet, and number all together 209 ... In the large enclosures of these blocks it is intended to erect palaces for some of the King's children. This is entirely in accordance with the Siamese ideas. The houses of the upper classes are generally hemmed

---

[39] N.A. R.5 M. of Agriculture 6/6153 (1913).
[40] Tasaka (2003, chapter 7).
[41] Chollada (1986); Sayomporn (1983); Porphant (1999*a*; 2008).

in by a collection of more or less inferior looking buildings, occupied by dependents. A row of better class buildings, suitable for European stores and dwellings, has been built on the principal city road, under the supervision of the Public Works Department ... The new military college was completed during the year. It is a handsome building, measuring 360 feet by 40 feet, partly two and partly three-storied. The total cost was 5,000*l* ... Sundry rows of inferior shop buildings have also been built by the Government, as well as many detached villas on newly-opened roads intended for the residence of Europeans. Such houses are much needed in Bangkok, as the house accommodation has always been limited, of very inferior description, and ridiculously expensive.[42]

Income from renting prime shophouses in Bangkok reflected the expansion of the market. Shophouse rents varied depending on location. Those along Ratchawong Road rented for 10 baht a month whereas shops at intersections rented for 40–60 baht a month. Monthly rent for buildings on Si Phraya Road, intended for European stores, started at 100 baht. When comparing the investment cost and the rent, it was clear that the Privy Purse Bureau would break even in approximately ten years' time. While investing in shophouses was no doubt a long-term source of rental income, it could not be said that it was a high-yielding investment, considering costs.[43]

In short, road construction and investment by the Privy Purse in shophouses and fresh markets were among the processes driving Bangkok's physical changes and growth. Bangkok was evolving into a residential, commercial, and industrial city covering several districts, namely Sampeng, Dusit, Sa Phatum, Bang Rak, Bang Kholaem, Bang Lamphu Lang, Bangkok Noi, Bangkok Yai, and parts of Bangsue west of *khlong* Prem Prachakon.[44] High density commercial and residential areas could be found where large numbers of Chinese lived: Phra Nakhon, Samphanthawong, Bang Rak, and Pom Prap districts.[45] Population density in *amphoe* Phra Nakhon was 37.6 persons per *rai*, 93.7 persons

---

[42] BCR, *Bangkok* (1892).
[43] Tasaka (2003).
[44] N.A. R.5. M. of the Capital 4.1 (1906–2453).
[45] N.A. M. of Finance 0301.1.1/13 (1931).

in Samphanthawong, 25.9 persons in Bang Rak, and 53.4 persons in Pom Prap. These districts had only a small portion of agricultural land.[46]

Centralization also affected Bangkok's growth. Throughout much of the latter part of the nineteenth century, colonialism was a real threat to Siamese sovereignty. Several other Asian countries had already become colonies of either Great Britain or France. King Chulalongkorn (Rama V) oversaw administrative changes and reforms to finance, education, and the governmental system intended to thwart this threat. After the 1870s, the King tightened his grip on power. Prior to the establishment of Revenue Office (*hor ratsadakon*) in 1873, tax collection, for instance, depended on tax farmers and was dispersed among various government agencies. Revenue Office centralized and unified tax collection, thus enabling the government to have better control over the country's finances.[47] In the 1870s, a governor was appointed to administer affairs in *mueang* Chiang Mai, a move which further consolidated the capital's administrative power [48] and which was extended to other regions such as Phuket, Phra Tabong, and Nong Khai in the years that followed.[49] The 1890s saw additional reforms of the local and regional governments controlled from Bangkok, under the leadership of Prince Damrong (*Khrom Phraya* Damrong Rachanubhap). The construction of railroads linking Bangkok with other regions after 1900 gave additional momentum to the growing economic and political centralization taking place.[50]

This centralization also strengthened and empowered the monarchy. Financial reform meant more control and resources at the King's disposal than ever before. Increased revenues translated into greater investment in infrastructure projects, especially in and around Bangkok. The construction of roads, large canals linking the capital and the Central Plain, as well as railways linking Bangkok and other regions all accelerated the process of centralization.

---

[46] Calculated from Ibid.

[47] Chaiyan (1994, p. 85).

[48] Tej (1977, pp. 61–63).

[49] See Tej (1977); Grabowsky, ed. (1995).

[50] See Tej (1977) for issues concerning government and bureaucratic system reform.

Population and Labour

After 1855, Bangkok's population increased rapidly, from roughly 100,000 to 365,000 by 1913 (see Table 2.1). This high rate of increase was due mainly to an influx of Chinese migrant labour. Meanwhile, no other city in the country experienced a comparable increase in population. The difference between the number of people in Bangkok and Chiang Mai, the second largest city, increased from 11 times in 1900 to 12 times in 1910, 13 times in 1920, and 14 times in 1930.[51] Bangkok had thus become the primate city with escalating influence over the Thai economy.

TABLE 2.1
Bangkok's Population, 1855–1937

Year	Population	Annual Average Rate of Increase (%)
1855	100,000	–
1883	169,300	1.90
1913	365,492	2.60
1929	702,544	3.92
1937	890,453	3.44

Source: N.A. R.6. M. of the Capital 27/3 (1909–14); N.A. M. of Finance 0301.1.1/13 (1931); Terwiel (1989, p. 223); Sternstein (1982, p. 32); Wilson (1983, p. 32), cited by Porphant (1997, p. 248).

Chinese Population in Bangkok

During this time, the Chinese comprised the majority of Bangkok's population, at more than 50 per cent.[52] The 1880s marked the beginning

---

[51] Sternstein (1982, p. 78).

[52] Skinner (1957, p. 81); N.A. M. of the Capital 30/9 (1922–23). In practice, it is rather difficult to state the exact number of Chinese in Bangkok because of the definition of "Chinese". Chinese children born in Siam would be classified as either "Chinese" or "Siamese". Moreover, there were no definite statistics of Chinese emigrants and immigrants. Above all, the Chinese were an ethnic group that had been well assimilated with the Thais. Prior to 1932, the Siamese State did not classify the Chinese as foreigners like other Asians or Westerners. A Chinese had almost the same rights as a Siamese. For more on migrant Chinese statistics, see Skinner (1957).

of not just continued growth but greater economic diversity. Statistics from the 1883 Bangkok Postal Census (*sarabanchi*)[53] make clear that Bangkok was already a centre of trade and the market economy. More than 28 per cent of the heads of households in the city were engaged in the non-agricultural sector including "trade and manufacturing", "marketing", and "professional". Only 20 per cent were engaged in the agricultural sector, and 9 per cent were government officials. If one looks at the specific occupations of the heads of households in Bangkok (excluding Thon Buri, which remained a largely agricultural-rural area), the proportion in the non-agricultural sector was as high as 60 per cent.[54]

---

[53] The 1883 Bangkok Postal Census (*sarabanchi*) was published by the Department of Post and Telegraph to expedite the postal service. To facilitate the mail service, a register of the population was needed. The Census is significant for understanding the economy and society of Bangkok in the latter half of the nineteenth century. It recorded the names of the residents (household heads) and their occupations and/or economic activities, social relation of masters and their corvee labour, ethnicity, type of houses, owner or renter status, payment of Chinese head tax, and addresses classified by roads, irrigation canals, and clustered villages and rivers, the departments to which household heads were attached, the title and/or rank of household heads. The Postal Census also provides information on the public infrastructure in Bangkok, including bridges, forts, city walls and gates, hospitals, hotels, schools, canals, rivers, theaters, temples, churches, rice mills, rice warehouses, fresh food markets, and so on. The Census was divided into four volumes, with varying titles. Broadly speaking, volumes 2, 3 and 4 divide the area not according to location but to the type of communication artery. Thus, volume 2 records the residences along "roads and lanes" (*tanon lae trok*). This classification covered many residences in the central districts, especially along roads such as Charoen Krung, Bamrung Mueang, and Fueang Nakhon. Volume 3 records residences in "clustered villages along rivers" (literally clustered villages and rivers, *ban mu lae lamnam*). Volume 4 covers residences along "irrigation canals" (*ku lae klong lumpradong*). These were usually very small and scattered groups. It should be remembered that Bangkok had spread steadily through the extension of such canals since the beginning of the nineteenth century, with the irrigation canals usually leading from the larger canals. As far as the Census is concerned the areas covered in volume 4 were then rural areas, especially on the Thonburi side of the Chao Praya River (Department of Post and Telegraph 1883*a*, 1883*b*, 1883*c*).

[54] Porphant and Tsubouchi (2001, pp. 390–92).

In 1883 an ethnic division of labour was the main employment characteristic in Bangkok, as recorded in the Bangkok Postal Census of households surveyed. The economic sector, especially "commerce and manufacturing", was dominated by the Chinese, who outnumbered the Thais. As many as 4,242 Chinese migrants owned non-agricultural businesses in Bangkok, representing 53.1 per cent of all Chinese, compared to only 1,675 Thais, or 7.9 per cent of all Thais (see Table 2.2).

The growth of business and industry provided employment opportunities for other ethnic groups: specifically, 174 Indians and Malays, 14 Westerners, eight Burmese, three Vietnamese, and three Laotians operated businesses in the non-agricultural sector. In the "fresh market" sector of the economy, both Thais and Chinese had equally important roles. One in five of Chinese heads of households (about 1,612 persons) were involved in this sector, compared to 6.8 per cent of Thais (about 1,441 persons), followed by Indian and Malay heads of households (see Table 2.2).

More Thais (2,746 persons) were government officials (including corvée service), compared to 92 foreigners (Chinese, Westerners, Indians, and a very small number of other Southeast Asians). Furthermore, approximately 30 per cent of all Thais were engaged in the agricultural sector compared to 13.8 per cent or 1,100 Chinese. Small numbers of Indians, Malays, and Burmese were also involved in agriculture (see Table 2.2).

The growing number of Chinese spurred the construction of dwellings in Bangkok, especially shophouses or row houses (*hong taew*). At more than 80 per cent, the Chinese were the largest group of tenants in the city, both for accommodation and small shops for various businesses. The Thais were second, followed by Indians and Malays (see Table 2.3).

As demand for rental property grew, especially for row houses that could be used both as a residence and a place of business, construction of row houses or shophouses was a major investment among noblemen, the Privy Purse, and rich citizens. The Chinese were the main factor in this aspect of Bangkok's commercial development. Shophouse construction was closely linked to land investment or, in particular, land speculation by the Privy Purse and the aristocracy. Shophouses were usually built along main thoroughfares such as Charoen Krung, Bamrung Mueang,

TABLE 2.2

Occupations of Heads of Households in Bangkok (including Thon Buri) by Ethnic Group, 1883

	Thai	Chinese	Westerner	Indian and Malay	Lao	Burmese	Vietnamese	Mon	Total
Agriculture (e.g. rice farmers)	6,281 (29.5)	1,100 (13.8)	1 (<1)	94 (15.1)	0 (–)	63 (80.8)	3 (9.4)	2 (16.7)	7,544 (24.9)
Fresh market[1]	1,441 (6.8)	1,612 (20.2)	4 (2.7)	55 (8.8)	0 (–)	0 (–)	4 (12.5)	7 (58.3)	3,123 (10.3)
Professionals[2]	612 (2.9)	269 (3.4)	23 (15.9)	30 (4.8)	0 (–)	1 (1.3)	0 (–)	1 (8.3)	936 (3.1)
Employees and workers[3]	517 (2.4)	363 (4.5)	30 (20.7)	38 (6.1)	0 (–)	1 (1.3)	0 (–)	1 (8.3)	950 (3.1)
Commerce and manufacturing[4]	1,675 (7.9)	2,630 (32.9)	14 (9.6)	174 (27.9)	3 (27.3)	8 (10.2)	3 (9.4)	0 (–)	4,507 (14.9)
Government officials and other state employees	2,746 (12.9)	62 (<1)	5 (3.4)	4 (<1)	1 (9.1)	1 (1.3)	19 (59.4)	0 (–)	2,838 (9.4)
Corvée service	4,245 (19.9)	0 (–)	0 (–)	9 (1.4)	1 (9.1)	0 (–)	0 (–)	0 (–)	4,255 (14.1)
Others (e.g. retired government officials, servants)	329 (1.5)	30 (<1)	1 (<1)	7 (1.1)	4 (36.4)	0 (–)	0 (–)	0 (–)	371 (1.2)
Unknown	3,458 (16.2)	1,909 (23.9)	67 (46.2)	213 (34.1)	2 (18.2)	4 (5.1)	3 (9.4)	1 (8.3)	5,657 (18.7)

Note: Numbers in brackets are percentages.

[1] E.g. food, dessert, seafood, fruits, spices, meats, and grocery dealers

[2] E.g. physicians and midwives, tax farmers, engineers, and skilled workers

[3] E.g. heads of coolies, boat builders and shipping, accountants and clerks, guards, rice mill and saw mill workers

[4] E.g. trading and manufacturing involving rice milling, saw milling, textiles, liquor, opium and lottery, rice, brothel owners, pawnshop owners, gamblers, and managers

Source: Bangkok Postal Census, vols. 2–4 referred to by Porphant and Tsubouchi (2001, p. 391).

TABLE 2.3
Residence Status of Heads of Households in Bangkok by Ethnic Group, 1883

Status	Thai	Chinese	Westerner	Indian and Malay	Lao	Burmese	Vietnamese	Mon	Total
Owner	20,019	4,431	81	597	9	74	36	6	25,253
Tenant	941	3,714	26	120	0	1	1	0	4,803
Dependent	567	197	5	25	0	0	0	0	794
Unspecified	515	170	26	16	0	1	1	2	731
Total	22,042	8,512	138	758	9	76	38	8	31,581

Source: Porphant and Tsubouchi (2001, p. 395).

Fueang Nakhon, roads within the city walls, and roads around commercial centres like Sampeng.[55] Some 226 shophouses could be found along Bamrung Mueang Road, 380 along Charoen Krung, and 186 along Fueang Nakhon.[56] These constituted Bangkok's central business district, which was dominated by the Chinese who rented these shophouses.

Information from the 1883 Bangkok Postal Census clearly shows the chief characteristics of dwellings across Bangkok, especially those of shophouses or row houses, which were built of brick and/or wood and occupied mostly by the Chinese. Chinese households living in all types of shophouses (brick and wood) (449 persons) outnumbered Thai (133 persons). There were 326 Chinese and 292 Thai households living in shophouses owned by the Privy Purse while 876 Chinese and 693 Thai households resided in shophouses owned by private landlords. Settlement along major thoroughfares together with the increasing number of shophouses both inside and outside the city walls were, therefore, the catalyst for rapid economic growth and changes in Bangkok's physical composition from a "water-based city" to a "land-based one", which, in turn, contributed to further business expansion.[57]

The influx of Chinese migrant labour into Bangkok continued to grow. The number of Chinese in-migrants at the Bangkok Port was around 16,000 a year in the 1880s, 25,000 in the 1890s, 60,000 between 1900 and 1920, and over 100,000 a year in the 1920s.[58] Perhaps not surprisingly, nationalistic feelings against the economic dominance of the Chinese began to emerge around 1910. The Thai government itself

---

[55] See the position and location of shophouses in the Bangkok Postal Census, vols. 2–4 (Department of Post and Telegraph 1883a, 1883b, 1883c). Row houses, both brick and wooden ones, were a unique characteristic of Chinese housing for a long time. They were present not only in Bangkok but also in other regions as well as in parts of Southeast Asia. For instance, in the thirteenth century row houses were living quarters and retail stores of Chinese merchants in Angkor Wat, Kingdom of Cambodia.

[56] Bangkok Postal Census, vol. 2 (1883).

[57] Porphant and Tsubouchi (2000b, p. 11).

[58] Skinner (1957, p. 173). Prior to 1910, most Chinese migrant workers were young men rather than family migrants. These young men would accumulate enough wealth from working in Bangkok and return to their home town in China. After 1910, Chinese women began to migrate with their husbands. There was a strong tendency for the Chinese migrants and their families to settle down in Thailand permanently.

expressed concern over the role of the Chinese in the nation's economy. The Chinese migrant influx was not only motivated by a desire to seek economic opportunity but also facilitated by the availability of fast, efficient, and inexpensive international shipping lines. In 1897, passage between Swatow and Bangkok cost only $1.50 Mexican, thus further accelerating migration from China to Thailand.

The Chinese were involved in all levels of commercial life in Bangkok, from the lowest to the highest: they were rice mill owners, merchants, exporters, and bankers, as well as unskilled and skilled labourers. In 1900, each rice mill in Bangkok hired about 100–200 Chinese workers.[59] The total employment in the mills on the eve of the First World War, according to one estimate, was about 10,000. This increased to 14,400 in 1920, to over 16,000 in the mid-1920s, fell to 14,200 in 1930, and then increased again to 16,400 in 1937.[60] The Chinese were intermediaries in trade linking Bangkok to foreign markets and the Thai countryside. Western businesses located in Bangkok all depended on Chinese compradors. In 1920, there were 39 export firms in Bangkok: 18 were British or British–Indian operated, nine were Siamese, three Danish, two French, and one each Norwegian, Swiss, Italian, American, Indian, Belgian, and Japanese.[61] Manufactured goods were imported from Europe by a Chinese wholesale network and sold to provincial customers.

MINISTRY OF THE CAPITAL AND THE ADMINISTRATION OF BANGKOK, 1892–1922

The increasing power of the monarch coupled with Bangkok's economic growth had made Bangkok the governmental and economic centre of the nation. In 1892, the Ministry of the Capital (*krasuang nakhonban*) was established to oversee Bangkok's autonomous administration and to accommodate population growth after the 1880s. Economic and commercial changes — the shift from a water-based city to a land-based one — increased Bangkok's income and taxes, while political motivations

---

[59] N.A. R.6. M. of the Capital 31.3/48 (1919).
[60] Sompop (1989, p. 167).
[61] *Importers and Exporters Directory for Siam* (1920, pp. 10–17).

— the desire to portray Bangkok as a modern capital and financial hub —
prompted the need to reform the city's administration. The establishment
of the Ministry of the Capital, with cooperation from the Privy Purse,
was a response to the state's and the monarchy's interests.

In fact, the new Ministry helped to expand the economic role of
the Privy Purse. Not only could the Privy Purse garner its own income
and sizable state budget, it also worked very closely with the Ministry
on issues relating to trade, transfer of land ownership, and investment
in assets such as roads and shophouses, as well as other developments
in Bangkok.[62] The growth of Bangkok, therefore, was closely linked to
the monarchy through the investments of the Privy Purse and the work
of the Ministry of the Capital. The powers and responsibilities of the
Ministry were also crucial to the economic growth of the Privy Purse
and Bangkok. The Ministry of the Capital was more of an adviser to
the King than an independent local government body, like those which
had existed in London and other cities in Europe in earlier times. Siam
at the time was an absolute monarchy, and because the Ministry of the
Capital was essential to the direction of changes taking place in Bangkok
in particular and in Siam as a whole, the close connection between the
Bangkok administration and the monarchy's interests greatly affected
Bangkok's economic, physical and other types of development.

Prior to 1892, Bangkok's administration was subject to the City
Traditional Law (*kot mai charit nakhonban*), which was enforced by
an appointed City Committee (*committee nakhonban*) in charge of law
and order and the court of justice. But in 1892, the City Committee
was abolished, and the Ministry of the Capital oversaw Bangkok's
administrative affairs through six *krom* (departments): *amphoe, mueang,
sukha phiban, phon tra wen, sanphakon nai,* and *chao tha* (see
Table 2.4).

---

[62] See Sayomporn (1983); Thaweesilp (1985); Chollada (1986).

TABLE 2.4
Responsibilities of the Ministry of the Capital, 1892–1922

Department	Responsibility
Krom Amphoe (district)	Administration of eight inner city districts (amphoe) and eight outer districts, population census, immigrant-emigrant statistics, vital statistics, vehicle registration, etc.
Krom Sukha Phiban (sanitation)	Road construction, repair and maintenance; canal maintenance; hospital and abattoir management; garbage collection; markets; street lighting, etc.
Krom Chao Tha (harbour)	Boat registration, verification of immigrants entering the country by boat, lighthouses, hospitals, etc.
Krom Sanphakon Nai (internal revenue)	Tax collection, tax tolls (phuk phi), boathouse and building tax collection, vehicle fees for horse-drawn wagons and trams, fines, etc.
Krom Phon Trawen (police)	Peacekeeping, crime prevention and suppression, overseeing pawnshops, etc.
Hua Mueang Monthon Krung Thep	Administration of mueang Nonthaburi, mueang Samut Prakan, mueang Nakhon Khuean Khan (Phra Pradaeng), mueang Pathum Thani, mueang Thanyaburi, mueang Min Buri

Source: *Royal Thai Government Gazette*, vol. 23 (1907, pp. 494–500); Carter (reprinted 1988, pp. 103–26).

The scope of authority of the Ministry of the Capital was as follows:

(1) Areas within Bangkok consisted of inner and outer districts. Inner districts were Phra Nakhon, Sampeng, Bang Rak, Sa Pathum, Dusit, Bangkok Noi, Bangkok Yai, and Bang Lam Phu Lang. Outer districts were Bang Kapi, Bang Sue, Bang Khen, Bang Khun Thian, Rat Burana, Taling Chan, Phasi Charoen, and Nong Khaem.

(2) Areas surrounding Bangkok consisted of Nonthaburi, Samut Prakan, Phra Pradaeng (Nakhon Khuean Khan), Pathum Thani (1892–1915), and Min Buri (1892–1922).[63] In 1922, however, the Ministry of the Capital was abolished and Bangkok's administration was transferred to the Ministry of Interior. In 1937, the Bangkok Municipality was created to oversee the capital's administrative affairs.

Under the Ministry of the Capital, densely populated areas were designated as "amphoe" (district) and/or "khet sukha phiban" (sanitary subdistrict). In 1897, the first Sanitary Law was promulgated and enacted inside the city walls. Later the law was extended to *khlong* Phadung Krung Kasem.[64] The Ministry of the Capital was in charge of sanitation, road and canal construction as well as associated problems, among other responsibilities. Its chief functions also included garbage and waste disposal, sewer installation, pipe water production, street lighting, fresh market and abattoir management, enforcement of sanitary laws, general sanitation, peacekeeping and crime prevention, and canal maintenance. The Ministry was also responsible for raising revenues and/or taxes to meet Bangkok's increasing budgetary demands.[65] Between 1892 and 1908, the Ministry's expenditures rose annually by 6–9 per cent and by 11–15 per cent for the period from 1914 to 1922.[66]

---

[63] *Royal Thai Government Gazette*, vol. 23 (1907, pp. 494–500); Carter (reprinted 1988, pp. 103–26).

[64] N.A. R.6. M. of the Capital 7.1/23 (1917–22).

[65] N.A. R.5. M. of the Capital 5.4 (2440); Carter (reprinted 1988, pp. 103–26).

[66] *Statistical Yearbook of the Kingdom of Siam (1930–1931)*. Statistics for tax collection by the Ministry of the Capital in selected years are as follows: in 1903, the Sanitation Department collected 10,000 baht from the abattoirs; in 1904, the Revenue Department collected 1.8 million baht. There were about 100,000 Chinese workers who paid tax

MANUFACTURING INDUSTRY

Free trade, established after 1855, resulted in an influx of cheap goods from industrial countries into Siam. Local manufacturing was slowly destroyed. The textile industry, for instance, could not compete with a major producer like Britain.[67] Meanwhile, Siam's rice exports continued to grow in tandem with "the great international division of labour" resulting from the Industrial Revolution and the expansion of colonialism.[68] Developing countries became the major market for manufactured goods. The growth of rice exports led to an increase in the number of rice mills — one of the important economic investments for Western merchants, Chinese traders, and tax farmers.

Rice mills were first introduced by Westerners. In 1858, the first mechanized rice mill, the American Steam Rice Mill (sometimes called *rong si chak american*), began operations on Thanon Tok. The second rice mill, the "Bangkok Company", was located opposite the first rice mill. The third rice mill was a German one, called "A. Markwald's Mill", which started business in 1864. The fourth rice mill was "Scott and Company", established in 1866. The fifth rice mill began operations in 1867.[69] Between 1858 and 1867, mechanized rice mills were operated by Westerners while the Chinese ran manual rice mills. The Chinese began to take charge of mechanized rice mills in 1870, when they ordered a rice milling machine from Britain. By 1877, the Chinese rice mills strongly competed with those owned by Westerners, resulting in decreasing revenues for the latter. In 1880, there were six Chinese rice mills, and in the years that followed, the role of the Chinese in rice milling continued to expand. As noted by the 1897 British Consular Report, "The rice business — that is buying from cultivators, the milling

---

toll in 1903. This figure rose to 101,000 in 1907, 126,000 in 1908, and 121,000 in 1909 (Carter reprinted 1988, pp. 119–20; N.A. R.5. M. of Interior 28.2/4.8 (1910)). In 1913 revenues from "kha ratchakan" (government fees) amounted to 1.67 million baht, collected from 74,786 Chinese, 52,708 Thais, 4,985 Indians, 56 Westerners, and 506 others (N.A. R.6. M. of Interior 1/25 (1913)).

[67] Chatthip and Suthy (1981, pp. 2–3).
[68] Findlay and O'Rourke (2009, pp. 365–428).
[69] Thaweesilp (1985, p. 289).

and the export — is now entirely monopolised by Chinese merchants, many of whom have command of very large capital."[70] In 1897, "Of the 26 steam rice mills in Bangkok only four are European, two British, belonging to one firm, one German, and the fourth nominally registered as French."[71] Finally, in 1924, all rice milling businesses were owned and operated by the Chinese.[72]

Investment in rice mills was considered very costly. For instance, the Markwald Mill — the largest and most modern in Bangkok at that time — was valued at 790,000 baht in 1924.[73] Rice mills in Bangkok became mechanized in the 1890s, and were electrified starting by the 1920s. Rice milling also expanded into other regions, especially those connected to the capital by river or rail. The rice mill industry, especially large mills, was dominated by the Chinese. For instance, Koo Seng, or Lee Tech Oh, who owned and leased 14 rice mills in 1920 also employed thousands of Chinese workers. The production capacity of his rice mills reached 1,360 tonnes per day. Hang Nguan Huat Seng and Wang Lee owned five mills and four mills with the production capacity of 990 tonnes per day and 600 tonnes per day, respectively.[74]

Apart from the British and Chinese, Siamese nobles and aristocrats also owned rice mills. The nobility, however, did not operate the mills themselves but usually leased them to Chinese entrepreneurs. For example, Queen Savang Vadhana leased her rice mill at *tambon wat* Ratchasingkhon for 4,000 baht per month. The mill belonging to Prince Nakhon Sawan at *tambon* Bang Phlat was also leased. More than half of the rice mills in Bangkok were owned by the Privy Purse.[75]

After 1857, ice manufacturing led by European companies like Markwald and Edward Knox, both of which built their own factories, began to replace imported ice from Singapore.[76] The business developed

---

[70] BCR, *Bangkok* (1897).
[71] Ibid.
[72] Thaweesilp (1985, p. 290).
[73] Hewison (1988, p. 392).
[74] Suehiro (1996, p. 85).
[75] Thaweesilp (1985, p. 291).
[76] Hewison (1988, p. 392).

further in 1877, when Chaloem Phinitchakkraphant set up an electric ice factory with French machinery that could supply 1,600 pounds of ice daily. In 1889, Siamese nobles and European entrepreneurs established a joint ice-making firm under the name "Bangkok Manufacturing Company" with a registered capital of 80,000 baht.[77] The Company increased its capital and expanded the factory, with investment from the Setabutra family (led by Lert Setabutra) and Hun Kim Huat (head of the Huntrakul family). This Company had a three-storied factory with 5,000 square feet of floor space capable of producing 40 tonnes of ice per day (after expansion) or 100 tonnes for refrigeration in cold storage.[78]

In 1887, a soda manufacturer named the Oriental Soda Company was established by Anderson and Co. The Company imported both the machinery and raw materials (soda) from Hong Kong. Unfortunately, it remained in business for only a short time because Thai consumers did not like soda. Efforts to develop beverage production in Bangkok were revived in 1925, when the Fraser and Neave Company and the Bangkok Manufacturing Company resumed soda water production using local water as raw material.[79]

Electric power was practically confined to Bangkok, as it was already in 1887. The larger and older station was under Belgian–Danish management with a normal running capacity of 12,000 kW and a reserve capacity of 15,000 kW, part of which was periodically employed. Apart from lighting most of the town, this plant owned and operated the city tramways and provided power for two suburban tram services operating the road bridge across the Chao Phraya River, for oil refinery, tobacco factory and soap works, and for part of the power needs of several rice mills and industrial establishments (in the 1910s). The other station, Samsen station, was owned by the government. It had a capacity of about 10,000 kW and supplied light and power to the Northern part of the city. About half of the output served to drive cement factory (operated

---

[77] Ibid., p. 392.
[78] Ibid., p. 393.
[79] Ibid., p. 394.

in 1915) and also provided power to the airfield establishment at Don muang and the military arsenal.[80]

In 1913, the Siam Cement Company was established and began operations in 1915. The first five years saw very high profits of around 5–10 per cent per share.[81] The Privy Purse was the major shareholder with half of the total one million baht in shares, meaning that it earned as much as 25,000–50,000 baht per annum in returns.[82] In 1917, the Company increased its capital by three million baht and imported modern machinery from abroad to expand its production capacity.[83] In 1923, Siam Cement employed 150 Thai workers (some of them women) and 95 Chinese workers. In 1925, the Company further expanded its capacity and began exporting to Singapore.[84] Even during the global depression, the Company made as much as 6–12 per cent annual profits.[85] The Company's success was due partly to several construction projects in Bangkok, especially shophouses along main roads, and partly to other infrastructure projects like the construction of the Rama VI Bridge in 1924, that fuelled demand for as many as 1,000 bricks per day.[86]

After the First World War, oil-based machinery and motors came to play an increasingly vital role in manufacturing owing to the growth of both heavy and light industries in Europe and America.[87] Foreigners and Thais alike invested in mechanized manufacturing in Bangkok such as the British–American Tobacco Company, established in 1920, to produce cigarettes. Other factories producing ice, soft drinks, soap, coconut oil, peanut oil, tanned leather, and hand-woven textiles were set up in Bangkok

---

[80] *Siam Resources* (c. 1940).

[81] For fuller discussion, see Porphant (2015, pp. 481–86).

[82] N.A. Royal Secretariats 20/13 (1921).

[83] Ibid.

[84] BTWM (18 June 1923; 3 July 1925; 3 December 1925).

[85] N.A. R.7. Royal Secretariats 206/77 (1928).

[86] Hewison (1988, p. 395).

[87] Progress in manufacturing led to a massive accumulation of weaponry and eventually the First World War between the Allies, comprising Great Britain, France, Russia, the United States, Japan, and Siam, etc. and the Central Powers of Germany, Austria–Hungary, and Turkey (Anonymous 1985a, p. 74).

and Thonburi.[88] In 1923, the government established an automated paper plant. This factory, attached to the Royal Thai Survey Department in the Ministry of Defense, was located in *tambon* Samsen and had a one-tonne daily production capacity.[89] In the 1920s, the government took an enhanced role in the economy with the establishment of the Royal Thai Railways, in which it was a major shareholder and which proved to be highly profitable. The government was also a major shareholder in the waterworks at Samsen.[90]

In 1928, the Min Se Company, with Chinese merchants as major shareholders and a registered capital of 0.2 million baht, set up a factory to produce matches on a 20-*rai* plot of land on Rama IV Road. This factory employed 700 workers, 600 of whom were Chinese women and children hired on a daily basis whereas the Thai workers were hired to work at home. Production was partly mechanized and partly manual. The Min Se Company predicted that it would have approximately 20 per cent of the market share by 1931.[91] A rival firm, the Siam Match Factory, was opened in 1931 by the Swedish Match Company in partnership with the Borneo Company. This factory employed more than 300 labourers on the day shift and 225 at night. Most of the work was automated, and the Chinese and Siamese labourers were employed on a piecework basis. It was said that an expert worker could make about 100 baht a month on this basis. Local wood was used for both matches and boxes. Siam currently used 3,800 cases a month.[92] By 1933 the Company was producing seven brands, all at 37 baht per case of 7,200 boxes. The excise on these was about 49 per cent, but new excise rates, which caused the temporary closure of the factory, raised this to 195 per cent.[93]

In 1932, *Phraya* Bhirom Bhakdi (Boonrawd Setabutra) established the Boon Rawd Brewery in Bangkok with a registered capital of approximately 600,000 baht. Apart from *Phraya* Bhirom Bhakdi, other

---

[88] Ibid.
[89] Ibid.
[90] BTWM (15 December 1924).
[91] BTWM (25 November 1929); Hewison (1988, p. 389).
[92] BTWM (2 March 1931).
[93] BTWM (23 March 1933).

major shareholders were the Privy Purse, the Hong Kong Bank, and the Shanghai Bank. The company was very successful and highly profitable, so much so that in its first nine months, the company paid a dividend of 6 per cent to its shareholders.[94] In 1934, Thailand set up its first local brewery, the Boonrawd Brewery in Bangkok, marking the debut of the well-known Singha Beer brand.

SERVICES

After 1855, the service sector also expanded, especially import–export enterprises, shipping, insurance, warehouses, and commercial banks. In 1888, European trading firms controlled 5.15 million *hab* of Thai rice for exports, representing 68.4 per cent of the total. They also dominated rice exports to Europe and 77 per cent of exports to Singapore.[95]

Road construction in Bangkok attracted other businesses such as shops, pharmacies, repair shops, tram services, railroads, hotels, bookshops, and printing houses. European trading firms were mostly British and included Windsor (1871), Berli Jucker (1882), Diethelm (1904), East Asiatic (1897), and Louis Thomas Leonowens (1905). Apart from their businesses in the service sector including insurance companies, agents for contacts with their headquarters, and agricultural exporters, some of these trading firms also owned rice mills and saw mills (for example, Berli Jucker and Borneo).[96] Domestic market expansion attracted western trading firms, who opened offices in Siam. For instance, the Berli Jucker Company was founded by a Swiss businessman named Albert Jucker, with an office on the Chao Phraya River. The Company imported consumer goods from Europe for sale to the nobility and exported teak wood and leather to Europe.[97]

The success of the East Asiatic Company was also due to the expansion of international trade. Its various businesses included trading, import and export, insurance, and manufacturing (rice mill and saw mill). Rapidly

---

[94] Chollada (1986, p. 165).
[95] Suehiro (1996, p. 48).
[96] Ibid., p. 45.
[97] Orawan (2004, p. 68).

expanding shipping services led to the establishment of warehouses, private docks, repair services, engine rental, engineering works, and various port services such as carriers. Employment in the shipping business required large inputs of labour both unskilled for loading and cleaning ships, and skilled such as captains, mechanical engineers, and workers at private dockyards. In 1883, there were 186 heads of households employed in shipping-related activities such as sailors, boat rental, boat repair, and mechanical engineers.[98] If unskilled labour working in shipping lines and at private dockyards was taken into account, the number would likely to have been much higher. In 1929, Bangkok had more than 40 private dockyards, 25 of which were located in Phra Nakhon while another 27 were on the Thonburi side of the Chao Phraya.[99] These dockyards were operated by various companies such as the Bangkok Dock Company, the Borneo Company, and the Wang Lee Company.

Another business that emerged as a result of the expansion of international trade was the hotel trade. The Oriental — the first luxury hotel in Siam — was established in the middle of the nineteenth century. It started as an accommodation for seafarers who docked at Bangkok and was developed into a hotel by C. Salje, a Danish sailor. The Oriental changed owners several times, eventually becoming a branch of the East Asiatic Company, with one million baht initial registered capital. Forty per cent of the shares were sold to Thai investors at 200 baht per share in 1919.[100] The Oriental hosted guests on several occasions including Crown Prince Nicholas of Russia, who later became Czar Nicholas.[101]

Road construction in Bangkok affected transportation of both cargo and passengers. The first tram line in the city was operated by a Danish company after it was granted a concession from the Siamese government in 1878. In the beginning, the tram was drawn by horses. Later it was electrified and run by Siam Electricity with a registered capital of 725,000 baht.[102] It operated several lines: Dusit (10.05 km), Hua Lam Phong

---

[98] Porphant and Tsubouchi (2000a, pp. 67–94).
[99] *Directory for Bangkok and Siam 1929* (1929).
[100] Chollada (1986, p. 163).
[101] Orawan (2004, p. 38).
[102] N.A. Department of Railways 2/10.

(6.03 km), and Kamphaeng Mueang (2.65 km).[103] Tram tracks in Bangkok in the years between 1897 and 1906 were only 17.3 km long, but the service greatly stimulated trade and travel while promoting settlement in the outer city. The expansion of tram services was a major feature of the Bangkok transportation scene after 1910, with five companies in operation. Trams, which required high capital input involving imported technology from western countries, created a large number of jobs. The average registered capital for a tram venture was approximately three million baht, with an annual passenger load averaging about ten million in 1900. There were at least 300 people working for tram companies in 1922, earning average monthly wages of 65–70 baht (including bonuses), which was higher than the wages for workers in rice mills in the years beginning in 1917.[104]

Railways were as important as trams in the development of Bangkok's transportation network since they, too, required large investments, relied on imported technology, and created large numbers of jobs. The first private rail service began in 1891, operated by the Danish firm, Bangkok–Pak Nam Railway Line Company, with an initial registered capital of 120,000 baht. The second line, run by the Mae Klong Thun Railway Ltd. Co. (*Tha Chin* Railway) with an initial registered capital of 1.78 million baht, opened in 1900.[105] Other transportation developments in the years that followed included the first public buses, initiated by Lert Setabutra and serving the Charoen Krung area and later extended to Yot Se, Pratu Nam, and Bang Lamphu.[106]

Trade and services in Bangkok expanded significantly in the years after 1900, attributable to changing consumption patterns influenced by the influx of western culture, urban growth, and increasing incomes. Table 2.5 clearly shows how Bangkok's economic activities diversified from rice exports to investment in new economic sectors such as land, real estate, services, and import and export.

---

[103] Wright and Breakspear (1908 reprinted 1994, p. 192).
[104] N.A R.6. M. of the Capital 120/18 (1922).
[105] N.A. Department of Railways 2/10.
[106] Porphant (1999a, pp. 463–64).

TABLE 2.5
Selected Stores and Services in Bangkok, 1930

Name	Year of Establishment	Type of Business	Registered Capital (baht)
Royal Hotel	1925	hotel	120,000
Jowras	1919	pharmacy	500,000
Khiam Hua Seng	1921	liquor and tobacco store	640,000
Lam Phun Land & Syndicate	1920	real estate	60,000
May Beth Pharmacy	1925	pharmacy	20,000
Nguan Ha Seng	1922	loan service	200,000
On Weng	1924	cleaning service	600,000
Oriental Store	1920	general store	1,000,000
Phatthanakan Cinematograph	1916	photography studio	200,000
Rundery Buromkham	1916	real estate	300,000
Rattana Mala	1921	general store	450,000
Thanon Rong Mueang Syndicate	1914	real estate	350,000
Saha Mit	1925	benzene, lubrication, and automobile spare parts	30,000
Siam Hide & Leather	1917	leather	100,000
Siam Observer	1925	printing house and newspaper	125,000
FW Special	1922	clothing and engineering equipment	100,000

Source: *The Record* (1930, pp. 205–6).

In summary, between 1855 and 1932, Bangkok grew into an outward-looking port city. The expanded rice trade led to increased import–export activities, warehousing, port development, and shipping lines. The urban population swelled with the influx of Chinese migrant workers. This resulted in greater economic opportunity and investment by the nobility, the Privy Purse, and others. After this period, Bangkok would change its economic, political, and social roles to become a more inward-looking metropolis.

BANGKOK, 1932–60

Bangkok's development was affected by the change from an absolute monarchy to a constitutional monarchy on 24 June 1932, the global depression of the 1930s, the expansion of state capitalism under the leadership of Field Marshall Phibun Songkhram, and the outbreak of the Second World War. Bangkok changed from an outward-looking port city into an inward-looking metropolis, with increasing roles of trading, business, and finance. The city also became a fledging manufacturing centre spearheaded by state enterprises.[107]

After the end of the absolute monarchy, a general election was held for the first time in Thai history. In 1932, elected representatives from the provinces had the unique opportunity not only to enter parliament for the first time, but also to bring local and regional concerns, such as those affecting the Northeast, to the attention of the parliament.[108] The role of Bangkok as capital and seat of government grew stronger as public policy and other aspects of national development were formulated there. Heightened feelings of nationalism, which emerged after 1932, especially after 1938, directly impacted Bangkok as the centre of development. The government under the leadership of Phibun introduced propaganda campaigns against the Chinese while supporting the economic role of Thai businesses and services through the mass media and educational system.

---

[107] Falkus (1993, p. 151).
[108] Keyes cited by Falkus (1993, p. 151).

Two major factors affecting Bangkok as an inward-looking metropolis have been of particular significance. Firstly, the political change that occurred in 1932 led to changes in the structure of elite Thai capitalists. The importance of rice traders such as the Wang Lee family began to decline, whereas new Chinese–Thai groups had a greater role in business under the state capitalist system.[109] Bangkok's economy was also better connected with the country's domestic economy. In 1936, extraterritoriality imposed under the Bowring Treaty and other "unequal treaties" came to an end. This enabled Thailand to utilize policies on taxes and duties to protect its manufacturing sector. Bangkok became an important base for the country's economy, finance, trade, and manufacturing. Secondly, the 1930s marked the beginning of major highway construction linking Bangkok with other regions. A five-year highway construction plan for 1936–41 provided for the capital to be connected with regional centres such as Samut Prakan, Sattahip, and Rayong. Moreover, interprovincial highways were linked, both directly and indirectly, throughout the whole kingdom via rivers and canals. In total, the plan called for the construction of 2,880 km of highways and roads.[110] However, the economic depression of the 1930s and instability during the Second World War delayed all proposed construction. Even as late as 1940 there was not a single trunk road linking Bangkok to other provinces. The furthest distance a motor vehicle could travel comfortably from the centre of Bangkok was no more than 20 miles. Around 1940, Virginia Thompson commented on Bangkok's road conditions:

> Unlike most great cities, which are usually the centre of a network of roads, Bangkok has vehicular isolation. Its few hundred taxis circulate within the capital's confines, and even today one can leave Bangkok only by boat or by rail. Such roads as exist are limited to the frontier regions or to areas totally lacking in other transportation facilities.[111]

---

[109] Suehiro cited by Falkus (1993, p. 151).
[110] N.A. Office of the Prime Minister 02066.5/5 (1934–53).
[111] Thompson (1967, p. 507).

Once road construction got underway after the conclusion of the Second World War with the total length increased from 5,589 km in 1945 to 8,446 km in 1960,[112] vehicular transportation began to increase, thus boosting trade and distribution of agricultural and other goods between Bangkok and other regions of the country. Another consequence was greater migration into the capital. Moreover, with the victory of the Chinese Communist Party in 1949, the influx of Chinese migrants abruptly ceased. An annual quota of not more than 200 immigrants was set. The Chinese in Thailand stopped sending remittances to China and began to invest in and expand their businesses in Thailand, which they came to see as their permanent home. The Thai workers became more important as they slowly replaced the Chinese.[113]

Population Growth

The population of Bangkok grew gradually. In 1937, the city's population (*changwat* Phra Nakhon) was only 533,000[114] and in 1944, the combined population of Phra Nakhon and Thonburi stood at 843,000. This figure rose to more than one million in 1952 and to 1.8 million by 1960 (see Table 2.6).

---

[112] *Statistical Yearbook of Thailand* (various years).

[113] During the Great Depression, import and export values declined, trade was slack, rice mills had to shut down, some of the Chinese workers became unemployed, stores had to cut wages and salaries (N.A. R.7. M. of Interior 12/3 (1930)). The Depression led to a decrease in Chinese immigration. In some years, there was more emigration than immigration, such as in 1933 and 1934 when emigrants exceeded immigrants by 14,528 and 13,349 respectively (N.A.(2) Office of the Prime Minister 0201.76/2 (1932–38)).

[114] This represents the population living in Bangkok Municipality only, excluding the population outside the municipality such as Phra Khanong and Thonburi Province.

TABLE 2.6
Population in Bangkok, 1937–60

Year	Bangkok (Phra Nakhon and Thonburi)	Phra Nakhon	Thonburi
1937		533,104	
1941		653,364	
1942		674,172	
1943	843,431	696,097	147,334
1947	781,652	608,520	177,132
1952	1,072,964	845,374	227,590
1957	1,526,715	1,204,894	321,821
1960	1,800,678	1,419,492	381,186

Source: *Reports on Bangkok and Thonburi Municipality Operation* (various years).

Migration contributed significantly to population growth in the capital. For instance, Bangkok's population increased by 53,230 in 1948, 58,282 in 1956, but by only 29,190 in 1959. Natural population increase was partly due to medical advances and improvements in sanitary conditions. The birth rate increased from 3.64 per cent in 1946, to 4.7 per cent in 1960, whereas the death rate fell continuously, from 2.3 per cent to only 0.5 per cent.[115] Thai migrant labour gradually replaced Chinese labour. Prior to 1941, Bangkok was characterized as "a Chinese City".[116] Increasingly, Bangkok became the capital of the Thai populace.

In 1937, those engaged in various branches of the service sector, namely commerce, transportation, public service, professions, domestic workers, and clerks, accounted for 55.6 per cent of all workers in Bangkok. The manufacturing sector contributed only 15.4 per cent of the workforce

---

[115] Paiboon (1973, p. 187).
[116] Thompson (1947, p. 242).

whereas the agricultural sector accounted for 30 per cent. The employment structure of Bangkok totally differed from that of the rest of the country, where 90 per cent of the workforce was employed in agriculture, 9 per cent in the service sector, and only 2 per cent in the manufacturing sector.[117] The male/female ratio of workers in Bangkok was 7:3 (see Table 2.7).

TABLE 2.7
Employment in Bangkok by Economic Sector, 1937

Sector	Male	Female	Total	Thailand
Agriculture and fishery	54,723	49,123	103,846	6,028,792
Forestry	341	156	497	20,407
Commerce	66,080	22,224	88,304	357,336
Manufacturing	41,859	10,530	52,397	129,954
Mining	33	2	35	15,071
Transportation and communication	25,983	661	26,644	58,857
Public service	20,117	348	20,465	62,876
Professional	10,209	3,419	13,628	49,474
Domestic workers	15,358	11,522	26,880	82,590
Clerical service	7,371	296	7,667	17,923
Total	**242,074**	**98,289**	**340,363**	**6,808,212**

Note: Persons ten years and older.
Source: 1937 Population Census.

---

[117] See Porphant (2013*b*, pp. 157–75).

In 1937, only 4 per cent of the labour force worked in the professions, signifying the beginning of skilled labour earning regular salaries. The establishment of higher education institutions, namely Chulalongkorn University (1917) and Thammasat University (established as the University of Moral and Political Science — *mahawitthayalai thammasat lae kan mueang* — in 1934), vocational schools, and other secondary preparatory schools ensured that females would be among the professionals. In 1937, there were 3,419 female professionals in Thailand.[118] Despite increasing demand for university and college education, the number of students enrolled in higher education was still very low. Both Chulalongkorn and Thammasat Universities had a prime directive of producing personnel for the government service. Chulalongkorn University offered courses in the faculties of Arts, Science, Engineering, Architecture, Nursing, Pharmacy, and Veterinary Science. Thammasat University offered courses in Economics, Political Science and Diplomacy, and Commerce and Accountancy. In 1937, both universities produced 5,056 graduates, 4,000 of whom resided in Bangkok, reflecting the fact that most of the modern higher education institutions were concentrated in the capital. Moreover, in 1937, the professionals included physicians, dentists, nurses, lawyers, engineers, electricians, technicians, actors, architects, artists and other artisans.[119] Occupations in the service sector with high employment were trades involving food and beverages (64,177 persons), retail and wholesale trade (11,702), transportation (25,508), and domestic workers (13,609). Workers in the manufacturing sector were mostly employed by the rice mills (5,040 persons), saw mills (2,435), savory food and sweets production (1,513), printing (2,895), and construction (1,894).[120]

Although the number of Chinese immigrants continued to decline after 1930, ethnic division of labour was still the dominant characteristic of Bangkok's economy until 1947. Chinese workers were essential in non-agricultural activities, namely trade, finance, manufacturing, skilled crafts, and unskilled, manual labour. On the other hand, most Thai workers were government officials, professionals, and farmers.[121]

---

[118] 1937 Population Census.
[119] Ibid.
[120] Ibid.
[121] Skinner (1957, p. 309).

Manufacturing Industry

After 1932, the government adopted economic nationalism, which emphasized the role of government as a major investor in key manufacturing ventures in a capitalist economy. At the time, the government believed that industrialization and economic growth in general must be led by the government sector. Therefore, the government was involved in various manufactures such as tobacco, paper, textiles, sugar, fuel, mining, and founded the company, namely the Thai Industrial Promotion Ltd. Co. (*borisat songserm utsahakhamthai chamkat*).[122] Statistics for manufactures in Bangkok are provided in Table 2.8.

In 1939, most of Thailand's manufacturing plants were concentrated in Bangkok. The manufactures listed in Table 2.8 were mainly small, low value-added, light industry producing for local markets (except rice mills). Most of the entrepreneurs were Chinese and Europeans while the workers were mainly Chinese. Light manufacturing plants in other provinces were rice mills (except one paper manufacturing plant in Kanchanaburi and one sugar mill in Lampang). Some areas were the sites for traditional manufactures such as ceramics, textiles, pottery, food preservation, and food processing, supplying only for the local markets.

The manufacturing sector was not significant to the Thai economy before the Second World War. From the end of the First World War to the beginning of the Second World War, the structure of the Thai economy changed very little. Most of the population lived in rural villages (in 1929, more than 80 per cent of the Thai population lived in rural areas and were mostly farmers). In 1937, there were 145,000 people engaged in the manufacturing sector, representing only 2.13 per cent of the total labour force.[123]

---

[122] Under the economic nationalism aiming for state capitalism, the government still permitted the running of private enterprises. The government invested in and managed large manufactures and other enterprises involved with state security. Nevertheless, the government also encouraged joint ventures with private manufacturing firms. If there was any manufacture that the private sector was not able to establish, the government was prepared to do so in order to promote domestic industrialization. Laws were enacted to handle domestic loans for manufactures so that Thai entrepreneurs could apply for investment in various enterprises (Panit 1984, p. 659).

[123] 1937 Population Census.

TABLE 2.8
Industrial Establishments in Bangkok, 1939

Enterprise	No.
Tanneries	32
Power rice and timber mills	27
Textile factories	26
Food canning and bottling	21
Machinery shops	20
Ice factories	12
Coconut oil plants	5
Match factories	4
Toothpaste and toothbrush factories	4
Soap factories	3
Cigarette and tobacco factories	1
Brewery	1
Glazing works	1
Paper mill	1
Cement plant	1
Metal shops	285

Source: Hewison (1988, p. 402).

Limitations to Industrialization Prior to the Second World War

What were the reasons for the limited industrialization in Bangkok and in Thailand generally before the Second World War? Four factors have been of particular significance.

Firstly, the development of the Thai economy from the signing of the Bowring Treaty to the Second World War was based on an abundance of land and a shortage of labour. Thailand's chief advantage lay in agricultural production, especially rice cultivation, rather than in manufacturing. Furthermore, Thai industrialization differed from Lewis' concept of economic development with unlimited supplies of labour, and H. Mynt's model of vent for surplus suggested in the book *The Classical Theory of International Trade and Underdeveloped Countries*. These two ideas emphasize the absence of a stimulus for industrialization arising from an excess labour supply or from the expansion of demand for local manufactured goods within the country, including backward linkages resulting from "vent for surplus",[124] or from increased income in the internal market, which could have led to increased use of more modern technology. Thai rice exports from the 1870s led to only a slight increase in the income of rural farmers and was not sufficient to increase the national per capita income. Demand for manufactured goods increased only marginally as a result of the export of agricultural products.

Secondly, the Thai government had a rather limited role in industrialization partly because of the Bowring Treaty (1855), which prevented Siam from setting import taxes above 3 per cent. In 1926, Thailand achieved some rights to set these taxes and it gained full power by 1936. Although the Thai government increased import taxes or put in place tax barriers to protect manufactured goods and income earnings, these tax rates were raised only slightly. Low import tax rates could not stimulate the growth of Thai manufacturing. The proportion of revenues from import taxes and duties compared to the value of imported goods increased from 3.7 per cent in 1926 to 22 per cent in 1935, representing an increase from 7 per cent to 25 per cent of total government revenues in the same period.[125] J.C. Ingram points out that the purpose of import taxes was to increase government revenues rather than to serve as a catalyst for industrial expansion. True, tariff levels were raised on a number of occasions after 1926. But, these tariffs were imposed to raise revenues, and any impetus to local industries (which included, for example, cigarettes, soap and matches) was unintended.[126] Not only were import tax rates low but the Thai government at that time did not have any policy to stimulate industrial expansion. Under these circumstances, Thailand had no need to pursue the policies which led to significant import substitution elsewhere. Thailand's foreign reserves were primarily tied to the gold standard and the pound sterling.[127]

In Southeast Asia the implementation of a tax policy to restrict imports and prevent foreign exchange outflows resulted in lessening the impacts of the economic depression and stimulated industrialization in several

---

[124] Myint (1958, p. 324).
[125] Ingram (1971, p. 183).
[126] See ibid., pp. 182–84.
[127] Ibid., pp. 182–84.

countries. Boomgaard and Brown point out that trade barriers such as high taxes and cheap labour had a considerable impact on industrial expansion in many countries.[128] For instance, Clarence-Smith noted that in Indonesia, or the former Netherlands East Indies, "One of the clearest effects of the recession [of the 1930s] was to push the Dutch authorities into a flurry of activity to support industrialization."[129]

Thirdly, prior to 1932, the government under the absolute monarchy did not promote industrialization as much as it should have. Professor Chatthip Nartsupha has argued that the Thai government could have done more to promote the development of industry. Writing of the interwar years, he noted that "The government ignored some private initiatives in promoting local industry" while "many local enterprise proposals for promotion were not given any substantial support".[130] After the 1932 revolution the government implemented policies to promote and support industrialization by investors from the elites and to oppose the Chinese at the same time (particularly after 1938) during Phibun's administration. However, these policies had a limited effect because important trade and manufacturing in Bangkok were firmly in the hands of the Chinese. A significant portion of profits (such as from rice trading) was sent to China, and, therefore, "capital accumulation" in the Bangkok economy was limited. W.G. Skinner concludes that 20 million baht or one-sixth of the total value of rice exports between 1927 and 1937 was sent back to China.[131] Capital accumulation, essential for industrialization, was slight. Investments in road construction and other economic infrastructures were also low. The Thai economy was still dependent on waterways for long haul transport.

Fourthly, the orthodox financial policy implemented by the government at that time further contributed to delayed industrialization. The threat of colonialism in Southeast Asian countries made it clear that the government had to guard against economic and political intervention by the colonial powers, and hence, the orthodox economic policy. This policy consisted

---

[128] Boomgaard and Brown, eds. (2000, p. 8).
[129] Clarence-Smith (2000, p. 234).
[130] Chatthip, Suthy and Montri, eds. (1981, pp. 7–8).
[131] Skinner (1957, pp. 225–26).

of a balanced budget, stable currency, restricted foreign debts, and the ability to pay all loans on time. After Siam joined the gold standard in 1902, the policy was implemented, upon the recommendation of a British financial advisor, to stabilize the value of the baht so that it could be exchanged freely for any other currency, to balance the budget, and to accumulate foreign exchange reserves (the pound) and gold to support the baht.[132] Prior to 1940, the Thai government borrowed from abroad only five times and in small amounts. The orthodox policy described above limited Thailand's industrialization in particular and the country's economic development as a whole.[133]

One question remains: why didn't the low import duties in Siam prior to 1940 lead to substantial industrialization? The answer is that the global depression in the 1930s had less impact on Siam than on many other countries. Siam did not have a current account deficit nor crippling foreign debts.

In the context of the international economy, throughout the years of the Great Depression, export-oriented countries had to levy high import duties because of lower exports and services. Some countries left the international exchange system, severing ties between the local currency and key foreign currencies and thus destabilizing international trade. Under these conditions, coupled with high import taxes, many countries supported nascent industrialization. Many governments also encouraged reduced imports in order to avert a foreign exchange drain.[134]

Many countries faced trade and service deficits but Siam managed to stay aloof even though the value of rice exports continued to decline. Lower prices for rice from Siam were not as low, however, as prices for other primary export goods, namely coffee, rubber, and wheat. Furthermore, the decrease in rice prices was slight compared to those for imported industrial goods. Consequently, the balance of trade and services in Siam remained free from the problems faced by other countries (rice accounted for 65–70 per cent of total exports from Siam). Siam was also able to sustain a trade surplus throughout the period between 1927

---

[132] See Mayuree (1977, pp. 56–89).
[133] Swan (2009, p. 3).
[134] See Porphant (2012, pp. 45–64).

and 1937. Again, pressure to increase import duties or to introduce other measures to promote industrialization, thus, did not emerge.[135]

The world depression, which affected all countries within the international economy in the 1930s, might have been expected to have had a considerable impact in Thailand. While we cannot detail the impact of the depression, a few relevant points may be noted. First, countries dependent on the export of primary products were severely hit through the shrinking of world trade and the fall in price levels for primary products. Their exports in volume and value fell. Second, such countries were usually dependent on imports of industrial products. Prices of industrial products tended to fall less than primary products. Third, primary producing countries were often heavy international debtors, and it was difficult for them to service loans with export revenues declining. Fourth, primary producing countries were typically dependent on one or two export markets. If these markets collapsed, the economies of primary producers suffered particularly.[136]

For example, in 1929, no fewer than 18 countries sent one-third or more of their exports by value to the United States (Malaya sent much of its rubber and Brazil nearly all its coffee). When demand from the United States collapsed, prices of coffee and rubber, for example, fell by more than three-quarters; the trade balance of overdependent countries suffered accordingly. Major primary goods exporters — Australia, New Zealand, the Dutch East Indies, Argentina, Brazil, and Malaya — all had trade imbalances followed by defaults on foreign debt payment.[137]

To mitigate these problems, many countries during the years of the depression imposed steep import taxes, restricted imports, devalued their currency, promoted bilateral trading, and abolished foreign debt repayments in order to balance their trade deficit. These policies and measures consequently promoted considerable expansion of the manufacturing sector. As one author has written,

---

[135] See Porphant (2012, pp. 46–65); Porphant (2013a, pp. 120–33).
[136] Porphant (2013a, p. 127).
[137] Falkus (1975, pp. 81–82).

[t]hus, sheltered behind the barrage of tariff restrictions, quotas, exchange controls, and the like industries of all kinds mushroomed in agricultural countries. In Argentine, Brazil, South Africa, India, and many others the depression sparked off enforced industrialization. Total industrial production in India, for example, passed its 1929 level in 1933, and by 1938 was 50% higher again.[138]

During the Second World War, the Thai government began to realize the necessity of self-reliance in industrial production and expedited industrialization to increase supplies of manufactured goods since shortages of imports were creating considerable difficulties. Many of the country's trading partners were involved in the war. Inflation sky-rocketed to more than 1,000 per cent towards the end of the war. Wages paid to unskilled labourers also rose rapidly. For instance, unskilled workers in a rice mill were paid 0.80 baht per day in 1936–38. Their daily wages increased to 2.05 baht in 1945, 5.46 baht in 1946, and 7.33 baht in 1947. Yet, in fact, real wages were decreasing.[139] After the commencement of the Second World War, the government established a number of state enterprises in Bangkok. In 1942 the Ministry of Industry was established, emphasizing manufactures that were essential to the people's lives and livelihoods. The establishment of the Bank of Thailand, which was put in charge of industrialization, also dates to 1942.[140] Between 1946 and 1948, the industrial output in Bangkok rose quickly: cement and cement products grew by 133 per cent, ice by 67 per cent, matches by 160 per cent, paper by 155 per cent, leather goods by 79 per cent, and tobacco by 299 per cent.[141]

After the Second World War, the government pushed for rapid industrialization in order to meet internal demand. Several industries

---

[138] Ibid., p. 79.

[139] *An Economic Survey of Thailand, 1946–47* (n.d., p. 51).

[140] Panit (1984, pp. 659–60). Inflation not only led to decreased wages for labourers but it also reduced the real income of government officials. The rapid decline in government officials' income triggered widespread malfeasance and corruption since officials had to find other sources of income to offset their losses. Such behaviour of seeking economic rent was rampant, for instance, many senior officials were committee members in several private as well as state enterprises.

[141] *Statistical Yearbook of Thailand* (1952); N.A. Ministry of Finance 0301.2.2/3 (1957).

such as tanneries, textile, and glass, were promoted (see Table 2.9). At the time, the major problem facing government factories was that actual output was significantly less than full capacity, partly because of depressed and often fluctuating demand as well as low working capital.[142]

TABLE 2.9
Selected Statistics for Manufactures in Bangkok, 1952–55

Manufacture	Investment Capital (million baht)	Real Capacity (daily)	Employment (no. of workers)
Umbrella Factory (1952)	0.86	10 umbrellas	7
Glass Factory, Glass Organization (1952)	36.40	20 tonnes of glass and 10–15 tonnes of fire-resistant material	400
Battery Factory, Battery Organization (1953)	5.03	50 sets of battery	101
Pins and Clips Factory (1953)	1.18	20 kg of pins and 58 kg of clips	6
Textile Factory of Textile Organization (1953)	70.90	1,330 kg of thread; 4,472 metres of fabric; 2,205 metres of dyed cotton yarn; 114.4 pounds of cotton balls; 4,394 metres of gauze	967
Pottery Factory (1954)	4.85	1,000–2,000 bowls	54
Tanning Factory, Tanning Organization (1955)	49.16	450 pieces of fabricated hides and 400 pairs of combat boots	449

Source: N.A. Ministry of Industry 0201.2.1831 (1959–60).

---

[142] N.A. M. of Industry 0201.2.1/31 (1959–60). The Battery Factory (attached to Battery Organisation) had a real daily production rate of 50 sets of batteries (its full capacity was 350 sets per day), representing only 15 per cent of full capacity. Other manufactures recorded similarly low outputs: Weaving Factory (10 per cent below full capacity and 17 per cent below full thread spinning capacity); Tanning Factory (23 per cent below full finished leather capacity and 25 per cent below full combat boots production capacity); Bang Yi Khan Distillery (10 per cent below full production capacity for 30 per cent liquor); Sam Sen Paper Factory (35 per cent below full paper production capacity). Some factories ran at a loss and were deeply in debt such as the Tanning Factory and the Battery Factory (N.A. M. of Industry 0201.2.1/31 (1959–60).

In 1960, the privately-owned cement factory employed the largest number of workers at 521, followed by the matches factory (321 workers), and the soap factory (42 workers), as shown in Table 2.10. Most of the factories were traditional manufactures such as hardware, printing, saw mills, and rice mills that were mostly run by Chinese entrepreneurs.

TABLE 2.10
Number of Manufacturing Plants in Bangkok and Thonburi, 1960

Type of Manufacture	No. of Plants			No. of Workers	Workers per Plant
	Total	Thai	Foreigner[1]		
Hardware	1,024	285	739	5,926	5.8
Mechanized printing	530	290	240	5,014	9.5
Saw mills	317	89	228	4,771	15.1
Handlooms[1]	382	15	367	4,527	11.9
Rice mills	149	92	57	2,625	17.6
Candles and incense	111	34	77	2,148	19.4
Machinery repair	283	122	161	2,096	7.4
Power looms	185	16	169	2,052	11.1
Thread spinning	62	9	53	1,586	25.6
Pharmaceutical-related	228	85	143	1,562	6.9
Flour and food	196	32	164	1,448	7.4
Matches	4	1	3	1,283	320.8
Garments[2]	29	8	21	1,116	38.5
Beverages and soft drinks	47	14	33	1,005	21.4
Tobacco	94	23	71	825	8.8
Lac	24	7	17	558	23.3
Soap[3]	13	2	11	550	42.3
Cement	1	0	1	521	521.0
Ice	43	24	19	510	11.9
Liquor and beer	6	5	1	218	36.3
Total[4]	7,302	2,233	5,069	62,264	8.5

Notes: [1] Mostly Chinese
        [2] Plants with more than five looms.
        [3] More than five workers employed.
        [4] Including other businesses
Source: Suehiro (1996, p. 184).

Services

The Depression of the 1930s greatly affected the service sector in Bangkok. Prices of paddy dropped by as much as 66 per cent, leading to the closure of many rice mills. In 1924, there were 86 rice mills, but by 1930, only 71 remained in business.[143]

Trading in Bangkok was slow in general, and workers' daily wages decreased from 1 baht in 1930 to 80 *satang* between 1931 and 1938.[144] Wages of skilled labour also decreased. For instance, a carpenter's daily earnings fell from 2 baht in 1930 to 1.45 baht in 1934, an ironsmith's wages declined from 3 baht to 2.45 baht, and a typical office clerk's monthly salary fell from 95 baht to 64.87 baht.[145] These decreases occurred around the same time as the People's Party's (*khana ratsadorn*) focus on economic nationalism. In 1939, the government sought to promote Thai trade through the establishment of the Thai Ni Yom Phanit Company, which engaged in the wholesale and retail trade of imported goods. In the same year, the Provincial Commerce Company (better known as *"borisat changwat"* — The Provincial Company) came into existence, with a branch in every province. Even so, the role of native Thais in trade remained rather limited. In 1939, stores and companies run by the Thais and registered with the Ministry of Commerce comprised: 75 import–export firms, three photo studios, six sign-making shops, one commercial bank, 54 printing and newspaper firms, nine drafting shops, 127 pharmacies, seven wholesale and retail stores, and a few unclassified shops.[146] The 1947 Population Census indicates that there

---

[143] Thaweesilp (1978, p. 290).

[144] *Statistical Yearbook of the Kingdom of Siam* (various years). Report from a government official of the Port Authority Department stated that: "Some of the workers in Pak Khlong Bang Lam Phu Tai area were unemployed while 1,000 Chinese workers in the northern part of the district were laid off from the rice mills. In 1930, there were 2,000 people who did not pay the poll tax to the government—an increase of 1,500 persons from the year before. Among these, 80–85 per cent were Chinese workers and 15–20 per cent were Thai" (N.A. M. of Interior 12/3 (2473)).

[145] Skinner (1957).

[146] Ministry of Commerce (1939).

were some 229,000 people engaged in the service sector in Bangkok: 141,000 in trade and finance, 43,850 servants and service sector employees, and 43,630 government officials. In contrast, the Chinese worked mainly in trade and finance.[147]

In summary, between 1932 and 1960, Bangkok was an inward-looking metropolis with an increased role as the centre of trade, business, and finance, the beginnings of state-led industrial enterprise, and a more significant centre for Thais, as opposed to Chinese migrants. After 1960, Bangkok was the centre of almost all aspects of Thai economic, social and cultural life. It had become the centre of Thailand's society, economy, and culture — a true primate megalopolis.

BANGKOK AFTER 1960

The 1960s saw accelerated changes in Bangkok. Its economic development transformed Bangkok from a primate city into a primate megalopolis — the social, economic, and cultural centre of Thailand. Although Bangkok had continued to grow since its founding, prior to 1960, this growth was gradual both in terms of population and economic activity, especially manufacturing. Bangkok had not yet grown into a modern industrial city. There were no large industrial base nor influx of rural migrants to the city.[148]

Population and Urban Growth

After 1960, Bangkok dominated almost all aspects of Thailand's economic and social development. In 1960, its population was 1.8 million, increasing to 2.6 million in 1967, and to more than six million in 1988. By the

---

[147] Skinner (1957).

[148] Bangkok's population, in comparison with the rest of the country, increased slowly. From 1913–29, Bangkok's population accounted for 4–6 per cent of the country's total and slightly decreased to about 4.4 per cent in 1947. In the 1950s, the population rose to more than 5 per cent of the whole country (*Statistical Yearbook of Thailand*, various years).

beginning of the 1990s, there were approximately 10 million people living in Bangkok, making it the 34th largest city in the world.[149] Furthermore, Bangkok has remained as the centre for trade and industry, it is the country's educational centre, and the hub for land, water, and air transportation. Bangkok as a primate city is phenomenal and has very few rivals elsewhere in the world.[150]

In 1947, the population of Bangkok was 20 times larger than that of the second largest city, Chiang Mai. In later years, it grew to be 26 and then 30 times larger. (In 1988, Nakhon Ratchasima was the second largest city.) Bangkok's population in comparison to that of Thailand's four largest cities in 1947, 1967 and 1988 is shown in Table 2.11.

TABLE 2.11
Population of Thailand's Four Largest Cities in 1947, 1967, 1988

1947		1967		1988	
Bangkok	781,662	Bangkok	2,614,356	Bangkok	6,155,269
Chiang Mai	38,211	Chiang Mai	81,579	Nakhon Ratchasima	204,982
Lampang	22,952	Nakhon Ratchasima	73,030	Chiang Mai	164,030
Nakhon Ratchasima	22,384	Hat Yai	49,327	Hat Yai	138,046

Source: *Statistical Yearbook of Thailand* (various years).

---

[149] Falkus (1993, p. 144).

[150] Bangkok is not only the "primate city" in Thailand, but also on a global scale. In 1960, Ginsburg established the Degree of Primacy Index in 104 countries, both more developed and less developed, on the basis of the proportion of the population in the largest city in comparison to the four largest cities in each country. Thailand was ranked first in the Index, with 94.2 per cent, followed by Uruguay (87 per cent), and Guatemala (84 per cent). At the same time, the average population proportion of the 104 countries in the Index was 60 per cent (Ginsburg cited by Anderson 1970, p. 42).

From 1960 to 1990, the major characteristic of Bangkok's urbanization was its high level of population concentration while urbanization elsewhere in the country was rather low. In 1947, Bangkok was home to 45.4 per cent of Thailand's urban population, increasing to 52.0 per cent in 1960, 60.9 per cent in 1970, and 60.0 per cent in 1980 (this was approximately 10 per cent of Thailand's total population). Bangkok accounted for 32 per cent of Thailand's GDP, 75 per cent of the manufacturing output, 55 per cent of manufacturing enterprises, 95 per cent of sea-borne foreign trade, and 70 per cent of personal income tax in 1980.[151]

Throughout the 1960s, Bangkok saw very rapid expansion, with the construction of hotels, commercial and residential buildings, offices, and shopping centres, resulting from the growth of the service sector and tourism. In 1961, the government embarked on its first economic development plan, which led to a growth in imports and increased private sector investments in a variety of major infrastructure projects. These policies encouraged and supported Bangkok's growth at the expense of rural areas since a large portion of the tax collected in the provinces was spent on urban development. Consequently, many young migrants were attracted to the capital and the new opportunities it offered. Jobs were by no means solely or even mainly in the industrial sector, but were spread across a wide range especially in services. The 1960s in particular was a time of immense physical change in Bangkok under the rebuilding enthusiasm of Field Marshall Sarit.

In the 1960s, many of the capital's canals such as *khlong* Silom and *khlong* Hau Lam Phong (Rama IV) were filled in and paved over. In the years immediately after the conclusion of the Second World War, there were approximately 100 canals in Bangkok and Thonburi,[152] but this number had dwindled by one-third by 1970. The disappearance of the canals was the major physical change that occurred in Bangkok during the 1960s. The central business district around *tanon* Charoen Krung spread from the Chao Phraya riverfront to *tanon* Silom, *tanon* Suriwong, and *tanon* Phra Ram Thi Si (Rama IV), making this the

---

[151] Falkus (1993, p. 145).
[152] Thepchu (1975, pp. 55–62).

highest growth area. Other businesses sprang up along Phloen Chit, Phetchaburi, and Asoke roads. Many of the old roads were repaved and enlarged to accommodate increasing traffic volume. Several new roads were built to link with the Bangkok Port at Khlong Toei and Don Mueang Airport owing to the expansion in imports and exports at Khlong Toei and tourism at Don Mueang. In the mid-1960s, the highway connecting Don Mueang and Saraburi was enlarged and resurfaced to mitigate traffic congestion and to facilitate urban growth. Another important fact was that this highway (Don Mueang–Saraburi) provided access through smaller roads to seven provinces in the Central Region, four provinces in the North, and several more in the Northeast.[153]

Bangkok's growth to the North after 1960 extended along Phahon Yothin and Vibhavadi Rangsit roads, to Pathum Thani, Nonthaburi, and Pak Kret. On the eastern side, urban growth was along Lat Phrao and Ram Kham Haeng roads to Bang Kapi and along Phetchaburi, Rama IV, and Sukhumvit roads into Samut Prakan Province. At the same time, urban growth to the West was along Charan Sanit Wong, Taksin, and Ekkachai roads. However, urbanization in Thonburi occurred much slower than in Bangkok. Parts of Thonburi were still orchards and rice fields.[154]

At the beginning of the 1960s, inner Bangkok, surrounded by city walls, slowly lost its population to other areas. Older business districts on Charoen Krung and Yaowarat roads declined in importance compared to newer centres, such as Pratu Nam, Ratchaprasong, Siam Square, Suriwong, Saphan Khwai, Wong Wian Yai (in Thonburi), Phra Khanong, and Bang Lamphu.[155] Urban growth also caused land prices to skyrocket. Prices for land in industrial areas were ten times higher than suburban rice fields.[156] Gross capital formation in the construction sector climbed steadily, especially for offices, factories, and hotels. Construction by the private sector rose from 1.66 billion baht in 1960 to 4.46 billion baht in 1970, while public sector construction increased

---

[153] See Porphant (2001, pp. 157–87).
[154] Chulalongkorn University (1991, p. 471).
[155] Paiboon (1973, p. 230).
[156] *Asian Industry* (1968, p. 41).

from 854 million baht to 5.47 billion in the same period, resulting in an increase in the total value of construction from 2.48 billion baht to 9.93 billion baht.[157]

The construction sector in Bangkok owed much of its growth to the spending of American soldiers on leave in Thailand during the Vietnam conflict, the hosting of the 5th Asian Games in 1966, and large-scale economic infrastructure projects, especially road construction in Bangkok. In the 1960s, the most obvious physical change in Bangkok was the construction of apartment buildings, offices for rent, bars, and housing units. An *Asian Industry* article in 1968 reported that "the numbers of houses in Bangkok doubled every 3 years".[158] The rapid rise in the number of housing units was due in part to the growing influx of rural migrants into Bangkok, which prompted the government to build cheap flats in such areas as Khlong Ton, Huai Khwang, and Din Daeng to accommodate them.[159] In 1970, there were approximately 200 office buildings for rent, many of them fully occupied and a quarter of which were quality offices with an excellent reputation.[160] Office buildings for rent greatly expanded along Phahon Yothin and Sukhumvit roads, around Lumphini Park, and other areas with high land rents. Office buildings for rent included Wang Li, Silom, Wong Wanit, A.I.A., Maneeya, Sarasin, Piya Thani, Dusit Thani, Olympia Thai, Thaniya, and Choke Chai.[161]

In the 1960s many department stores, such as Central, Daimaru, and Ratchadamri Shopping Arcade, were built in response to demand from the middle- and high-class customers both inside and outside the country. These department stores carried a diverse range of goods, most of them imported.[162]

Since Bangkok was the centre of manufacturing and services, economic changes of the country were certainly felt in Bangkok as well. In the 1980s, Thailand's average annual economic growth rate

---

[157] *National Income Account of Thailand* (various issues).
[158] *Asian Industry* (1968, p. 39).
[159] Ibid.
[160] *The Investor* (1971, p. 216).
[161] Ibid., pp. 218–19.
[162] See Anderson (1970).

was as high as 7 per cent, and the economic system was rapidly diversifying. There were tremendous changes, for example, in the manufacturing sector, especially export-oriented manufactures. In 1986, the value of exported manufactured goods overtook rice and other agricultural products for the first time. Manufactured goods accounted for only 2 per cent of all exports in 1960, but this figure had risen to 28.3 per cent in 1980 and 68 per cent in 1989. Exports of rice and other agricultural goods totalled 20.2 per cent in 1969, but it later dropped to 8 per cent. The top ten export items were textiles, rice, tapioca products, gems and jewellery, integrated circuits, canned seafood, shoes, sugar, and frozen shrimp. These items accounted for 54.5 per cent of all exports. The value of textile exports was double that of rice while revenues from international tourists were 2.5 times greater than rice exports.[163] After 1987, the influx of foreign direct investment, especially from manufacturing groups headquartered in the United States, Japan, and other Asian nations was key to growth in the manufacturing sector, exports, and the Thai economy as a whole. Comments that "Thailand would soon be the newest industrial country" or Asia's fifth tiger in the very near future (after 1988) became more and more frequent. Bangkok was like the capital of Asian NIEs (newly industrializing economies) because the city and its environs functioned as the manufacturing and assembly point for industrial goods bound for other newly industrialized countries in Asia as well.[164]

Ever since 1982, revenues from tourism have been the nation's number one income earner, bringing in a large amount of foreign exchange (overtaking revenues from rice exports). More than two million international tourists visited Thailand in 1982. This number grew to more than five million by the end of the decade.[165] Although the launch of new airlines (after 1989) made tourist attractions in other regions more accessible, as the capital, Thailand's air transportation hub, and a tourist destination in its own right, Bangkok reaped the benefits of

---

[163] Falkus (1991, p. 59).
[164] Askew (2002, p. 72).
[165] Ibid., p. 80.

the tourism boom most directly. More than 90 per cent of international tourists entered Thailand by air through Bangkok. Although the average length of stay in Bangkok was shorter than in other destinations such as Chiang Mai, Phuket, and Pattaya, Bangkok could still draw more than four times the number of tourists in each of these provinces.[166] Furthermore, as the country's financial centre, the financial liberalization at the beginning of the 1990s led to a tremendous inflow of capital to the Stock Exchange of Thailand (SET) because of Bangkok's ability to mobilize capital from the private sector. The SET was one of the fastest growing stock exchanges in the world. In the early years of the 1990s, the value of traded stocks increased from 38 per cent in 1991 to 109 per cent of GDP in 1993. The number of registered companies in the Stock Exchange rose from 21 in 1975 to 276 in 1991 and 347 in 1993. It is clear that the Stock Exchange was the principal capital market which fuelled the growth of banking, real estate, and construction.[167]

At the beginning of the 1990s, Bangkok was an Asian megalopolis, a centre of tourism and air transportation, investment, manufacturing, and finance. Bangkok's urban and industrial development not only extended to its peripheral provinces — Nonthaburi, Pathum Thani, Samut Prakan, Samut Sakhon, and Nakhon Pathom — but also to other provinces. A 1990 issue of *Far Eastern Economic Review* stated that:

> Like a magnet, the capital has drawn migrants from all over the country, and in some ways greater Bangkok now stretches 100 kilometers north to Ayutthaya, 50 kilometers to Chaschoengsao and 100 kilometers southeast to Sri Racha. With rapid industrialization of eastern seaboard, the latter should eventually stretch another 100 kilometers to Rayong.[168]

Industrial growth leapt with the eastern seaboard development project (started in 1981 when the industrial estate and a deep sea port were constructed). Economic activities, particularly industrialization,

---

[166] Ibid., p. 80.
[167] Pasuk and Baker (1995, p. 158).
[168] *Far Eastern Economic Review* (17 May 1990, p. 51) quoted in Falkus (1993, p. 160).

had moved from Si Racha to Rayong, meaning that Bangkok had extended its economic and industrial influence over 200 km.[169] Expansion of economic activities in the region led to rapid urban growth. On the other hand, population growth in Bangkok itself had slowed as people moved into suburban areas in peripheral provinces, creating urban communities there.

From the 1970s, many hotels were built to accommodate the increasing numbers of tourists.[170] These were accompanied by a boom in the construction of housing estates, both detached houses and townhouses, which had a considerable impact on the cityscape because of their adapted foreign architecture. As urban areas became more densely populated, land prices rose, leading to the rapid expansion of the condominium market. Households living in condominiums and apartments rose quickly from 2.6 per cent per annum between 1970 and 1980, to 9.7 per cent in 1990.[171] Between 1971 and 1990, built-up areas also expanded by 7.4 per cent annually. This annual average figure compares to 5.8 per cent in 1953–71 and 2.6 per cent in 1936–53. During these same periods, the population of the capital increased annually by 4.1 per cent, 5.5 per cent, and 1.6 per cent, respectively. The total administrative area of Bangkok increased from 66.7 square km in 1953 to 96.3 in 1958, 173.0 in 1965, 290.0 in 1971, and 1,560 in 1972.[172] A very large area expansion in 1972 was due to the annexation of Bangkok (*changwat* Phra Nakhon) and *changwat* Thonburi.

Significant factors explain the large expansion of built-up areas and areas of economic influence in Bangkok. Firstly, Bangkok's rise as a centre of finance, trade, and tourism occurred very rapidly. Activities in these sectors (for example, hotels, department stores, and offices) were most often concentrated in the inner city, leading to higher land prices. As a result, the population of the inner city increased slowly or decreased while the outer suburbs saw a larger increase.[173] Secondly,

---

[169] Falkus (1993, p. 160).
[170] Paritta (1993, p. 10).
[171] Askew (2002, p. 78).
[172] *Statistical Yearbook of Thailand* (various years).
[173] Falkus (1993, p. 157).

rapid industrialization especially in the outer suburbs benefited from lower land prices and from locational advantages, which included access to a large labour pool, the port, urban utilities, and economic infrastructure. Moreover, manufacturing benefited from the agglomeration of a large market resulting from a rapidly growing population. Industrial concentration in Bangkok, in turn, led to an increasing number of construction projects both for dwellings and other purposes. Thirdly, agricultural land occupied by rice fields was available for development. Agricultural sector earnings decreased in comparison to those in the manufacturing sector, which was vigorously promoted. At the same time, improved transportation effectively diminished the advantage of market proximity. Land for manufacturing and the service sectors became more profitable than agricultural land, which led to expansion, particularly in the construction of factories, warehouses, housing units, and offices. Fourthly, a lack of urban planning and the overlapping responsibilities of various state agencies led to urban sprawl. Fifthly, cheap labour from the rural areas also contributed to the growth of Bangkok.[174]

Migration

Rapid population growth in Bangkok was partly due to the natural rate of increase, attributable to better nutrition, public health, and medical care which caused the death rate to decrease. Meanwhile, the natural increase continued to decline from 2.8 per cent in 1970 to 2.6 per cent in 1975 and 2.0 per cent in 1981, respectively.[175] It was migration from the countryside into Bangkok, which remained at high levels, that more directly affected the city's population growth. In fact, Bangkok had higher migrant gains than any other region.[176]

---

[174] Ibid., p. 157; Porphant (1996; 1998).

[175] Chira (1983, pp. 11–12).

[176] There were 342,000 net migrants in Bangkok in 1960, 601,000 in 1970, and 202,000 in 1980. Bangkok's immigration rate was 7 per cent per annum during 1960–70 and 7.2 per cent per annum during 1970–80. The 1990 Population Census indicates that natural increase was still the major factor for Bangkok's population growth. In fact, 62 per cent of its population growth was from natural increase whereas another 38 per cent was from net migration. Such high rate of natural increase was

With the accelerated development of export-oriented industries between 1975 and 1980, migration into Bangkok grew quickly, with the number estimated at 212,000. Over the next five years, from 1985–90, this figure grew by an additional 366,000. Nevertheless, migration sharply declined during the economic crisis of 1997–2000. Instead, emigration, fuelled by business closures and subsequent layoffs of large numbers of workers increased, resulting in lower net migration (see Table 2.12). In the period that followed, migration continued to decrease partly due to regional economic growth that led to rapidly rising wages, both in money and in real terms, in other regions.[177]

TABLE 2.12
Net Migration in Bangkok, 1955–2000

Year	Net Migration (persons)	Changes (persons)
1955–60	67,000	
1965–70	64,000	–3,000
1975–80	212,000	148,000
1985–90	366,000	154,000
1995–2000	135,000	–231,000

Source: Chalongphob and Yongyuth cited by Kanchana (2012, p. 6).[178]

The gap between wages and job opportunities in Bangkok and other regions, especially before 1980, continued to grow, resulting in a high migration rate into the capital. Bangkok was a magnet that drew thousands of rural migrants with high hopes for their future. The image of Bangkok as a place where economic dreams came true was strengthened by

---

due to the large number of women of reproductive age in Bangkok (Chintana Phetcharanon et. al., cited by Kanchana 2012).

[177] World Bank (2005, pp. 96–97); Porphant and Siriporn (2001).
[178] Kanchana (2012).

radio and television programmes, movies, and the migrants themselves. Bangkok is very different from other cities in Thailand, with shopping malls, modern shops, and paved roads. A writer once said: "The magic spell of Bangkok is cast."[179] Migration from rural areas to Bangkok became an investment in human capital as an oversupply of labour from low-productivity rural areas flowed into a higher productivity area. Furthermore, as Bangkok was a centre of education with many leading universities and educational institutions, it drew a large number of young people from all across the country. Migration from the rural areas to Bangkok can be summarized as follows: firstly, economic factors, both "push" and "pull", can explain most of the migration from rural to urban areas. Secondly, migration is an indicator of the movement of people from areas with lower economic opportunity to places of higher economic potential. Thirdly, young people and the educated found better job opportunities and higher wages, making them the largest group of migrants. And fourthly, migrant labour was vital to population growth in Bangkok from the 1950s.[180]

---

[179] Paritta (1993, p. 31).

[180] For a literature review covering migration from rural areas to Bangkok, see Somboon (1985). Robert B. Texter studied Bangkok's Pedicap drivers in the 1950s and found that job opportunities in the city had tremendously increased for unskilled and semi-skilled labour and as a result, they could get a higher paying job. Pedicap drivers could earn three times as much as construction workers or gardeners. A later survey of 500 Pedicap drivers indicated that inadequate water supply was pressing farmers in the villages. On the other hand, Bangkok offered more economic opportunities, excitement, experiences, and esteem if a family member could move from the village to the urban area (Textor 1961). William J. Klausner studied migrants from the Northeast to Bangkok in the late 1950s. He found six major factors for migration: (1) demand for cheap labour in the industries with most of the investments from the United States and various international organizations; (2) a prolonged drought that lasted for four years in the Northeast; (3) improvements in transportation; (4) an obsession with city life in Bangkok; (5) a strong desire among the young generation to experience the civilization of the "City of Angels"; and (6) assistance given by monks in Bangkok to new immigrants. Klausner pointed out that immigrants from the Northeast had strong ties with their families and an obligation to send money back home to support their relatives (cited by Paritta 1993, p. 29). Marian R. Meinkoth studied immigrants from the Northeast in 1957 and found that economic reasons were paramount. Of the 415 interviewees, almost 80 per cent migrated to Bangkok in search of a job, while another 15 per cent migrated because

After 1987, migration into Bangkok declined due to the saturation of carrying capacity, traffic congestion, and the expansion of manufacturing and other economic activities to the perimeters of Bangkok and other provinces. This population spill-over led to the rapid growth of neighbouring provinces like Samut Prakan and Nonthaburi,[181] which had been the source of Bangkok's earliest migrants.

A migration survey for Bangkok conducted in 2009 by the National Statistical Office shows that there were only 42,885 immigrants against 452,782 emigrants, representing a net migration of −409,879 in 2009. This number was very high, in comparison to the South and even other parts of the Central Region, where emigration was likewise higher than immigration. It was the North and Northeast that attracted more immigrants. These migration statistics are a clear indication that economic growth from Bangkok and the Central Region continued to diffuse to other regions, especially the North and the Northeast. The number of migrants classified by region is shown in Table 2.13.[182]

---

of food shortages or rice crop failure. Moreover, 75 per cent of male interviewees were 20–24 years old, while another 12 per cent were younger than 20. On the other hand, 46 per cent of the female interviewees were older than 40, 48 per cent were 20–24 years old, and only 6 per cent were younger than 20. Meinkoth also discovered that almost 25 per cent had relatives in Bangkok, almost one-third migrated to find friends and relatives, only 2 per cent intended to live in Bangkok permanently, while some of them admitted that they might stay permanently if they could find a desirable job (Meinkoth reprinted 1971, pp. 6–9, 21, 31–33). A study conducted by Chulalongkorn University in 1974 indicated that 39.7 per cent of the immigrants in Bangkok were either looking for a job or had found a job and another 16.5 per cent wanted to further their education (Visid and Penporn 1974, p. 52). Factors for rural to urban migration in the case of Bangkok after those periods changed in accordance with the changing economy and society as well as the labour market. (For instance, cheap labour was followed by a labour shortage that led to higher wages in the years after 1987 when rural wages increased significantly, or the case of workers from neighbouring countries replacing local workers, etc.) Apart from economic factors and diverse job opportunities, there were other more complex factors involved in migration decisions. These included information, cost of adjustment, social network, educational attainment, etc., as well as various options in other provinces (reasons for migrating to Bangkok can be found in Apichat 1995 and several migration surveys for Bangkok).

[181] The number of immigrants in Nonthaburi doubled between 1960 and 1970, whereas those in Samut Prakan increased more than fivefold over the same period.

[182] Migration Survey (2009).

TABLE 2.13
Number of Migrants Classified by Region, 2009

Present Region of Domicile	No. of Immigrants	No. of Emigrants	Net Migration
Bangkok	42,885	452,782	−409,897
Central	166,220	330,069	−163,849
North	170,723	67,163	103,560
Northeast	592,425	101,955	490,470
South	41,082	61,366	−20,284
Total	1,013,335	1,013,335	0

Source: Migration Survey (2009).

Prior to 1980, migration from rural areas put a great deal of pressure on wages, especially for unskilled labour, as they did not increase as much as they should have. Average wages for unskilled labour in all types of manufacturing in Bangkok increased only slightly between 1950 and 1980.

In fact, from 1950–80, most real wages were on the decline, indicating that unskilled workers did not share in the economic benefits of Bangkok's rapid growth. The real wage was 16.7 baht per day in 1950, and 12.8 baht per day in 1980[183] (see Table 2.14). Low wages were a key factor in the profitability of many businesses and in the expansion of manufacturing industries in the capital. In fact, industrial development in Bangkok depended primarily on cheap labour (particularly before the beginning of the 1990s). A large, cheap workforce was also the basis for the expansion of export-oriented industries, most of which were labour-intensive.

Beginning in the 1980s, especially after 1989, however, both money wages and real wages increased rapidly. The money wage, which was 52.5 baht per day in 1980, rose to 276.3 baht per day in 1994 (or an increase of 520 per cent). At the same time real wages increased from 34.3 baht per day in 1980 to 98.5 baht per day (a 3.34-fold increase), as shown in Table 2.15. This rapid increase in wages reflects a rapid rise in the demand for labour due to the booming tourism sector and the influx of foreign direct investment after 1987.

---

[183] Nipon (1981).

TABLE 2.14
Money Wages and Real Wages for Unskilled Labour in Bangkok, 1950–80

(baht/day (1954=100))

Year	Money Wages	Real Wages
1950	16.1	16.7
1954	19.8	19.8
1955	21.1	16.7
1964	22.6	20.7
1967	22.6	15.8
1970	23.9	15.2
1975	33.9	13.4
1978	36.4	12.7
1979	41.7	12.8
1980	52.50	12.8

Note: As there was no consumer price index in the 1950s, real wages here are money wages adjusted by the wholesale price index.
Source: *State Railway of Thailand* (various years); Ministry of Interior (1959, pp. 13–14); Porphant (1996; 1998, p. 83); Nipon (1981).

TABLE 2.15
Wage Rates for Unskilled Labour in Bangkok's Manufacturing Industries, 1980–95

(1976=100)

Year	Money Wages (baht/day)	Real Wages (baht/day)
1980	52.5	34.3
1981	59.0	34.2
1983	80.5	41.4
1984	84.0	42.4
1989	129.5	66.1
1990	155.3	73.9
1993	219.5	82.1
1994	276.3	98.5
1995	289.2	114.9

Note: Real wages are money wages adjusted by the consumer price index.
Source: Labor Force Survey (various years).

Manufacturing Industry

The coup-d'état staged by Field Marshall Sarit Thanarat in 1957 directed Thailand's economy away from state intervention, or an economy whose growth depended largely on the state, towards one in which the "private sector" was given a key role in industrial and economic development. The government at the time was advised by the World Bank to reduce its role in the economy and encourage private sector investment. The country was to open up to foreign direct investment in industrialization, while the government's role was restricted to providing public utilities and public assistance.[184] Between 1960 and 1972, the government's industrialization policy emphasized import substitution, but after 1972 the policy became much more focused on exports. Expansion of the country's manufacturing sector in the 1960s was concentrated mainly in Bangkok. This was extended to peripheral and other nearby provinces in subsequent years. In 1967, Bangkok was home to 54 per cent of all manufacturing plants, followed by Samut Prakan (20 per cent), and Nonthaburi (less than 4 per cent).[185] In 1980, Bangkok was still the prime location with 46.5 per cent of all industrial plants, but this declined to 40.5 per cent in 1985 and 37.7 per cent in 1987.[186]

In 1981, half of the total number of manufacturing plants producing foodstuffs, textiles, chemicals, and metal products (17,470) were located in Bangkok. More than 80 per cent of the plants that produced apparel (excluding shoes), paper and paper products, plastics, and electrical appliances were likewise in Bangkok.[187] These are figures which reflect the locational advantages of consumer or market proximity. Then, in 1987, the Thai economy shifted its focus towards more export-oriented industrialization, and by 1989, industrial goods comprised 68 per cent of all exports. From the late 1980s, the influx of foreign direct investment, mostly from Japan and the United States, was directed mainly at export-oriented manufacturing industries and concentrated largely

---

[184] For details, see Pranee (1988, pp. 193–97).

[185] Donner (1978, p. 827).

[186] Industrial Works Department, Ministry of Industry, cited by Atchana (1989, pp. 61 and 63).

[187] Wilaiwan (1983, pp. 5–6).

in Bangkok and its environs. The rate of economic expansion in Bangkok and the surrounding areas far outpaced the rest of the country by almost 3 per cent.[188] Despite policies and measures to decentralize manufacturing, industrial expansion spurred by foreign direct investment still centred chiefly in and around Bangkok (Samut Prakan, Nonthaburi, Pathum Thani, Nakhon Pathom, and Samut Sakhon). As a result, GDP both in Bangkok and its environs skyrocketed. GDP of the greater Bangkok area accounted for 46.8 per cent of Thailand's GDP in 1986. This rose to 52.6 per cent in 1990 and 51.5 per cent in 1995.[189]

Bangkok and its environs became Thailand's centre for assembling and manufacturing industries, with ties to Asia's newly industrialized countries. The five peripheral provinces around Bangkok had the highest employment growth rate in the country.[190] The number of manufacturing plants in Bangkok rose from 16,920 in 1987 to 20,248 in 1991 — an annual increase of 4.55 per cent. If Bangkok was included with the five "inner ring" provinces, the number of plants grew from 21,894 to 28,049, representing an annual increase of 7 per cent.[191] In 1994, Bangkok and its environs contained 33 per cent of new industrial plants and 40 per cent of new investments. Even so, there was a growing tendency for more industrial plants, attracted by the ready supply of transportation and economic infrastructure such as the deep seaport, to relocate to the eastern seaboard provinces.

Bangkok's industrial labour force rose quickly from approximately 145,000 in 1960 to 257,000 in 1970 and 853,000 in 2005, equivalent to the share of overall labour force increases of 14.3 per cent, 18.62 per cent, and 22.7 per cent in the same period, respectively.[192] Small factories (1–5 employees) comprised the bulk of employers, but this decreased as a proportion of all labour from 63.8 per cent in 1987 to 57.8 per cent in 1991. Factories with 20–49 employees or more were on the rise, representing a 22.6 per cent increase.[193]

---

[188] Askew (2002, p. 72).
[189] Ibid.
[190] Ibid.
[191] Nipon (1995, p. 119).
[192] Population Census (various years); Labor Force Survey (various years).
[193] Nipon (1995, p. 122).

Foreign investment was key to stimulating the accelerated expansion of the industrial sector. Such investment both in import substitution and export-oriented industries (especially after 1987) involving assembly and manufacturing, tended to be concentrated in and around Bangkok due to locational advantages such as proximity to the port and the large market in Bangkok (especially import substitution industries).

A major factor for attracting foreign direct investment from 1960 was the relative political and military stability that set Thailand apart from Indonesia, Malaysia, Singapore, and the Philippines, all countries beset by political conflict and turmoil. In the case of Indonesia, between 1957 and 1965, the Sukarno administration nationalized all foreign assets, including foreign-owned enterprises, resulting in an unattractive atmosphere for foreign direct investment.[194] In Thailand, investment by the Japanese, who were seeking advantages in import-substitution industries, especially in textiles due to the large market in Thailand, accounted for most of the increase in foreign investment.[195] From 1985, economic changes in Japan and the newly industrialized countries (NICs) in Asia, along with the sharp rise in the value of the yen and higher production costs, were the push factors for the relocation of Japanese industrial plants to Thailand and other Southeast Asian nations. The Thai economy, with its comparative advantages in basic resources (for example, labour, raw materials, and economic infrastructure), made Bangkok and its environs the major manufacturing region in East and Southeast Asia.

---

[194] Yoshihara (1978, pp. 54–57).

[195] A comprehensive work on foreign investment in Thailand and other Southeast Asian countries was by Pasuk Phongpaichit. She found that the flow of investment out of Japan into Asia increased steadily from the mid-1950s onwards. In the period up to 1985, three major trends can be identified. First, Japanese investment sought to secure supplies of raw materials which were scarce in Japan. Second, Japanese firms relocated manufacturing processes to countries with lower production costs. Third, Japanese firms established subsidiaries in countries which had erected tariff barriers to encourage import substitution. Japanese capital began investing in import-substitution projects in ASEAN in the 1960s. This form of investment increased through the 1970s, and then tailed off. In the early 1970s, the Philippines was a favourite destination, but the investment subsequently declined and more flowed to Malaysia and Thailand (Pasuk 1990, pp. 29–30).

Although several manufacturing plants relocated from Bangkok to the peripheral provinces and the eastern seaboard after 1987, many — especially small-scale ones — remained concentrated in Bangkok to take advantage of the agglomeration economy and the easy availability of raw materials. They also enjoyed other positive factors such as a large pool of skilled labour, convenient access to economic infrastructures, production factors, and repair and delivery services. Locating near large businesses that often had contracts with small factories was another advantage.[196] These benefits were so numerous that many small firms remained in operation in Bangkok despite the high wages and high land rents. Factories in Bangkok ranged from large to small. The 1997 Industrial Census for the Kingdom of Thailand pointed out that:

> Bangkok and its environs has the highest proportion of factories producing textiles, garments, bleaching, etc. (28.6 percent and 17.4 percent, respectively); followed by fabricated metal products, furniture, printing and publishing, rubber products, and plastics. On the other hand, Bangkok's environs are producing foodstuffs, beverages, tobacco products, fabricated metal products, rubber products, and plastics.[197]

The Vietnam War, Tourism, and Services

Tourism and the service sector in Bangkok rapidly expanded as a result of massive spending by American soldiers between 1960 and 1972 — the period of the Vietnam War. The Thai government's involvement in the war signified the close military relationship between Thailand and the United States. In 1961, American bases were constructed in several provinces, five in the Northeast: Nakhon Ratchasima, Udon Thani, Nakhon Phanom, Ubon Ratchathani, and Khon Kaen; and two in the Central Region: U Ta Phao in Chon Buri and Nakhon Sawan.[198] This spending accounted for 4 per cent of Thailand's GDP or 20–40 per cent of total export values from 1966–70.[199]

---

[196] World Bank, cited by Nipon (1995, p. 125).
[197] 1997 Industrial Census (p. 11).
[198] Boonkong (1974, pp. 1–2).
[199] Ibid., p. 134.

The Thai government's support for anti-Communist expansion policies led to the selection of Bangkok as the site for several international organizations' offices/headquarters, international conferences for the business and private sectors, and various other international agencies — all reflecting the portrait of Thailand as the U.S.'s nominee. Major international organizations located in Bangkok included the Asia Foundation, the United Nations Economic and Social Commission for Asia and the Pacific (ESCAP), the Food and Agriculture Organization of the United Nations (FAO), the United Nations Educational, Scientific, and Cultural Organization (UNESCO), the Southeast Asia Treaty Organization (SEATO), and the World Health Organization (WHO).[200]

The expansion of hotels, restaurants, nightclubs, and bars was partly due to an increase in the number of tourists, spending by G.I.s and other personnel, and various war-related expenditures. The number of tourists as well as G.I.s and other personnel on R&R (rest and recuperation) increased from 169,000 in 1965 to 279,000 in 1968. G.I.s on R&R from Vietnam accounted for 11–16 per cent of all tourists between 1966 and 1968, with spending as high as US$6.8–10.8 million, or one-fifth of all tourist spending, and representing twice the per capita spending of non-military tourists in 1967. Tourism growth also led to physical changes in Bangkok. Rice fields and marshes in some areas, particularly along New Phetchaburi Road, were transformed into entertainment businesses, such as bars and nightclubs.

The 1969 *Bangkok World Annual Review* reported that:

> Petchaburi Road extension, dubbed the American strip, grew out of a swamp rice field and fruit orchards. The main activity along the five mile strip reflects the influence of American involvement in South Vietnam.[201]

The G.I.s' demand for entertainment led to changes in the Sukhumvit area, parallel to New Phetchaburi Road. Here, too, bars, hotels and other entertainment facilities were constructed. This development spilled into

---

[200] Porphant (2001, p. 159).
[201] *Bangkok World Annual Review* (1969, p. 70).

the Patpong area as well, and by 1977 Patpong was an internationally-known entertainment centre in Thailand. The entertainment industry spread into other areas in Bangkok as well.[202] In 1959, the Tourism Organization of Thailand was established to promote and develop tourism. Later international offices were opened in New York and Los Angeles, followed by Frankfurt, Tokyo, Sydney, Toronto, Paris, and London.[203]

In 1965, the government allocated a budget of 200 million baht to renovate the airport and air transportation facilities at Don Mueang.[204] Technological advances in aviation also contributed to the growth in tourism, especially the availability of jumbo jets capable of carrying large numbers of passengers. Bangkok's role as the regional air transportation hub also helped to boost tourism and make the city a centre for regional tourism.

By 1974, Bangkok had become one of the world's air travel hubs. There were only 11 other airports around the world with heavier traffic than Bangkok. The tourism industry ranked fifth in foreign earnings. Eighty per cent of tourists entered Thailand by air. Air transportation increased by more than 25 per cent annually owing to the Vietnam conflict.[205] New first class hotels were constructed at an increasing rate to accommodate the growing number of tourists. The year 1966 saw a boom in hotel construction with 14 new first class hotels.[206]

Hotels built between 1960 and 1969 to accommodate the increasing numbers of international tourists included the Nana, Century, Victory, Park, Imperial, Majestic, Manorah, Rex, Amarin, Federal, Crown, Siam Intercontinental, Rich, Peninsula, R.S., Monthien, President, Manhattan, Asia, Chavalit, Raja, Chao Phraya, Intercontinental, Bangkok Tower, First, Grace, Siam, and Narai.[207] In 1982, Thailand welcomed 2.2 million

---

[202] Askew (2002, pp. 257–61).
[203] *Thailand Yearbook* (1970–71, p. F6).
[204] Ibid.
[205] Muscat (1990, p. 131).
[206] *Thailand Yearbook* (1968–69, pp. G102–3).
[207] Ibid. The number of hotel rooms in Bangkok increased from 959 in 1960 to 1,843 in 1963, 2,634 in 1965, and 7,064 in 1967 (*Thailand Yearbook*, various years).

tourists, compared to 880,000 per year in the previous decade.[208] In 1984, large hotels in Bangkok had more than 19,000 rooms or three times more than in Chiang Mai.[209] In 2009, revenues from tourism in Bangkok were as high as 331 billion baht.[210]

Trade and services also expanded. In 1971, there were 5,461 wholesale, retail, and other service establishments. This rose to 12,230 in 1978, or more than double in only seven years. This growth clearly reflects the primacy of Bangkok since the city had more than 53 per cent of all of Thailand's trade and service establishments in 1971, but this quickly grew to 71.64 per cent in 1978. Bangkok had 73 per cent of the country's wholesale trade, 87.27 per cent of wholesale and services, and 70.96 per cent of wholesale, retail and services combined.[211] The trade and service sector not only grew in numbers but also in diversity with many new emerging businesses, such as computer and related services. In 2007, there were 241,000 small enterprises in Bangkok, each employing 1–15 workers (accounting for 95 per cent of all enterprises). Total employment by these small businesses was 1.6 million, 1.3 million of whom were paid employees while the remaining 300,000 people worked without pay.[212]

Bangkok's Growth and the Rise of Cheap Labour

Cheap labour was key to the growth of Bangkok from 1960, since it enabled export-oriented industries to be more competitive while supporting the expansion of the manufacturing and service sectors along with urban capital accumulation and urban population growth. The issue of cheap labour from rural areas must be given particular emphasis since

---

[208] Somchai (1995, p. 92).

[209] Paritta (1993, p. 10).

[210] Tourism Authority of Thailand <www.tourism.go.th>.

[211] Wanee (1983).

[212] The largest employers were hotels and restaurants with a total employment of 376,000, followed by retail trade with more than 370,000, and wholesale trade with more than 280,000. Trade and services had combined revenues of more than 3.8 trillion baht in 2007 (Business Trade and Services Survey in 2008 for Bangkok, Samut Prakan, Nonthaburi, and Pathum Thani).

it was the key factor to Bangkok's growth and its transformation from a pre-industrial city before the Second World War to a rapidly growing, commercial and industrial city after 1960.

Prior to the Second World War, the Thai economy was characterized by a "sparse population" and abundant land, which meant "indigenous labour was expensive". Unskilled labourers working at construction sites in the provincial rural areas could earn higher wages than unskilled Chinese labourers in Bangkok.[213] Incomes of farmers (broadcast rice fields in a 50-*rai* plot of land) were significantly higher than those of Chinese coolies working in Bangkok. In 1910, a rice farmer could earn 262 baht per six months, 303 baht in 1919, and 246 baht in 1929. On the other hand, the income of a Chinese coolie working in a Bangkok rice mill (per six months) during the same period was 158 baht, 180 baht, and 180 baht, respectively, as shown in Table 2.16.[214] Moreover, between 1860 and 1921, real wages in urban areas tended to decline whereas real incomes of rural people were on the rise.[215]

TABLE 2.16
Incomes of Farmers, Unskilled Labourers, and Hired Farm Labourers, Selected Years

(baht/six months)

Occupation	1905	1910	1919	1929
Farmer (50 *rai* of broadcast rice fields)	704	262	303	246
Farmer (12.5 *rai* of transplanted rice fields)	245	152	202	135
Chinese coolie in Bangkok rice mill	158	158	180	180
Hired farm labourer in the Central Plain	157	164	119	133

Source: Modified from Sompop (1989, p. 168); Porphant (1996, p. 60).

---

[213] Porphant (1996, pp. 51–58; 1998, pp. 78–108; 1999*b*).
[214] Sompop (1989, p. 168).
[215] Feeny (1982, p. 29).

The level of income or wages in Siam's rural areas was high in comparison to other countries. In 1883, a wage labourer in rural areas of the Central Region could earn 80 baht in nine months.[216] This was three times higher than that of an unskilled labourer in Japan.[217] In 1930/31, Zimmerman conducted a rural economic survey and found that Thai farmers had, on average, the highest income in comparison to farmers in any other Asian country.[218] Zimmerman also discovered that the real income level of Thai farmers was double that of a typical Chinese migrant coolie.[219] In the author's work, it was found that wages for government construction work in the countryside prior to 1950 were higher than those paid to a Chinese worker in Bangkok.[220] The major factor contributing to the high income levels of Thai farmers was high productivity in the Thai agricultural sector in relation to labour input caused by sparse population. Although using simple techniques to expand the amount of arable land would lead to low yields per *rai*, the output per worker per hour worked remained high.

In 1850, the population of Siam was five million, and it increased to 8.3 million in 1909 and 17 million in 1947.[221] Prince Dilok Nabarath estimated that in 1900, Siam had seven million people, living in an area of 634,000 square km, which represented a density of 11 persons per square km. In comparison, Burma had 16 persons, Indonesia (or the former Netherlands East Indies) had 21 persons, the Philippines had 25 persons, and India had 73 persons per square km in the same period.[222]

Landholdings in Siam were large in comparison to all other countries in Asia. Most farmers had their own land, with very few tenants. In 1931, as such as 78 per cent of the country's total land area was forested. Natural abundance included vegetables, aquatic animals, and numerous varieties of fast-growing fruits. These conditions had a positive impact on the country's economy, as follows. Firstly, most of the Siamese were engaged in the agricultural sector, especially in rice production (approximately 70–80 per

---

[216] Ibid., p. 133.

[217] Maddison and Prince (1989, p. 265).

[218] Zimmerman (1931, p. 318).

[219] Ibid., p. 227.

[220] Porphant (1996, pp. 50–60; 1998, pp. 85–90).

[221] Ingram (1971, p. 7); *Statistical Yearbook of Thailand* (various years).

[222] Chatthip (reprinted 1999, p. 25).

cent of the total labour force). Increases in rice production were achieved mainly through expansion of the cultivated areas using existing traditional techniques. It was estimated that from 1850 to 1950, rice fields increased, through land clearing, from six million *rai* in 1850 to 35 million *rai* in 1950.[223] This huge increase in cultivated lands led to an increasing trend in the ratio between rice growing areas and workers by about 1.19 per cent annually from 1905 to 1941.[224] Secondly, Siamese village economy was a subsistence one, except in the Central Region near Bangkok, where a market economy was in place. Natural fertility and vacant land enabled communities to utilize natural resources directly for consumption without having to trade for them. Household labour, therefore, was the most important factor of production. The subsistence economy was apparent in the North, the Northeast, and the South until 1932.[225]

These circumstances, then, prior to the Second World War had two consequences. First, rural to urban migration remained low especially in Bangkok because of comparatively higher wages — risks from uncertain and variable wages were higher in urban areas. Natural abundance and food availability enabled rural workers to work less with more time for leisure. Second, high opportunity cost of moving was a crucial factor in keeping Thai labour engaged in rural agriculture, especially rice production with the strong traditional village-base economy of the Thai peasant. On the contrary, Chinese immigration played an important role in developing the non-farming occupations in Thailand, especially in Bangkok. The influx of Chinese immigration helped to keep unskilled urban wages down.

After the Second World War, the golden age of high income and wages came to an end and was replaced by "cheap labour", resulting from rapid population growth. Thailand was becoming a country with a larger population and less available land than in previous periods. Natural resources deteriorated considerably, and it became more difficult to expand the available stock of arable land. Between 1911 and 1947, the Thai population rose slowly, doubling over the 36-year period. In 1911 the population of Siam was 8.3 million, and by 1947, it was 17.5 million. In 1986, Thailand's population stood at 52.6 million, having doubled in only 23 years. A

---

[223] Ingram (1964, p. 109).
[224] Feeny (1982, pp. 44–45).
[225] Chatthip (reprinted 1999).

high population growth after Second World War, especially in the 1950s and 1960s put pressure on rural incomes and wages. In the 1950s, as we have seen, rural unskilled wages now lagged behind unskilled wages. Farmers had to divide their land into smaller plots, so small that they could not provide an adequate living, forcing many rural farmers to become tenants. In 1930, the comparative ratio between farmers with rented land to the rural population was 15.7 per cent.[226] The ratio grew to 17.3 per cent in 1953 and 19 per cent in 1963, while it decreased to 18 per cent in 1963, before rising again to 20.8 per cent in 1976.[227] These farmers became landless, eventually having no choice but to work as hired labour. A crisis in Thailand's rural areas clearly emerged in the 1950s, when rice production fell below subsistence levels.[228] In 1962, about 61 per cent of the rural population lived below the poverty line. Rural poverty was widespread: 77 per cent in the Northeast, 66 per cent in the North, 46 per cent in the South, and 40 per cent in the Central Region.[229] Surplus labour in rural areas was the result of population growth. The country's workforce increased at approximately 2–2.5 per cent annually between 1950 and 1980, a rate higher than in more developed countries (1.2 per cent). The rural population increased by approximately 20 million from 1950 to 1980, 2.5 million of whom migrated to Bangkok and another six million to other regions. The remaining 11.5 million people worked in the countryside since the urban manufacturing sector could only absorb a 3 per cent increase in the labour supply annually.[230] Low productivity, the emergence of hired workers, landless farmers, and surplus labour in rural areas resulted in an unlimited non-agricultural labour market that, in turn, led to wages that increased only very slowly. Wages in Bangkok grew relative to those in the provinces, and the relations between rural and Bangkok unskilled earnings, favourable to the former in the pre-war period, became increasingly in Bangkok's favour after around the 1950s (see Table 2.17).

---

[226] Zimmerman (1931, p. 212).

[227] Ministry of Agriculture cited by Porphant (1996, p. 72).

[228] Madge (1958, p. 12).

[229] See Oey (1979, p. 52).

[230] See Suvinai (1989, p. 45).

TABLE 2.17
Wages by Occupations, 1954

(baht/week)

Occupation	Thailand	Bangkok	North	Central	Northeast	South
Academics	189.24	258.42	134.87	216.24	139.54	142.28
Managers and administrators	301.36	392.79	174.17	137.02	199.83	274.75
Clerks	167.81	184.60	119.05	170.46	123.15	140.64
Sales	131.15	140.49	74.07	133.74	93.72	143.63
Farming, fisheries, and forestry	89.51	85.40	47.65	79.70	37.85	94.23
Mining	101.11	–	70.38	145.38	127.69	104.49
Transportation	153.69	166.92	96.00	156.67	104.05	149.72
Mechanics	134.72	155.31	97.78	137.30	108.60	135.12
Factory workers	113.78	130.01	76.92	125.84	81.00	125.10
Service sector	91.50	107.49	74.77	91.05	77.77	105.49
Others	139.23	141.88	136.56	142.13	114.99	151.86
Thailand average	143.79	156.11	102.94	148.23	111.76	141.86

Source: First Report of the Economic and Demographic Survey (1954).

In 1954 farmers, whether in agriculture, fisheries, or forestry, were the lowest paid at about 89.51 baht per week. When comparing these regional wages to other occupations in Bangkok or in the same region, it is clear that the occupation with the lowest return was indeed farming, which accounted for the majority of the workforce. Cheap labour, therefore, was essential to Bangkok's continuous growth. Structural changes in the country's economy from one characterized by high-cost labour to one defined by cheap labour, mostly in rural areas in the 1950s, inevitably led to increased migration into Bangkok. Cheap labour was the primary factor that gave rise to competitiveness, exports, and the expansion of the service sector, which was centred in Bangkok. Cheap labour also enabled rapid expansion in the manufacturing sector,[231] hence, the emergence of labour-intensive industries and services, especially export-oriented ones in the second half of the 1970s. These industries included textiles and garments, which could compete well in international markets.

Conclusion

Bangkok, as the capital and a primate city, has been the seat of the monarchy, the centre of capital accumulation by domestic elites and foreign investors, the primary port, and the centre of internal and international trade. As such, it has always been the key to Thailand's economic development. Bangkok's population in the middle of the nineteenth century was about 100,000, already overtaking all other cities in the country. The signing of the Bowring Treaty with Great Britain in 1855 and of similar treaties with other countries afterwards had a great impact on the expansion of trade and economic changes in Bangkok.

As one of the most important ports in Southeast Asia, expansion in international trade especially rice exports contributed to the city's growth. Over time, there was increasing diversification of economic activities including rice milling, shipping, warehousing, and trading companies, as well as an influx of Chinese migrant labour, and western capital and ideas. Bangkok grew much more than any other city in the country, with the Chinese having important roles as labourers and entrepreneurs at all levels of trade.

By 1883, Bangkok was already the centre of the economy and trade. More than 28 per cent of the heads of households in Bangkok were in the non-agricultural sector including trade and manufacturing, marketing, and the professions. Household heads engaged in agriculture

---

[231] Real industrial production increased 14 per cent annually between 1960 and 1970 and between 1970 and 1980. The latter increase was mostly labour growth (or higher employment) rather than an increase in production efficiency such as technology or other capital factors (Sirilaksana 1988, p. 92).

constituted about 20 per cent of the population, whereas 9 per cent were government officials. If Thonburi is excluded, the proportion of household heads in non-agricultural occupations in Bangkok city proper would be as high as 60 per cent.

Bangkok's population grew from 360,000 in 1914 to 700,000 by 1930, more than half of this growth was due to the influx of Chinese migrants. Canal construction in the Central Plain was also important to Bangkok's growth. Canals were the main transportation routes carrying goods, especially rice for exports, from other regions into Bangkok.

Through growing centralization, Bangkok came to dominate the other regions. Financially, the tin mining economy of Chiang Mai and the Southern provinces was controlled and taxed by Bangkok. Bangkok dominated not only other regions in particular, but Thailand as a whole.

Road construction in Bangkok, particularly in the closing decade of the nineteenth century, was the major factor in changing Bangkok from a "water-based" to a "land-based" city. This not only increased land prices but also spurred investment by the Privy Purse in row-house construction. It boosted trade and investment and the development of land transportation. Bangkok grew in all directions, both in terms of population and the economy. The Ministry of the Capital, established in 1892, oversaw a large budget to administer Bangkok's affairs. The Ministry was also responsible for tax collection in Bangkok that would later be allocated for road construction and maintenance as well as other infrastructure projects, for example, piped water infrastructure and the construction of canals. At the end of the nineteenth century, the Privy Purse invested heavily in row houses and fresh markets for rent.

Between 1932 and 1960, Bangkok grew into a primate metropolis with an increasing role in the economic development of the country's other regions. The government's economic nationalism, especially after 1938, supported the growth of bureaucratic capitalism. Government officials formed close ties with Chinese businessmen, in particular, to expand their economic base. The construction of roads linking the capital with other provinces also enhanced the role of Bangkok as the economic and trading centre. Furthermore, after the Chinese Communist Party successfully took control of mainland China in 1949, the Chinese in Thailand stopped sending money to China and started to invest more in the Thai economy. As a result, trade and manufacturing continued to expand.

After 1960, Bangkok grew in all aspects, becoming a full-fledged "primate megalopolis". Its role and influence dominated the Thai economy, society, and culture. Bangkok grew rapidly both in population and build-up area. Major factors contributing to this rapid growth included R&R expenditures in Bangkok by American soldiers during the Vietnam War, the expansion of tourism together with the opening of new hotels and other businesses in the service sector, the government's economic development policy which strongly favoured Bangkok, and the influx of cheap rural labourers into Bangkok looking for work because of low productivity and low income and wages in the agricultural sector, which resulted from the pressure of rapid population growth. Cheap rural labour contributed to higher profits and increased competitiveness in business and exports, and thus the large concentration of business and manufacturing in Bangkok.

3

CENTRAL REGION

Background

The Central Region contains a vast fertile plain that is the Chao Phraya River delta. It is similar to other river deltas of the world such as those of the Mekong River in Vietnam and Cambodia and the Ayeyarwady River in Burma, all of which are important to population settlement.[1] Deltas are plains created by the accumulation of sediment carried by the river from mountains and other high areas. Delta soil is rich in natural fertilizers and is ideal for growing grains and crops to feed a large population.

The Chao Phraya River delta was first settled by communities of various ethnicities that migrated from abroad. It is suitable for building houses and for agriculture. The Central Region's delta has been deemed one of the most important "rice bowl" of the world. This reflects the area's richness and its suitability for rice cultivation with a potential to "feed" the people of the world. Other river basins exist in the Central Region, namely those of the Tha Chin and Pa Sak rivers. The western part of the region is not a plain but a continuation of mountain ranges

---

[1] For development and changes in the Chao Phraya River delta, see Srisakra (2000).

from the North. The area is also fertile because it is a confluence of the Mae Klong and Phetchaburi rivers with coastal basins along the Gulf of Thailand. The Central Region also covers the east coast, which is the southeastern part of Thailand. The area comprises deltas formed by small rivers such as the Rayong, Chanthaburi and *mueang* Trat. The upper watersheds next to the Gulf and in the eastern part of the Central Region are the Bang Pakong basin and the Prachin Buri basin.

Before 1855, the economy and commerce of the region was expanding. Sugarcane farming for sugar production flourished in Bang Pla Soi, Nakhon Chai Si, Bang Pakong and Chachoengsao. There were no less than 200 sugarcane processing plants in Chachoengsao, some with as many as 200 labourers. During the reign of King Rama III, sugar production extended to 19 major cities, most of which were in the Central Region. Pepper was another important export. Its main production sites in Chanthaburi were run by the Chinese. The amount of pepper exported to China in 1822 was 600,000 *hab*. The development of a market economy affected the growth of the region's population and economy.[2]

THE CENTRAL REGION UP TO 1941

After the signing of the Bowring Treaty in 1855, the Central Region saw a change from a subsistence economy to a commercial one, more so than any other region. The Central Plain was ideal for growing rice. It was in close vicinity to Bangkok, which was a port city linking local rivers to the world market. The average rural household income was the highest among the regions. Nevertheless, the Central Region did have its debt and agricultural land ownership problems. Also prevalent were problems with landless farmers having to rent farmland to make a living.

The growth of the rice economy had an impact on the development of rice mills, most of which were run by the Chinese. Thailand became a major exporter. In 1907, around 90 per cent of rice exports originated

---

[2]   See Nidhi (2000, pp. 141–44); Pallegoix (reprinted 2006); Crawfurd (1915, pp. 111–12).

from the Central Region. Economic growth encouraged the settlement of Chinese immigrants in various provinces. These immigrants sought to start businesses at every level in the non-agricultural sector. Most such businesses were in the area of commerce. As a result, the Central Region was more affected by the world economic depression in the 1930s than other regions.

Population and Settlement

Between 1847 and 1857, the population of the Central Region, based on the estimate made by M.E. Malloch, was 2.2 million (or 61 per cent of the population of Siam). The population consisted of 1.2 million Thais, 660,000 Chinese, 50,000 Lao, 40,000 Mon, 14,000 Malays, 10,000 Khmers, 7,000 Burmese and 10,000 other nationals. These figures include the population of Bangkok, too.[3] The presence of people of many ethnicities signified the region's economic significance. It was an area where international trade was expanding. War with neighbouring countries affected human settlement because of tight immigration laws. To protect Bangkok, the capital city, surrounding cities such as *mueang* In, *mueang* Phrom, *mueang* Sing, *mueang* San, *mueang* Nakhon Chai Si and *mueang* Nonthaburi had to extend their borders in order to strengthen their military command. The Chao Phraya River and its network of canals were important to agriculture, transportation, commerce and other governmental functions (such as tax collection, levies and general administration).[4]

In 1902, according to W.A. Graham, the population of some of the Central Region's *monthon* was made up of Chinese, Lao, Mon, Malay, Khmer, Vietnamese, Burmese, Shan and Karen[5] (see Table 3.1).

The 1909 census shows the population distribution among the region's *monthon*. Krung Kao had the largest population at 548,000. In second place was Ratchaburi at 426,000 (see Table 3.2).

---

[3] Malloch cited by Paitoon (1984, p. 316).
[4] See Hubbard (1977); Paitoon (1984).
[5] Graham cited by Prince Dilok (reprinted 2000, p. 19).

TABLE 3.1
Population of the Five *monthons* of the Central Region by
Ethnic Group, around 1902

	Nakhon Sawan	Ratchaburi	Nakhon Chai Si	Krung Kao	Prachin Buri
Siamese	200,000	59,000	100,000	189,000	181,000
Laotian	70,000	35,000	20,000	50,000	50,000
Chinese	10,000	40,000	43,000	50,000	50,000
Mon	–	40,000	–	10,000	–
Malay	–	10,000	–	10,000	–
Khmer/Vietnamese	–	–	5,000	10,000	40,000
Shan/Burmese	–	–	–	–	3,000
Karen/Hill tribes	20,000	80,000	–	–	–

Source: Graham cited by Baffie (2003, p. 29).

TABLE 3.2
Population of the Central Region, 1909

Monthon	Population
Krung Kao	548,465
Nakhon Chai Si	287,631
Phetchaburi	74,077
Prachin Buri	325,721
Ratchaburi	426,825
Chanthaburi	136,463

Source: *Statistical Yearbook of the Kingdom of Siam*
(1918).

In 1919, there were 2.2 million people in the Central Region (excluding *monthon* Krungthep). This number had risen to 3.3 million by 1937. Provinces (*changwat*) with the highest population were Ayutthaya (326,000), Suphan Buri (288,000), Ratchaburi (271,000) and Nakhon Pathom (225,000).[6] The Chinese had a major impact on the population increase. In 1919, there were 212,000 Chinese in the region (including the *monthon* of Krungtep). The number grew to 369,000 in 1929 and 390,000 in 1937.[7] The Chinese population in the Central Region made up 78.5 per cent of the Chinese population in the entire country. Provinces around Bangkok and those near the east coast had the highest ratio of Chinese nationals, namely Samut Prakan 3,581 (22.7 per cent of the population), Samut Songkhram 5,332 (11.6 per cent), Chon Buri 9,301 (17.4 per cent) and Chachoengsao 7,808 people (12.2 per cent).[8] The Chinese were involved in the rice trade, playing the roles of middlemen, traders, retailers and rice mill workers. In the Chao Phraya delta, the rice trade and other commerce were connected using the Chao Phraya and a network of canals. The Chinese were fruit and vegetable farmers and also grew sugarcane and pepper, among other crops. They worked in fishery along the east coast as well.[9]

In 1937, more than 80 per cent of all workers in the Central Region were engaged in agriculture, a majority as rice farmers. Other non-agricultural sectors, namely industry and services, were comparatively very small in size. Only 33,044 people worked in industry, or just 2.0 per cent of the region's workforce (see Table 3.3). Advanced agriculture was practised in the Central basin, primarily in Suphan Buri, Phra Nakhon Si Ayutthaya, Ratchaburi and Nakhon Pathom, which were areas most suitable for rice farming.

---

[6] 1937 Population Census.
[7] Skinner (1957).
[8] 1937 Population Census.
[9] See Skinner (1957).

TABLE 3.3
Central Region Employment by Sector, 1937

Province	Total	Agriculture and Fishery	Forestry	Commerce	Manufacturing	Metalwork	Transportation	Public Service	Professional Work	Domestic Work and Personal Service	Clerical Service
Kanchanaburi	51,128	45,100	1,114	2,397	566	238	301	322	336	249	95
Chantaburi	48,741	42,727	358	1,999	1,350	5	270	879	483	550	120
Chachoengsao	91,179	75,012	961	9,025	2,004	–	842	1,028	686	1,376	225
Chon Buri	69,672	55,308	1,127	6,778	2,156	5	744	1,131	619	1,654	150
Chai Nat	71,988	66,150	497	3,060	580	–	237	395	420	523	126
Nakhon Pathom	112,285	98,518	44	9,405	1,487	1	725	441	692	758	204
Nonthaburi	54,069	42,438	17	6,508	2,663	–	428	700	537	580	301
Pathum Thani	62,490	51,502	26	7,429	1,350	–	437	429	467	607	143
Prachuap Khiri Khan	24,326	20,278	503	1,360	292	237	652	214	189	514	61
Prachin Buri	91,696	79,348	394	5,613	871	–	574	3,346	401	187	163
Ayutthaya	149,858	118,624	106	18,890	5,041	–	1,908	879	1,562	2,437	409
Phetchaburi	70,931	58,895	786	5,190	2,599	2	718	825	747	1,019	150
Rayong	30,567	27,853	177	1,357	387	–	195	100	231	567	68
Ratchaburi	127,675	108,048	102	10,937	2,154	119	761	2,605	923	2,324	257
Lop Buri	77,429	64,598	145	7,274	1,167	–	459	2,144	474	990	171
Samut Prakan	57,999	40,167	904	5,726	895	–	434	1,491	552	1,620	210
Samut Songkhram	43,221	32,279	540	6,732	1,151	1	376	156	576	1,308	102
Samut Sakhon	34,677	26,324	1,209	4,093	1,383	–	456	287	291	537	93
Saraburi	90,690	77,283	552	7,823	1,159	–	774	1,035	519	1,387	176
Sing Buri	47,737	40,833	31	4,507	1,058	–	293	202	381	339	73
Suphan Buri	138,202	124,149	102	9,764	1,576	–	591	460	289	697	145
Ang Thong	62,422	54,444	31	5,134	1,155	–	247	194	538	589	130
Regional total	1,609,780	1,349,888	9,726	141,001	33,044	608	12,422	19,263	11,913	20,813	3,572

Note: Persons over the age of ten.
Source: 1937 Population Census.

Agriculture

The signing of the Bowring Treaty in 1855 triggered the transition of the Thai economy from one of subsistence to one based on commerce and money economy. This region's economy was more affected by the treaty than the other regions. Villages became more adept at rice farming for exports (being a river delta, the area was already suitable for the purpose). The expansion of rice farming leached labourers and resources away from traditional handicraft industries such as textiles. As a result, household industries began to decline. In 1910, almost all rice exports, around 90 per cent of the country's exports, came from the Central Region. Sugar production slowed because rice became more profitable than sugarcane. Sugarcane farming stagnated and sugar exports eventually ceased in 1878. According to J.C. Ingram, "In the two decades before 1850, the price of rice was between 0.30–0.50 baht per *hab*. After 1855, it rose to 2.00–2.50 baht per *hab*, and in 1900, the price became 5 baht per *hab*."[10]

The expansion of commercial rice farming began in the Central Plain, particularly in the areas around Bangkok such as Min Buri and Ayutthaya because of transportation advantages, etc. In 1909, there were about 1.9 million *rai* of farmland in *monthon* Krungthep (including the following *mueangs*: Krungthep, Thonburi, Nonthaburi, Samut Prakan, Nakhon Khuean Khan (Phra Pradaeng), Pathum Thani, Thanyaburi, Min Buri), half of which was dedicated to rice farming.[11] After 1900, once the railroad connected Bangkok to other provinces, rice farming started to extend to other regions. Commercial rice farming went on the increase because of lower transportation costs. More and more land was cleared to grow rice.[12] Between 1905 and 1909, there were 9.2 million *rai* of farmland in Thailand, with 6.8 million in the Central and 2.4 million in other regions. Between 1925 and 1929, farmland totalled 18.1 million *rai*, with 10.9 million and 7.2 million in the Central and other regions,

---

[10] Ingram (1971, p. 209). In 1860, Schomburg recorded that rice farming was more favoured among the Thais than other professions. A growing demand for rice from China, which came with the opening of the Chinese economy, boosted rice farming and drove up prices by 300 per cent. Ingram also noted that sugar production declined because it was not as profitable as rice. Furthermore, severe flooding in Nakhon Chai Si in the mid nineteenth century damaged many sugarcane plantations, causing sugarcane farming and sugar exports to cease altogether in 1878 (Paitoon 1984, p. 333).

[11] Sompop (1989, pp. 57 and 76).

[12] Ibid., p. 50.

respectively. The Central Region produced 0.75 million tonnes of rice in 1875. The figure increased to 1.7 million by 1910, which represented half of the country's total rice production that year.[13]

The digging of canals in the mid nineteenth century opened up millions of *rai* of potential farmland in areas such as Maha Sawat, Prem Prachakorn, Prawet Burirom, Damnoen Saduak and Rangsit. People from various regions migrated to the Central Plain to claim a piece of new farmland. This happened at the same time as the abolition of slavery. Almost two million *rai* of new farmland was allocated during the reign of King Rama V.[14] Infertile soil was one factor that pushed people to seek out new land. One report stated that the new houses erected along the Rangsit canals were "mostly relocated from seaside areas where farming was not possible due to salt-water floods and weeds that frequently destroyed crops".[15]

Migrant workers from the Northeast (Isan) contributed somewhat to the growth of the rice economy in the Central Region. Because rice production was labour intensive and the workforce was relatively small compared to the amount of farmland, labourers quickly became scarce as demand for rice grew. Workers' wages skyrocketed during certain seasons from 1 baht to 2–3 baht per day. Despite the wage increase, the labour force was still in short supply. In 1897, workers from Isan began to come to work in Thanyaburi. In 1901, there were 1,094 workers and in 1904, 5,000. They were paid 40–120 baht per season. On average the workers received 80 baht working and living with the farm owners. Due to higher wages, the method of rice farming was switched from transplanting to broadcasting.[16] As a result of worker migration from Isan, the population of Thanyaburi rose from 27,545 in 1900 to 40,000 in 1902 and 73,200 in 1909.[17]

The increase in volume of commercial rice production in the Central Region was more a result of allocating additional farmland rather than

---

[13] Ibid., p. 50.
[14] Pertaining to this topic, see Suntharee (1987); Chatthip (reprinted 1999).
[15] N.A. M. of Finance 0301.1.18/2 (1905).
[16] Johnston cited by Suwit (2005, p. 330).
[17] Suntharee (1987, p. 93).

improving the production yields per *rai* of existing land. Traditional production methods and tools — buffalos, cows, hoes and shovels — were still utilized. Although total production rose, yields per *rai* remained low. The lack of technology hindered the development of Thai agriculture. The situation was different in newly cleared farmland in developed countries such as the United States and New Zealand. Those countries constantly invested in new farming technology. Rice farming in Thailand, for both export and domestic consumption, was carried out by small-scale farmers. This was in contrast to that of developed countries where agricultural production was done on a large-scale or called "plantations".[18]

The yield per *rai* of each *monthon* during the years 1922–26 was as follows: Ayutthaya 3.98–5.10 *hab* per *rai*, Nakhon Chai Si 3.97–4.95 *hab* per *rai*, Prachin Buri 3.47–4.20 *hab* per *rai*, Ratchaburi 5.02–5.65 *hab* per *rai*.[19] However, yields per worker were high because the sparsely populated land allowed for nearly unlimited farmland reclamation. Dr Sompop Manarungsan shows that around 1900, Japanese rice farmers had to work twice as hard as Thai farmers in the Central Plain to produce the same amount of rice. This meant that the productivity of Thai farmers was relatively high. Furthermore, it was discovered that rice yields in 1890 were well ahead those in Java in the 1920s (see Table 3.4). As mentioned in the previous chapter, the income and wages in rural Thailand were apparently high compared to other countries. In 1883, hiring a Central rural worker cost 80 baht per nine months,[20] which was three times higher than in Japan.[21] In 1930/31, Zimmerman's rural survey shows that Thai rice farmers had high average income compared with the rest of Asia.[22] Before the Second World War, wages of these farmers were generally higher than those of unskilled Chinese labourers in Bangkok.[23]

---

[18] Ammar (1975).

[19] N.A. Department of Royal Railways 2/12.

[20] Feeny (1982, p. 133).

[21] Maddison and Prince (1989, p. 265).

[22] Zimmerman (1931, p. 318); also see Skinner (1957, pp. 28–32, 91–92).

[23] Porphant (1998, p. 86).

TABLE 3.4
Rice Yields Per Unit of Labour, Central Thailand, East Java and Japan

(kg/work hour)

Year	Central Thailand	Year	East Java	Year	Japan
1901–9	3.47	1920–29	2.40	1890	1.80
1930	3.41			1952	2.90
1965–67	2.52			1970	6.80

Source: Sompop (1989, p. 171).

Three key factors influenced the growth of rice exports from the 1870s. First is the development of international trade routes. The opening of the Suez Canal in 1869 significantly reduced the distance and cost of transportation between Europe and East Asia. Steamships replaced sailing ships because they were better equipped to handle heavy, bulky products. Shipping costs began to fall. Douglass North estimated that after the completion of the Suez Canal, freight costs fell 64 per cent between 1830 and 1905.[24] Steamships thus played an important role in the expansion of Thai rice exports. Furthermore, other Southeast Asian nations such as Malaya, the Philippines and the Netherlands East Indies (Indonesia) began to produce commodities such as tea leaves, coffee and coconut for exports. The expansion of these industries caused workers in those countries to switch from subsistence rice and crop farming to working on large plantations that grew these commodities for exports. Labour-for-hire was on the increase and these workers became an important consumer market for Thai rice.

Second, apart from new canals being built to support rice farming and stimulate exports,[25] irrigation projects in the Central Region also helped to make existing land more productive. Such undertakings included the Pa Sak Tai (1915–24), the Suphan (the Pho Phraya dam on the Tha Chin River in 1925) and the Chiang Rak–Bang Hia (completed in 1932)

---

[24] North cited by Sompop (1993, p. 22).
[25] Chatthip (reprinted 1999, pp. 46–48).

projects. These projects improved agricultural irrigation, solved drought problems and generally improved rice farming in the Central Plain.[26] The Chao Phraya River and the various canals linking Bangkok to rice fields played a major role in the shipment of rice and other heavy goods from other regions to Bangkok. For instance, in 1927, although 10,297 km of rail lines were laid to connect Bangkok to other regions, 86 per cent of rice shipments to Bangkok was still transported through the Chao Phraya and the network of canals.[27]

Third was the increase in population. The death rate decreased markedly as a result of advancements in science and medicine. The population of Asian and European nations increased. For example, between 1873 and 1920, the population of China increased by 80 million. During the same period, the number of people in Netherlands East Indies (Indonesia) and the Philippines grew 1.4 per cent per year.[28] The world population continuously increased, so export of rice expanded, particularly in the inter-war years.

The growth of commercial rice trading had an effect on the economy and population settlement. The settlement of many villages in the Central Plain was driven by noblemen and landowners. Until the 1860s, most of the population were still under the control of noblemen and royalty in a feudal, master–servant society. The growth of rice exports pushed the noblemen, particularly those living in the capital, to recruit more servants and slaves and settle them in villages to work in order to meet production demands. Kitahara found that many villages in Nakhon Nayok and the nearby vicinity were established by "lords". (In Nakhon Nayok there was a village called "*rong chao*" or "Nobleman's building".)[29] These villages were founded by noblemen, often in areas close to the capital. They laid claim to land in Rangsit, Ayutthaya, and Pathum Thani, and invested in rice farming. Even though slavery was legally abolished in 1905, some slaves and servants willingly continued to serve under their master. With the growing rice trade, ownership of the land around

---

[26] Pendleton (1962 reprinted 1976, p. 143).
[27] N.A. R.7. M of Commerce 8.1/1929.
[28] Sompop (1989, p. 58).
[29] Kitahara (1996, p. 54).

communities in the Chao Phraya delta near Ayutthaya and Bangkok fell to the noblemen. Most ordinary farmers became tenant farmers rather than owners of their land.[30] Those that did own farmland possessed small patches no more than 5–10 *rai* in size. As time passed, major landowners were able to gradually take more control of the canal areas near Bangkok and rice fields near Ayutthaya. In the 1880s, three families owned one-third of the rented farmland around Bangkok, each possessing 41,000 *rai* of land on average. Other families, numbering around 120, owned 1,000 *rai* on average.[31]

In the early 1930s, important commercial rice production areas were Rangsit, Thanyaburi, Ayutthaya and Suphan Buri. Farmers in these areas owned on average 25 *rai* of land per family.[32] In other areas, such as Saraburi, Petchburi and Chanthaburi, the figure was 6–18 *rai* on average and farmers were able to produce scarcely more than what their household consumed.[33] The economy of the villages in Rangsit and around Bangkok changed more rapidly than other villages in the Central Region. Land close to the capital was often used for commercial farming because it was closer to export markets. Production was mostly on a larger scale than the outer surrounding areas. The landowners and farmers here had to constantly improve their productivity. A network of canals made up the geography, allowing for lower transportation costs than in more remote areas. Shipment points were easily accessible by large cargo ships that could carry the heavy rice. The growing rice trade profited the landowners and farmers, creating an incentive for commercial farming to generate cash. The increasing cash revenue allowed the farmers to consume more goods, prompting a demand for more merchandise from Bangkok, where people enjoyed a lifestyle that rural consumers sought to emulate.[34]

---

[30] See Suntharee (1987); Johnston (1987); Thaweesilp (1978).

[31] Pasuk and Baker (1995, p. 26). In 1895, Prince Narathip owned 10,000 *rai* of land under cultivation in Rangsit, all of which were irrigated (BTWM, 14 December 1931).

[32] Zimmerman (1931, pp. 25–28).

[33] Ibid., p. 116.

[34] Dilok (reprinted 2000, p. 91).

In Thanyaburi in 1930, 90 per cent of the farmers were tenants. Land was mostly owned in large patches.[35] Landlord–tenant relationships were characteristics of the Central delta area around Rangsit. In the Central Region as a whole, tenants who owned no land made up 36 per cent of all farmers. The region's farmers (both tenants and those who owned land) had on average 24 *rai* of land to work with.[36] Outside Bangkok and the Rangsit canal area, there were few major landowners because land there was relatively cheap. Rice transport costs were high, particularly at villages without connecting canals such as those in Saraburi, Phetchaburi, Lop Buri, Suphan Buri and Chanthaburi. These villages were created when smallholder farmers occupied land in other provinces. Outside the Rangsit area, 90 per cent of the farmers worked for themselves. The ratio of farmers who owned their own land was very high, which meant that only a small percentage rented their land.[37] The size of land in each farmer's possession was therefore up to the production capabilities of the owner.

The Central Region was the major area for commercial rice production. The average cash revenue generated by farming families from each region in 1930 was as follows: Central Region (279 baht), North (176 baht), South (126 baht) and Northeast (83 baht). The national average was 168 baht. Though the Central Region had the largest commercial rice production with the highest productivity among the regions, it still had land ownership issues along with debt per household that was higher than in the other regions of Thailand (see Table 3.5).

The economic downturn that set in in the beginning of 1929 affected the rice economy in the Central Region more than anywhere else due to its commercial nature. As the price of rice fell, so did wages. The average wage for hired farm labour in the Central Region was normally 60–80 baht per season. This was reduced to 30–50 baht, or a 37–50 per cent reduction. The price of rice decreased by one-third in 1929. In Lop Buri, some farmers saw their land repossessed and put

---

[35] Zimmerman cited by Pasuk and Baker (1995, p. 26).
[36] Zimmerman (1931, p. 18).
[37] Seksan (1989, p. 207).

TABLE 3.5
Socio-economic Status of Rural Siam, 1930

	Regional Average			
	Central	North	South	Northeast
Land owned (*rai* per family)	28	10	3	6
Families owing no land (%)	36	27	15	18
Rice produced (litre per family)	8,253	6,583	2,619	3,312
Rice sold (% of crop)	61	43	15	20
Outstanding debt (per family, end of 1930, baht)	190	30	10	14
Cash income per family (baht)	279	176	125	83
Cash income from crops (% of total)	55	39	31	21

Source: Zimmerman cited by Larsson (2012, p. 95).

on the open market. But even so the land was still difficult to sell, for example, land that cost 1,000 baht could be resold for only 200–300 baht. The decline in farmers' income caused many stores in the city to close their doors.[38] The effect of the low price of rice in Ang Thong was that some farmers lost ownership of their land and had to sell their savings in gold jewelry. In 1931, five stores in downtown Ang Thong that sold consumables and foreign liquor went out of business.[39] Some areas also experienced crop damage. In 1929, some districts (*amphoes*) in Chai Nat Province were faced with drought and groups of citizens declared that they were starving. Some started to plant solanum and yams instead of rice. Some even resorted to begging. About 4,000 people were affected. The Interior Minister approved a budget of 20,000 baht to aid, relieve, and provide rice to the farmers.[40] However, by 1930, the situation had not changed. The Ministry negotiated an additional 40,000 baht to help the farmers.[41] There was also news of food shortages in

---

[38] N.A. M. of Commerce 7/10 (1932).
[39] Ibid.
[40] BTWM (2 September 1929).
[41] BTWM (9 September 1929; 7 October 1929; 27 January 1930).

Ratchaburi and Nakhon Pathom.[42] In the same year, due to the slump in rice production in Suphan Buri, farmers demanded that they be allowed to postpone paying their capitation taxes (or taxes that were imposed on males who had not served in the military). The government agreed to a six-month extension of the payment.[43] In May 1930, 70 representatives of the farmers travelled to Bangkok to personally inform the government of their plight. After the meeting, the government subsidized the travel expenses for their return trip.[44] In 1930, a proposal was made to the government to lift rice transportation taxes in order to make Thai rice more competitive in the world market.[45] In the same year, Halls Patt, a government treasury advisor, suggested passing a law to prevent exorbitant profits, especially the exceedingly high interest rates offered by Chinese middlemen.[46]

A second survey of rural Thailand in 1934/35 carried out by James M. Andrews shows that the Central farmers had an average household debt of 163 baht at the end of 1929. The amount grew to 190 baht at the end of 1930, 234 baht in 1932 and remained relatively level at 233 baht at the end of 1933. Farmers' debt in other regions is shown in Table 3.6.

TABLE 3.6
Thai Farmers' Debt, 1929–33

(baht)

Region	End of 1929	End of 1930	End of 1932	End of 1933
Central	163.24	190.36	234.45	233.82
North	23.67	29.91	14.66	17.12
South	7.97	10.32	6.48	9.59
Northeastern	12.11	14.20	5.96	6.75

Source: Andrews cited by Suntharee (1993, p. 21).

---

[42] BTWM (9 September 1929).
[43] BTWM (6 January 1930).
[44] BTWM (19 May 1930).
[45] BTWM (24 November 1930).
[46] *Siam Financial Position* (1930).

Andrews' report also provides province-level debt information. He found that the province with the highest increase in household debt was Chachoengsao, which suffered the highest losses in the rice trade in 1933. On average each family lost 70.07 baht. In 1929/30, the province's debt was considerably higher than in 1933. Two other provinces in the Central Region that showed an increase in debt were Suphan Buri and Nonthaburi. Suphan Buri grew little rice for several years, while Nonthaburi saw very low fruit prices and farmers were unable to collect money for the goods sold. Provinces where household debt actually decreased were Saraburi, Ayutthaya and Thanyaburi. The lower debt in Saraburi and Thanyaburi was due to land mortgage defaults. Without the defaults, the amount of debt in 1933 would have been more or less the same as in 1932. In Ayutthaya, the decrease in debt was because payments were being made in cash, which was a sign of general prosperity. In Phitsanulok, cooperatives played a role in deferring farmers' debts.[47]

Compared to neighbouring countries such as Burma, where rice exports were expanding, the global depression had less effect on the Central Plain. David Johnston indicates that farmers were able to choose which farmland to rent. He provides an example of farmland conditions in the east of the plains (in the Rangsit area) in 1926:

> He [the landlord] who owned much farmland and had land tenants were few in number. Many had no tenants. Farmers could freely choose which patches of land to rent. If one was unfavourable, they could go elsewhere because there was much vacant farmland. Some managed to grow rice without even renting the land. Once the harvest was done, they moved away. The owners never knew because they lived far away [in Bangkok].[48]

Farmers in many areas of the Central Region grew rice only for their family's own consumption, with little in excess. They were able

---

[47] Andrews cited by Suntharee (1993, p. 22).
[48] Johnston (1987, p. 226).

to adapt their subsistence farming to changing conditions and were not overly affected by the economic downturn. This was evident in the absence of any repossession of large plots of farmland or bankruptcy cases in the rural areas. In 1932, a law was passed to prohibit the repossession of subsistence farmland if the owners were unable to pay land taxes.

Little changed in the farmland ownership landscape between 1930 and 1937. Many farmers in the areas close to Bangkok were tenants.[49] Most of the farmland belonged to the nobles. Village land was owned by the Privy Purse. The rest belonged mostly to descendants of the royal family or was privately owned. Further out, the ratio of land rental decreased. For example, in Uthai Thani, Prachin Buri and Kanchanaburi, about 11.9–19.6 per cent of farmers rented their farmland, while in the areas around Bangkok and nearby provinces such as Thanyaburi, Nonthaburi, Pathum Thani and Samut Prakan, Nakhon Nayok, Nokorn Pathom and Chachoengsao, the ratio was between 28.8 and 67.0 per cent.[50]

Manufacturing Industry

Industries in the Central Region were small in size and employed few workers. For instance, in 1937, there were only 33,044 labourers in the industrial sector, which was 2.0 per cent of all workers in the region.[51] Rice milling was an important industry of the region at the time. The first rice mill in the Central Region, located on the bank of the Bang Pakong River in Chachoengsao, began operations in 1877. Charles S. Leckie wrote the following in 1894:

> Of late years, the Bangkok and Patriew [approximately 30 miles from Bangkok] rice mills have been a favourite investment of Siamese princes

---

[49] Seksan (1989, p. 206).
[50] Ibid., p. 207.
[51] 1937 Population Census.

and nobles, who now own many of the mills, or hold mortgages on them.[52]
In 1879, there were five European and five Chinese or Siamese mills on
Bangkok river, and one on the Eastern River [Bang Pakong River]. After
fifteen years, …. [there were] three on the Eastern River.[53]

Beginning in the early 1910s, rice mills started expanding beyond
Bangkok into other areas of the Central Region and eventually into
other regions of the country. The expansion led to various forms
of capital accumulation by the Privy Purse, high-ranking officials and
other government officials. King Rama V paid 120,000 baht to buy
Phraya Phisanphonphanit's mill, located in *tambon* Saimoon,
Chachoengsao. He then gave it to his son, Crown Prince Vajiravud.[54]
In the 1920s, the expansion of rice mills became more rapid in the
Central Region. The growing rice trade meant that more land was
cultivated for rice farming. Between 1920 and 1929, there were 394
rice mills, more than during the period from 1908–19 when there
were 83, a 474 per cent growth rate. In 1929, there were 477 mills
in the Central Region, or 62 per cent of the country's total (see
Table 3.7). New rice mills were generally built along suitable
riverbanks to take advantage of transportation via the waterways. This
helped to reduce the shipment cost per unit as rice was a "bulky"
commodity.

Most rice mills in the Central Region were owned by the Chinese.
Small and requiring little investment, they produced rice for sale within
the province or in neighbouring provinces. The mills in this region
consisted of both steam and engine-powered ones. Most were less than
30 horsepower.[55] The mills hired 4,092 workers. Table 3.8 shows the
worker distribution among the Central provinces.[56]

---

[52] Lekies cited by Chaiyan (1994, p. 69).
[53] Ibid., p. 70.
[54] Tanom (1984, p. 123).
[55] N.A. Personal File 2.41/27 (1929).
[56] 1937 Population Census.

TABLE 3.7
Number of Rice Mills in the Central Region, 1929

Province/City	Mills Completed between 1908 and 1919	Mills Completed between 1920 and 1929	Total
Samut Prakan	3	12	15
Nonthaburi	5	16	21
Min Buri	1	14	15
Phra Pradaeng	–	11	11
Ayutthaya	26	36	62
Saraburi	–	25	25
Lop Buri	2	21	23
Ang Thong	4	15	19
Pathum Thani	4	7	11
Sing Buri	–	8	8
Thanyaburi	1	7	8
Chachoengsao	8	25	33
Chon Buri	1	26	27
Prachin Buri	–	12	12
Nakhon Nayok	–	10	10
Nakhon Pathom	5	42	47
Suphan Buri	16	17	33
Samut Sakhon	3	13	16
Ratchaburi	1	43	44
Petchaburi	2	15	18
Samut Songkhram	1	17	18
Kanchanaburi	–	2	2
Central Region total	83	394	477

Source: N.A. Personal File 2.1/27 (1929).

TABLE 3.8
Worker Distribution Among the Central Provinces, 1937

Province	No. of Workers
Chantaburi	82
Chachoengsao	458
Chon Buri	138
Chai Nat	18
Nakhon Pathom	418
Nonthaburi	179
Pathum Thani	251
Prachin Buri	76
Ayutthaya	649
Petchaburi	122
Rayong	35
Ratchaburi	361
Lop Buri	142
Samut Prakan	210
Samut Songkhram	76
Samut Sakhon	256
Saraburi	220
Sing Buri	49
Suphan Buri	187
Ang Thong	96

Source: 1937 Population Census.

Up until 1847, the sugar industry also expanded. The sugar mills used relatively dated production technology. In 1859, sugar exports totalled 12.18 tonnes, but after that exports began to decline. There were two large sugar production plants. The first was in Nakhon Chai Si which operated from 1862 to 1870. This plant closed down because one of its engines was relocated to a rice mill in Bangkok.[57] The factors that contributed to the decline of the sugar industry were: (1) the fall in exports; (2) soil alkalinity due to salt water breaches; (3) lack of control over productivity and price, decreases in global prices and reallocation of farmland for other uses; (4) higher wages. Labour, which had been cheap, became more expensive as work opportunities opened up in other sectors; (5) factory owners, who were generally revenue farmers, were no longer able to impose their own terms to labour and supply of cattle and came under an improving administrative control; (6) extension of rice cultivation at the expense of cane plantations owing to the opening of rice mills at Bangkok, and that Chinese labour flocked to these mills where conditions were better; and (7) fierce competition from higher-quality Java sugar made it impossible to compete.[58]

Prior to 1932, the Thai government paid little attention to industrial development. But after the 1932 revolution, efforts were made to create new sugar production plants. For example, in 1934, the establishment of Thai Sugar Co. Ltd. at Si Racha, Chon Buri, was proposed. The area was vast, totalling more than 20,000 *rai* and was suitable for planting sugarcane. *Phraya* Mahaisawan requested that the government subsidize the investment and provide protection. The initial investment capital was one million baht. At the time, the government agreed to buy no more than 25 per cent of the Company's shares. The Company's conditions were that the plant must be able to process 500 tonnes of sugarcane per day, which meant a medium-sized factory. In other words, it would have to be able to produce 50 tonnes of sugar, or 840 *hab* per day, which was one-sixth of the amount of imported sugar (in the year 1934). The

---

[57] Hewison (1988, p. 393).
[58] Ibid., p. 391; *The Record* (1922, pp. 7–8).

Company was expected to have revenues of 108,000 baht per year, with no less than 15 per cent profits annually.[59] However, the plant never became operational because not enough capital was raised.

From 1938, the government became more involved in developing the industrial sector. Factories were built in the Central Region such as a pulp and paper factory in Kanchanaburi (1938) and a leather factory (1943). The Kanchanaburi factory was the first pulp and paper factory outside of Bangkok and the country's second. After the establishment of the Royal Thai Survey Department at Samsen, Bangkok in 1917, the Kanchanaburi factory was able to use advanced machinery to produce quality paper from bamboo. However, it was consistently unprofitable. In 1942, the two factories were reassigned to the newly established Department of Industry and received more investment, but they continued to lose money.[60]

Services and Tourism

In 1937, the service industry employed 208,000 workers, representing 12.9 per cent of all labour in the Central Region. Trade was the most important sector of the region's service sector, employing 67.4 per cent of the workers in that sector. This percentage was the highest among the regions. In other regions, the percentage of trade workers was as follows: the North at 56.3 per cent, the Northeast 38 per cent and the South 53.8 per cent. The high ratio shows that the growth of the rice economy in the Central Region affected the expansion of trade, retail and wholesale businesses, transportation, middlemen, agents and financial intermediaries, etc. The Central Region's service sector was, therefore, more diverse than in other regions. Statistics of employed workers in the Central Region in 1937 are shown in Table 3.9.[61]

---

[59] N.A.(2) Office of Prime Minister 0201.22.2.7/4 (1933–37).

[60] In 1954, the two factories combined had a yield of 2,000 metric tonnes and employed 600 workers (Ingram 1971).

[61] 1937 Population Census.

TABLE 3.9
Distribution of Workers Engaged in the Service Sector
of the Central Region, 1937

Industry	No. of Workers
Trade	141,000
Transportation	12,422
Public service	19,263
Professional work	11,913
Domestic and personal service	20,813
Clerical service	3,572

Source: 1937 Population Census.

Hua Hin: Tourist Attraction

An important tourist destination of the Central Region was Hua Hin. After 1897, the royal family and high-ranking government officials from the capital started to seek out and purchase seaside land to build beach houses, mostly near key cities close to Bangkok. The houses were used for recreation and as vacation getaways, a concept borrowed from the West. After the completion of the railway connecting Bangkok to the South, Penang and Singapore in 1917, the Department of Royal Railway opened a southern rail route that made a stop at *tambon* Hua Hin, facilitating the travel there. The number of tourists rose as a result and the beautiful beaches added to Hua Hin's popularity. Prince Naret built Phra Tamnak Sukavet Palace as his vacation home at Hua Hin and invited his relatives to do the same. King Vajiravudh (Rama VI) initiated the construction of a golf course at Hua Hin in 1921. The Department of Royal Railway built the luxurious and modern Hua Hin Railway Hotel, which quickly became popular among the rich and the elites. Members of the ruling class, such as Prince Nakhon Sawan, Prince Pitsanulok, Prince Chanthaburi and Prince Naret, started to build personal homes and bungalows along the beach. During his reign, King Prajadhiphok (Rama VII) built Klai Kangwon Palace to be used as his alternative home. Hua Hin became a tourist attraction and the most popular seaside destination in Thailand.

In 1925, one committee was established, with Prince Kamphaengphet as its Hua Hin division head. The aim was to oversee the city's planning, infrastructure, land expropriation and intra-/inter-city road construction. Sir Edward Cook even proposed a road cutting through Klai Kangwon Palace, for which the budget would be borrowed from the Privy Purse and then repaid.[62] A majority of the Hua Hin development budget went to building a market (15,000 baht), improving the road connecting Hua Hin to Nong Khae (40,000 baht) and building a slaughterhouse (2,000 baht). A market by the name of Chatchai was built in Hua Hin (it was named after Prince Kamphaengphet's former name) on the Privy Purse's land. The Hua Hin Development Plan stated that Hua Hin had tourism and economic potential and therefore revenue from taxes was higher than its neighbours. In 1925, its income was 49,397 baht, compared to Cha Am (8,731 baht), Huai Sai (20,827 baht) and Nong Khae (4,297 baht). Much of the collected taxes came from opium and local liquor, which accounted for 23.7 per cent and 44.9 per cent of the total taxes, respectively. Railway revenue generated by the Hua Hin station was 21,688 baht compared to Cha Am (8,836 baht), Nong Khae (4,996 baht) and Khao Tao (4,718 baht).[63] In 1926, more land was purchased for the city's waterworks, electricity production and transportation. City projects were also planned on the newly acquired land.[64] In 1937, the Hua Hin Municipality was established and Hua Hin was assigned to Prachuap Khiri Khan Province.

The Hua Hin Railway Hotel was modern and luxurious, with 16 rooms, a lobby, a lounge and billiards room, a wine storage room and a balcony. It cost a staggering 128,000 baht to build, which was an enormous amount at the time. The hotel began operations in 1923.

---

[62] N.A. M. of Finance 0301.1.37/37 (1926–27).

[63] Ibid.

[64] The details are as follows: "The 204th kilometer milestone of the railway was the center of the area's development. To the North were the Huai Sai Tai station, Huai Sai Nuea station, Bo Kham train stop, Ban Cha-am station, up until the 182nd kilometer. Southward, there were the Bo Fai, Hua Hin, Nong Kae, and Kao Tao stations down to the 226th kilometer. To the East of the railway up to the shore... Westward, up to three kilometers from the rail tracks perpendicular to the 182nd kilometer and 226th kilometer milestones" (N.A. M. of Finance 0301.1.37/37 (1926–27)).

Tourists increasingly flocked to Hua Hin, partly because: (1) of its proximity to Bangkok and the convenience of transport, particularly when the railway connected it to southern destinations such as Hat Yai and Padang Besar (in 1919) and to Butterworth and Penang (in 1926). Express trains and imported European sleeping compartments provided faster and more comfortable long-distance travel for tourists. (2) The Department of Royal Railway promoted tourism in Hua Hin through various media such as newspapers, magazines and directories, elaborating on its beautiful natural setting and the luxurious accommodations. After 1926, particularly when the Bangkok–Butterworth rail line was completed, train ticket revenues rose by a factor of four. A report by *The Record* described the growth of Hua Hin in 1929 as follows:

> The months of October, November, December and January are winter months. Many foreign tourists visited Siam around the middle of December and during the New Year. Many traveled to Hua Hin. The State Railway Hotel was full of vacationers, most of whom were from Bangkok, the Straits Settlements and Malaya. This showed the increasing popularity of Hua Hin as a top vacation destination in the eastern part of this region. It was so popular among foreigners that the hotel was fully booked during the last New Year. The Royal Railway has therefore decided to expand the hotel. Work will commence soon.[65]

Hua Hin became the Central Region's seaside destination and an attraction for Thai and foreign tourists, creating a constant revenue stream for the local economy and the country.

To summarize, before 1941, there was a major shift to a commercial and money economy in the Central Region, more so than any other region of Thailand. The Bowring Treaty (1855), signed by Thailand and Great Britain, and similar treaties by other countries, had the effect of transforming Thailand into a world leading rice exporter. At the beginning of the twentieth century, 90–95 per cent of exported rice came from the Central Region. The growth of rice exports was

---

[65] N.A. Department of Royal Railways 2/21.

facilitated by the cultivation of more farmland using simple and traditional techniques.

The expansion of rice exports benefited related businesses such as rice milling which was the largest non-agricultural business sector in the country at the time. Although the rural economy of the Central Region was affected by the Great Depression, which caused rural debt problems and farmer bankruptcy, the region fared better than some countries such as Burma, with farmers quickly adapting to the situation by, for example, resorting to subsistence farming.

THE CENTRAL REGION AFTER
THE SECOND WORLD WAR

After the Second World War, the Central Region underwent greater economic changes than the other regions because it was close to Bangkok, the economic and labour centre of the country. It was here that the Green Revolution originated, which saw the growth of upland crops, the expansion of a market economy, and the gradual shift from an agricultural to a non-agricultural economy.

Because provinces in the Central Region are close to Bangkok, the growth of the city after the Second World War was an important factor in the economic diversification of the region. As Bangkok was a merchandise market, a large consumer of agricultural products and, more importantly, a domestic and international transportation centre, it was the most important market for agricultural goods. Apart from local consumption, Bangkok's advantage of location enabled goods to be transported to other regions as well as trading them with other countries.[66] As the population of Bangkok grew, the demand for agricultural goods such as vegetables, fruits, shrimps, shellfish, crabs, fish and rice, likewise, grew. The agricultural production of villages in the Central Region increased as a result. The growth of industrial goods from Bangkok from 1960 contributed to the decline of the local industries. Bangkok was continuously

[66] Chermsak (1983, pp. 6–20).

modernizing. The industries of export-led growth, import-substitution, leading service sectors such as banks, hotels and so on were centred in Bangkok. Bangkok remained overwhelmingly the leading port and it increased its share of both Thailand and urban populations. Jobs were by no means solely or even mainly in the industrial sector, but were spread across a wide range of sectors especially in services. Demand for labour increased considerably, especially unskilled labour. Manual jobs in the service sector constituted most of the non-professional urban jobs especially from the 1960s. Bangkok became a magnet for young men and women from the Central and other regions.

Bangkok's growth had an impact on the concentration of some types of food processing plants. Plants that produced products with little or no weight reduction after processing, plants that processed perishable agricultural produce such as fruits and vegetables, cold storage plants, plants processing heavy goods and farms that produced goods whose demand was dependent on consumer income such as pork, chickens, and ducks (as well as animal feed production plants) were located in Bangkok and its periphery. Various areas in Nakhon Pathom, Pathum Thani and Samut Prakan were allotted for this purpose, and food processing plants flourished. Farmers raised livestock and grew fruits and vegetables to meet rising demand. Pathum Thani's land was cultivated for fruits and vegetables. As a result, less land was used for rice farming. Rice fields decreased 11 per cent between 1979 and 1983 and land used for fruit orchards grew 19 per cent.[67] Fruit growing expanded to more remote villages in provinces such as Nakhon Nayok, Prachin Buri and Chon Buri, where flat farmland was converted to orchards. In the Central Region, the total fruit farming area increased by 1.66 per cent per annum between 1980 and 1990. Fruit production grew by 69.5 per cent in the Central Plain.[68]

The growth of Bangkok was a stimulant for nearby villages to produce and sell handicrafts and local products (such as fish nets, dried

---

[67] DORAS (1996, p. 113).
[68] Ibid.

and pickled foods)[69] because of the large number of customers. Trading was easy because transportation and communications were convenient. This and the expansion of capitalism as well as the introduction of local markets were incentives for villagers to produce their own products to meet market demands. In 1978–79, non-agricultural income (which included making products for sale) accounted for around 36 per cent of the total income of a farming household.[70] Revenue from non-agricultural products became increasingly important for agricultural households in the Central Region.

The construction of new roads and highways linking Bangkok to the Central Region boosted the expansion of upland crops. The World Bank indicates that "Before 1936, highways were practically non-existent. If they were present, they were in very bad condition."[71] Between 1936 and 1941, the government embarked on a five-year project to build a total of 2,880 km of roads and highways.[72] The plan was to construct highways linking Bangkok to various provinces in the Central Region (and to highways around the country) such as the Bangkok–Samut Prakan–Chachoengsao-Sattahip–Rayong highway,[73] but construction was delayed due to the 1930s economic depression and the outbreak of the Second World War. In 1941, there were still no roads linking Bangkok to other Central provinces (except for shorter roads connecting the capital to Samut Prakan and one linking Bangkok to Nonthaburi).[74] There were few highways in the Central Region, especially those that connected to Bangkok because of the lack of demand for such transportation. Rice was shipped via the rivers and canals. Rice, a heavy commodity, benefited from the cheaper transport costs made possible by the waterways. Subsistence farming was common in many parts of the region and it produced little excess goods for sale, hence little need for more roads.

---

[69] Nipon (1983, p. 33).
[70] World Bank (1983, p. 166).
[71] World Bank (1960, p. 157).
[72] N.A. Office of the Prime Minister 02066.5 (1934–53).
[73] Ibid.
[74] Department of Fine Arts (1994, pp. 320–24) .

In the late 1940s and the 1950s, new roads were built in the Central Region, an important one being the Bangkok–Nakhon Pathom–Ratchaburi–Phetchaburi–Cha-am–Nong Khae–Prachuap Khirikhan highway. Other roads included the Lak Si–Min Buri–Chachoengsao, Rayong–Chanthaburi, Chai Nat–Nakhon Sawan, Chachoengsao–Prachin Buri, Kanchanaburi and Suphan Buri highways.[75] After that, the Suphan Buri–Si Prachan, Sing Buri, Kanchanaburi and Chedi Sam Ong routes were built.[76] An important road in the Central Region was the Friendship Highway (*tanon* Mittraphap) connecting Saraburi to Khorat. The highway was opened to traffic in 1958, making Saraburi (and Nakhon Ratchasima) a favoured site for growing high-elevation upland crops, particularly maize. Maize made up 90 per cent of all crops in Saraburi. Between 1957 and 1968, due to the expansion of upland crops cultivation, farmers began to occupy land on the sides of the Friendship Highway. Rice growing and production expanded more slowly,[77] while upland crops flourished in Saraburi. The products made from these crops were for exports and the highway acted as the link for trucks to cheaply transport them to markets in Bangkok. Robert J. Muscat writes: "The Friendship Highway was one of the most extensively used roads in the country. Half of the vehicles going through checkpoints were trucks and 60% were vehicles entering and leaving Bangkok… Maize shipments at Saraburi and Khorat became cheaper by 20%."[78] Construction of the Chachoengsao–Sattahip (127 km) and the Chachoengsao–Nakhon Ratchasima (264 km) highways had similar stories. They had an effect on upland crops farming, land cultivation and the migration of thousands of people from other regions into the area.[79]

---

[75] N.A. Office of the Prime Minister 0201.71/18 (1955–56).

[76] Ibid.

[77] Visit (1971, p. 35).

[78] Muscat (1990, p. 121).

[79] Ibid., p. 29. The improvement of the Bangkok–Nakhon Pathom highway linking the capital to the southern transport lines. This highway was 50 km long. Vehicular traffic was less than on the Bangkok–Saraburi route. Muscat observed that "the two highways [the Bangkok–Saraburi and Bangkok–Nakhon Pathom] could become the center of the highway system in a 150-km radius around Bangkok. In 1984, 50% of goods transported by road were on these two highways" (Muscat 1993, p. 127).

In 1953, a report called "The Thailand Road Investment Program" stated the following regarding the impact of highways on increased crop production:

> The reduced cost of transportation made possible by new highways will stimulate farmers to produce more fruits, vegetables, crops and other commercial plants, particularly in Bangkok and other major cities. Farmers earn more and consumers benefit from cheaper prices. Equally important is the fact that the linked highways allow for growth in inter-region trade. More trucks can be used to transport high-value and perishable goods between Bangkok and the Central Plain, to Chiang Mai and Lamphun and to Songkhla and Hat Yai, etc. Domestic markets, some of which are newly established, have expanded, allowing producers, processors and merchants to benefit. Furthermore, the highways create a connection with some underdeveloped areas that were previously cut off from the rest of the country. The roads help to promote population settlement through land cultivation and livestock farming in new areas.[80]

Population, Migration and Economic Change

The population of the Central Region grew very rapidly from 5.4 million in 1947 to 9.7 million in 1980 and 18.1 million in 2010.[81] In 2010, the three largest provinces in the region were Samut Prakan (1.82 million), Chon Buri (1.54 million) and Nonthaburi (1.33 million).[82] From 1947, due to population pressure, the fertility of the Central Plain began to deteriorate and eventually became unproductive. The result was a migration of people, especially from the southern part of the region, to other areas in search of new farmland on higher ground. The success of the Malaria eradication project in the plateaus and the expansion of highways and export markets in the 1960s caused a quick expansion of agricultural land.

Agricultural production increased by 5.5 per cent per annum between 1960 and 1969. The six provinces with the highest net migration rate

---

[80] N.A. of Finance 1.3.3.2/1 (1954).
[81] Population Census (various years).
[82] 2010 Population Census.

(in-migration subtracted by out-migration) in Thailand between 1955 and 1960 were Sing Buri, Chachoengsao, Chainat, Samut Songkhram, Ang Thong and Ayutthaya. The migration rate was between 3.2 and 4.2 per cent of the entire population.[83] These migrants settled mainly in the northern part of the Central Region, while some moved to Bangkok and its surrounding areas. Between 1955 and 1960, migrants from the Central Region made up 56 per cent of all migrants moving into Bangkok (the total number of newcomers in Bangkok between 1955 and 1960 was about 300,000).[84] Kamphaeng Phet in the Northern region was a major destination because a self-help settlement called "Thung Pho Thale" was set up. The population of Kamphaeng Phet doubled between 1960 and 1970. Overall, the Central Region had a negative net migration rate against all other regions except the Northeast.[85] The total number of migrants for the five-year period from 1955 to 1960 was 48,776, while between 1965 and 1970, the number was 80,370.[86] Nevertheless, between 1965 and 1970, some provinces in the region had a high number of incoming migrants, namely Nonthaburi and Samut Prakan, because they were close to Bangkok and relatively close to the provinces along the east coast — Chon Buri, Rayong, Trat and Chanthaburi.[87]

People continued to move away from the Central Region. The net number of migrants leaving the rural areas of the region was 91,017 between 1975 and 1980 and 90,522 between 1985 and 1990. Their destinations included Bangkok and other regions of the country. These migrants occupied land and worked in areas with a high industrial growth

---

[83] Molle and Thippawal (1999, p. 19).

[84] ESCAP (1976, p. 21).

[85] Ibid., p. 16. Permanent emigrants outnumbered permanent immigrants. The net population loss was 345,000 in 1960 and 516,000 in 1970.

[86] ESCAP (1976, p. 18).

[87] Ibid., p. 22. Rayong's net immigration was 102.3 per 1,000 people. Other provinces also experienced high immigration rates. Factors included the expansion of agricultural and industrial farmland (particularly agricultural processing), the establishment of U.S. military bases and self-help settlements, the gemstone rush, and the development of resorts. Prachuab Khirikhan was among the provinces with very high immigration rates, equivalent to 100 and 140 per 1,000 people in 1960 and 1970, respectively. This was due to sugarcane and pineapple farming in much of the newly cleared land (ESCAP 1976, p. 22).

rate such as Chon Buri, Rayong, and Bangkok.[88] Between 1975 and 1980, about 262,000 people in rural parts of the Central Region moved away. About 47 per cent relocated to Bangkok, 14 per cent to nearby provinces and 39 per cent to the Northern provinces.[89]

After 1990, the Central Region experienced a positive net migration,[90] however, most of the resettlement was internal. In 2004, this region had the country's highest rate of internal migration at 460,000 individuals, or one-third of the country's total, primarily because it was close to Bangkok. (The total number of internal migrants was 1.35 million with 25.3 per cent in the Northeast, 21.5 per cent in the North and 18.9 per cent in the South.)[91] In 1987, two-thirds of the economy of Bangkok and its vicinity was non-agricultural.[92] In 2004, most migrants in the Central Region worked with machinery or on assembly lines in factories. About 74.6 per cent were company employees.[93]

Out-migration and a lower birth rate caused a contraction in the population growth rate in the rural areas. The percentage of people working in the agricultural sector against the entire population of the Central Region shrank very rapidly from 70 per cent to 40 per cent between 1960 and 1990. The percentage of people working in agriculture in the Central Plain decreased from 48 per cent in 1990 to 33 per cent in 1996.[94]

Between 1980 and 2010, the number of non-agricultural workers rose very quickly in all industries (except in ore and rock mining). The percentage of workers working in industries and services grew from just 27.4 per cent to 76.6 per cent. Agricultural workers decreased from 62.4 per cent to 23.4 per cent, indicating that industry and services had become more important to the region. The industrial sector with the

---

[88] Migration Survey (various years).

[89] Molle and Thippawal (1999, pp. 10, 12–20).

[90] Net immigration was 24,000 people in 1990–92 and 42,000 people, 278,000 people and 199,000 people in 1992–94, 1995–97 and 1997–2002, respectively (1994, 1997 and 1998 Migration Surveys).

[91] Migration Survey (2005).

[92] DORAS (1996, p. 54).

[93] Migration Survey (2005).

[94] Molle and Thippawal (1999, p. 124).

highest employment rate was manufacturing with 3.71 million employed workers, or one-third of all workers. Agricultural workers numbered merely 2.57 million, or 24.5 per cent of the total (see Table 3.10). The number of agricultural workers had been declining both in total number and percentage since 1990. This shows a general shift away from agriculture towards more non-agricultural sectors.

The Central Region was significant for the country's economic development. Between 2001 and 2008, industrial production and services made up 57.4 per cent of the region's total production, an increase of 62.3 per cent. The eastern coast was significant to the region's product manufacturing, contributing 63.5 per cent of the regional output.[95] In 2011, the region's production, if Bangkok was included, made up 71.2 per cent of the country's GDP and clearly reflected the Central Region's position as the centre of the country's economy.[96]

TABLE 3.10
Central Region Employment by Economic Sector, 1980–2010

(thousand workers)

Sector	1980	Per Cent	1990	Per Cent	2000	Per Cent	2010	Per Cent
Agriculture	3,183	62.4	3,780	54.8	2,806	35.3	2,572	23.4
Mining	43.4	0.9	23.9	0.3	14.6	0.2	14.8	0.1
Manufacturing	458.3	9.0	909.7	13.2	1,526.0	19.3	3,711.1	33.8
Construction	108.4	2.1	230.7	3.3	326.2	4.1	438.2	4.0
Utilities	15.9	0.3	32.4	0.5	35.5	0.4	58.8	0.5
Commerce	427.0	8.4	625.6	9.1	1,123	14.2	1,574.9	14.4
Transport	109.4	2.1	160.5	2.3	253.2	3.2	281.8	2.6
Services	482.7	9.5	602.9	8.7	837.9	10.6	2,077.3	18.9
Miscellaneous	271.3	5.3	529.1	7.7	431.2	5.5	242.1	2.2
Total	5,100	100.0	6,895	100.0	7,909	100.0	10,971	100.0

Source: Population Census (various years).

---

[95] Gross Regional and Provincial Product (various years).
[96] Krirkkiat (2006, chapter 6, pp. 16–19).

Although the share of agricultural production in GRP in the Central
Region declined from 12.2 per cent in 2001 to 5 per cent in 2008, the
region was nevertheless still regarded as Thailand's most important
agricultural zone — Asia's "rice bowl" — that could produce enough
to feed the country and for exports. In 2007, the total amount of rice
produced in the region was 9.41 million tonnes, or 38.1 per cent of
the country's output. The other regions' yields were as follows: the
North in 2nd place at 31.0 per cent, the Northeast 27.1 per cent and the
South 3.68 per cent.[97] The eastern coast of Thailand had always been
the country's leading producer of durians, mangosteens and rambutans.
In 1971, durian farmland in Chanthaburi totalled 14,700 *rai*, rambutan
29,100, orange 23,100 and mangosteen 1,840.[98] Fruits accounted for
47 per cent of the agricultural income of Chanthaburi, while rice
contributed only 18.8 per cent.[99] The growing of perennial fruits began
to spread from the eastern coast to the Central and other regions. In the
2000s, the east coast provinces produced a significant amount of fruits,
especially durians. In 2006, durian production in the three east coast
provinces — Chanthaburi, Rayong and Trat — was 0.314 million tonnes
in total, or 84 per cent of all durian production in the Central Region,
nearly half of the nation's total.[100] Similarly, rambutan production in the
three provinces in 2006 was also high at 0.31 million tonnes in total,
virtually all of which was grown in Chanthaburi and yielding 99 per
cent of the nation's output.[101]

Freshwater and marine fishing were also an important industry
along the eastern seaboard. In 1968–70, freshwater fishing produced
17.6 per cent of the country's total, while marine fishing contributed
15 per cent.[102] Chachoengsao was able to produce 81 per cent of the
freshwater fish in the region. The region produced 18.9 per cent of the

---

[97] Somporn (2010, p. 13).
[98] Donner (1978, p. 365).
[99] Ibid., p. 367.
[100] Agricultural Statistics of Thailand (2007).
[101] Ibid. 2009.
[102] Donner (1978, pp. 378–79).

country's freshwater fish in 1969, an increase of 5.1 per cent from 1962, while in 1969 the marine fish yield was 20 per cent of the country's total.[103] Shrimp farming began to play a role in the regional economy in the 2000s. The east coast continued to be an important producer of marine fishes. In 2003, shrimp culture production in these provinces was 82,812 tonnes, or 25 per cent of the nation's total.[104]

Agriculture

After the Second World War, farmland expansion in the Chao Phraya delta was reaching its limit. Farmers expanded their farmland and cleared forest land for cultivation in the outer new areas. The average farmland per person had not decreased from 1961, despite high population growth rate. On the contrary, it was rising at a stable rate. The average agricultural land in the Central Region was 7.62–10.59 *rai* per person. Between 1961 and 1985, the figure was 8.21–11.07 *rai* per person and 5.70–8.20 *rai* per person for the Central Plain and western parts of the region, respectively.[105] The amount of farmland and farms in the region rose rapidly. In 1954, the total farmland area was 23.8 million *rai*. This grew to 27.5 million in 1975 and 29.0 million in 1985.[106]

In 1977–86, important agricultural production systems in the Central Plain were: (1) the rice-centred system in most farmland in the plains and the middle and eastern areas of the Chao Phraya River delta, totalling about 7.5 million *rai*.[107] This system was also used for

---

[103] Ibid.

[104] Agricultural Statistics of Thailand (2007).

[105] Ammar (1987, p. 13).

[106] Agricultural Statistics of Thailand (various years).

[107] Rice-centric production systems could be subcategorized as follows: (1) Lowland rice farming, where rice could only be grown once a year. This system of rice farming could be found in Sing Buri, Lop Buri, Ang Thong, Ayutthaya, Nakhon Nayok, and Chachoengsao. (2) Rice farming in moderately irrigated areas, where rice could be grown twice a year. Such farmland could be found in parts of Lop Buri, Ang Thong, Suphan Buri, and Ayutthaya. (3) Intensive rice farming where rice is grown three times per year. This type of system is found in Chai Nat, Sing Buri, Suphan Buri, Nakhon Pathom, Nakkhon Nayok and Chachoengsao (for details, see Thippawal and Molle 2000, p. 13).

the most part in Singaburi, Lop Buri, Ang Thong, Ayutthaya, Nakhon Nahok, Chachoengsao, Suphan Buri, Chai Nat and Nakhon Pathom. (2) The sugarcane-centred system was primarily used in the highlands west of the Central Plain in Kanchanaburi, Suphanburi, Chai Nat and Nakhon Pathom. These areas received water from the Mae Klong Yai River irrigation system. This system was also found in some areas north of the Central Plain in Singaburi and Ang Thong. (3) A system centred around fruits and vegetables. This could be found in the southwestern side of the plains in Ratchaburi and in some parts of Nakhon Pathom, Nonthaburi and Nakhon Nayok. (4) Freshwater fish farming, including giant freshwater lobsters and other fishes. This could be found in the west of Samut Prakan and Chachoengsao. (5) Brackish water fish farming and salt production. These fisheries reared species such as tiger prawns and could be found near the coastal areas of Samut Songkram, Samut Sakorn and Samut Prakan. (6) Mixed cropping and plantations. These mixtures of plant and livestock farming included rice, sugarcane, fruits and vegetables, orchids, flowers, baby corn and beef and dairy cattle. They were particularly common in Nakhon Pathom and Samut Sakorn.[108]

The diversification of agriculture meant reduced rice production, both in the amount and ratio of rice produced against other crops. There were 482,000 rice-producing households in 1993 and 365,000 in 2003, a decrease from 37.3 per cent to 30 per cent (see Table 3.11). The number of families growing other crops — fruits, vegetables, herbs and ornamental plants — grew rapidly. These two main types of families made up 60 per cent of all farming households in the Central Region in 2003 (in 1993, the percentage was 50 per cent).

---

[108] Thippawal and Molle (2000, p. 13).

TABLE 3.11
Number of Holdings by Land Use, 1993–2003

	1993		1998		2003	
	No. of Holdings	rai	No. of Holdings	rai	No. of Holdings	rai
Total	1,295,918 (100.0)	24,127,818 (100.0)	1,183,044 (100.0)	21,339,253 (100.0)	1,013,460 (100.0)	21,592,365 (100.0)
Rice	482,915 (37.3)	10,826,521 (44.9)	447,827 (37.8)	9,723,401 (45.6)	365,318 (30.0)	8,541,412 (39.6)
Rubber	33,440 (2.6)	1,002,668 (4.1)	35,797 (3.02)	1,049,918 (4.9)	32,952 (3.2)	980,168 (4.5)
Perennial plants, fruits, forestry	302,369 (23.3)	3,425,767 (14.2)	277,013 (23.4)	3,186,947 (14.9)	313,740 (30.9)	3,986,821 (18.5)
Upland and other field crops	267,127 (20.6)	7,120,369 (29.5)	206,644 (17.5)	5,807,834 (27.2)	186,299 (18.4)	5,754,882 (26.7)
Vegetables, herbs and ornamental plants	78,269 (20.6)	402,337 (29.5)	99,822 (17.5)	542,297 (27.2)	111,716 (18.4)	512,345 (26.7)
Pasture land	13,548 (1.0)	281,515 (1.2)	6,257 (0.5)	121,350 (0.6)	n.a. (–)	205,407 (0.9)
Freshwater farms	n.a.	n.a.	n.a.	n.a.	n.a. (–)	741,661 (3.4)
Others	118,250 (9.1)	1,068,641 (4.4)	109,681 (9.3)	907,506 (4.3)	3,425 (.31)	869,669 (4.0)

Source: 1993 and 2003 Agricultural Censuses.

Pertaining to land ownership, in the Central Region between 1975/76 and 1992/93, the number of land tenants was on a downward trend from 30.7 per cent to 25.2 per cent. This was due to the increasing use of agricultural land for industrial and residential purposes.[109] However, the rental percentage was still high compared to other regions which were 17.7 per cent for the North, 5.2 per cent for the Northeast and 3.17 per cent for the South. Provinces with the highest rental percentages were Pathum Thani at 53.8 per cent, Samut Prakan at 62.9 per cent and Nakhon Nayok at 54.69 per cent.[110]

From 1993 to 2003, 64.1–66.6 per cent of farming households in the Central Region owned the land they worked in. Most (76.2 per cent)[111] had ownership documentation (title deeds/ *NS 5/ NS 3/ NS 3K/ NS 3khor*) for their land. In 2003, 16.6 per cent of land-owning farmers used their own as well as others' land for farming. Farmers without any land of their own made up 19.3 per cent of the total. Nevertheless, compared to 1998, the number of landless farmers rose by 37.4 per cent.[112] This shows a tendency for farmers to sell their land for a profit, taking advantage of the urban expansion of Bangkok, its periphery and other major cities. In many cases, once sold, land was used to build accommodations, golf courses, new roads and to widen existing roads.

Between 1993 and 2003, the largest group of holdings in the Central Region had between 10 and 39 *rai* of land. This group made up about 44.6–50.4 per cent of all holdings. The second most numerous group consisted of those who holded less than 6 *rai*, making up 19.1–28.4 per cent of all holdings in the same period. Taken as a whole, agricultural holdings who holded 39 *rai* of land or less made up 82–85 per cent of all holdings. Between 1998 and 2003, the number of holdings rose in all parts of the holding demographic, with those holding a small piece of land (less than 6 *rai*) having the highest increase at 57.5 per cent (the only exception was the group owning 10–19 *rai*, which fell by 17.3 per cent) (see Table 3.12)

---

[109] Apichai (1996, p. 14).
[110] Ibid., p. 15.
[111] 2003 Agricultural Census.
[112] Ibid.

TABLE 3.12
Agricultural Holdings by Land Size, the Central Region,
1993–2003

Size of Land (*rai*)	No. of Holdings		
	1993	**1998**	**2003**
Total	934,024 (100.0)	852,253 (100.0)	902,759 (100.0)
Less than 6	205,200 (22.0)	163,103 (19.1)	256,848 (28.4)
6–9	92,113 (9.9)	78,395 (9.2)	88,341 (9.8)
10–39	470,736 (50.4)	486,537 (57.1)	402,452 (44.6)
40–139	154,241 (16.5)	115,606 (13.6)	142,825 (15.8)
More than 140	11,734 (1.2)	8,612 (1.0)	12,293 (1.4)

Source: 2003 Agricultural Census.

The rising number of small holdings shows a general increase in the number of small farms and the tendency to divide farmland into smaller pieces. As many as 84,085 households disappeared from the 10–39 *rai* group, and the group with less than 6 *rai* added as many as 93,745 new households. This phenomenon ought to have caused a shrinkage in the average land size per household; instead there was an increase from an average of 26.8 *rai* per household in 1963 to 31.8 *rai* per household in 1991 and eventually to 25.0 *rai* in 1998 and 23.9 *rai* in 2003. The increase in land size was due to the migration of people from villages to cities and other areas.[113]

Rice

Although rice production had been on the increase, the role that rice played in the economy had been declining due to the increase in production of such crops as maize, cassava and sugarcane. The expansion was both in

---

[113] Agricultural Census (various years).

terms of land use and output. The agricultural output of the Central Plain rose by 5.5 per cent yearly between 1960 and 1970.[114] Nevertheless, the rice economy was still important to the region as a source of employment. Rice still occupied the most agricultural farmland in terms of area. It was an important source of carbohydrates. It also supported other related businesses such as rice mills, the rice trade, harvesting businesses, as well as agricultural technology. An important change in the economy of the Central Region was the Green Revolution.[115]

The Green Revolution and the construction of the Chao Phraya dam (1952–62) both had an impact on rice and agricultural production in the Central Region. The Chao Phraya irrigation project consisted of the construction of a dam, irrigation canals, and a drainage system. Land in the irrigated areas was consolidated. The irrigation system had a tremendous impact on the economy of the villages in the rural Central region. Not only did productivity increase because rice could be grown two to three times per year, there was also more space for transplanting as opposed to broadcasting. The areas where rice could be damaged by floods or droughts were reduced. The increase in productivity and income, along with new land consolidation, allowed for better agricultural technology to be applied. Tractors replaced working animals. Chemical fertilizers and new varieties of rice seed were introduced. Hired labourers replaced the use of family members, causing traditional customs like *"long khak kiao khao"* (exchange labourers for rice growing) to decline. Farmers increasingly used new, high-yielding rice varieties (HYVs). These varieties were quick to produce grains and were not photosensitive, allowing multiple yields per year. One example was the *kor khor* rice high-yielding variety.[116] The use of HYVs required more sophisticated production technology. More fertilizers were needed and more pest

---

[114] Molle and Thippawal (1999, p. 17).

[115] The "Green Revolution" refers to the agricultural revolution or the raising of agricultural productivity by utilizing new technologies, particularly the use of scientifically researched seeds like miracle rice (created by the International Rice Research Institute (IRRI) in the Philippines), the use of scientifically proven fertilizers, and pesticides.

[116] For details, see Ammar and Viroj (1990, p. 97).

control was required. Good irrigation and land management were essential for high productivity. The government invested more in irrigation in this region than in any other region because the Central Region has always been the most important rice-growing zone both for consumption and exports.

The Central Region used more agricultural machinery and chemical fertilizers than other regions. In 1968/69, the ratio of the use of tractors (with emphasis on four-wheel tractors with 45 horsepower or less), two-wheel tractors and water pumps,[117] and related tools such as ploughs, scarifiers and threshers to manual labour was 69:31 in the Central Region, 12:88 in the North, 38:62 in the Northeast and 56:44 in the South.[118] The amount of chemical fertilizers used in the Central Region was 13.88 kg per *rai*, in the Northeast 9.36 kg per *rai*, and the South 8.96 kg per *rai*.[119] The use of buffalos, once the main work animal in the irrigated zone, began to disappear, particularly in the areas north of Chao Phraya such as Chai Nat, Sing Buri and Ang Thong. The irrigation system made the rice farming schedule more time-intensive. Income from agriculture increased more than other sectors. The income of farmers in Ban Wang Nam Yen, Ang Thong province, rose fivefold once they were able to grow rice twice per year (between 1968 and 1974). The increased income and higher price of rice allowed farmers to invest in expanding production and improving productivity.[120] In 1978, 73 per cent of the country's irrigated land was concentrated in the Central Region (63 per cent of the rainy season rice farmland received irrigation).[121] The high percentage of irrigated land and the widespread use of agricultural machinery affected the income and the production resource allocation of farming households.

---

[117] Waranya (1974, p. 256).
[118] World Bank (1983, p. 66).
[119] Thanet (1974, p. 228).
[120] Gisselequist (1976, p. 109).
[121] Dow (1984, p. 13).

At the end of the 1960s, rice production for trade expanded. Storing rice for household consumption was no longer practised.[122] Rice was grown more than once per year. Labour was needed in the rice fields only during the planting and harvesting seasons. Wages on rice farms rose. The daily rate of hired labour in rice farms in some areas such as Rangsit was 33 baht per *rai*. In some cases the rate was twice the amount paid on rice farms in the North and Northeast (see Table 3.13).

TABLE 3.13
Wages on Rice Farms in the Central Region, 1965

(baht)

	per day[1]	Harvest (per *rai*)[2]	per year[3]
Rangsit		33/1	1,200
Ayutthaya		33/1	
20 km south of Saraburi	10/1		
Near Lop Buri	8/1, 10/1		
Chai Nat	7–10		
Nakhon Pathom	10–15	20/1	
Minburi	10–12	20–15/1	
Chachoengsao	3–7	(70 in three working days and 20/1) 26/1	
Between Chachoengsao and the Chao Phraya River		20/1	
Kabinburi	5–7		
Prachin Buri		20	
Trat			500 per *rai* six-month harvesting season

Notes: [1] 10/1 means ten baht and one meal.
　　　　[2] One *rai* usually takes 1.5–2 days to harvest.
　　　　[3] Usually one year, including board.
Source: Usher (n.d., pp. 2–3).

---

[122] Although there was an increase in commercial rice farming, the ratio of subsistence rice production was still high, at least until the early 1960s. Farmers in the Central Region not only produced rice to sell, but also kept some for consumption. Farmers further away from the cities tended to grow rice for consumption as their first priority,

After 1965, wages for hired farm labourers had an upward trend. This points to an expansion in rice farming, particularly in the northern part of the Chao Phraya basin. The nominal wage for a rice field worker in 1965 was 10 baht per day and it rose to 12 baht and 25 baht in 1972 and 1975, respectively. It continued to soar, reaching 52.4 baht per day in 1980. The real wage was relatively stable between 1965 and 1972, but then increased again afterwards (see Table 3.14).

TABLE 3.14
Central Region Farm Wages, 1965–80

Year	Nominal Wage (baht/day)	Real Wage (baht/day) (1965 Prices)
1965	10.0	10.0
1970	12.0	10.4
1972	12.6	10.6
1975	25.0	13.6
1976/77	30.0	15.6
1980	52.4	17.8

Note: Real wage is the nominal wage adjusted against the consumer price index.
Source: Revised from Nipon (1981, p. 95) and Bertrand (1980, p. 493).

Although the Green Revolution brought about an increase in income and valuable assets such as production tools and machinery, increased land holdings and growth in local markets and businesses, and new jobs in villages, it produced some undesirable effects on the Central Region's community-level economy. Farmers did not understand and had little knowledge of how to use new technology such as irrigation systems, chemical fertilizers and pesticides, leading to higher costs and eventually to debt and bankruptcy.[123] Farmers who had little capital and small farmland were unable to cope with the increased rice-farming expenses that were the result of the revolution. The country's higher

---

and then sold whatever remained. This continued to be the practice of the farmers. The proportion of total household consumption for villagers in the Central Region in 1962/63 reached 72.8 per cent of the total output (Silcock 1967, p. 237).

[123] Apichai (1996, p. 62).

productivity put pressure on the price of rice, preventing it from rising in relation to production costs. Small-scale farmers were severely affected. Running out of capital and land for farming, they soon became landless and eventually ended up being workers for hire on other farms and in factories in the same province, the neighbouring provinces, or even in Bangkok.

The Green Revolution also resulted in an increase in class differentiations in village communities. Groups of investors, loan sharks and merchants began to emerge. These groups were able to make use of the interests in technology and machinery for rice production. Studies in numerous villages by Thai and Western researchers revealed that farmers who were able to promote themselves to village investors managed to see the opportunities in the market. For example, they bought or rented tractors and trucks, constructed roads leading into their farmland, dug canals that irrigated their land, expanded their plantations and hired additional workers. Some of these rich farmers switched their farming methods from broadcasting to transplanting. For instance, farmers whose land had access to the irrigation system were able to consistently control the water level in their farmland. The technology change was widely applied and these farmers were able to accumulate enough capital to adjust their land for the farming season.[124] Smallholder farmers without access to larger funds often ended up in bankruptcy because of the higher cost of production compared to the relatively small increase in the price of rice. The rate of land loss (farmers having to sell their land) increased. In 1969, the Ministry of Agriculture and Cooperatives concluded that one in five farmers who had to rent farmland lost their own land due to debt and default on mortgages that originated from the previous generation. A village study in Ayutthaya found that 30–50 per cent of all land were being held under tenancy.[125] In summary, the situation of the villages in the Central Plain was as follows:

---

[124] Apichai (1996, p. 62). See also Pasuk and Baker (1995, pp. 38–43).
[125] Pasuk and Baker (1995, p. 38).

These seemed to be what amounted to be a law in the agricultural economy of the area as to the minimum size a farm holding must have to be exploited profitably. The break off point seemed to be about 15 *rai*. If a farmer had less than this, he could not survive economically as a full-time farmer without acquiring additional land. Failing this possibility, if he was an owner he either sold or rented out his land; and if he was a renter he withdraw from farming. In either case, land was made available for other more successful farmers to purchase or to rent.[126]

The expansion of the irrigation system affected the income and allocation of production resources within farming households. In 1981, the income of farmers in three villages in the Suphan Buri irrigated area was 70.8 per cent of the net total (or 29,232 baht from a total of 41,311 baht).[127] On average, 63.4 per cent of the working hours of a male worker was spent on rice farming (1,018.4 hours) and 27.2 per cent (277.0 hours) was dedicated to activities away from their own land (such as being hired labour on other farms or in goods production and services in other areas). Only about 9.4 per cent (95.8 hours) was used for non-agricultural work (such as arts and crafts and working in the city). The hours a female worker spent on rice farming were 67.7 per cent of the year's total average (equivalent to 554.2 hours). The hours spent outside the farm and outside of agriculture were 19.0 per cent (156 hours) and 13.3 per cent (109.2 hours), respectively.[128]

The prevalence of agricultural machinery and labour-saving devices rose rapidly. For example, between 1993 and 1998, the number of tillers went up from 310,000 to 511,000 units. Tractors rose from 54,511 to 179,000 units and water pumps from 864,000 to 1.67 million. Other agricultural tools such as pesticide spreaders (with and without an engine) and threshing machines (excluding two-wheel tillers) also saw rapid growth.[129] Four-wheel tillers, threshers and harvesters were used on virtually every farm, both on and off season. From 1987, the growth of

---

[126] Amyot quoted in Pasuk and Baker (1995, p. 38).

[127] Narongchai (1983, p. 12).

[128] Ibid., pp. 32–33.

[129] Agricultural Statistics of Thailand (various years).

agricultural machinery showed the farmer's adaptation to rapidly rising costs in the sector, a result of the lack of labour.

A study on three villages in Suphanburi reveals that farm workers' wages rose very quickly. The wages for growing seedlings at Ban Wang Yang, Bang Sa Krachom and Ban Chorakhe Yai were 109 baht, 64.5 baht and 103 baht per day, respectively, in 1987. These figures rose to 120 baht, 100 baht and 120 baht per day in 1998. Higher wages were the reason that farmers in the three villages started using labour-saving agricultural machinery or direct seeding rice.[130]

With more widely available irrigation, increased use of machinery and HYVs, and better roads and other means of transportation, aided in no small part by the relative closeness to Bangkok, the largest consumer market, the productivity of the Central Region's rice and upland crops became the highest of all regions.[131] Labour productivity, expressed in tonnes per worker, was the highest in Thailand at 2.87 from 1968–72 and it grew to 3.55 and 7.66 in 1988–92 and 2003–7, respectively (see Table 3.15). The Northeast and the South had low productivity because little agricultural machinery was utilized. Many areas, especially the Northeast, relied on rainwater alone.[132] The higher productivity made the income of Central farmers the highest among the regions.[133]

TABLE 3.15
Labour Productivity of Thai Rice Farming, 1968–2007

(tonnes/worker)

	Northeast	North	Central	South	Whole Kingdom
1968–72	1.01	1.51	2.87	1.15	1.45
1988–92	1.29	1.85	3.55	0.76	1.69
2003–7	1.73	3.57	7.66	1.25	2.87

Source: Somporn (2010, p. 18).

---

[130] Somporn and Hossain (2003, pp. 115–16).
[131] Ammar (1987, p. 13).
[132] Somporn (2010, p. 18).
[133] Ibid.

The income of farmers in irrigated and non-irrigated areas was not equal. In 1998/99, farmers within irrigated areas earned 18,557 baht from the household's agricultural produce, 12.8 per cent higher than rain-fed farmers (16,492 baht). The larger the farmland, the higher the farmer's income. In other words, there was a disparity between the incomes of large-scale and small-scale farmers (see Table 3.16).

TABLE 3.16
Net Income of Farming Households in the Central Region
by Irrigated Area and Farm Size, 1998–99

Item	baht Per Person
Had access to irrigation	18,557
No access to irrigation	16,492
Average	17,528
Farm size (*rai*)	
Less then 10 *rai*	14,040
10–29 *rai*	14,066
30–59 *rai*	20,113
More than 59 *rai*	29,432
Average for every farm size	17,528

Source: Somporn (2001, pp. 31–32).

A village study in 2000 shows that the income disparity between farmers in rain-fed and irrigated areas was as much as 2.8–8.7 times. The net income from agriculture in a Suphan Buri village with access to irrigation was 7,195 baht per *rai*, which was more than villages in flood-prone areas in Lop Buri and Ayutthaya which earned a net 2,560 baht per *rai* and 822 baht per *rai*, respectively.[134]

Agricultural Diversification

After the Second World War, agricultural diversification has been the characteristic of the Central Region. Highways helped to reduce the cost of transportation, boosting the expansion of upland crops. Upland crops such as maize, sugarcane, and cassava grew rapidly in terms of area and production. The farmland used for these crops in the Central Region expanded from 400,000 *rai* in 1950 to 4.8 million *rai* in 1967[135]

---

[134] Molle et al. (2001, p. 47).
[135] Pasuk and Baker (1995, p. 54).

(more than a tenfold increase). In 1968, the Central Region yielded 83 per cent and 70 per cent of the country's total cassava and sugarcane production, respectively. In 1982, the figures declined to 39 per cent and 66 per cent, respectively. The decrease shows that the upland crops had started to extend to the Northeastern Region.

Between 1989 and 1990, Central farmers planted 2.8 million *rai* of maize, 2.7 million *rai* of sugarcane and 2.8 million *rai* of cassava (see Table 3.17). Rice farmland in the Central Region increased as well. During 1950–52, in-season rice farmland totalled 16.9 million *rai*. This increased to 20.0 million *rai* between 1965 and 1967 and then decreased to 11.9 million between 1988 and 1990. Off-season rice farming flourished in the late 1970s and occupied 3.8 million *rai* between 1988 and 1990.[136] Upland crops farmland in the Central Region was a significant part of the country's total (see Table 3.17). Aside from upland crops, fisheries, livestock, fruits and vegetable farming also expanded.

TABLE 3.17
Area Under Major Upland Crops in the Central Region, 1950–90

(thousand *rai*)

Year	1950–52	1959–60	1965–67	1980–81	1989–90
Maize					
Central	102 (40.0)	699 (54.0)	3,453 (83.9)	2,016 (22.5)	2,866 (25.6)
Total	255 (100.0)	1,275 (100.0)	4,133 (100.0)	8,960 (100.0)	11,165 (100.0)
Sugarcane					
Central	247 (59.9)	513 (56.3)	603 (69.7)	2,267 (77.4)	2,779 (64.6)
Total	412 (100.0)	911 (100.0)	865 (100.0)	2,927 (100.0)	4,298 (100.0)
Cassava					
Central	–	327 (88.1)	597 (76.8)	2,704 (35.5)	2,894 (30.2)
Total	–	371 (100.0)	777 (100.0)	7,596 (100.0)	9,562 (100.0)

Note: Parentheses indicate percentages.
Source: Calculated from Pasuk and Baker (1995, p. 54).

---

[136] Ibid., p. 34.

Important sugarcane plantation sites in the Central Region were the western side of the region in the Mae Klong River irrigation zone in Nakhon Pathom, Kanchanaburi and Suphan Buri. The sites in the eastern part of the region were in Chachoengsao and Chon Buri. In 1979/80, the western area produced 47 per cent and the eastern area yielded 19 per cent of the country's total sugarcane production.[137]

In the late 1980s and early 1990s, sugarcane production increased. This was due to the expansion of sugarcane farmland into areas above the Mae Klong River Basin and the Chao Phra River delta. These areas included Song Phi Nong, Sam Chuk and Tha Chang districts in Suphanburi and some areas of Ang Thong and Sing Buri. The expansion followed the extension of the irrigation system.[138] Sugarcane expansion meant the growth of sugar production plants, too. There were about 30 such plants in the Central Region (and 42 plants nationwide). Most were located close to the sugarcane farms which were next to roads and riverbanks, particularly the banks of the Mae Klong River.[139] Farm cash income from upland crops became more and more important. The revenue from these crops in some years during 1980/81 to 1991/92 was close to the amount earned from rice farming (see Table 3.18).

---

[137] World Bank (1983, p. 55).

[138] DORAS (1996, p. 109). Fast-expanding sugarcane farmland such as in *amphoe* Sam Chuk, Suphan Buri. In 1958, sugarcane farmland totalled 3,600 *rai*. This rose to 20,000 *rai* in 1964, 30,000 *rai* between 1980 and 1989 and 50,000 *rai* in 1995. In a project in Krasiew, sugarcane farmland increased from 15,000 *rai* to 35,000 *rai* between 1990 and 1999. The farmland area in Tha Bot rose from 300 *rai* to 6,000 *rai* between 1990 and 1995. In *amphoe* Baromathat, the increase was from 700 *rai* to 17,000 *rai* between 1985 and 1994. In *amphoe* Song Phi Nong and *amphoe* Phanom Thuan in the northern area of the Mae Klong River basin, sugarcane plantation increased by 162,000 *rai* between 1985 and 1994 (DORAS 1996, p. 109).

[139] World Bank (1983, p. 54).

TABLE 3.18
Average Farm Cash Income in the Central Plain, 1980/81–1991/92

(baht)

	1980–81	1982–83	1986–87	1987–88	1988–89	1991–92
Total crop income	36,479	33,722	28,640	38,939	35,537	56,318
Rice	14,904	14,076	13,134	20,338	9,790	21,862
Upland crops	14,902	11,553	8,529	13,731	9,946	19,063
Vegetables	783	1,188	1,187	3,732	3,451	4,333
Fruits/trees	2,757	2,657	3,073	7,366	7,630	9,295
Flowers	n.a.	n.a.	601	704	270	774
Livestock income	3,884	4,310	5,605	4,657	7,424	11,120
Aquaculture	306	234	1,472	592	1,433	3,425

Source: DORAS (1996, p. 104).

In 1998/99, the three highest contributors to the net income per person of a Central Region village farmer were freshwater farms (40,448 baht), livestock (38,595 baht) and upland crops (15,971 baht)[140] (see Table 3.19). Other sources of agricultural income aside from rice farming were becoming increasingly important to the overall income. For example, in Ban Lat Salee, Lopburi, the income from livestock was 43.4 per cent of the total income from agriculture, or 29 per cent of the total household income.[141]

Looking at village-level data reveals the details of net income. In 1996/97, farmers in Khok Klang village, Damnoen Saduak District, Ratchaburi, earned a net income of 152,330 baht per *rai* from grape farming. The other leading income generators were lime (86,700 baht per *rai*), sapodilla (59,100 baht per *rai*), rose apple (51,150 baht per *rai*), guava (14,200 baht per *rai*), shrimps (7,520 baht per *rai*), coconut (5,460 baht per *rai*) and rice (1,880 baht per *rai*).[142] The net income from rice was the lowest among other plant-based agricultural products. This is an important factor that led farmers away from rice farming towards other types of jobs in and outside the agricultural sector.

Farmers began to use their land for other types of production, growing various kinds of plants and animals, aside from rice. In 1937, across villages in six provinces in the Central Plain (Sing Buri, Ayutthaya, Ang Thong, Suphanburi, Pathum Thani and Nakhon Pathom), 96 per cent of the farms were rice farms. This dropped to 90 per cent in 1963, and 30 years later in 1993, the figure was 70 per cent. Land used for farming other crops grew from 16 per cent in 1978 to 18 per cent in 1993 (see Table 3.20).

---

[140] Somporn (2001, p. 33).
[141] Molle et. al. (2001, p. 49).
[142] Amphan (2000, pp. 85–86).

TABLE 3.19
Net Agricultural Income of Central Region Farmers, 1998–99

Item	baht per person
Rice	14,279
Upland crops	15,971
Vegetables and ornamental plants	13,538
Fruits and trees	12,990
Livestock	38,595
Freshwater farming	40,448
Mixed farming	9,532
Total	17,528

Source: Somporn (2001, p. 33).

TABLE 3.20
Evolution of the Percentage of Farms Growing Rice
in the Central Plain, 1937–93

Province	All Farms Growing Rice					Farms with Only Rice		Rice/Mixed Farms	
	% of Total in 1937	% of Total in 1947	% of Total in 1963	% of Total in 1978	% of Total in 1993	% of Total in 1978	% of Total in 1993	% of Total in 1978	% of Total in 1993
Ayutthaya	98	97	95	96	91	88	79	8	12
Ang Thong	98	93	9	93	79	79	55	14	24
Pathum Thani	94	95	93	78	64	64	48	14	18
Sing Buri	97	95	95	95	84	81	65	14	19
Suphan Buri	95	91	n.a.	72	67	66	48	6	20
Nakhon Pathom	96	81	79	61	46	41	31	20	15

Source: Molle and Thippawal (1999, p. 66).

After 1993, more land was allocated to vegetable and fruit farming. In Damnoen Saduak, west of the Central Plain, the amount of land allocated to growing fruits and vegetables grew from 312,000 *rai* in 1963 to 621,000 *rai* in 1995. Oranges were grown in Rangsit. Farmers grew vegetables on the outskirts of Bangkok. Shrimp, fish, pig, poultry and cattle farming were scattered around the Central Plain.[143] These production activities required more investment per *rai* than rice farming. In 1996/97, the approximate cost for each activity was 96,480 baht per *rai* for freshwater fish farming, 27,670 for grapes, 12,900 for sapodilla, 11,850 for rose apples and 11,300 for limes. In comparison, the variable cost of rice farming was 470 baht per *rai*.[144] The high investment per *rai* indicates that these commerce-oriented crops required more management, skills and care. Maintenance required more time, particularly in the shrimp industry such as giant tiger prawn farming. Contract farming was also on the rise. This, likewise, required large capital investments and used less labour. These types of farms included shrimp, poultry, pig, fish and asparagus. The distinctive features of these farms were that they were care and management intensive and required a high level of skills.

Rural Service Sector

Another important change in the agricultural rural economy in the Central Region, particularly after 1987, was the expansion of "small shops". Rural agricultural households began to invest in these types of businesses, for example grocery stores, car/motorcycle/bicycle repair, television/radio/electrical appliance repair and agricultural machine/metal repair shops etc. The number of such businesses grew from 85,845 in 1992 to 99,777 in 2001 and 112,000 in 2005 (see Table 3.21).

---

[143] Thippawal and Molle (2000, p. 13).
[144] Amphan (2000, pp. 85–86).

TABLE 3.21
Small Shops in the Villages in the Central Region, 1992–2005

Category	1992	1994	1999	2001	2003	2005
Grocery store	71,347	77,096	65,060	70,386	76,715	79,103
Car/motorcycle repair	6,927	8,018	11,493	13,456	13,488	13,579
Television/radio repair	1,612	2,121	2,328	2,720	3,525	3,429
Electrical appliance repair	1,178	1,223	1,866	2,269	n.a.	n.a.
Agricultural machinery repair	n.a.	n.a.	n.a.	n.a.	2,028	2,244
Welding and lathing shops	2,228	2,213	2,888	3,315	4,042	4,064
Building construction and repair and sales of construction materials	n.a.	n.a.	1,212	1,469	2,361	2,503
Sales of agricultural production materials*	n.a.	n.a.	n.a.	3,987	3,807	4,024
Others (construction/ repair related)	2,553	2,556	1,697	2,175	2,908	3,161
Total	85,845	93,237	86,544	99,777	108,874	112,107

Note: *Agricultural production materials such as seeds, fertilizers, and machinery.
Source: Department of Community Development (various years).

The information in Table 3.21 does not fully cover the number of "small businesses" such as barbers, tailors, picture frame makers, local commuter (car and motorcycle) services, karaoke bars, household industries, street vendors, peddlers, gasoline stations, pharmacies and book rentals.

Table 3.21 shows an interesting pattern. The data confirm that peasant families have turned their attention to other forms of non-agricultural activity to make a living. Peasants showed a remarkable ability to adapt to changing conditions while at the same time maintaining their established patterns of behaviour and particular modes of survival. Indeed, it is at this point that the peasant workers, far from disappearing, increasingly imposed themselves on the village economy. Peasants provided the workforce and often the entrepreneurship which lay behind the expansion of a multitude of new small businesses. The growth of small service activities in the village created a different structure of production and form of enterprise. The enterprises relied solely on family workers and the resources of the peasant family, with the characteristics of a small capital and minimal levels of skills. In many ways the new forms of enterprise built further on traditional skills and traditions, such as marketing and bargaining.

In many villages where land was scarce or productivity was low, householders would intensify their labour by diversifying their production, adding animal husbandry or other products such as vegetables or fruit trees cultivation. Some worked on a seasonal basis in factories in nearby towns and Bangkok, while others worked in family trade and service businesses in the villages.[145] Although the farm family allocated labour to off-farm work, a substantial portion of income was remitted to their households in the villages. Some of these remittances were invested in agricultural production; here, the off-farm work was part of the household's plan for utilizing its labour and sustaining their households. Living in the city and working in the factory did not separate individuals from their households in the countryside. On the contrary, the mix of the activity (so-called "pluri-activity" of households) helped peasants to survive on the land. In some instances, off-farm income helped equalize income distribution in the villages.

The growth of these small businesses became an important source of employment for the rural and village-level economy. Their growth was increasingly important as a source of non-agricultural income throughout the region, making up 18–19 per cent of household income between 1991/92 and 1995/96.[146]

---

[145] Porphant (2003, pp. 246–48).
[146] Agricultural Statistics of Thailand (1994 and 1998).

Three factors contributed to the growth of small stores and service businesses in the Central Region.

First, village families adapted to the lack of available labour and shrinking farmland that had been the trend over the past two to three decades. The annual population growth rate of the Central Region had dropped dramatically from more than 2.5 per cent in the late 1950s to 1–1.2 per cent in the 1990s. Young workers who moved away to find work caused a shortage of labour in their villages. The average size of the family had shrunk to 3.7 people per household in 2005 from 4.1 people per household in 1994.[147] The percentage of young and old in the population increased rapidly. The average age of the head of an agricultural household shows an upward trend, rising from 51.02 years old in 1994 to 53.89 years old in 2004.[148] When young workers failed to enter the agricultural sector to offset the shrinking size of farming households, the number of families engaged primarily in agriculture dwindled. The number of young workers decreased, while the age of heads of households increased. The deterioration of farmland caused families to adapt in order to maintain their village productivity. Because stores and service businesses did not require a large workforce and were open to workers of all ages and genders, this form of "household" economy became the solution for families struggling to cope with changes in the village economy. These types of production coincided with the resources that were available locally such as groceries and food that could be obtained from rice farms and rivers.

Second, the emphasis on agricultural development from the 1960s resulted in higher income for farming families. The growing use of agricultural machinery and other production resources such as seeds and chemical fertilizers made the income of Central Region farmers higher than in any other region. They were able to grow rice two to

---

[147] Office of Agricultural Economics (2005, p. 38).
[148] Ibid., p. 34.

three times per year. The farmers used more agricultural machinery than in other regions and together owned the most agricultural and non-agricultural assets (value-wise) at 1.85 million baht per household in 2001. The figure was 0.753 million baht per household for Northern farmers, 1.18 million for Southern farmers and 0.753 million for Isan farmers.[149] The higher income brought about by the use of machinery and agricultural resources allowed for the expansion of stores and service businesses, particularly those that provided resources for production (for agriculture, fisheries and forestry) such as seeds, fertilizers and machinery and production services such as engine repair, metal welding and lathing and agricultural machinery repair.

Third, the growth of small service businesses indicates that efforts were made by members of farming households who had migrated to work elsewhere to maintain the village's productivity and way of life. They brought in knowledge and experience from the urban economy where they were factory workers or had studied at vocational schools and universities. They sent back their income from these urban occupations to aid the villages. For more than a decade, workers from villages received considerably higher education thanks to expanding educational opportunities in all the regions, particularly at vocational and university levels.[150] These workers gained higher skills and expertise from their education and industrial work experience. They returned to their homes and transferred their knowledge. They became entrepreneurs in the aforementioned stores and service businesses. The youngsters also had business ventures engaged in other "household" ventures such as coffee shops, organic food stores, resorts accommodation, construction services and ornamental plant shops. These businesses grew very rapidly. Their expansion could partly be attributed to the economic growth in the cities that created demand for these products. For example, the real estate boom generated the need for construction services and ornamental plants etc.

---

[149] Ibid., p. 60.
[150] Department of Community Development (various years); Labor Force Survey (various years).

Resorts and accommodations in the Central Region proliferated to serve the growing tourism industry. Tourists flocked to homestay-style lodging. These and other family-based businesses benefited from the knowledge and experience of household members who had been working elsewhere. They were "management-oriented" businesses that did not require extensive labour the way agriculture did. They primarily needed only the right managerial and operational skills that the households' youngsters had.

Kitahara revisited his 1979 research site in Lan Laem, a village in Naknon Pathom in 1995–96 and found that the villagers were increasingly connected to the urban economy. Rice production was declining because of low rice price and there was an increase in non-agricultural and part-time agricultural work. Work in factories and in the formal sector was most common for the younger generation, while middle-aged and old people, as well as housewives, were found predominantly in the informal sector and daily wage work.[151]

Manufacturing Industry

During the Second World War, many breweries were set up in the Central provinces such as Prachin Buri, Saraburi, Ratchaburi, Chachoengsao, Phetchaburi, Nakhon Pathom and Chonburi, though output and employment were still low.[152]

In 1951, the government established a hemp sack factory in Nonthaburi. It had the capacity to produce 6,767 sacks per day, or two million sacks per year.[153] There were two other privately-owned sack factories (their locations were unknown) and combined they could produce six million sacks per year by the mid-1950s.[154] The government founded a sack-weaving factory in Saraburi in 1955 with a capacity of

[151] Kitahara (2003, pp. 267–76).
[152] N.A. M. of Finance 0301.2.2/3 (1957).
[153] N.A. M. of Finance 0201.2.1/31 (1954).
[154] N.A. M. of Finance 0301.2.2/3 (1958).

3,000 bags per day,[155] a distillery in Ayutthaya that produced 30,000 liters of pure alcohol per day,[156] a paper factory in Bang Pa In in Ayutthaya in 1961, and two sugar factories in Chonburi — all produced for domestic consumption. Important statistics regarding industries in the Central Region are as shown in Table 3.22.

TABLE 3.22
Central Region Factory Statistics, 1938–61

Industry	Investment Capital (million baht)	Product	Capacity	Employment Size (no. of workers)
Paper factory, Kanchanaburi (1938)	12.9	Paper	3,000 tonnes per year	483
Sack-weaving factory, Saraburi (1946)	22.0	Sack	3,000 sacks per day	415
Thai Sugar factory, Saraburi (1951)	n.a.	White sugar	150 tonnes of sugarcane processed per day	44
Chonburi Sugar Industry factory, Chonburi (1956)	126.1	White sugar	8,000 tonnes of sugarcane processed per year	490
Suphan Buri Sugar Industry factory, Suphan Buri (1958)	193.3	White sugar	1,500 tonnes of sugarcane processed per day; 160 tonnes of sugar produced per day	815
Paper factory, Bang Pa In (1961)	380	Paper	40 tonnes per day; 13,200 tonnes per year	294

Source: N.A. M. of Finance 0201.2.1 (1954); N.A. M. of Industry, 0201.1.11/3 (1960).

---

[155] Ibid.
[156] Ibid.

At the beginning of the 1970s, the manufacturing industrial sector was still relatively small with 1,193 businesses operating in 1970 (see Table 3.23). There were 289 businesses employing ten or more workers scattered in the Eastern Region (or eastern Central Region) comprising Nakhon Nayok, Prachinburi, Chachoengsao, Chonburi, Rayong and Chanthaburi) and 905 businesses in the southern Central Region (the remaining provinces).[157] The most dominant industries at the time were food (571 factories) and non-metals (239 factories). These businesses were mainly situated in key cities of the region such as Ratchaburi (170), Ayutthaya (118), Saraburi (118), Nakhon Pathom (56) and less than 50 businesses in the other southern provinces. Aside from food manufacturing industries, non-metallic production was mainly situated in Ratchaburi (76) and Saraburi (62).[158]

TABLE 3.23
Factories in the Central Region
(Employing Ten or More Workers), 1970

Industry	No. of Factories
Food	571
Beverages	10
Tobacco	6
Textiles	85
Textile goods	57
Wood and cork	75
Furniture and fixture	15
Printing and publishing	6
Chemicals	23
Non-metallic products	239
Metallic products	14
Machinery and repair	27
Transportation equipment	47
Others	18
Total	1,193

Source: 1970 Industrial Census.

---

[157] 1970 Industrial Census.
[158] Ibid.

Important factors that affected the sites and types of industrial businesses in the eastern Central Region were the natural environmental factors of each area and the locally available raw materials. Wood processing (saw mills), agricultural processing (cassava and sugar) and fishery products could mainly be found in Chonburi (making up 36.7 per cent of all businesses in the eastern Central Region), while fish production was largely concentrated in Rayong (23.9 per cent).[159] Chonburi was home to the largest number of sugar factories in the country. In 1970, nine out of twelve sugar factories in the eastern area were located in that province. Together they had 0.652 million tonnes of capacity, or 23 per cent of the country's total. The number of workers in key provinces in the Eastern Region was as follows: 5,841 in Chonburi, 2,350 in Rayong, 1,451 in Chachoengsao, 1,165 in Prachinburi and 298 in Nahkon Nayok. However these numbers were much less than the actual number of workers because only businesses with ten or more employees were included in the count.[160]

The economic boom that began in 1986 boosted the expansion of industry from Bangkok and its periphery to the surrounding provinces, including Ayutthaya and Saraburi to the north, Ratchaburi and Kanchanaburi to the west and Chachoengsao and Rayong along the eastern shoreline. During the boom between 1987 and 1991, the annual growth rate of factories in provinces along Bangkok's inner ring was 11.91 per cent and 11.17 per cent for the outer ring. Growth in all other parts of the Central Region combined was 10.9 per cent annually (see Table 3.24).

In the 1990s, factories in the Central Region were concentrated in the following areas: (1) East of Ayutthaya, which were Saraburi and Lop Buri. The density of the factories was still low. In 1994, there were about 32–94 factories per district, which was lower than the Central Region's average of 125. Factories started to be built in the northern part of the region, which included Ayutthaya, Saraburi and Lop Buri. Between 1981 and 1989, the industry grew at 9.5 per cent annually. In 1991, there were 3,172 factories in the northern part of the Central Region.[161]

---

[159] Donner (1978, pp. 291–92).
[160] Ibid., p. 392.
[161] DORAS (1996, p. 62).

TABLE 3.24
Number of Factories in Some Provinces of the Central Region, 1981–91

Province	1981	1987	1991	Annual Growth Rate (%)	
				1981–87	1987–91
Inner Ring	3,733	4,974	7,801	4.90	11.91
Samut Prakan	1,950	2,526	3,716	4.41	10.13
Samut Sakhon	446	767	1,317	9.46	14.47
Pathum Thani	364	462	800	4.05	14.71
Nonthaburi	473	609	871	4.30	9.36
Nakhon Pathom	500	610	1,097	3.37	15.80
Outer Ring	4,259	3,986	6,089	−1.10	11.17
Ayutthaya	267	300	411	1.96	8.19
Ang Thong	137	76	208	−9.35	28.62
Saraburi	328	326	490	−0.10	10.72
Nakhon Nayok	45	48	97	1.08	19.23
Chachoengsao	347	331	529	−0.78	12.44
Chonburi	1,237	1,030	1,344	−3.01	6.88
Suphanburi	367	584	786	8.05	7.71
Ratchaburi	883	624	922	−5.62	10.25
Kanchanaburi	522	574	1,134	1.60	18.50
Samut Songkhram	126	93	168	−4.94	15.03
Others	2,290	2,673	3,927	2.61	10.09

Source: Nipon (1995, pp. 118–19).

(2) Chachoengsao, Chonburi and Rayong had been developing rapidly since 1984, aided by the government's policy to develop the eastern seaboard with an emphasis on natural gas drilling. Natural gas separation plants attracted a host of other factories to the vicinity. These provinces' manufacturing structure was largely dependent on industry and services. The production value of each province grew very quickly. The growth of industry helped to increase the non-agricultural production sectors such as construction, transportation, wholesale and retail trade, banking, real estate and general services. (3) In the Central Region, factories were mainly situated throughout Ban Pong District, Ratchaburi.

After the economic recession of 1997, industrial growth was lower than before. The rate of increase in factories across the region was only 2.44 per cent per year. Some provinces saw a negative rate of increase such as Samut Songkram and Nakhon Nayok (see Table 3.25).

TABLE 3.25
Number of Factories in Some Provinces of the Central Region, 2002–9

Province	2002	2006	2009	Annual Growth Rate (%)
Samut Prakan	7,057	7,034	7,452	0.93
Samut Sakhon	3,439	4,519	5,140	8.24
Pathum Thani	2,234	2,563	2,875	4.78
Nonthaburi	1,457	2,007	2,089	7.22
Nakhon Pathom	2,829	2,843	2,763	−0.38
Ayutthaya	1,351	1,609	1,932	7.16
Ang Thong	448	457	461	0.48
Saraburi	1,265	1,301	1,487	2.92
Nakhon Nayok	296	295	295	−0.16
Chachoengsao	1,385	1,542	1,725	4.09
Chonburi	2,486	3,178	3,715	8.23
Suphanburi	1,308	1,135	1,141	2.12
Ratchaburi	1,684	1,372	1,555	1.27
Samut Songkhram	348	290	262	−4.11
Kanchanaburi	1,423	1,397	1,431	0.09
Rayong	1,513	2,155	2,107	6.54

Source: *Statistical Yearbook of Thailand* (various years).

Between 1996 and 2006, the number of industrial businesses in the Central Region with 11 or more employees rose from 3,778 to 5,909 (56.4 per cent), creating 80 per cent more employment. The value of gross output and value added increased by 156 per cent and 120 per cent, respectively (see Table 3.26). In 2006, the total number of industrial businesses in the region (including those with 1–12 employees) was 46,338. Important businesses in the region were textiles, wearing apparel, leather products and food, beverages and tobacco, with 19.6 per cent and 16 per cent of businesses belonging to these two categories, respectively. Other leading industries were furniture (15.4 per cent), wood and wood products (13.3 per cent), and basic metals and fabricated metal products (12.1 per cent).[162] Most factories, 89.6 per cent to be exact, were small in size, having just 1–15 workers.[163]

---

[162] 2007 Industrial Census.
[163] Ibid.

TABLE 3.26
Important Industrial Business Statistics in the Central Region,
1996 and 2006

Items	1996[1]	2006[2]	Change (%)
No. of businesses	3,778	5,909	56.4
No. of employees (thousands)	566.9	1,030.7	81.8
No. of workers (thousands)	563.5	1,022.9	81.5
Average per business (thousand people)	149.2	173.1	16.0
Gross output (thousand million)	111.5	2,855.8	156.5
Average per business (thousand baht)	294,753.4	483,299.1	64.0
Average per worker (thousand baht)	1,964.3	2,770.5	41.0
Added value (million baht)	294,738.2	648,405.0	120.0
Average per business (thousand baht)	78,014.4	109,731.8	40.7
Average per worker (thousand baht)	519.9	629.0	21.0

Notes: [1] 1997 Industrial Census — only industrial businesses employing ten workers or more.
[2] 2007 Industrial Census — only industrial businesses employing 11 workers or more.
Source: 2007 Industrial Census.

Tourism

Tourism has always been important to the economy of the Central Region. The eastern Central Region has the coastline as an advantage. A rich mangrove forest extended from the mouth of the Bang Pakong River (Chonburi) to the border of Cambodia. Many provinces have beautiful beaches that are important to tourism. Important tourist destinations include Bang Saen, Pattaya and Trat. Other provinces in the region have historical attractions such as the ancient ruins in Ayutthaya. Hua Hin and Cha-am are major attractions on the west side, attracting droves of Thai and international tourists. Tourism has played a major role in the economic development of the Central Region, which has the advantage of being relatively close to Bangkok, the country's tourism centre and a transportation hub of Asia. The Central Region has benefited from this and other related industries. Hotels and accommodations have burgeoned. In 2006, the number of hotel rooms and accommodations in the region was 105,000, making up

30 per cent of the country's total and the highest of all the regions.[164]
Hua Hin and Pattaya can be considered world-class tourist destinations.

The Growth of Hua Hin

The construction of the Phetchakasem highway linking Bangkok to the
Southern Region in the 1950s allowed tourists to travel in cars and
other rented vehicles, reducing the use of railways. Flights connecting
Bangkok to Hua Hin also became available. Hotels, bungalows, and
commerce in Hua Hin flourished. Hua Hin's major income has been
from tourism and continues to be so to the present day.[165] The city
expanded along the Phetchakasem highway, boasting numerous
attractions, hotels, accommodations, restaurants and other tourism-
related businesses. The number of tourists and travellers has been on
the increase.[166] In 2007, an estimated 1.6 million people visited the city.
Foreign tourists made up about 320,000 of that figure and they spent
6,988 baht per day on average, making Hua Hin richer by 6,204 million
baht. This was a very high income figure in comparison to the size of
the city with a population of just 50,000–70,000. In 2010, 1.04 million
tourists stayed in hotels in Hua Hin. Of these, 714,000 were Thais and
329,000 were foreigners.

The economic structure and growth of Hua Hin had been dependent
on the income from tourism. In 2008, there were 152 hotels, 19 banks,
two department stores, 1,880 various shops and 87 restaurants. Some
hotels could be considered world class, such as the Sofitel, Centara Grand
(formerly the Hua Hin Railway Hotel), Intercontinental, Hilton, Dusit
Thani, Imperial, Hyatt, Marriott, Sheraton and Ibis hotels. There were
22 five-star hotels. These businesses required hundreds of millions of
baht in investment and generated enormous value in the construction
sector. They physically changed Hua Hin into an important tourist
destination.

---

[164] *Statistical Yearbook of Thailand* (2010).
[165] Hua Hin municipality, available at <www.huahin.go.th>.
[166] Tourism Authority of Thailand.

The Growth of Pattaya

Before 1961, Pattaya was a small fishing village located on the eastern coast of Bang Lamung District, Chonburi. Changes started to take place in the city in the early 1960s. In 1961, American servicemen fighting the Vietnam War stationed at a military base in Nakhon Ratchasima and went on holiday trips to Pattaya. Because the city is also close to the U-Tapao military base in Sattaheep, it started to become a popular recreation destination for the American military's "R&R" (rest and recuperation). After that, no less than one million travellers entered Pattaya annually in the period from 1987–96. The figure increased to five million between 2005 and 2007, generating 48,000–59,000 million baht in income. Tourists, particularly from abroad, have had tremendous impacts on the city's economic growth. Pattaya has changed very rapidly. Russian travellers make up a good portion of the tourists with tens of thousands visiting the city each year. The fall of the Soviet Union in 1989 meant that residents of the former member countries had more freedom to travel. It also meant the growth of a new moneyed class. A trip from Russia (and other countries such as Ukraine, Kazakhstan and Uzbekiztan) to Pattaya or to the Don Mueang or Suvarnabhumi Airport takes a relatively short time, in some cases as little as four hours. Cold winters often propel tourists to make the trip.

After the economic crisis in 1997, the weak Thai baht made travelling to Thailand much more affordable and tourists arrived in droves. Pattaya saw very rapid growth. New restaurants and attractions were open for business. Signs in Russian were put up to cater to this group of tourists. The growth of tourism helped fuel the expansion of five-star hotels such as the Dusit Thani, Montien, Marriott and Sheraton, as well as the opening of a well-known department store, Central Department Store. In 2007, there were 38,085 hotel rooms in Pattaya. The average occupancy rate was 57.4 per cent. The average duration of stay was 2.71 days. Entertainment and tourism businesses boomed — new hotels, department stores and resorts were quickly constructed. Income from tourism continued to boost Pattaya's economy, including growth in commerce and services such as retail, wholesale, hotels, bungalows, condominiums, housing, department stores, restaurants, entertainment, attractions, motorcycle rental, jet-ski rental, boat rides and parasails.

Conclusion

After the signing of the Bowring Treaty in 1855, the Central Region went through a change from a subsistence economy to a commerce one, more so than any other region. This region is situated in a river delta suitable for rice farming and in close vicinity to Bangkok which, through canal and river-based transportation, is considered to be the gateway to world markets. The growth of the rice economy allowed for the expansion of the primarily Chinese-owned rice mills. Thailand became a major exporter of rice. In the late 1900s, around 90 per cent of rice exports came from this region. Although the yield per *rai* was low, rice output per worker per hour worked was relatively high. The limited number of workers, together with abundant farmland, led to high labour productivity as long as the land frontier remained.

After the Second World War, an important economic change in the region was that farmers in the delta began to occupy new and "higher" ground. Forests were cleared to grow crops such as sugarcane, cassava and maize (because land in the plain was mostly already under cultivation). This led to higher output for these plants as well as higher exports. Farmers' income increased from the sale of upland crops, production of which increased very rapidly. The Green Revolution and the expansion of irrigated areas in the Central Plain in the 1960s led to an increase in commercial rice farming. New agricultural machinery was used and more farm labourers were hired. Central farmer productivity and income were the highest of all the regions.

The construction of roads linking Central villages to the rest of the country, particularly Bangkok, in the years after the Second World War helped to boost the interactions between them in terms of markets, migration and rice and crop farming for exports. Villages around Bangkok started to move away from rice farming in favour of fruits and vegetables, poultry and livestock. Village industries, particularly those whose products did not lose weight after processing, were on the increase. More and more land was allocated to fruit farming, reaching into nearby provinces. Rice farmland was converted to plots for fruits, and fruit production increased. The Central Region was an important market for industrial goods, partly due to its vicinity to Bangkok. As these goods reached village markets, they started to displace those products which were produced locally in households.

After the 1970s the region's industrial sector grew very rapidly because of the expansion of Bangkok-based factories. The eastern part of the Central Region saw the highest growth rate because of its superior economic infrastructures such as the Laem Chabang deep sea port. By the end of the 2000s, products made in the Central Region and Bangkok combined made up 80 per cent of Thai industrial GDP. The Central Region, therefore, was important to the industrial development of the country. Though the agricultural share in GRP of the region was steadily decreasing, it nevertheless was still considered an important agricultural zone and a "rice bowl" of Asia. It remains capable of producing food for the whole country with enough left for exports. Important tourist destinations and major sources of income for the country are the cities of Hua Hin and Pattaya.

The expansion of stores and service businesses in rural villages using family labour was a distinct characteristic of the economic changes in the region. These businesses, such as grocery stores, car repair, radio and television repair, electrical appliance repair, metal welding and lathing and building construction and repair, relied on labour within the household. They leveraged the city work experiences of family members to raise internally-sourced capital. These businesses have allowed the village economy to carry on because they are flexible and can easily be adapted to changing environments.

4

THE NORTH

Background

Prior to 1809, the upper Northern Region[1] or "Lanna Kingdom" (Lanna means the land of a million rice fields) with Chiang Mai as the capital had a close relationship with Burma after which relations with Bangkok developed and grew stronger.[2] As Siam's vassal state, Lanna had to send royal tributes, gifts, and soldiers in times of war to Bangkok. Lanna was granted autonomy by the Siamese government thus the kingdom could appoint its own governor and viceroy.[3] Lanna was free from being governed by Bangkok until the 1860s. The Northern Region extends to the upper Central Region, or the part that is usually called the lower Northern Region, covering the area occupied by nine provinces today: Nakhon Sawan, Tak, Sukhothai,

---

[1] Consisting of the areas covering the present provinces of Chiang Mai, Chiang Rai, Lampang, Mae Hong Son, Phrae, Nan, Lamphun, and Phayao.
[2] For a full discussion of the meanings and boundaries, see Sarassawadee (2005, pp. 11–52).
[3] See Chaiyan (1994) and Sarassawadee (2005, pp. 312–84).

Uttaradit, Phitsanulok, Kamphaeng Phet, Phichit, Phetchabun, and Uthai Thani.[4]

In the nineteenth century, the population of the Northern Region comprised of Thais, Chinese, and various minority groups such as Khmu, Lau, Karen, Meo, Yao, and other ethnic groups. The Northern Region's subsistence economy focused mainly on rice cultivation. Households made various goods mostly for their own consumption through exchanges within the villages. Exchanges also took place between northern villages and nearby regions such as Yunnan and Burma due to the limited access of the mountainous terrain and because waterway transportation was prohibitively expensive. The North traded with Yunnan Province in China and the city of Moulmein in Burma, using mules and horses. Yunnanese and Shan merchants brought iron, opium, brass pans, and beeswax from Yunnan and would buy salt, areca nut, and raw cotton from the North and lac, ivory, and tobacco from Moulmein.[5]

The North traded with Burma and China more than with Bangkok because of better transportation. Bowring stated that in 1855 the river flowing to Bangkok, from Chiang Mai to Rahaeng [Tak], was treacherous.[6] Intercity trade was very limited, most of which was through exchanges of goods. Bowring therefore concluded that:

> Currency was rare and it could almost be said that trade was through the exchange of goods. Salt was highly lucrative and could be exchanged with any goods. Salt, one of Bangkok's goods, was sold at very high prices in Chiang Mai.[7]

---

[4]   The issue of defining the Northern Region still persists. Some thought that the North should mean the upper North which was the ancient Lanna Kingdom, or *monthon* Phayap. Officially, the North, according to the National Statistical Office (NSO), is the combination of the upper North and the upper Central Region amounting to 17 provinces. For analytical purposes, this book uses the NSO's definition of the North.

[5]   Chatthip (reprinted 1999, p. 60).

[6]   Bowring, vol. 2 (2007, p. 43).

[7]   Ibid., p. 44.

In comparison to other regions, the North was heavily forested. Forest products had long been important to agricultural production since the ancient times, especially as tributes paid for exports as well as materials in the construction of houses, temples, bridges, boats, and in daily life. The North had the best teak that was highly valuable. John Crawfurd noted in 1821 that Siam had the potential to export teak: "Siam has abundant teak forests and would be very valuable if they could contact us [Great Britain]."[8] Teak was not exported to other countries until the nineteenth century. The teak industry was mostly handled by the Chinese who paid rents to "*chaos*" (local rulers) in the Northern provinces in exchange for the rights to work in the forests.[9]

THE NORTH UP UNTIL 1941

Chiang Mai was an important city in the North. It was the centre for trade and government in the North, especially after Bangkok's centralization. Teak business was significant for the North's economic development, generating significant export revenue. From the early 1880s, most investment in teak business was from Europe. Growth in the business led to an expansion of saw mills and the employment of mostly Khmu and Shan workers. Such growth was also the cause of bankruptcy of small locally-owned timber businesses, especially those of local *chaos*.

Prior to 1921, when the railway reached Chiang Mai, the North (particularly the upper North) traded with China and Burma more than with Bangkok due to obstacles in waterway transportation as well as a lack of roads and rail links with Bangkok. After the railway construction, trade between the North and Bangkok expanded while those with China and Burma declined. Commercial rice cultivation also expanded. Railways had significantly replaced waterway transportation and this resulted in the growth of businessess and trade. Imported manufactured goods from Bangkok began to take over the market whereas the local industry slowly declined and eventually went bankrupt

---

[8] Crawfurd (1967, p. 427).
[9] Ingram (1971, p. 16).

No official population statistics for the North existed in the nineteenth century, although there was an official survey of the population census in 1909 but the results were unsubstantiated.[10] There was no register for the different ethnic groups, namely Chinese, Burmese, and Khmer, nor was there any identification of the various hill tribes.[11] Prior to such survey, there was no clear boundary definition of the nation-state, particularly for the northern part bordering Burma.

In 1909 the population of the North was 1.53 million or 18.8 per cent of the total population. *Monthon* Phayap alone accounted for 1.21 million people or 80 per cent of the Northern Region's population (see Table 4.1), signifying its dominance in the economy of the upper North. Government-wise, *monthon* Phayap had seven cities, 50 districts (*amphoe*), and 603 sub-districts (*tambon*).[12] Such political divisions represented the largest government unit in the "*thesaphiban*" system in Siam at that time, reflecting its importance in the country's administration. *Monthon* Phayap was heavily forested and teak was the major revenue earner. Taxes and revenues of *monthon* Phayap were 1.36 million baht in 1904 and 1.83 million baht in 1905, the highest provincial revenues in the country.[13]

TABLE 4.1
Population of the North, 1909

Monthon	Male	Female	Others[1]	Total
Phayap*	566,142	614,843	35,832	1,216,817
Phitsanulok**	116,648	126,912	4,490	248,050
Phetchabun***	34,082	36,700	1,880	72,662
Total	716,872	778,455	42,202	1,537,529

Notes: [1] This group included priests, monks, missionaries, and others in monkhood.
    * *Monthon* Phayap comprised of Chiang Mai, Lampang, Lamphun, Nan, Phrae, and Mae Hong Son.
    ** *Monthon* Phitsanulok comprised of Phitsanulok, Uttaradit, Sawan Khalok, Sukhothai, and Phichit.
    *** *Monthon* Phetchabun comprised of Lom Sak and Phetchabun.
Source: *Directory for Bangkok and Siam 1914* (1914, p. 192).

---

[10] See Skinner (1957); Sternstein (1966); Sompop (1989); Grabowsky (1996, pp. 49–85).
[11] Grabowsky (1996, p. 51).
[12] *Directory for Bangkok and Siam 1914* (1914, p. 191).
[13] N.A. M. of Finance 0301.1.1.4/4 (1902–14).

In 1919 the North had 2.01 million people and this grew to 2.52 million in 1929 and 3.22 million in 1937. The upper Northern Region in 1937 made up 60 per cent of the North's population, with Chiang Mai having the largest population of 0.543 million, followed by Chiang Rai (0.443 million) and Lampang (0.308 million). The lower Northern Region provinces with large population were Nakhon Sawan (0.300 million), Phichit (0.177 million), and Phitsanulok (0.164 million).[14]

In 1937, the North had 1.34 million people who were economically active with 1.26 million engaged in agriculture and 5,922 people in forestry, accounting for 94 per cent of the Northern workforce. Those engaged in the agricultural and forestry sectors of the upper Northern Region accounted for 62.8 per cent of all workers in the North. Most of the workers in the agricultural sector were in three upper Northern provinces: Chiang Rai (0.206 million), Chiang Mai (0.202 million), and Lampang (0.13 million).[15] There were some 21,640 workers in the manufacturing industry (or 1.60 per cent of all workers). Some 0.105 million workers (7.1 per cent) were in the service sector, namely trade, transportation, public service, professional, domestic and personal, and clerical services.[16]

Non-agricultural workers in 1937 also concentrated in the upper North, indicating the significance of the manufacturing industry and service sectors. Chiang Mai had 14.3 per cent of all workers in manufacturing and services, followed by Lampang with 9.4 per cent, and Lamphun with 10.7 per cent. Nakhon Sawan had 9.17 per cent of non-agricultural workers in the lower Northern Region (see Table 4.2).

The Chinese played an important role in the commercial development of the region. Even though their number was small in comparison to all economically active workers, they dominated major economic activities, especially in the branches of trade and services at all levels.

---

[14] Wilson (1983, pp. 33–34).
[15] 1937 Population Census.
[16] Ibid.

TABLE 4.2
Number of Workers in Various Economic Sectors of the Northern Region, 1937

Province	Agriculture and Fishery	Forestry	Trade	Manufacturing	Mining	Transportation	Public Service	Professional Work	Domestic Work and Personal Service	Clerical Service	Total
Upper Northern Region											
Chiang Rai	206,100	328	6,580	1,485	7	341	588	654	2,099	176	218,358
Chiang Mai	202,304	1,024	16,660	6,066	19	1,796	2,008	1,573	5,444	466	237,360
Nan	85,242	62	898	1,018	–	121	368	419	369	107	98,600
Phrae	74,835	510	2,614	1,999	–	577	349	439	837	160	81,550
Mae Hong Son	30,087	520	998	480	–	130	319	142	441	86	33,203
Lampang	130,088	815	5,117	2,214	–	1,129	1,283	689	2,966	240	144,541
Lamphun	68,522	68	3,591	1,647	–	493	274	329	1,348	93	76,365
Total	797,178	3,327	36,458	14,909	26	4,587	5,189	4,245	13,504	1,328	889,977
Lower Northern Region											
Kamphaeng Phet	24,304	721	1,070	367	9	139	187	179	442	61	27,870
Tak	35,214	339	2,033	920	–	1,176	362	328	1,641	59	42,087
Nakhon Sawan	122,718	590	6,680	2,332	1	1,246	722	690	1,491	206	136,693
Phichit	78,500	59	4,644	864	–	330	251	519	737	109	86,014
Phitsanulok	82,239	405	3,807	609	–	529	852	577	408	165	38,183
Phetchabun	22,411	44	919	815	–	95	427	254	316	109	15,950
Uttaradit	66,829	378	1,836	379	–	430	277	387	278	120	70,914
Uthai Thani	37,780	59	1,850	445	–	171	201	283	300	91	41,191
Total	469,995	2,595	22,839	6,731	10	4,116	3,279	3,217	5,613	920	458,902
Grand Total	1,267,173	5,922	52,927	21,640	36	8,703	8,468	7,462	19,117	2,248	1,348,879

Note: Persons older than ten years of age.
Source: 1937 Population Census.

Most of the Chinese lived in the urban areas. The distribution of the Chinese in the major provinces in 1937 was 1,801 in Chiang Mai, 1,701 in Chiang Rai, and 1,934 in Lampang. The distribution of the Chinese in the lower Northern Region was 3,148 in Phichit and 1,659 in Phitsanulok and Sukhothai.[17]

Chiang Mai had long been the centre of the North. Bishop Pallegoix estimated that some 0.5 million people lived in Chiang Mai city in the mid nineteenth century.[18] But Bowring believed that there could be around 50,000 people.[19] The 1891 British Consular Report noted: "Many people from Chiang Mai City have moved to the outskirts. There are many new buildings indicating the city's growing prosperity that has been attracting people to rapidly settle there."[20] Also, according to the British Consular Report, in 1898

Chiang Mai is the most enterprising of all provincial centres of Siam, and the town with its numerous stores, some of which are handsome brick buildings, has quite a prosperous look. The Chinaman is the moving spirit in the Bangkok trade, and the stores here were originally offshoots from Chinese firms in Bangkok.[21]

Prince Usdang reported to King Vajiravudh (Rama VI) during his trip to oversee *monthon* Phayap in 1920 that:

Chiang Mai City is immense and grand, suitable to be the Northern City in the Kingdom. There are nice houses, buildings, and stores that one is inclined to think that it could have been Bangkok. One unusual feature is that all lively places are along the river banks. Within the city wall that the locals call '*nai wiang*', it is more like a wilderness with more temples than anywhere else. There are also many large tracts of vacant land. Places where people stay underground are those with government houses

---

[17] Ibid.

[18] Pallegoix (reprinted 2006, p. 49).

[19] Bowring (2007, p. 40).

[20] BCR, *Chieng Mai* (1891).

[21] BCR, *Chieng Mai* (1898).

and other government buildings within the city wall. So people have to commute. There are some people selling food and stuff there but most are in decline. At present, the inner city looks more like the outer city ('*nok wiang*') whereas the real city is outside the city wall.[22]

Three major trade routes existed before the railroad reached Chiang Mai in 1921. Firstly, trade with Burma was handled through pack animals. Secondly, internal trade (from other parts of the country to the South) was via boats and/or linked with the southern part by rail. Thirdly, trade with southern China, mainly Shan and Yunnan, used pack animals, and also trade with Indochina.[23]

Chiang Mai continued to grow in importance from the 1870s owing to many factors. Firstly, Chiang Mai's growth was partly due to teak exports that resulted in foreign investment mainly from Britain. Chiang Mai became the site for trading companies involved in teak exports. The emergence of the British in teak exporting businesses from the 1880s attracted economic interests. Teak became one of the most important exports of Siam. Secondly, as the centre of the North, government reform resulted in centralization that led to Chiang Mai's growth, especially after 1892. Bureaucratic system expansion in the form of '*thesaphiban*' (the lieutenant governor of a circle) consequently affected the city's prosperity and growth because major government agencies such as the international court, post offices, police stations, hospitals, schools, district offices, etc. were usually established at Chiang Mai first before moving to other cities. Thirdly, the Bangkok government supported the British teak business to expand its dominance over the Lanna Kingdom. British forestry officials settled the conflicts between timber concessionaires and the Northern aristocracy. This further indicated the importance of the Lanna Kingdom to the government in Bangkok. Fourthly, after the 1921 construction of the railroad linking Bangkok and Chiang Mai, both import and export markets further expanded due to all season accessibility which enabled cargoes to be transported faster and cheaper by rail than by boat. After

---

[22] N.A. R.6. M. of Interior 27/10 (1920–24) cited by Worachat (2013, p. 212).
[23] Kakizaki (2007, p. 13).

the opening of the Northern Line, trade with Bangkok increased whereas trade with Moulmein decreased.

The Northern Economy

Prior to 1921, transportation difficulties were major obstacles in the trade between Bangkok and the North, especially the upper North. Most of the upper Northern trade was over land to Moulmein and Yunnan because of geographic advantage and the distance involved. In 1905 travelling between Chiang Mai and Moulmein took 40 days for the return trip: 15 days to travel to Moulmein, ten days for trading and business dealing, and 15 days to travel back to Chiang Mai. In comparison, travelling between Chiang Mai and Bangkok took a lot longer, amounting to 70 days for the return trip (including ten days of trade) during normal times or at high tides and could be as long as four to five months in the dry season. Moreover, exports to Moulmein were tax-free compared to the 3 per cent tax collected at Bangkok.[24] Difficulties in travelling and transportation resulted in higher cost and more expensive goods. Waterway transportation for goods between Bangkok and Uttaradit was rather smooth but parts of the north of the Nan River were not navigable.[25] At the end of the nineteenth century, the amount of imported goods from Moulmein, such as textiles, was equivalent to those imported from Bangkok.[26] In 1900, the value of imports from Bangkok to Lamphun was 95,300 baht while that from Moulmein was 61,000 baht. Imports from

---

[24] BCR, *Chieng Mai* (1895).

[25] BCR, *Chieng Mai* (1896). The British Consular Report noted: "It is, of course, the difficulties and expenses of transport which account for these high prices. Goods can be carried without much difficulty from Bangkok to Utaradit in boats of fairly large capacity, but above this point the course of Nam Nan (Nan River) is interrupted by several impassable rapids. The boats which ply between Utaradit and Nan are of dugout pattern formed a single log. They are about 30 feet in length by about three feet in width. It may be understood then that their capacity is very limited. A loaded boat even of this class cannot be dragged up the rapids on this upper portion of Nam Nan; at three points goods have to be landed and carried to the head of the rapid up which it is only safe or possible to haul up a boat empty" (BCR, *Chieng Mai* 1896, p. 16).

[26] Kakizaki (2007, p. 13).

Moulmein were mostly textiles and yarns.[27] The value of silk exports from *monthon* Phayap to Burma in selected years was as follows: in 1910 it was 1,822 pounds and it sharply increased to 9,556 pounds in 1914, but fell to 4,850 pounds in 1921.[28]

Centralization led to significant economic changes in the North by merging with Bangkok's economy. Government reforms gave rise to intermittent modernization that subsequently resulted in the power decline of various local princes. Centralization involved the economy, politics, and military with the *thesaphiban* system as the major mechanism for merger with the national economy. In the 1890s, commissioners were appointed from Bangkok to rule the North, namely Chiang Mai, Lamphun, Phrae, Nan, Mae Hong Son, Chiang Rai, and Chiang Kham.[29] Government reforms also brought modern Siamese society to the North. Education development led to a standardized educational system with central Thai as the language of instruction and the common language in establishing the modern nation-state. Centralization could be said to be partly successful because of the North's military weakness. Finally, the Bangkok government achieved full control of the North in 1900.

The construction of the Northern Line in 1901–21 brought growth in trade and economy to the North. Rice was produced for export to Bangkok by rail. In 1925 as much as 650,000 *hap* of rice was transported from the North, accounting for 10 per cent of the North's total rice production. In 1935 this amount rose to 1.3 million *hap* or 9 per cent of total rice exports.[30] In 1924 *monthon* Phayap imported raw silk from Burma valued at 11,000 pound sterling. The finished silk fabric was exported to Burma but could fetch only 8,000 pounds. The British Consular Report mentioned that "the amount exported to Bangkok could have been higher because traditional tube skirts made with Chiang Mai silk was very popular among well-to-do ladies in

---

[27] Ibid.
[28] BCR, *Chieng Mai* (1922).
[29] Tej (1977, p. 141).
[30] Chatthip (reprinted 1999, p. 62).

Bangkok."[31] However, until 1930 apart from rice, farmers in the upper North could not export many goods to Bangkok by rail even though the freight rates had already been lowered. Revenues from selling vegetables were not worth exporting to the Bangkok market.[32]

Although rice farming in the North had begun to change from subsistence to commercial, many households still grew glutinous rice for their own consumption. Rice was cultivated only once a year. Zimmerman explained that for rice production in the North "some areas could be used for cultivation twice a year but most of the rice farmers were not interested in the second rice crop except when the first crop failed or there was some unavoidable situations that forced them to grow the second crop."[33] As it turned out, Northern rice farmers grew the second rice crop only if the price of agricultural produce was low, making income from the first rice crop inadequate for expenditure and to repay debts.[34]

The expansion of commercial rice production led to the emergence of related businesses such as rice milling, stores, imports and exports, etc. When the railroad reached Pak Nam Pho in 1905, Chinese merchants and Western companies began to send their goods by rail and then continued by rivers to the North. After the Northern rail line had been extended to Uttaradit in 1909, caravans from the Shan State and Yunnan could travel all the way to the terminal by rail to connect with the major cities in the North, instead of going to Moulmein as before. In fact, transportation of light cargoes such as textiles had been handled this way. When the Northern rail line finally reached Lampang and Chiang Mai, waterway transportation eventually ended, except for logs, because Chinese merchants had switched from waterway to rail transportation.[35] Other reasons were the lower cost, trade expansion, and the merging of the Northern trade with Bangkok's.

---

[31] BCR, *Chieng Mai* (1925).
[32] Zimmerman (reprinted 1999, p. 164).
[33] Ibid.
[34] Ibid.
[35] BCR, *Chieng Mai* (1910 and 1913); Kakizaki (2007).

Before the advent of the railway, transportation cost was prohibitively high. In the 1900s, waterway transportation from Chiang Mai to Bangkok cost 152 baht per tonne while the rice farmers could sell their products for only 50 baht per tonne. But transportation cost decreased when the railroad reached Chiang Mai. The cost of transportation by rail was as low as one-third that of the waterway transportation, resulting in much reduced role of the latter.[36] After 1921 hand-woven fabric production in *monthon* Phayap changed from household and community consumption to a more commercial one. Complex production processes such as growing mulberry to feed silkworms as well as growing cotton and hand spinning were abandoned in favour of raw silk bought from Burma and Yunnan and yarn from Chinese merchants who brought them from Bangkok for sale in the North.[37]

The establishment of commercial banks further stimulated the Northern economy. In 1927 Siam Commercial Bank opened their Chiang Mai branch, followed by the Lampang branch in 1930. Prior to 1927 there was no commercial bank in the North. Merchants had to take a loan from old-time Chinese merchants who had accumulated their wealth from waterway transportation. Notable Chinese families who were creditors, mortgagees, and pawnbrokers included the Chutima (*Luang* Anusan Sunthon), the Nimmanahaeminda (Khimho Nimmanahaeminda), the Shinawatra (Chiang Shinawatra), and the Wibulsanti (Madaeng). Teak trade and tobacco industry in Chiang Mai led to higher demand for money. At that time, the North had short supply of the baht and Thai coins making it necessary to use rupee imported from Burma. Commercial bank establishment, thus, was the means to support the expansion of the Northern trade and investment.[38]

Agriculture

Rice cultivation was the dominant economic activity in the North. More than 80 per cent of the population grew rice mainly for household

---

[36] Sompop (1989).
[37] Poonporn (1987).
[38] Lowy (2007, p. 31).

consumption, not for sale. Glutinous rice was grown in the upper North whereas rice was grown in the lower North. Rice cultivation in the North was both on the lowlands and uplands. Apart from rice, vegetables such as shallot, garlic, and soybean were grown for household consumption together with fruits. Local tobacco varieties were also grown mainly for household consumption. Natural abundance and mountainous terrain were suitable for hunting and gathering, including fishing and catching frogs, prawns, mollusc, and crabs in the rivers. Agricultural labour for rice production and other activities were mostly family members as well as exchanged and shared labour when family members were in short supply.

Before the Second World War, fertile land and sparse population in the North resulted in overproduction of rice. Major problems that occurred included unsuitable weather conditions, unseasonal rain, water shortages, and various pests. Parts of the North are plateaus which are suitable for upland rice and shifting cultivation once a year. But productivity was lower than both transplanted rice and broadcast rice cultivation. Upland and field crops (maize, taro, sweet potatoes, chili peppers, etc.) were planted in three-to-four-year rotating plots.[39] Such shifting cultivation was popular among the hill tribes. Landforms in the lower North are mostly lowland, slightly above mean sea level and suitable for transplanted and broadcast rice fields. There are also flood plains, undulating plains, and terraced hills. Major rivers in the North are connected to Ping, Wang, Yom, and Nan.

The upper North has a private irrigation ditch system called *"mueang fai"* that has been in existence for more than 700 years. This is a water management system run by the villagers to ensure adequate water supply. This irrigation system shows the local wisdom and local technology that has existed for a long time to resolve the limitation of small landholding and ensure fair water distribution. After the Second World War this system was still widely utilized. The irrigation ditch system has been successful because the villagers all participated in its construction.[40]

---

[39] Dilok (reprinted 2000, pp. 114–15); Suwit (2005, pp. 381–82).
[40] Zimmerman (reprinted 1999, p. 163).

When the railway reached Lampang and Chiang Mai, the economy began to change in the lower North due to the expansion of rice fields in the Central Region. Land speculations in the lower North accelerated. Lao Song from *monthon* Ratchaburi and Nakhon Pathom, forced by a lack of land and high land prices in the Central Region, settled in Phitsanulok. Moreover, migrants could also be found in Nakhon Sawan, Sukhothai, and Pichit provinces.[41] Increasing migration into the lower North resulted in higher population density in 1919–29. Population density in *monthon* Phitsanulok and *monthon* Nakhon Sawan each rose from nine persons to 14 persons per square km.[42] Land under rice cultivation in the Northern *monthon* expanded, as shown in Table 4.3.

TABLE 4.3
Rice Cultivated Area of Northern *monthon*, 1925–37

(1,000 *rai*)

Year	Upper North	Lower North	Total Area
1925	1,291	1,811	3,102
1928	1,398	2,195	3,593
1937	1,746	1,983	3,729

Source: *Statistical Yearbook of the Kingdom of Siam* (1937); *The Record* (various years).

Rice yields per *rai* of *monthon* Phayap were rather good, more than 6 to 7.19 *hap* per *rai* in 1916–26, while *monthon* Phitsanulok's was mostly more than 5 *hap* per *rai*, and *monthon* Nakhon Sawan had the lowest yields in comparison to the other two *monthons* (see Table 4.4). High yields in the North were partly due to fertile Chiang Mai valley and the easily accessible irrigation ditch system of *monthon* Phayap. In R.L. Pendleton's opinion: "the irrigation ditch system ensured higher certainty and consistency of rice cultivation and production than in other parts of the country. Rice farmers in the North [upper part] were the best in the country."[43]

---

[41] Jiraporn (2003, p. 61).
[42] *Statistical Yearbook of the Kingdom of Siam* (1933–34).
[43] Pendleton (1962 reprinted 1976, p. 152).

TABLE 4.4
Average Rice Production in the North, 1916–26

(*hap/rai*)

Year	Monthon		
	Phayap	**Phitsanulok**	**Nakhon Sawan**
1916	7.19	4.49	4.29
1923	6.65	5.15	4.46
1924	6.48	7.06	5.68
1925	6.82	5.68	4.96
1926	6.05	5.78	5.41

Source: *The Record* (various years).

The expansion of commercial rice cultivation could not be handled by the local irrigation ditch system. The private sector, both the Chinese merchants and the Northern aristocrats, jointly invested in the construction of irrigation ditches and charged certain fees for their usage. In 1922 the Bangkok government allocated one million baht for the development and improvement of the irrigation ditch system but no action was taken. Later in 1927 the irrigation construction plan in the Chiang Mai and Lampang plains was allocated a budget of one million baht each, totalling two million baht in 1928. Weir across the Ping River at Mae Taeng district was constructed and completed in 1936 after which the previous Mae Ping project was revived and completed in 1940. Weir across the Wang River in Lampang to irrigate the Wang River basin was completed in 1935.[44] These projects provided adequate water supply to 0.245 million *rai* of rice cultivation and approximately 0.06 million *rai* of dry season cultivation of other crops. They also enabled better control of the water level on the left bank of the Ping River.[45] Although many areas in the North had converted to market economy, most production was for household consumption more than for sale. They used household labour and in

---

[44] Poonporn (1987, p. 120); N.A. of Finance 0301.1.385/5 (1927).
[45] World Bank (1960, p. 52).

small landholdings — around 10 *rai* per family.[46] In 1930 cash income from agriculture in the North was 176.30 baht (excluding the lower North).[47] The economic depression in the 1930s had some impacts on the Northern farmers, especially those who produced rice commercially. Decreasing rice prices badly affected their revenue. Farmers tried to offset such disparity by cutting their consumption of finished products and switching to making items themselves for household use, such as making cloth instead of purchasing garments. Beeswax was bought from Yunnan merchants to make candles for household consumption.[48]

Teak and Business Enterprise

Prior to the 1880s, timber concession or rent was handled by the local *"chaos"*.[49] In the North, forestry was in the hands of the Mon, Burmese, and Chinese. The *chaos* rented them the forest in Chiang Mai, Lampang, and Lamphun. From the 1880s forestry and teak business drastically changed due to increasing involvement of the British in the business which was supported by the Bangkok government.

British timber business that expanded into Burma faced teak shortage before 1880 and this prompted the need to seek new suppliers such as Northern Thailand. The shortage of oak wood in Britain was the major reason the British needed more teak. Teak was also required for the

---

[46] Zimmerman (1931).

[47] Ibid., p. 69.

[48] Poonporn (1987, p. 153).

[49] Traditionally, the law allowed the Prince to exercise his own rights solely in the forest of his province, i.e., all forests such as those in Lampang belonged only to the Prince of Lampang. Therefore, any forest was within the Prince's prerogative to be given to his relatives in any size or portion, depending on his desire. It was customary that the person given such forest could exploit it on his own or passed it on to others who would have to pay the owner only the stump tax. The law and the tradition of Siam recognized the rights to forest that could be passed on to others as rightful. The forest owner used to exploit it himself or was paid the stump tax all along. And even though the person who was given the forest by the Prince had passed away, his successor or heir could carry on such rights (N.A.(2) Office of the Prime Minister 0201.58/1(1934)).

construction of railroad sleepers in India and for ship building. Britain further needed to exploit the timber business because of the expansion of the teak market in Europe, Asia, and Latin America. The Britishers' attempt to enter the business started before 1880 via renting or hiring contractors and drawing various contracts. But their major obstacle was that the North was autonomous and under the rule of princes that did not protect British nationals, nor grant them any special privileges as stipulated by the Bowring Treaty. The North was far away from Bangkok and hence travelling there was inconvenient. In the 1860s the British rented a forest from Prince Kawilorot, *chao* or the ruler of Chiang Mai. Later on, a British national was murdered. Turmoil around Lanna's border towns coupled with robbery, including elephant stealing, caused damages to the British and their subjects. T.G. Knox, the British Consul at the time, demanded the Bangkok government to maintain law and order and to be vigilant in protecting the British and their property. He also pressured for the appointment of a Vice Consul for Chiang Mai (at that time the British Borneo Company tried to rent the forest in the North but was unsuccessful).[50]

The government at Bangkok had to decide whether to side with the British that had rapidly expanded commercial and political influences or to intervene in the timber business under the Northern princes to solve the forestry problems. In 1874 the Anglo–Thai Treaty was signed in Chiang Mai. The crux of this treaty lies in the directing and controlling of the renting or granting of the concession for the Salween Forest and to empower the Bangkok government to solve the conflict in the North and to establish a mobile police force in Chiang Mai. However, the outcome of the treaty was rather limited until 1883 when the Chiang Mai Treaty was signed which gave the Bangkok government more control over the Northern cities.[51] The government at Bangkok was also entitled to oversee renting contracts and teak production. The major issues in the treaty were as follows. Firstly, the treaty had expanded (amended) the benefits from the Bowring Treaty to cover the North as well as the

---

[50] Falkus (1989, p. 136).
[51] Chaiyan (1994, p. 20).

appointment of the Vice Consul at Chiang Mai. Secondly, it gave the Bangkok government the rights to formulate measures to control forest renting contracts and a proportion of the subsequent revenues. And thirdly, the treaty allowed Westerners to handle the logging themselves without having to buy from the locals. Nevertheless, the first few years of the treaty saw limited outcome because the Northern princes still held partial ruling power.[52] Subsequently, the British influence in the timber business quickly grew. In 1905 three British companies controlled most of the Northern timber business. The Bangkok government chose to support the British partly to have more power and partly to lessen the control of the Northern princes. Under centralization, the Royal Forest Department was established in 1896. Legally, the department was under the control of the King, but in reality it was under the administration of British and Indian officials, with Mr Herbert Slade as the first Director and eleven other British officers. The department was responsible for the overseeing of the forest renting system and regulating contract terms as well as profit sharing between the state and the private sector. Up to 1895 forest renting was mostly in the hands of the Burmese and seldom in the hands of the Thai. The newly amended regulations meant the Bangkok government could control and own the resource as well as reap more revenues from the royalty sent to Bangkok. In 1898, the Royal Forest Department had eleven Europeans as its staff, one of whom was stationed at Pak Nampo [in Nakhkon Swan Province] and another at Kado-Moulmein.[53] In 1900 Bangkok had complete control of the administration of Chiang Mai and Lampang — the major teak production areas. Centralization thus favoured the British companies to handle forest renting through the Royal Forest Department and not the local *chaos*. Renting contracts were renewed for a longer term, from three or six years to 30 years. These changes tremendously benefited the British timber business.

Teak production continued to grow. Teak exports from Siam rose from less than 20,000 tonnes (worth 130,000 pounds) in 1882–84, to

---

[52] Falkus (1989, p. 137).
[53] BRC, *Chieng Mai* (1898).

an average of 90,000 tonnes (almost one million pounds) from 1903–4 to 1908–9.[54] Teak was one of the dominant exports of Siam, representing 5.5 per cent of all exports in 1890 and it grew to 11.2 per cent in 1906. Teak exports in 1914–34 grew both in value and volume. Export volume was 68 million cubic metres and valued at 6.90 million baht in 1915–19. It grew to 83 million cubic metres worth 7.60 million baht in 1920–24, and 92 million cubic metres worth 9.20 million baht in 1925–29.[55] Revenues from royalty and logging charge was 0.686 million baht in 1886 and it slowly rose to 1.9 million baht in 1921–25 but fell to 1.4 million in 1932–35, due to the economic depression. However, it bounced back to 1.5 million baht annually in 1936–38. Apart from being exported, teak was also used domestically in fluctuating amounts, depending on the volume cut and exported.[56]

After teak trees were cut, they would be bound into rafts and floated down rivers before berthing at Pak Nam Pho checkpoint to pay royalty to the Bangkok government. After that they would be floated down to Bangkok and sent to saw mills to be processed into small pieces or teak boards. Around 30–40 per cent were produced for the domestic market while the rest were exported to India, China, Ceylon, and Europe. In 1910–15, there were as many as 0.1 million teak logs passing through Pak Nam Pho annually. Teak from the North was also exported to neighbouring countries by floating down the Mekong River to Saigon, and down the Salween River to Moulmein in Burma.[57] At the beginning of the twentieth century timber business was controlled by foreign capital, most of which were British companies, namely the Bombay Burmah Company, Borneo Company, Siam Forest Company, and L.T. Leonowens. Teak sent to Bangkok in 1902 was as follows (see Table 4.5).

---

[54] Falkus (1989, p. 138).

[55] Ingram (1971, p. 96).

[56] In 1896, teak used in Siam amounted to 82,115 metric tonnes, or 58 per cent of the total output. In 1926–30 the volume of teak for domestic utilization was 68,564 metric tonnes, or 38 per cent of output (Sompop 1989, p. 135).

[57] N.A. Department of Railways 2/1.

TABLE 4.5
Annual Teak Output Sent to Bangkok (*circa* 1902)

Producer	No. of Logs Per Annum
Bombay Burmah	35,000
Borneo	10,000–12,000
Siam Forest	6,000–7,000
L.T. Leonowens	8,000
East Asiatic (Danish)	3,000–4,000
Chinese producers	10,000–12,000
"Native" producers	20,000–25,000

Source: Macaulay cited by Falkus (1989, p. 143).

Table 4.5 indicates that of the 0.1 million logs produced in the North, two-thirds were owned by European companies, most of which were British. The two British companies, Borneo and Bombay Burmah, owned more than two-thirds of the logs but the real figures could have been much higher. The Bombay Burmah Company controlled most of the Salween timber plots that could produce as many as 40,000 logs annually. For Moulmein, most of the trees cut down by the locals and the Chinese were bought by the Europeans. Local forests in the area were also rented by the Europeans.[58]

In 1899 investment in the teak industry was as high as 2.5 million pounds, two million pounds of which were British capital. In 1924 European companies (four British, one each of France and Denmark) invested in the business with a total value of three million pounds.[59] Investments in timber business (including saw mills) by British companies accounted for a significant share of the investment value in Thailand. In 1900 British investment was 0.826 million pounds and it increased to 1.64 million,

---

[58] Falkus (1989, p. 114).
[59] Ingram (1971, p. 107).

6.25 million, and 11.1 million pounds in 1914, 1927, and 1938, respectively. They represented 84 per cent, 73 per cent, 32 per cent, and 22 per cent, respectively of the investments in the teak industry.[60]

Investments in the timber industry required large amounts of capital with a long return period. Each teak tree must pass through complex processes from selecting, stamping, to ring barking and cutting. Logs would be hauled by elephants from the forest and floated down the river. Moreover, teak log must be girdled (*kan mai*) for two to three years before they could be floated.[61] Teak must be cut only during the rainy season from July to October. Not only were there labour cost, but also the cost of buying elephants for log-hauling. *The Times* suggested that "probably no business in the world is more absolutely dependent on the services of an animal than is the teak industry on those of the elephant".[62] Elephants used in the logging business were worth 500–600 pounds each and as many as 50–60 elephants were needed in one forest to haul all the logs from the forest to the river. Each year there would be around 1,900–2,000 elephants working in the forest. From 1896 to 1914, the cost of elephants in timber business rose from 4.5 million baht in 1896 to 12 million baht in 1914.[63] The price of teak in Bangkok also rose, leading to logging of other varieties of wood for the construction of dwellings and the making of furniture but they were inferior in comparison to teak. The British Consular Report in 1898 noted:

> In 1897, only 494 logs other than teak passed Pak Nam Pho, but in the following year the number increased to 39,000. Four leases of about 10 squares miles each have been granted in the Raheng [Tak] and Kampeng Pet districts for the extraction of timber other than teak, and there are good prospects at present of such a business proving remunerative.[64]

---

[60] Falkus (1989, p. 123).

[61] "*kan mai*" or girdle means to let the tree stand dying for two years. This method requires cutting the tree down to its heartwood in a two- to three-inch strip and let the tree stand. It will die within two to three years. If the entire tree fell when it is still fresh, it will be too heavy and will sink (Slairat 1985, p. 55).

[62] Quoted in Falkus (1989, p. 134).

[63] Sompop (1989, p. 130).

[64] BCR, *Chieng Mai* (1898).

In comparison to rice exports, the expansion of teak exports only slightly affected the local economy and the Siamese way of production because capital, entrepreneurship, and labour were all foreign. In 1898 the British Consular Report stated that:

> [T]he mass of the population here have taken no active share in the development of great riches of their forests. The inhabitants here are Lao, a race differing in speech very considerably from the Siamese, and they lack in a singular degree the trading instincts which distinguish the Burman to the west of them, and the Shan to the north. They are quite content to live a hand-to-mouth existence and leave trading and money-making in their country to foreigners. There is not entirely due to their own fault, though the Lao are notorious in the East for laziness, but partly due to the fact that the people are all dependents of some chief and have not been in a position to engage in business for themselves.[65]

The main reason why the Siamese did not like working in forestry was because it was dangerous, fraught with malaria, and they had to leave their homes for long periods of time. Hence they were contented to grow rice or be government officials more than entrepreneurs. Labour shortage was mostly caused by immobile Siamese labour who refused to move away from their farms or rice fields to work in timber plots. As a result, foreign labour — mostly Khmu, Shan, and Burmese — were hired in the logging business. Khmu workers, mostly black skinned, were from Luang Prabang and worked as mahouts, spoke a language similar to Khmer, and were enduring and trustworthy. They usually came in groups of 5 to 50 people, worked for one to three years, and earned variable wages depending on labour demand and supply — whether labour shortage was severe or not. Their wages were 83 rupees (102 baht) per year in 1898 but it used to be 120 rupees (212 baht) in 1889. After that, their annual wages levelled off at 97 baht from 1891 to 1910 with the employer providing meals and accommodations as well. The number of Khmu workers in timber business was estimated to be around 4,400 to 5,700 per year from 1896 to 1941, amounting to an annual labour cost of 0.316 to 0.553 million

---

[65] Ibid.

baht.[66] Some of these Khmu workers migrated from Luang Prabang to Chiang Mai on a regular basis in the late 1890s. The main reason for migration was the heavy poll tax that had to be paid to the French at $8.00 per head. Furthermore, labour demand for road construction and other public works in Siam led to good wages of 50–90 rupees, excluding the amount of rice that the employer must also pay. Khmu workers migrated in groups led by "*nai roi*" (labour broker).[67] In the 1920s, other local labour, such as the Karen, began to be hired for various works. Apart from the Khmu, there were also Kha, Tongsu, and Shan. Kha and Tongsu were mainly hired in Phrae and Nan. They were experts in floating log rafts in Yom River. The Shan were more skilful than the Khmu so they were usually hired as foremen and were paid higher wages that could be as much as 240 rupees per year.[68]

Expansion of the teak business, controlled by foreign capital, sent small local operators into debts and they had to shut down. One of them was *Chao* Bunwat Wongmanit, the chief of Lampang, who had a debt of 0.145 million baht.[69] Timber business also caused widespread deforestation. Teak around Chiang Mai and Lampang became scarce and more expensive and those left standing were mostly in the deep forest. This was partly due to the British companies' political influence as well. They controlled the whole process, from forest renting to distribution and transportation — all of which were dominated by the British trading companies.[70]

After the First World War, Western companies still had influences over Thai capital, especially the local ones, because the concessions granted each year were mostly to the Westerners. In 1934, Western companies were granted the concession (the number of stamped logs) to cut as many as 0.37 million tonnes of teak — equivalent to 91 per cent of all the concessioned wood. The Northern timber business had high demand for labour (most of whom were Khmu), together with elephants and trucks or carts to haul the logs. There were 2,508 Khmu workers in the

---

[66] BCR, *Chieng Mai* (1897).
[67] Ibid.
[68] BCR, *Chieng Mai* (1899); Poonporn (1987, p. 30).
[69] Sarassawadee (2008, p. 525).
[70] Ibid., p. 526.

timber business or 81.9 per cent of all labour hired for logging. They used 518 elephants or 64 per cent of all the elephants involved in teak logging (see Table 4.6).

TABLE 4.6
Teak Concessions in the North, 1934

Company	No. of Logs	Factors of Production		
		Elephant	Truck or Cart	Worker
Bombay Burmah	96,383	241	540	1,400
Anglo Siam	178,224	135	10	541
Borneo	31,799	30	45	151
Louis Leonowens	32,942	54	5	242
Asiatic	30,665	58	1	174
Private* (small)	36,122	289	320	551
Total	406,135	807	921	3,059

Note: *For example, *Chao* Chularatana Na Chiang Mai, *Chao* Thippawan Kridakorn, *Chao* Ratchasamphan Na Lampang, Luang Prasarnmaitrirat, Mr Bunmee Kitkoson, Mae Chao Chankhamburirat, Lamsam Company.
Source: NA. Office of the Prime Minister 0201.58/6 (1934–40).

Apart from private investments in timber business, the government also got involved as a concessionaire in the 1910s. The government operated four forests, namely Pa Saed in Phrae Province, Pa Mae Raka in Tak Province, and Pa Mae Ta and *mueang* Long in Lampang Province. The investment was small and made a loss of 0.363 million baht in 1928–35 with a total investment of 1.49 million baht and the revenue of 1.12 million baht.[71]

Timber business growth under the Westerners undermined the economic dominance of the princes and their families. Revenues as well

---

[71] N.A. (2) Office of Prime Minister 0201.58/6 (1934–40).

as stump tax or concessions that the princes used to receive before 1897 were severed along with the rights to operate in their own forest. Many princes became heavily indebted and eventually became bankrupt.[72] Efforts were made to demand the rights and benefits to exploit the forest from the Bangkok government. For instance, nine descendants of the princes sent their grievances to *Phraya* Manopakon Nithithada, the Prime Minister, requesting the rights to own a forest or to receive certain revenue from the government.[73]

The growth of timber business had little impact on the local economy in the North. The apparent impact was the increasing number of saw mills that were mostly located in Bangkok before the Second World War. In 1941 there were about seven large saw mills, two of which were Chinese-owned and employed mainly Chinese workers. In 1937 there were 21,000 workers in forestry, hunting and animal trapping, and 16,000 workers in "manufactures of wood".[74] Such numbers well illustrated the limitation of teak business on employment and economic growth.

Manufacturing Industry

After the signing of the Bowring Treaty in 1855, the amount of goods exported from Europe, India, and China sharply rose, especially manufactured goods that were more diversified. The local industry began to decline because cheap goods had invaded the market; imports from Britain were cheaper than those from Chiang Mai. Therefore, textile producers such as the North could not compete with Europe. The value of imported garments continued to climb. Increase in imported textile products directly affected the decline of the local textile handicraft, particularly when the railroad had reached Chiang Mai in 1921.[75] The impacts on local manufactures in the North

---

[72] See Poonporn (1987, pp. 157–58).
[73] N.A. (2) Office of Prime Minister 0201.58/1 (1934).
[74] Ingram (1971, p. 107).
[75] Suehiro (1996, p. 36).

became apparent in a short period of time when Japan began to export their products to Siam. Difficulties caused by the First World War enabled Japan to export cheap products especially textiles and garments. Japanese goods quickly replaced European goods.[76] Household handicraft, on the other hand, was still strong. Bamboo was found in almost every village. The villagers used them as construction materials for their dwellings and basketry as well as fishing gears. Basketry was a male duty during the off-season period while females would weave cotton fabrics for household consumption.[77]

A major local industry of the upper North was silk fabrics, a highly demanded product in Bangkok. Raw silk was imported from the Shan State and Burma as a raw material in the production of silk fabrics in the upper North.[78] Households with looms for home-grown cotton and silk

---

[76] William L. Swan concluded that Japanese goods had quickly replaced European goods for the following reasons. (1) Japanese companies extended credit to sell Japanese goods for a long period of time. (2) Japanese goods were inexpensive, thus requiring smaller investment for the inventory compared to European goods. Selling inexpensive goods enabled the merchants to get quick returns. (3) Japanese goods were available in large varieties and qualities in comparison to European and American goods. (4) Apart from contacting the merchants, Japanese companies also hired Chinese clerks, service personnel, low-level personnel, brokers, and trade representatives to work in their office regularly. They also drew personal contracts with various merchants in the Chinese communities. Japanese companies could utilize the Chinese who were experts in commerce to their advantage. Similar to the European merchants entering the business before them, the Japanese companies hired Chinese associates to contact their customers and business groups. These Chinese personnel could forge better trade deals between Thailand and Japan (Swan cited in Pannee 2002, p. 99).

[77] Poonporn (1987, p. 18).

[78] N.A. Ministry of Finance 0301.1.28/15 (1923). The value of exporting silk fabric from *monthon* Phayap to Burma is as follows. It was worth 1,822 pounds in 1910, 9,556 pounds in 1914, and 4,850 pounds in 1921 (BCR, *Chieng Mai*, various years). Chinese merchants were instrumental in initiating silk weaving for sales. The Shinawatra was an old family that had initiated silk weaving in Chiang Mai, starting from Seng, who was a tax farmer. His son, Chiang Shinawatra, settled in San Kamphaeng village, Chiang Mai and bought raw silk yarn from Burmese and Yunnanese merchants. He then hired the villagers to weave the yarn into silk *sarongs* and silk tube skirts.

weaving contributed to the textile industry in the North.[79] Apart from silk and textiles, well-known products from the North included silverware, gems, umbrellas, mats, paper made from Siamese rough bush, tiles and ceramics, and boats. These were made by Shan and Burmese workers, most of whom were females and more skilful than the Laotian or the locals. Gem mines were located at Chiang Khong in Nan Province. Workers in these mines were mostly Burmese and Shan who migrated from Chiang Mai.[80]

After the 1920s, Northern manufactures expanded both in urban and rural areas, mainly Chiang Mai, Lampang, and Nakhon Sawan, owing to electrification. Other manufactures included ice, tanning products, soda, textiles, polished wood, cotton and cotton products.[81] The cigarette industry also grew. The British-American Tobacco Company established tobacco plantations in the North with a curing facility. The Company also distributed seeds to local tobacco farmers. Later, the Siam government nationalized the Company by buying over the entire operation at a cost of 5.5 million baht.[82] Khmu workers were employed to grow tobacco at Phan District in Chiang Rai. Under the government's economic nationalism, from the mid-1930s, two sugar mills were established in Lampang (1937) and Uttaradit (1941) to produce refined sugar.[83]

---

[79] Ingram (1971, pp. 114–15). Efforts were made to encourage cotton cultivation. The government sent students to study in the United States in 1910. Experiments with cotton varieties and model cotton farms were carried out at Phrom Phiram District in Phitsanulok Province in the same year. Exports of Thai cotton to the world market were disrupted by the First World War. The following Depression led to the closing of the Phrom Phiram experimental station in 1925. After the reign of King Rama VI, cotton development was revitalized in 1935 when the Agricultural and Fishery Department, headed by *Luang* Suwan Vajokkasikij, encouraged farmers to grow cotton. The Department established an experimental station at Khlong Tan Subdistrict in Si Samrong District, Sukhothai Province, and collaborated with the Ministry of Defence to establish a cotton gin in the same area. The ginned cotton was sent to a spinning and weaving factory, set up by the Ministry in 1934. The resultant cotton fabric was woven at a factory located at Kiak Kai in Bangkok and supplied to the domestic market (Suthanm 1994, p. 140).

[80] BCR, *Chieng Mai* (1891).

[81] Hewison (1988, p. 396).

[82] Ingram (1971, p. 137).

[83] Ibid., p. 140.

Commercial rice production also expanded. Rice was sent to Bangkok after the railroad had reached Lampang and Chiang Mai in the early 1920s. Rice mills sprang up along the railways. *Monthon* Phayap had five fully operational rice mills in 1919–25 and six new mills in 1926–29, totalling 11 mills in 1929. *Monthon* Phitsanulok had eight and 23 mills during the same period, totalling 31 mills in 1929, whereas *monthon* Nakhon Sawan (excluding rice mills in Chai Nat) had 21 and 14 mills during the same period, totalling 25 mills in 1929.[84] Most of these rice mills were small and operated by the Chinese, with a daily production capacity of approximately 30–40 tonnes. The total number of workers in the Northern rice mills was 1,198.[85] Nakhon Sawan had the largest number of rice mills at 19 in 1929, employing 336 workers — 330 males and six females.[86] Nakhon Sawan rice mills were located in different districts: five in Phayuha Khiri, four in Pak Nam Pho, three each in Chum Saeng and Banphot Phisai, two in Krok Phra, and one each in Ta Tako and Lat Yao.[87]

The sawmill industry also expanded in the North owing to its proximity to the forests. Most of them were small and operated by the Chinese.[88] Statistics concerning sawmills in the North are not available. The 1937 Population Census recorded 1,839 persons who worked in saw mills. Workers in rice mills and sawmills were mainly in the major provinces (see Table 4.7).

The abundance of forest resource in the North led to the expansion of construction-related local industry such as carts, furniture, and polished wood. Polished wood was very popular in Bangkok even though the quality was inferior compared to imported polished wood from Japan and Burma. Therefore, they were produced only for the domestic market.[89] Another construction-related occupation in the North was carpentry. In 1937 there were carpenters in several provinces such as Chiang Mai (1,194), Lampang (471), Nakhon Sawan (381), and Phrae (246). Basket

---

[84] N.A. Personal File 2.41/27 (1929).
[85] 1937 Population Census.
[86] Ibid.
[87] N.A. Personal File 2.41/27 (1929).
[88] Skinner (1957).
[89] Department of Royal Railways 2/10.

TABLE 4.7
Number of Workers in Rice Mills and Sawmills in the North, 1937

	Rice Mill Workers	Sawmill Workers
Kamphaeng Phet	23	72
Chiang Rai	217	111
Chiang Mai	76	523
Tak	97	206
Nakhon Sawan	336	186
Phichit	139	79
Phitsanulok	79	58
Phetchabun	–	39
Phrae	30	28
Mae Hong Son	29	79
Lampang	25	216
Lamphun	–	121
Sukhothai	39	72
Uttaradit	51	23
Uthai Thani	57	26
Total	1,198	1,839

Source: 1937 Population Census.

weavers were mainly in Chiang Mai (948), Lampang (574), and Nakhon Sawan (179).[90] In summary, there were some 21,640 people engaging in the Northern manufacturing sector in 1937, 14,909 of whom worked in the upper North, representing 68.8 per cent of the manufacturing workers. At the same time there were 6,731 people working in the lower North or only one-third of all manufacturing workers. Industrial workers of the upper North mainly concentrated in Chiang Mai (6,066), Lampang (2,214), and Phrae (1,999), amounting to 68.9 per cent of all workers in the upper North or 47.5 per cent of those in the North. Only Nakhon Sawan in the lower North had a significant proportion of industrial workers (2,332), the rest of the provinces had less than 1,000 workers

---

[90] 1937 Population Census.

each.[91] The number of workers in the manufacturing sector in the North in 1937 was as follows (see Table 4.8).[92]

TABLE 4.8
Number of Manufacturing Sector Workers in the North, 1937

Chiang Mai	Lampang	Nakhon Sawan
Rice mills (76)	Sugar maker (146)	Rice mills (336)
Sawmills (523)	Sawmills (216)	Sawmills (186)
Brick maker, tile maker, and potter (187)	Stone grinder (91)	Stone grinder (321)
Blacksmith (117)	Blacksmith (89)	Yarn maker and weaver (90)
Carpenter (1,194)	Carpenter (471)	Carpenter (381)
Embroiderer (3,936)	Tailor (182)	Tailor (128)
Tailor (394)	Weaver (166)	Basket weaver/wicker maker (179)
Weaver (740)	Goldsmith, silversmith and nielloware maker (107)	
Basket weaver/wicker maker (948)	Shoe repair and shoemaker (80)	
Goldsmith, silversmith, and nielloware maker (172)		
Lacquerware maker (116)		
Hat and palm leave hat maker (177)		
Potter (184)		

Source: 1937 Population Census.

---

[91] Ibid.
[92] Ibid.

Almost all manufactures in the North were for the home industry. Many handicrafts involved local resources such as earthen bricks, tiles, and earthenware; carpentry; stone grinding; yarn making and weaving. Furthermore, many manufactures were traditional ones such as silverware, golden ware, and lacquerware. The reasons that industrialization in the North lagged behind other regions are as follows. Firstly, the main means of transportation until 1921 was waterway transportation that had prohibitively high cost, especially the route from Bangkok to the upper North when the direction was up-stream. Such high costs led to very high expenses in importing raw materials. These constraints, in turn, could not attract the necessary investment. Although the railroad was constructed to link Bangkok to the North, passing through major provinces, the available transportation could not stimulate trade and investment as much as it should have. The problems lie in the lack of feeder roads to support or connect with the railroad. Existing roads in the North at the time were not suitable for all weather, especially during the rainy season. Such poor road conditions were the major obstacles to motorcar and truck utilization. In 1928 the upper North had only 680 cars, 174 of which were private cars and 506 passenger vehicles and trucks.[93] The lower North had even fewer number of vehicles. In 1937 there were only 1,180 vehicles in the entire Northern Region.[94] Poor road conditions and the small number of vehicles, compounded by a small market size, were the major hindrances to transportation and industrialization. Secondly, the market economy in many areas of the North was still subsistence in nature with very limited use of the currency as the means of exchange. The North still used "rupee" up to the 1920s as an active money in its economy. Zimmerman's survey of the rural economy in 1930 reiterated that even though the economy of the lower North had changed to a market economy by emphasizing rice production for exports, many households still produced rice for their own consumption with very little left to be sold. The villagers had to find materials such as firewood and decorative items

---

[93] BCR, *Chieng Mai* (1930).
[94] *Statistical Yearbook of the Kingdom of Siam* (1937–38).

for their dwellings. Farmers in many areas weaved their own clothes instead of buying them from the market.[95]

Services

The transition to a market economy and urban community and an increase in income affected the service sector such as wholesale and retail trades, transportation, professions, and services. In 1937 some 96,809 workers were engaged in the service sector, with the distribution as shown in Table 4.9.[96]

TABLE 4.9
Distribution of Workers Engaged in the Service Sector, 1937

Trade	59,279
Transportation	8,703
Public service	8,468
Professional work	7,462
Domestic and private service	19,117
Clerical service	2,248

Source: 1937 Population Census.

Those engaged in trade had the highest proportion in the service sector totalling 59,279 or 56.3 per cent of all workers. Chiang Mai and Lampang had a combined workforce of 21,777 in trade or 59.7 per cent of all workers in the upper North, or 36.7 per cent of those in the North.[97] On the other hand, among the lower Northern provinces, Nakhon Sawan had the highest number of those working in trade (6,680), followed by Phichit (4,644), and Phitsanulok (3,807).[98]

---

[95] Zimmerman (reprinted 1999).
[96] 1937 Population Census.
[97] Ibid.
[98] Ibid.

In summary, centralization at the end of the nineteenth century coupled with the construction of the railroad to Chiang Mai in 1921 had profound effects on the Northern economy. In particular, the growth of Chiang Mai as the major economic and administrative centre of the North led to a merger with the national economy, especially with Bangkok. Trade with Burma and Southern China was in decline. Expansion of timber business was operated mostly with Western capital and Karen and Khmu labour. Teak was essential to the Siamese economy as one of its major export earners.

THE NORTH AFTER THE SECOND WORLD WAR

Geographical features affected the agricultural and economic development of the North. Differences exist between the upper North and the lower North. The upper North had less landholdings than the lower North and any other regions in Thailand because of its mountainous terrain and forest cover. On the other hand, the lower North had larger landholdings than the upper North which has been a major producer of upland crops, horticultural crops, flowering plants, and various fruits. The upper North's landform is ideal for natural tourism. The limitation of landholdings in the upper North, therefore, has profoundly constrained the increase of agricultural income even though the region has diversified from rice cultivation to growing other crops such as shallots, garlic, beans, and fruits.

Road construction connecting Bangkok with other provinces in the North after the Second World War effectively reduced the significance of waterway transportation while manufacturing and tourism have expanded. Border trade in the North has grown rapidly since the beginning of the 2000s, particularly with Myanmar that has been essential to the economic development of the North. Such trades also resulted in the growth of the economy, trade, and investment in the manufacturing and the service sectors, foreign labour movement, as well as urban growth in the North. Undoubtedly, border trade has been a major factor of provincial growth.

Population

After the Second World War, the North's population increased from 3.62 million in 1947 to 5.2 million in 1960, 7.4 million in 1970, and 8.9 million in 1980. In 2010 its population was 11.43 million.[99] The North had high annual population growth rates of 3.1 per cent in 1950–60 and 2.1 per cent in 1960–70, compared to only 1.8 per cent in 1940–50.[100] The three most populous provinces in 2010 were Chiang Mai (1.73 million), Chiang Rai (1.17 million), and Nakhon Sawan (0.992 million).[101] In 1961–67, the annual rate of natural increase was 3.1 per cent but it dropped to 1.8 per cent in 1974–76. The immigration rate was only 1.05 per 1,000 population. After that the North's population continued to decline.[102] From 1990 to 2000 the annual population growth rate was 0.77 per cent but from 2000 to 2010 the rate was a mere 0.001 per cent which was extremely low. Many Northern provinces had annual negative growth rates from 2000 to 2010: Lamphun (–0.17 per cent), Lampang (–0.6 per cent), Uttaradit (–0.8 per cent), Nan (–0.3 per cent), Phayao (–2.09 per cent), Mae Hong Son (–0.87 per cent), Nakhon Sawan (–1.11 per cent), Uthai Thani (–0.47 per cent), Phichit (–0.77 per cent), and Phetchabun (–0.36 per cent).[103] The North had the lowest population density in the country, especially the upper North with 44 persons per square km in 1970 whereas the Central Region (including Bangkok) had 102.5, the Northeast 70.6, the South 60.9, and the national average at 67.[104] In 2010, the North's population density remained the lowest in the country, with 68.7 persons per square km.[105]

The major population issue and a national concern in the North is the minority ethnic groups. They are hill tribes who have been living in the mountainous areas for a long time. In the past there were hardly any changes to the social system and the livelihoods of the hill tribes

---

[99] Population Census (various years).
[100] ESCAP (1982, p. 14).
[101] 2010 Population Census.
[102] ESCAP (1976).
[103] 2010 Population Census.
[104] Ibid.
[105] Ibid.

but after the Second World War the population increase put pressure on their landholdings. People in the lowland tried to find landholdings in the upland, while people in the upland tried to do the reverse. Hence, conflicts arose.[106] All these while, immigrants continued to pour in from China due to unrest after the Second World War. Workers from Southern China migrated to the upper Northern Thailand and other countries in Southeast Asia. The number of hill tribes also rose. Estimations of the hill tribe population were inconsistent, ranging from 50,000 to 200,000 in 1960–69.[107] The United Nations estimated that in 1965 there were 0.275 million hill tribes of different ethnic groups living at 600 metres above sea level. The distribution of the hill tribes in 1965 was as follows: Karen (44.8 per cent), Meo (19.3 per cent), Yao (5.9 per cent), Lahu (5.8 per cent), Lisu (3.4 per cent), and other tribes (20.8 per cent), representing 2.1–5.7 per cent of the upper Northern population.[108]

A report of the National Statistical Office entitled, "The Hill Tribe Population: Chiang Mai, 1986" offered interesting insights into the socio-economic background of the hill tribes that could be extended to the Northern hill tribes in general. In 1986 the hill tribe population in Chiang Mai was 0.141 million, with the Karen as the largest group (61.1 per cent), followed by Lisu (15.2 per cent) and Meo (10.2 per cent).[109] Chiang Mai hill tribes were engaged mostly in upland crops (50 per cent), followed by rice cultivation (26.5 per cent), vegetable cultivation (8.8 per cent), hired farm labourers (3.6 per cent), commerce (0.7 per cent), and the unemployed (4.4 per cent). When classified by ethnic group, most of them were engaged in farming. Upland rice was cultivated by 76.1 per cent of all hill tribe households, followed by transplanted rice (9.2 per cent) and maize (2.5 per cent). All hill tribes were engaged mostly in upland rice cultivation as compared to other occupations, with the exception of the Yao with 72.7 per cent of them growing vegetables but only 2 per cent grew upland crops. The Akha had the highest proportion of field crop farmers

---

[106] For this discussion, see Ammar (1973).
[107] Donner (1978, p. 697).
[108] Ibid., pp. 697–98.
[109] *The 1986 Hill Tribe Population Survey Report: Chiang Mai* (1987).

(87.2 per cent) whereas the Lahu had the highest proportion of merchants (3.7 per cent).[110]

The hill tribe households mostly had small holdings of 4.2 *rai* per household. The Yao had the largest holdings of 11.5 *rai* per household, followed by the Akha (10.5 *rai*), Lau (6.8 *rai*), Lahu (5.5 *rai*), and Meo (5.4 *rai*).[111]

Most landholdings of the hill tribes have encroached public land and reserved forests, amounting to 61 per cent of all households, followed by legal ownership (29.1 per cent), allocation by the state (6 per cent), and renting (1.1 per cent). Encroached landholdings were the largest proportion held by the hill tribes, with the Akha having the highest amount (76 per cent), followed by Meo (74.2 per cent), Lisu (69.2 per cent), and Lahu (65.6 per cent).[112] Attempts were made to classify the hill tribes into opium poppy growers and non-growers. The growers were the Meo, Yao, Lahu, Lisu, and Akha. The non-growers were Lua, Kha, Khmu, and Karen.[113]

Apart from the minority hill tribes, the Chinese were also crucial in commercial development, including those who migrated from the Central or other regions, both before and after the construction of the railroad connecting Bangkok and Chiang Mai and those who migrated into the upper North (and further into Burma).[114] After the victory of the Chinese Communist Party over the mainland in 1949, Kuomintang troops fled into the border area of the North. The number of migrants quickly rose after the Burmese government pushed them into the Northern border near Burma. These Chinese got married to the local Thai and later became Thai themselves. The Chinese and the Thai-Chinese were engaged in agriculture, commerce, opium poppy growing and trading, counterfeiting, etc. Other migrants such as those from Yunnan in Southern China were mostly Muslims and Christians and were generally called "*Chin Haw*" or Yunnanese and estimated to be as many as 15,000 in 1980.[115]

---

[110] Ibid.
[111] Ibid.
[112] Ibid.
[113] Ibid.
[114] Ammar (1973).
[115] Van der Meer (1981).

Migration

After the Second World War, migration of the Northern Region population was mostly over short distances, mainly within the same region. In 1965–70, the Northern province with the largest number of immigrants per head was Kamphaeng Phet with 200 immigrants per 1,000 inhabitants, resulting in the net migration rate of 142.2. Such high immigration rate was due to the establishment of the Thung Pho Thale Self-Help Settlement in Kamphaeng Phet.[116] The 1970s saw the effect of immigration on the rapid expansion of arable land in the North, especially the lower North where forests were turned into maize fields and for other field crops cultivation. Some of the migrants went to Bangkok which was growing at a tremendous speed. In 1975–80 intraregional migration continued (especially between the rural areas) because of population pressure and limited landholdings. Most migrants increasingly went in search of landholdings in nearby provinces. There were more emigrants than immigrants in the North — 217,000 emigrants versus 115,000 immigrants. Most emigrants from the North went to Bangkok and its vicinity, including other parts of the Central Region adjacent to Bangkok.[117]

---

[116] ESCAP (1976). Phetchabun was another province with a high immigration rate affecting the net migration rate. This province attracted migrants from neighbouring provinces that had high population density, namely Ayutthaya, Nakhon Sawan, and Phichit. People have settled in these provinces for a long time.

[117] Torres (2004, p. 52). Migration rate in the North was low. In 1995–2000 there were 0.495 million migrants who moved within the North and the other regions, representing 4.3 per cent of the North's population. Up to 84.2 per cent were born in the North. Only 15.8 per cent were immigrants from the same province. In 2000 there were 0.495 million people in the North who migrated within five years, among them were 0.294 million people who moved within the North (both in their current province and other Northern provinces), representing 59.4 per cent of all migrants. The rest of the migrants were from other regions and other countries as well. In 2005–10 approximately 0.9 million people in the North migrated, accounting for only 7.7 per cent of the population (Population Census, various years).

Urban Growth

Chiang Mai has been the economic as well as land and air transportation centre of the North. In 1947 Chiang Mai's urban or municipal population was 38,211 and it continued to grow to 81,579 in 1970, 0.164 million in 1988, and 0.336 million in 2010.[118] Chiang Mai was the second largest city in Thailand until the mid-1980s. The major factor contributing to Chiang Mai's urban growth was the road network connecting the Northern districts and provinces. Field crop production also increased rapidly (including commercial rice production). New field crops of the 1960s were tobacco, groundnut, garlic, and soybean.[119] There were 40,000 *rai* of tobacco and 41,000 *rai* of groundnut cultivation in 1964.[120]

Such increases in field crop production led to the emergence of wholesale and retail trades, financial institutions, banks, and other related businesses such as tractors. Agricultural expansion was enhanced by the Mae Tang Irrigation Project in Chiang Mai which enabled year-round crop production, especially for the 0.15 million *rai* of rice fields in Mae Tang, Hang Dong, Mueang, and San Pa Tong districts. Arable land in Chiang Mai increased to 0.629 million *rai* in 1978.[121] Chiang Mai's industrial growth was also heightened through the establishment of the Lamphun Industrial Estate in 1985 which occupied 1,788 *rai* of land. Such industrial estate boosted Chiang Mai's economic importance because of its proximity to Chiang Mai — only 40 km away. Thus, industrial growth in Lamphun reinforced economic growth in Chiang Mai at the same time.[122]

Tourism was one of major factors of Chiang Mai's urban growth since the city has long been foremost in the North's tourism. Chiang Mai is an old city and the former capital of the Lanna Kingdom with beautiful scenery that has attracted millions of tourists, especially from abroad.

---

[118] *Statistical Yearbook of Thailand* (various years).
[119] Sarassawadee (2008, p. 593); Silcock (1970, pp. 136–43).
[120] Silcock (1970, p. 137).
[121] Sarassawadee (2008, p. 593).
[122] Ibid., p. 607.

Hotels, resorts, shopping centres, and other tourism related businesses all grew accordingly. During the economic boom in the early 1990s, many construction projects were approved, including 60 high rises, 32 large hotels, and 120 housing estates. Land prices increased many folds. The urban areas rapidly expanded from 100 square km in 1980 to 429 square km in 1989.[123] Chiang Mai was also ranked as one of the world's most attractive city for tourism.[124] The establishment of Chiang Mai University in the 1960s also played a part in the city's growth. Chiang Mai has been the centre of education judging from the various higher education institutions, both public and private, located in the province.[125]

In 1985 the GPP of Chiang Mai was 20,547 million baht or 15.9 per cent of the North's GRP with high proportions of GPP in the manufacturing (84 per cent) and service (86 per cent) sectors from 1985 to 2005. Such figures indicate the dominance of Chiang Mai in the economy of the non-agricultural sector and the economic centre of commerce, services, and manufacturing. Chiang Mai had 201 branches of commercial banks — the fourth highest in the country with one-third of all deposits and credits of the entire Northern Region.[126]

Nakhon Sawan dominates the lower Northern Region as the place where the Chao Phraya River originates from its four tributaries — Ping, Wang, Yom, and Nan Rivers flowing from the North. Nakhon Sawan

---

[123] Ibid., pp. 612–14.

[124] In 2010, Chiang Mai was ranked fifth among the world's top tourism destinations. *Travel and Leisure*, a travel magazine published in the United States in 2010, conducted a survey regarding the World Best Award-Top Ten Cities (<th.wikipedia. org/wiki/changwatchiangmai>). It stated that: "Chiang Mai was ranked fifth among the world's top tourism destinations judging from the place, scenery, beauty, shady and cool, arts, culture, tradition, food, and shopping areas."

[125] There are 12 higher education institutions, most of which are located within Chiang Mai Municipality. The increasing number of these higher education institutions affected Chiang Mai's urban growth in terms of its physical and economic changes. Each year there would be tens of thousands of students pursuing higher education in these institutions. It was reported that in 2005–10, most of the immigrants in Chiang Mai were students (25.8 per cent), followed by those who changed their domicile (22.4 per cent), and job seekers (14.0 per cent) (2010 Chiang Mai Population Census).

[126] Bank of Thailand, Northern Branch.

had been the centre of waterway commerce. Statistics of waterway transportation through the Chao Phraya indicate that Nakhon Sawan was the origin of 10,944 trips and the destination of 7,284 trips in 1964. Waterway transportation had declined after the construction of the Phahon Yothin Highway connecting Bangkok to the lower Northern provinces. The Asian Highway linking Nakhon Sawan, Kamphaeng Phet and Tak resulted in higher land transportation and directly affected the expansion of transportation between Chai Nat and Nakhon Sawan. From 1964 to 1972 the volume of land transportation increased from 1,180 to 3,789 trips daily.[127] Such transportation expansion strengthened the role of Nakhon Sawan as the economic and transportation centre of the lower North. Furthermore, Nakhon Sawan was also the commercial centre linked to economic growth, such as the expansion of upland crops in Uthai Thani. The growth of rice cultivation business in Kamphaeng Phet from the 1930s led to the expansion of finance and banking and other service sector businesses in Nakhon Sawan. The proportion of GPP in manufacturing and service sectors increased from two-thirds in 1985 to three-quarters in 2005, signifying the dominance of non-agricultural economy in Nakhon Sawan's economy.[128]

The Northern Economy

The structure of Northern economy increasingly changed from agricultural to manufacturing and service sectors. The proportion of the agricultural sector in the GRP continued to decline, from 40 per cent in 1981 to 26.2 per cent in 2010. At the same time the proportion of GRP in manufacturing and service sectors strongly increased, especially the share of the manufacturing sector which grew from 9.0 per cent to 21.6 per cent in 2010. The proportion of agricultural labour also decreased from 80 per cent to 57.0 per cent of the Northern labour force whereas the proportion of labour in the service sector rapidly increased from 17.9 per cent to 35.4 per cent during the same period (see Table 4.10).

---

[127] Donner (1978, p. 298).
[128] Gross Provincial Product (various years).

TABLE 4.10

Economic Structure of the Northern Region, 1981–2010

Year	Agriculture	Manufacturing	Services	Total
Gross Regional Product (million baht)				
1981	38,794 (40.3)	8,955 (9.0)	48,403 (50.3)	96,152 (100.0)
1990	52,220 (23.8)	32,089 (10.4)	134,983 (61.6)	219,292 (100.0)
2000	69,787 (17.9)	84,537 (21.6)	236,149 (60.4)	390,473 (100.0)
2010	218,361 (26.2)	179,943 (21.6)	433,570 (52.1)	831,874 (100.0)
Employment ('000 persons)				
1981	4,148 (80.0)	109 (2.1)	931 (17.9)	5,188 (100.0)
1990	4,868 (75.6)	274 (4.3)	1,294 (20.1)	6,436 (100.0)
2000	3,463 (53.6)	362 (5.6)	2,639 (40.8)	6,464 (100.0)
2010	3,829 (57.0)	511 (7.6)	2,378 (35.4)	6,718 (100.0)

Source: Population Census; Gross Domestic Product; Labor Force Survey (various years).

In comparison to other regions, the Northern economy was the smallest in the country, at 7.4–7.7 per cent of the national GDP in 1990–2010.[129] In 2010 most of the employed workers in the North were entrepreneurs without any employees, representing 38.5 per cent, followed by those who worked as employees of the government, the state enterprises, and the private sector (32.4 per cent).[130]

The rapid growth of the service sector that resulted from tourism expansion had affected the North's economic growth and generated numerous related activities, from hotels to various kinds of accommodation, guesthouses, restaurants, souvenirs, and tour operators. However, income increased only slightly, which was lower than the national average per capita income of the North's population. For instance, per capita income was 10,039 baht in 1981, and it continued to rise to 27,759 baht in 1995 and 68,321 baht in 2010 while the national per capita income during the same period were 15,933 baht, 70,884 baht, and 81,304 baht, respectively.[131]

Agriculture

One of the dominant features of the Northern economy was shifting cultivation or swidden agriculture that was mainly subsistence. However, farmers had increasingly turned to commercial agriculture partly due to limited resources and the government policy to construct roads to remote mountain villages for security reasons, to lessen Communists influence (before the mid-1980s), to prevent deforestation, and to decrease opium poppy cultivation by substituting with other commercially viable crops for the hill tribes. Shifting cultivation usually moved from plot to plot by clearing and burning all covered vegetations before new varieties were planted successively and doing so until all nutrients were depleted, before a new plot would be exploited. Major crops for shifting cultivation

---

[129] Gross Regional and Provincial Product (various years).
[130] 2010 Population Census.
[131] Gross Regional and Provincial Product (various years).

were opium poppy, maize, and other upland crops such as potatoes, sorghum, beans, chillis, and vegetables. From the late 1980s, the major commercial production of the hill tribes was temperate crop cultivation and contract farming that has been supported by the government. Development of upland irrigation was carried out together with electricity generation.[132]

Until the 1970s, the agricultural sector was dominant in the Northern Region's economic development and also a major source of employment. In 1970 there were 3.71 million workers in the agricultural sector with 2.73 million rice farmers, representing almost 80 per cent of the Northern workforce. Other field crops were less important in terms of employment: there were 0.179 million people growing maize; 0.128 million people growing tobacco, cotton, tea, coffee, and kenaf; and another 40,463 people growing vegetables.[133]

The agricultural sector was another major source of income contributing more than 40–52 per cent of the GRP in the 1970s.[134] Expansion in arable land was the result of increasing rice and field crop cultivation, especially in the lower North. In 1963–78 landholdings expanded from 9.17 million *rai* to 15.17 million *rai*, or an increase of 64.9 per cent. Such rate of expansion was the highest holdings in the country. The upper North's holdings expanded from 3.38 million *rai* to 4.81 million *rai*, representing a 42.2 per cent increase.[135] Up to 1963 most farmers (74.16 per cent) in the North were landowners (meaning they owned their land or partially rented the land) covering 73.7 per cent of all land.[136] Such proportion remained almost unchanged. For instance in

---

[132] See Pratueang (2009, pp. 126–48).

[133] 1970 Population Census.

[134] World Bank (1983, p. 72).

[135] The Central Region (8.8 per cent), the western Central (25.2 per cent), the upper Northeast (53.3 per cent), the lower Northeast (53.3 per cent), the upper South (0.4 per cent), and the lower South (12.2 per cent) (World Bank 1983, p. 44).

[136] This indicated a larger proportion of landowners than in the Central Region, but smaller than in the Northeast and the South (74.10 per cent of farmers in the Central Region were landowners, 90.30 per cent in the Northeast, and 89.90 per cent in the South) (1963 Agricultural Census, cited by Nipon 1974, p. 385).

1971, 76 per cent of Northern farmers owned their agricultural land while 19 per cent were full-time tenants.[137]

Land use for agriculture in the North varied from place to place. The upper North had lowland irrigation system, forestry, upland rotation cropping, and permanent crops. The lower North with its lowland was suitable for rice cultivation and the hilly areas were fit for upland crops.[138] Mountainous terrain in the North is the major obstacle to farming, hence the lowest proportion of farming land use in comparison to other regions. In 1963–64 the average size of holdings in the North was 16.6 *rai* while that of the upper North was much lower: 7.6 *rai* in Chiang Mai, 11.1 *rai* in Chiang Rai, 7.4 *rai* in Lampang, 8 *rai* in Lamphun, 7.4 *rai* in Mae Hong Son, 8.3 *rai* in Phrae and only 6.2 *rai* in Nan.[139] The national average for the same period was 21.6 *rai*. In 1975 the average size of holdings slightly increased to 23 *rai* per household for the North while the upper North's was much lower (see Table 4.11).[140]

TABLE 4.11
Upper North's Average Landholding Per Household, 1975

Chiang Mai	10 *rai*
Chiang Rai	17 *rai*
Mae Hong Son	7 *rai*
Phrae	12 *rai*
Nan	15 *rai*
Lamphun	8 *rai*
Lampang	8 *rai*

Source: van der Meer 1981, (p. 20).

---

[137] van der Meer (1981, p. 195).
[138] For this issue, see Wanpen (2004).
[139] Silcock (1970, p. 137).
[140] van der Meer (1981, p. 68).

Even though the average size of holdings was small, but yields per *rai* of the North were high. In 1976–77 rice yields per *rai* were the highest, particularly the upper North that had very high yields of 462 kg per *rai*, or higher than the national average by 1.71 fold (see Table 4.12).

TABLE 4.12
Average Rice Yield per *rai* in the North, 1976–77

Region	Kg. per *rai*	Upper North	Kg. per *rai*
North	377	Chiang Mai	448
Northeast	197	Chiang Rai	500
Central (Central)	358	Mae Hong Son	434
Central (East)	270	Lamphun	398
Central (West)	270	Nan	405
South	291	Phrae	467
Thailand	269	Lampang	379
		Upper North Average	462

Source: Office of Agricultural Economics, cited by van der Meer (1981, p. 20).

High rice yields per *rai* were partly due to the small irrigation ditch system scattered in every province of the upper North. Arable land in irrigated areas (both the irrigation ditch system and the government irrigation scheme) of the upper North was as shown in Table 4.13.[141]

Although the North's yield per *rai* was higher than in many regions, when considering labour productivity (rice yields per head), it is clear that the North's labour productivity was lower than the Central Region simply because the Central farmers utilized more agricultural machinery per unit of arable land and the irrigation system was much more complete.[142]

---

[141] Silcock (1970, pp. 136–37).
[142] Somporn (2010).

TABLE 4.13
Percentage of Irrigated Area by Province
in the Upper North in the 1970s

Province	Percentage of Irrigated Area
Chiang Mai	92
Chiang Rai	76
Lampang	73
Lamphun	89
Mae Hong Son	79
Nan	52
Phrae	71

Source: van der Meer (1981, pp. 136–37).

The increased agricultural holdings had a negative effect as the proportion of tenants rapidly increased from 0.8 per cent in 1960 to 16 per cent in 1978.[143] From 1963 to 1978 the number of agricultural holdings in the North rose by 0.67 million, totalling 1.03 million while the agricultural landholdings rose from 12.4 million *rai* to 19.9 million *rai*, with the lower North having higher increase both in terms of numbers and areas under holding.[144] Most agricultural land expansion was for rice and field crops cultivation whereas the proportion of landholdings for other agricultural purposes (tree planting and other forests) had clear declining tendency.[145]

The 1960s onward saw an expansion of the upland crops in the North. Various factors contributed to this expansion. Population growth, highway construction in the North (and elsewhere in the country), land clearing for rice cultivation in the Central Region (especially in the Central Plain) had come to an end. Expansion of upland crops, such as sugarcane and cassava in the Central Region, had reached the saturation point.

---

[143] Medhi (1986, p. 40).
[144] World Bank (1983, pp. 44–45).
[145] Ibid.

Land utilized for new varieties of field crops rapidly expanded, particularly maize, sugarcane, cassava, tobacco, and fruits such as longan. Such expansion was aided by an increase in the utilization of farm machinery. Tractors had replaced animal labour and helped farmers to better expand their arable land, especially for cultivation of upland crops. However, expansion in field crop yields was also partly due to demand from abroad.

Road construction also reduced transportation obstacles in the rainy season and led to the increasing number of trucks and other motor vehicles connecting the villages and transporting rice from the fields. In the 1950s and afterwards the major highway constructed in the North was Phahon Yothin which was constructed in fragments such as Nakhon Sawan–Kamphaeng Phet, Sawankhalok–Tak, Sukhothai–Phitsanulok, Denchai–Phrae–Nan, Chiang Mai–Chom Thong–Hot, Saraburi–Nakhon Sawan, and Chiang Mai–Lampang.[146] Highway construction led to lowered transportation cost and the expansion of markets linking the upper and the lower Northern Region, including Bangkok and other parts of the country. It was expected that agricultural produce from the North for exports to Bangkok would increase by 25 per cent in the mid-1950s.[147]

In 1976 the length of roads in the North totalled 11,038 km and it increased to 12,898 km in 1978.[148] The construction of Phitsanulok–Nakhon Sawan Road in 1982–83 enabled direct travelling from Phitsanulok to Bangkok.[149] Road construction not only resulted in linking the economy of the upper North with the lower North, but also reduced the dominance of waterway transportation on the Chao Phraya, Ping, Wang, Yom, and Nan Rivers. Road expansion was followed by increasing number of motor vehicles, the emergence of roadside commercial areas, and the expansion of urban communities in Phichit, Sukhothai, and Nakhon

---

[146] N.A. (2) Office of Prime Minister 02.066.5.5/35 (1934–53); N.A. M. of Finance 0201.2.2/1/52 (1961–62).

[147] N.A. (1) M. of Finance 1.3.3.2/1 (1953).

[148] World Bank (1960, p. 52).

[149] Jiraporn (2003, p. 67).

Sawan. Settlements began to concentrate along the newly constructed roads such as the Asian Highway which was built in 1979 and resulted in the expansion of Phichit to the outlying areas.[150]

The expansion of the irrigation system in the North had significant effects on the increased production of rice and field crops. The irrigation project on the right bank of Mae Tang in Chiang Mai (1959–64) could supply irrigated water to 0.23 million *rai*.[151] The Tha Nam Lao irrigation project near Chiang Rai (1951–61) was under construction. Upon completion, it was expected to irrigate 0.47 million *rai*.[152] Moreover, there were two large multipurpose dams — the Bhumibol and the Sirikit — that supplied water to the lower North and the upper Central Regions, totalling 7.3 million *rai* of irrigated areas in 1978. However, irrigated areas in the North were still limited covering only 19.9 per cent of such areas, with 17 per cent being actual irrigated areas. Thereafter, arable land expansion began to decrease due to depletion. The number of agricultural holdings also decreased from 1.40 million in 1993 to 1.30 million in 1998 but it rebounded to 1.37 million in 2003.[153]

About 41 per cent of the Northern farmers had 10–39 *rai*, followed by 32.4 per cent with less than 6 *rai*. Large holders with more than 140 *rai* comprised only 0.6 per cent. From 1998 to 2003 the number of Northern holdings had a 4.9 per cent increase to 64,512, with notable increase among those with 40–139 *rai* (2.6 per cent) and under 6 *rai* (1.6 per cent). On the other hand, holdings with 6–9 *rai* and 10–39 *rai* decreased in numbers (see Table 4.14).[154]

Rice cultivation occupied more than half of all agricultural land-holdings with a tendency to decrease. The area under rice cultivation totalled 14.5 million *rai* in 1993 and it dropped to 13.3 million *rai* in 2003 (a decrease from 58.1 per cent to 53.2 per cent). The area under upland and other field crops also decreased by 7.4 million *rai* (29.9 per cent of the total area under holdings) to only 6.8 million *rai* (or 27.0 per cent).

---

[150] Ibid., p. 99.
[151] World Bank (1960, p. 52).
[152] Pendleton (1962 reprinted 1976, p. 146).
[153] 2003 Agricultural Census.
[154] Ibid.

TABLE 4.14

Agricultural Landholding by Land Size, Northern Region, 1993–2003

Size of Land (*rai*)	No. of Holdings			Per Cent			Per Cent Change	
	1993	1998	2003	1993	1998	2003	1993–98	1998–2003
Total	1,408,363	1,307,069	1,371,581	100.0	100.0	100.0	–7.2	4.9
Under 6	409,650	403,154	445,137	29.1	20.8	32.4	–1.6	10.4
6–9	219,921	201,657	197,294	15.6	15.4	14.4	–8.3	–2.2
10–39	629,028	580,114	562,759	44.7	44.4	41.0	–7.8	–3.0
40–139	143,706	117,106	158,632	10.2	9.0	11.6	–18.5	35.5
Over 140	6,058	5,038	7,759	0.4	0.4	0.6	–16.8	54.0

Source: 2003 Agricultural Census, Northern Region.

The proportion of land use for the cultivation of fruit trees, vegetables, herbs, and decorative and flowering plants had a slight increase but still far behind the land used for rice and upland crops (see Table 4.15).

Landholdings for agriculture owned by farmers accounted for 64.8 per cent, most of which or more than half had land deeds or title deeds (*NS 5/NS 3/NS 3K/NS 3khor*).[155] Most of the agricultural holders (64.1 per cent) only worked in their own land while 19.5 per cent worked in both their own and in others' land. There were as many as 16.4 per cent landless farmers from 1998 to 2005. Their proportion continued to rise to 19.3 per cent or 36,341 persons.[156]

In the mountainous terrain of the upper North, rice cultivation occupied only 6.5 per cent of the total rice production area in the country in the 1960s. The small area under rice in the upper North could produce 11–12 per cent of the country's rice due to the rather high yields per *rai*.[157] The restricted topography of the upper North slowed down the expansion of rice fields which fluctuated between 2.3 and 2.9 million *rai* in 1950–70. At the same time, rice production increased from 0.327 million tonnes in 1950 to 1.4 million tonnes in 1970.[158] Rice cultivation in the North could be divided into rice and glutinous rice (sticky rice). Land under glutinous rice in the North was about 7–10 per cent of the country's rice production areas from 1973 to 2007. Glutinous rice was mostly grown in the upper North and mainly for household consumption. In 2007 glutinous rice was harvested in 2.3 million *rai* with yields of 1.2 million tonnes or 38.4 per cent of the country's glutinous rice production. Land for both rice and glutinous rice cultivation in the North was 11.05 million *rai* in

---

[155] Ibid.

[156] Ibid.

[157] Donner (1978, p. 706); Pendleton (1962 reprinted 1976). A major geographic feature of the upper North was the unclassified forest and other areas totalling more than 50 million *rai* or 91.8 per cent of all agricultural land use in 1965 while such proportion for the whole country was only 74 per cent, signifying the high proportion of forest to the unused land (Donner 1978, p. 703).

[158] Donner (1978, p. 706).

TABLE 4.15

Agricultural Landholding, Classified by Land Use in the North, 1993, 1998, and 2003

Category	Area ('000 rai)			Per Cent		
	1993	1998	2003	1993	1998	2003
Total	25,042.3	23,223.2	25,020.8	100.0	100.0	100.0
Rice	14,561.6	13,686.3	13,302.0	58.1	58.9	53.2
Para rubber	13.6	13.1	20.9	0.1	0.1	0.1
Perennial, fruit trees, forest	1,920.6	2,217.8	3,230.9	7.7	9.6	12.9
Upland and other field crops	7,483.3	6,313.9	6,886.2	29.9	27.2	27.5
Vegetables, herbs, decorative and flowering plants	251.9	472.6	468.4	1.4	2.0	1.9
Pasture	209.8	47.0	227.8	0.8	0.2	0.9
Freshwater aquaculture			126.6			0.5
Others	511.0	472.1	757.5	2.0	2.0	3.0

Source: 2003 Agricultural Census.

1973–77 and it increased to 12.82 million *rai* in 2003–7 while the yields increased from 3.23 million tonnes to 5.57 million tonnes in the same period.[159] Labour productivity of the Northern rice farmers from 1961–2007 continued to increase, from 1.58 tonnes per farmer in 1968–72 to 1.85 tonnes in 1988–92 and 3.57 tonnes in 2003–7, which were higher than the national average as well as the Northeast and the South.[160] In 2010, top Northern rice producing provinces that were among the top ten of the country were Phichit, Phitsanulok, Nakhon Sawan, Kamphaeng Phet, Sukhothai, and Chiang Rai.[161]

Upland Crops

Maize expanded very rapidly, mostly for exports. Land under maize cultivation in the North was concentrated in the lower North, mainly in Nakhon Sawan, Phitsanulok, Kamphaeng Phet, and Phetchabun. Land under maize cultivation increased from 15,000 *rai* in 1950–52 to 0.16 million *rai* in 1965–67 and between 4.4 and 5.1 million *rai* in 1989–90 and 1998–99 (see Table 4.16). Land under maize in 1979–80 accounted for 41 per cent of all maize cultivation areas in the country,[162] and increased to 47 per cent in 1998–99.[163] Nakhon Sawan, the most important maize producer of the North, had extensively increased its maize cultivation land. For instance, in 1959 the maize planted area was 52,800 *rai* (82 per cent in sweet maize while hard maize occupied only 18 per cent). But in 1964 the maize planted area increased to 0.97 million *rai* as a response to world market demand.[164] Apart from maize, sugarcane production was expanded to supply the world market as well.

---

[159] Somporn (2010, p. 11).
[160] Ibid., p. 18.
[161] <www.nso.go.th>.
[162] World Bank (1983, p. 65).
[163] Agricultural Statistics of Thailand (2000).
[164] Silcock cited by Ingram (1971, p. 262).

TABLE 4.16
Area under Upland Crops in the North, 1950–2010

('000 *rai*)

	1950–52	1965–67	1980–81	1989–90	1998–99	2005	2010
Maize	15	160	4,658	5,156	4,429	3,961	4,597
Sugarcane	41	52	366	851	1,322	1,806	1,796
Cassava	–	14	255	721	938	938	1,155
Soybean	66	62	683	2,295	1,038	642	529

Source: Ingram (1971, p. 260); Pasuk and Baker (1995, p. 54); Agricultural Statistics of Thailand (various years).

Sugarcane expanded rapidly to satisfy world market demand. Land under sugarcane increasingly expanded from the Central Plain to the North especially in Uttaradit, Nakhon Sawan, and Lampang in which a sugar mill was located. Table 4.16 also shows that land for sugarcane cultivation increased from 41,000 *rai* in 1950–58 to 366,000 *rai* and 851,000 *rai* in 1980–81 and 1989–90, respectively.[165] In 1979–80 sugarcane production was 2.2 million tonnes or 18 per cent of all production and it grew to 26.6 million tonnes or 27.7 per cent of the country's sugarcane production in 2010. Major sugarcane producers were Nakhon Sawan, Kamphaeng Phet, and Phetchabun.[166] Sugar mills also expanded along with sugarcane cultivation. In 1975–76 there were eight sugar mills in the North.[167]

One of the dominant crops in the North was tobacco[168] and it remained so until the 1980s when it began to decline. Tobacco cultivation after the Second World War was mainly contract farming to supply the curing operation in the North. This was under the administration of the Thai Tobacco Company which had its office and curing sheds in all provinces where tobacco was cultivated. Under contract farming, farmers were supplied with Virginia tobacco seedlings, insecticides, and fertilizers by

---

[165] Pasuk and Baker (1995, p. 54); Agricultural Statistics of Thailand (various years).
[166] Agricultural Statistics of Thailand (2012).
[167] World Bank (1983, p. 55).
[168] Tobacco grown in the upper North were mostly Virginia. Burleigh type of tobacco was grown in Sukhothai Province.

the Company for free. When the tobacco leaves were harvested they would be delivered to the Company.[169] Major tobacco cultivation areas in the North were Chiang Rai and Phrae, with a combined production of more than 50 per cent of the North. Tobacco was grown in 62,500 *rai* and it quickly expanded to 0.334 million *rai*; the yield of tobacco leaves was 6,600–58,000 tonnes in 1950–70.[170] There were three factories in Bangkok for the manufacture of tobacco and cigarettes.[171]

Forestry

The North contains the largest forested area in the country. In 2011 the Northern forest accounted for 55 per cent of the forest in the country while covering 56 per cent of the total area of the North. Forested area differed from province to province. For instance, in 1970, 50 per cent of Chiang Rai was forested while the forests in Mae Hong Son covered as much as 79 per cent of the province.[172] Forests have long been an important resource base for the people in the North. Its biodiversity supplies food, medicine, charcoal for cooking and as fuel; it maintains the climate condition and creates massive economic values. In 1970, forest products were worth 842 million baht or about 5 per cent of the Northern Region's GRP.[173] Also in 1970, there were 6,830 people engaged in forest-related businesses and 19,467 people were involved in handicraft and forest product manufactures, including furniture. The latter group worked in saw mills, plywood factories, wood and cork production, furniture and fixtures.[174] After 1980 the forest-related economy began to decline. Deforestation from shifting cultivation was the culprit. In 1967–70 shifting cultivation in the North covered 16,891 square km, representing

---

[169] The cigarette industry has been operated by the government. Thirty-five per cent of tobacco leaves produced by the farmers were used by domestic cigarette factories while the other 65 per cent were sold overseas. The Tobacco Act was promulgated in an effort to maintain the quality through contract farming that could control every stage of its production and distribution (Ammar and Chermsak 1986, p. 43).

[170] Donner (1978, p. 708).

[171] Ibid., p. 749.

[172] Ibid., p. 716.

[173] Ibid., p. 716.

[174] 1970 Population Census.

18.9 per cent of all arable land. The proportion of shifting cultivation varied from province to province: 22.8 per cent in Chiang Mai, 25.3 per cent in Nan, and 22.1 per cent in Phrae.[175]

Income and Wages

Although the agricultural output in the North continued to increase, the income of the farmers grew at a very slow pace and was lower than those in the non-agricultural sector. In 1954, agricultural labour — farmers and forestry workers — were paid the lowest wages of 47.07 baht per week in comparison to the average weekly wages of 102.94 baht in other occupations in the North and 143.79 baht for the whole country.[176] The International Labour Orgnization's (ILO) survey on the labour condition in Thailand in 1954 indicated that:

> The teakwood and tobacco industries employ unskilled and semi-skilled workers at the lowest wages found in Thailand. In the teakwood camps, footmen with elephants receive between 70 and 100 baht per month. Drivers of elephants (mahouts), experienced men doing a perilous job, receive between 90 and 130 baht. At one camp, Sob Prob *amphur* in the *Changwat* of Lampang, a driver was reported to be employed at a rate as high as 180 baht. In Camp Me Pe in the jungle of Chomtong *amphur*, some 50 kilometres south of Chiang Mai, the cook and assistant cook each received 50 baht per month, the lowest single wage for adult workers the expert noted anywhere in Thailand.... In the tobacco industry in the north and northeast, wages vary somewhat between outside growers and Thai Tobacco Monopoly stations. Some outside growers employ men of the Kamouk tribes from Laos. The expert visited a station in Pharn *amphur* in the *Changwat* of Chiang Rai. Thai paid Kamouk workers between 650 and 800 baht per year, that is 54–66 baht per month. The same station also employs local women at the rate of 2.50 baht per day with the head girl receiving 4 baht; male workers at 4 baht per day; and strokers at 5 baht for two shifts of six hours each. A neigbouring station paid women 3 baht and male workers 4 baht per day.[177]

---

[175] Donner (1978, p. 682).
[176] Central Statistical Office (1954).
[177] ILO (1954, p. 32).

In 1965, the wages for rice growers in some Northern provinces were 5 baht per *rai* in Chiang Rai (including one meal), 4 baht per *rai* in Phayao (plus one meal), 5–7 baht per day in Lampang, 6 baht per day in Lamphun, and six baht per day for harvesting longans and working in sugar mills in Chiang Mai.[178] Workers in some non-agricultural occupations in 1965 were paid much higher; unskilled labour in Lampang rice mills earned 180–360 baht a month, those in Nakhon Sawan earned 10–15 baht per day while machinery operators at Chumsaeng and Mae Chan were paid 600–1,000 baht per month.[179] Silversmith in Chiang Rai earned 25–30 baht per piece of design (working 1.5–2 days), Nakhon Sawan carpenters earned 15–20 baht per day whereas Chiang Rai carpenters were paid 10 baht per day while head of intra-provincial bus drivers in Phitsanulok earned 500–700 baht per month.[180]

The cash income of Northern agricultural households slightly increased from 1,611 baht in 1953 to 2,693 baht in 1970, representing an annual increase of only 3.9 per cent during this period.[181] In 1975–76 the upper Northern rice farmer's income was 2,849 baht per person but it dropped to 2,501 baht per person in 1985/86 whereas the lower Northern farmers' income was 3,548 baht per person and it grew to 4,110 baht per person in the same period. Other farmers earned 3,054 baht per person and this slightly increased to 3,119 baht.[182] In 2002, the income of rice farmers and other farmers was much lower than the national average (28,541 baht per person).[183]

The slowly rising income resulted in the large proportion of the poor in the North, second only to the Northeast. The North's poor were as many as 1.35 million in 2008,[184] most of whom were farmers. Only 21.4 per

---

[178] Usher (n.d., pp. 2–3).

[179] Ibid., pp. 2–3.

[180] Ibid., p. 14.

[181] Krirkkiat (1974, p. 567).

[182] Ammar and Viroj (1990, p. 146).

[183] Office of Agricultural Economics (2005, p. 113).

[184] In 1962–63, the proportion of the poor or those with income below the poverty line was 65 per cent and it dropped to 33 per cent in 1975–76 and 23 per cent in 1988–89. However, the proportion of the poor remained high (15.16 per cent in 2004, 13.26 per cent in 2008, and 11.08 per cent in 2009). The Northern poor in 2009

cent of the agricultural households earned their living solely from rice farming while those who earned from agriculture as well as other sources were 78.6 per cent. It was also discovered that agricultural households with rice farming as their sole income source decreased by half from 1998 indicating that agricultural households had to rely on supplementary income aside from agriculture.[185]

Farmers had adapted in many ways by diversifying their income sources to compensate for the decreasing income in agriculture. In the upper North, farmers began to grow other crops such as shallot, garlic, beans, and fruits. Some of the workers migrated to non-agricultural occupations or to agricultural products distribution and sent remittances back to invest in the rural areas in small trades and service businesses that mostly utilized household investments and labour. Such small businesses included grocery stores; motor vehicle, motorcycle, and bicycle repair; radio set and television set repair; electrical appliance repair; agricultural machinery repair; metal lathe, welding, and repair shops, etc. They grew from 90,039 in 2001 to 95,814 in 2003 and 98,747 in 2006.[186] Furthermore, some farmers were involved in contract farming whereby the farmers produce certain crops and animals to be delivered to the contractor when they were harvested. Contract farming is one form of agro-business that has expanded considerably in the North. The contract could be a joint-venture or simply producing crops and animals such as hogs and chickens for the contractor. Contract farming is capital-intensive and emphasizes good management.

---

totalled 1.35 million. Mae Hong Son had the highest proportion of the poor in the North (0.183 million), followed by Phetchabun (0.177 million), and Lampang (0.147 million) (Medhi 1986, p. 21; Somchai 2004; NESDB 2015, pp. 1–6).

[185] In 2003, agricultural holders in the North with income from agricultural production between 20,001 and 50,000 baht were the largest group (31.4 per cent), followed by 10,001–20,000 baht (19.1 per cent), and 50,001–100,000 baht (16.0 per cent). Agricultural productivity in the North was low compared to the non-agricultural sector. Consequently, income from the agricultural sector compared to the wages and salary for the household continued to decrease: from 62 per cent in 1986 to 50.0 per cent in 2000, and 49 per cent in 2004. These proportions were slightly higher than the Northeast's (2003 Agricultural Census; Nipon 2007, p. 51).

[186] Department of Community Development (various years).

Manufacturing Industry

Manufacturing industry in the North remained small with low employment numbers until the 1970s. There were 0.109 million manufacturing workers or 3 per cent of all employment in 1970. Manufactures with high employment numbers were handicraft, food, beverages, and tobacco, with 29,082 workers. Wood handicrafts and wood products industries employed 19,489 workers while 28,016 people were employed in handmade textiles, garments, finished textiles, leather and leather products industries, and 13,707 people were employed in metal handicrafts and metal products industries.[187] Most manufacturing enterprises were located in Chiang Mai (144 establishments with 15,750 workers), Chiang Rai (96 establishments with 11,891 workers), and Lampang (78 establishments employing 10,183 workers).[188]

A growth of rice trading resulted in the expansion of rice mills, particularly in the lower North with plains that are suitable for commercial rice production which is unlike the mountainous upper North with smaller agricultural landholdings. There were numerous rice mills in the lower North further south from Nakhon Sawan which is near Bangkok — a large market with ports for international exports. Construction of highways linking Bangkok and the Northern provinces stimulated the expansion of rice mills, especially in the lower North where rice mills continued to flourish. In 1970 there were approximately 250 rice mills in the North, employing 8,563 workers.[189] Indeed, the rice mills were a major employer in the manufacturing sector, accounting for 7.8 per cent of all employment in the sector. In 2008, there were 422 rice mills, 262 of which were located in the lower North, representing 62 per cent of the Northern rice mills. Nakhon Sawan had the largest number of rice mills (92), followed by Kamphaeng Phet (46), and Phetchabun (35). Rice mills in Nakhon Sawan had a daily capacity of 11,892 tonnes while the production rate of each mill was as high as 129.26 tonnes per day with an average of 7.76 rice mills in each district.

---

[187] 1970 Population Census.

[188] Donner (1978, p. 742).

[189] 1970 Population Census.

Phichit had fewer rice mills than Nakhon Sawan — only 34 mills — but its daily production capacity was 8,199 tonnes with the production rate of each mill at 241.14 tonnes per day, signifying the largest producer in the North (see Table 4.17).

Manufacturing industry in the North relied heavily on natural resources and labour. In 1970 there were 499 factories with more than ten employees in the upper North (almost 50 per cent of which were located in Chiang Rai and Chiang Mai), and 285 factories in the lower North about half of which were located in Nakhon Sawan, Kamphaeng Phet, and Phichit.[190] However, the industrial statistics are lower than in reality because most of the factories employed less than ten people, especially small factories and those using household labour. The 1970 Population Census reported the employment of the Northern manufacturing sector at 0.1 million.[191] Major manufactures in the North were tobacco, processed food, and wood products. In the 1980s, the Northern manufactures increasingly expanded due to the following factors. Firstly, roads along with the transportation system and economic infrastructure had been linked to the Northern provinces. Secondly, the government's policy emphasizing the distribution of growth to the provinces through the 4th and 5th National Economic and Social Development Plans in 1977–81 and 1982–86 had designated the primary economic centres of the North (Chiang Mai, Phitsanulok, and Nakhon Sawan) and the secondary centres (Lampang and Chiang Rai). Thirdly, in 1985 the establishment of an industrial estate at Lamphun had stimulated industrial development and the subsequent employment.

During the economic boom in 1990–97, the Northern industries had experienced tremendous expansion — as high as annual growth rates of 25.41 per cent compared to other sectors in 1992–96: 8.23 per cent in the construction sector, 1.16 per cent in the agricultural sector, and 5.31 per cent in the commercial sector.[192] Such growth led to the increase in the GRP of the Northern manufacturing sector from 8,955 million baht in

---

[190] Donner (1978, p. 742).
[191] Ibid.
[192] Rattanaporn (2003, p. 227).

TABLE 4.17
Number of Rice Mills in the North, 2008

Province	No. of Rice Mills	No. of District with Rice Mills	No. of Rice Mills Per District	Total Production Capacity (tonne/day)	Average Production Per Mill (tonne/day/mill)
Chiang Mai	15	11	1.36	737	49.1
Lampang	16	8	2.00	159	9.9
TLamphun	9	5	1.80	169	18.7
Phrae	10	2	5.00	234	23.4
Phayao	31	6	5.17	2,189	70.6
Chiang Rai	34	10	3.40	3,625	106.6
Mae Hong Son	1	1	1.00	8	8.0
Nakhon Sawan	92	12	7.67	11,892	129.2
Uthai Thani	30	7	4.29	3,478	115.9
Kamphaeng Phet	46	9	5.11	8,127	176.6
Tak	8	4	2.00	504	63.0
Sukhothai	14	8	1.75	1,247	89.0
Phitsanulok	24	7	3.43	5,377	224.0
Phichit	34	11	3.09	8,199	241.1
Phetchabun	35	7	5.00	2,020	57.7
Nan	1	1	1.00	15	15.0
Uttaradit	22	5	4.40	2,464	112.0
Northern Region	422	114	3.70	50,444	119.5

Source: Somporn (2010, p. 102).

1981 to 48,202 million baht in 1992 and 79,384 million baht in 1996.[193] The proportion of manufacturing in the Northern GRP rose from 6.5 per cent in 1986 to 11.9 per cent in 1992 and 13.5 per cent in 1996. Production had diversified more than before, with large investments in new industries such as electronics parts, processed food products, zinc smelting, and cement. The 1997 Industrial Census noted that:

> The total value of manufacturing products in the North is 111.0 billion baht. The value of production in food products, beverages, and tobacco is 51.1 billion baht and machinery and equipment is 30.1 billion baht, representing 46 percent and 27.1 percent of the North's industrial output, respectively. Most factories are concentrated in Chiang Mai, Lamphun, Lampang, Nakhon Sawan, Phitsanulok, and Chiang Rai. When classified by market, it is found that only 367 factories or 17.3 percent of all Northern factories exported their products, 99 of which are in the food, beverages, and tobacco group.[194]

In the 2000s, the Northern manufacturing sector accounted for 4 per cent of the country's manufactures. The upper North was known for electronics and handicrafts while the lower North was notable for the agro-industry and foods such as rice milling, processed agricultural goods, sugar, beverages, and flavour enhancers. Eighty per cent of the Northern manufacturing base has been in three major areas: (1) Chiang Mai–Lamphun–Lampang, (2) Kamphaeng Phet–Nakhon Sawan–Phitsanulok, and (3) Mae Sot–Chiang Rai (Lamphun is the largest industrial base of the North, followed by Kamphaeng Phet).[195]

In 2006 there were 92,210 industrial establishments with more than one employee in the North; 97.1 per cent of which had 1–15 employees. Major manufactures included woods and wood and cork products

---

[193] Gross Regional and Provincial Product (various years).

[194] 1997 Industrial Census, the Northern Region, cited by Economic News, <http://www.ryt9.com/s/ryt9/269081>.

[195] Bank of Thailand, Northern Branch, <http://ww.bot.or.th/Thai/EconomicConditions/Thai/North/EconConditions/EconomicsStructure/Pages/Econstructure.aspx> (accessed 11 September 2013).

(excluding furniture) (24.6 per cent), food and beverages (21.8 per cent), and garments and dyed and decorated wool (21.0 per cent). There were approximately 0.392 million people working in those establishments in 2006, 0.225 million of whom were employees.[196]

From around the 1990s, labour shortage in the rural area due to lower birth rate, emigration, and the expansion of the manufacturing and service sectors all led to rapidly rising wages. Businesses and manufactures in the North resolved such labour shortage by hiring foreign labour such as Burmese in Mae Sot, Chiang Rai Province. Consequently, factories were attracted to agglomerate while the influx of foreign workers continued. In the 2010s, there were 0.17 million registered foreign workers, more than half of whom worked in the upper North. Foreign workers had thus become the crucial factor in the development of the industrial and service sectors in the North.[197] The unequal distribution of the Northern manufactures resulted in significantly different income in the various provinces. Major industrial locations included Chiang Mai, Lamphun, Chiang Rai, Phitsanulok and Nakhon Sawan. These five provinces together accounted for 30–40 per cent of the North's industrial output from 1985 to 2009.[198]

---

[196] For instance, there were 22 companies producing electronics parts in the Northern Region Industrial Estate with export values of 22 billion baht. The zinc industry has been operated by only one company: Padaeng Industry Public Company Limited that produces high grade zinc ingots from zinc ore mined in the North, with an average export value of two billion baht. The sugar industry in the North had an average production of 1.2 million metric tonnes, 0.4 million tonnes (worth five billion baht) of which were exported. Processed vegetable and fruit products from the North were worth 9.3 billion baht; 40 per cent of the factories exported their products overseas. Exports of Northern ceramic products were worth at least two billion baht per year. Other manufactures included tobacco curing, jewelry and ornaments, local handicrafts, and furniture (2007 Industrial Census, the Northern Region, <http://student.lcct.ac.th/~51137915/job/7>).

[197] The Northern Region Strategic Plan in the 11th National Economic and Social Development Plan (2012–16).

[198] Gross Regional and Provincial Product (various years).

Home Industry

Local handicraft, the Northern traditional home industry, continued to decline. Rapid industrialization under the import substitution policy in the 1960s led to the expansion of consumer products that had replaced the home industry. The World Bank's study reports that in 1968–69 only 4 per cent of all Northern households still used handlooms. Other goods that could be produced for Northern village consumption such as plastic buckets, soaps, mats, and kitchen utensils had all been replaced by manufactured goods from Bangkok. Despite declining local manufactures, local handicrafts[199] could be found everywhere involving many generations in the household production. These handicrafts included ceramics, hill tribe's handicraft, *khaep mu* (fried pork rind) and *naem* (pickled pork sausage), pottery, palm leave hats, mulberry paper, fishing gear basketry, etc.[200]

In 2001, there were 0.239 million (or 7 per cent) Northern households involved in the home industry with 0.47 million workers. Among them, 0.185 million worked in the home industry producing food, beverages, and tobacco followed by 0.115 million in textile, knitted wares, garment, and leather products.[201] Most of the workers were household members (82.4 per cent). Income from the home industry was supplementary rather than the primary household income. In general, income from the Northern home industry was 16 billion baht but its value-added was only 8.05 billion baht. The average household income from the home industry in 2001 was 70,004 baht. The highest income generators of the home industry were metal products (157,810 baht), followed by food, beverages, and tobacco (151,798 baht), as shown in Table 4.18. Income from the home industry accounted for 31.1 per cent of the total household income.[202]

---

[199] World Bank (1983, pp. 79–81).
[200] Rattanaporn (2003, pp. 286–88).
[201] Home Industry Survey (2001).
[202] Ibid.

TABLE 4.18

Number of Households and Income from Home Industry, 2001

Category	No. of Household	baht Per Household
Food, beverages, tobacco	57,954	151,798
Textile, knitted wares, garments, leather products	88,924	35,196
Wood and wood products	59,612	27,979
Paper, paper products, printing	2,592	66,321
Chemicals, rubber, and plastic	1,132	118,188
Non-metallic products	2,773	157,810
Metal products, machinery, and equipment	6,435	174,638
Other manufactures (including furniture)	19,963	64,923
Total	239,385	70,004

Source: Home Industry Survey (2001).

Tourism

Tourism is vital to the economic development of both the upper and the lower North with Chiang Mai as the tourism centre of the North and the country. The lower North has the cultural World Heritage site at Sukhothai and the natural World Heritage site at Huai Kha Khaeng in Uthai Thani. Apart from the distinctive culture, both the upper and the lower North are abundant in mountains and forests — natural resources that facilitate natural tourism, ecotourism, and health tourism, etc.

Construction of roads linking Bangkok to the Northern provinces after the Second World War coupled with the upgrading of Chiang Mai Airport into an international airport had positively stimulated tourism. Furthermore, the establishment of the Tourism Organization of Thailand by the private and the public sectors had reinforced Chiang Mai as a tourist attraction. Tourists, both domestic and international, continued to pour into the North, particularly Chiang Mai. Tourism in the North had focused not only on the urban areas but also the remote mountain areas. In 2009, 1,547 Northern villages, or 10 per cent of the total number of villages in the North, had tourist attractions in the form of home stays or other activities that could translate into income. It was estimated that 54,849 households in the Northern villages, or 2.80 per cent of all Northern village households, drew their income from tourism.[203]

Chiang Mai's Tourism

Chiang Mai's diverse tourist attractions attracted a large number of tourists. Attractions in Chiang Mai can be classified into five groups: urban attractions such as temples, city gate, city wall, old markets, local goods centre, etc.; attraction sites in Doi Suthep such as *wat* Doi Suthep and the Bhubing Palace; waterfalls and caves; natural attractions; cultural, arts, and traditional festivals such as Songkran and Yi Peng, etc. At first, the tourism promotion concept in Chiang Mai was to develop Doi Suthep

---

[203] Department of Community Development (2009).

into a tourist attraction.[204] Later, the promotion extended into cultural tourism spurred by the establishment of the Chiang Mai Cultural Centre in 1971 to offer Lanna culture and arts with *khan tok* dinner catering. In 1973 there were 0.106 million tourists in Chiang Mai and this grew to 0.201 million in 1975.[205] The proclamation of 1987 as the "Visit Thailand Year" and 1988–89 as the "Year of Culture and Arts" resulted in a continued influx of tourists. In 1994 there were 2.18 million tourists in Chiang Mai and this rose to 3.62 million in 2007. Foreign tourists increased from 0.885 million in 1994 to 1.57 million in 2007, or almost doubled. The weakness of the baht from 1997 also contributed significantly to the increasing number of tourists in Chiang Mai. Hotel business rapidly expanded, from 86 hotels in 1994 to 299 hotels in 2007 (or a 3.35-fold increase). Hotel rooms increased from 11,407 to 20,203 (or almost doubled) during the same period (see Table 4.19). If guesthouses and resorts were included, there would have been more rooms available: 2,645 in the guesthouses and 783 in the resorts.[206]

The tourism sector, therefore, has been essential to Chiang Mai's rising income and employment. The hotels and restaurants sector accounted for 7.3 per cent of Chiang Mai's GPP in 1995 and it grew to 10–11 per cent in 2005–9, representing the highest proportion in the country during that period. Chiang Mai's GPP in the hotels and restaurants sector was third in the country, after Phuket and Bangkok, with a value of 5,657 million baht in 1995 and it rose to 8,282 million baht in 2009.[207] The total employment in the hotels and restaurants sector in Chiang Mai increased from 27,908 in 2000 to 53,243 in 2010 (or almost doubled). The proportion of workers in the hotels and restaurants sector in Chiang Mai in 1999 was also high, representing 37.2 per cent of all employment in trade and services in the province.[208]

---

[204] For this issue, see Sarassawadee (2008, p. 598).
[205] Ibid., p. 599.
[206] Tourism Authority of Thailand, Northern Office, Division 1.
[207] Gross Provincial Product (various years).
[208] 1999 Survey of Trade and Services.

TABLE 4.19
Number of Hotels and Tourists in Chiang Mai, 1994–2007

Category	1994	2002	2003	2004	2005	2006	2007
No. of hotels	86	199	195	214	218	228	299
No. of rooms	11,407	13,466	13,625	14,103	16,673	16,430	20,203
No. of tourists	2,186,308	3,197,790	3,146,194	3,623,395	3,708,795	4,405,720	4,181,873
Thai tourists	1,321,164	1,639,473	1,714,843	1,877,194	1,922,042	2,592,420	2,598,041
Foreign tourists	885,997	1,558,317	1,431,351	1,746,201	1,786,853	1,876,300	1,583,837

Source: Chiang Mai Tourism Office.

Growth in tourism affected the income and employment of related businesses such as souvenir shops, furniture-related businesses, tour operators, bars and nightclubs, department stores, etc. Tourism expansion in Chiang Mai also had tremendous effects on its physical environment, both in the urban areas and the surrounding districts, with the construction of hotels, accommodations, and shopping malls, particularly in 1992–97 when 32 projects to construct large hotels in Chiang Mai were approved. In the meantime, land prices rose many folds.[209]

The socio-economic impact of tourism expansion was felt both in the urban and the rural areas. Many villages and households in Chiang Mai drew their income from tourism. At the village level the income was mainly from home stays, production of souvenirs, cultural shows, tour guides, etc. Despite the positive impact of tourism on income and employment, such income was concentrated mainly in the high income group and was not distributed to the lower income group. Income distribution disparity leaned towards the wealthy such as those who could invest in the production of souvenirs. Income from tourism tended to concentrate in well-to-do villages more than from agricultural and non-agricultural sectors.[210] Moreover, other major tourism impacts included environmental degradation, expansion of the sex industry in both the urban and rural areas, child prostitution, and the proliferation of illicit drugs had heavy tolls on the local culture and could be regarded as too high an economic cost.[211]

---

[209] Sarassawadee (2008, p. 613).

[210] Akarapong cited by Mingsan (2011, p. 52).

[211] For studies concerning the tourism impact on the Northern economy and society, see Mingsan (2011) and Cohen (2001).

Border Trade

Border trade between the North and its neighbours, Myanmar and Laos, had long been in existence, not to mention the even-longer trade with China. But its expansion was rather limited prior to 1987. Most trade involved consumer products such as flavour-enhancers, fish sauces, tonics, dried food, savoury and sweet condiments, etc. Such limited trade was partly due to the Cold War and political unrest. When the Cold War drew its close in the early 1990s, the Thai government's policy was to support and encourage free trade. This was especially during General Chatichai Choonhavan's government when the policy "turning battlefields into marketplaces" and the policy to open the country to more trade had been introduced. Economic quadrangle or "the 5 Chiang's Strategy" consisting of Chiang Mai–Chiang Rai–Chiang Tung (Burma)–Chiang Rung (Yunnan)–Chiang Thong (Luang Prabang–Laos) was a joint project to link the economy, commerce, investments, labour, and transportation between four countries, namely Thailand, Burma, Laos, and China (Yunnan Province). This project was initiated by the private sector and was supported by the neighbouring countries. The major aim was to create cooperation and transport connections in the area of more than 100 million people and to facilitate the movement of goods, services, and labour that would bring about economic growth. In 1992 the Greater Mekong Subregion (GMS) Economic Cooperation Program, initiated by the Asian Development Bank, was established to strengthen the economic cooperation as well as to open and expand the free market among the six member states, namely Thailand, Burma, Laos, Cambodia, Vietnam, and Southern China.

In 2003, the Thaksin Shinawatra's government had reached a strategic economic cooperation agreement with Cambodia, Laos, Myanmar, and Vietnam under the Ayeyarwady–Chao Phraya–Mekong Economic Cooperation Strategy (ACMECS). The agreement identified cooperation in eight areas: (1) facilitation of trade and investment, (2) agriculture, (3) manufacturing and energy, (4) transportation linkage, (5) tourism, (6) human development, (7) public health, and

(8) environment.[212] Many projects were encouraged to support true development and cooperation such as the construction of 3A (R3A) highway in 1995 which is part of the modern Silk Road linking China–Laos–Thailand to stimulate trade, investment, tourism, cultural exchanges, etc. The R3A highway, over 1,800 km long, was completed in 2011.[213] The Thai government supported the agreement by establishing the border economic zone as well as implementing regional economic development along various economic corridors. Furthermore, an agreement was signed

---

[212] The 11 planning priorities of GMS were: (1) Southern Economic Corridor, (2) East–West Economic Corridor, (3) North–South Economic Corridor, (4) Telecommunication Interconnection, (5) Power Trade and Power Transmission Interconnection, (6) Trade and Cross-border Investment Facilitation, (7) Private Sector Participation and Competitiveness Enhancement, (8) Human Resource and Specialization Development, (9) Environmental Development Strategic Framework, (10) Flood Mitigation and Water Resource Management, and (11) Tourism Development. The economic corridor development involved construction of highways linking the six-member states (including economic infrastructure such as waterworks, roads, and energy) that had been partially implemented. This is the top priority plan under the GMS regional collaborative framework, aiming to expand the benefits of transportation interconnection to remote areas in GMS in order to stimulate economic activities with growth nodes for the development of the surrounding areas. Such plan gave the opportunity for investment both inside and outside GMS so as to provide the prioritizing mechanism as well as infrastructure investment collaboration.

[213] Tsuneishi (2008, pp. 12–16) mentioned ten road construction projects to enhance the collaboration. In 2005, nine economic corridors were identified to better cover the areas with higher potential. Thailand is involved in four routes: R1, R2, R3, and R10. R1 is in the Southern Economic Corridor, connecting Bangkok–Phnom Penh–Ho Chi Minh City–Vang Tao (1,000 km long). R2 is the East–West Corridor from Moulmein (Myanmar) through Thailand at Mukdahan into Lao PDR to Vietnam at Danang. R3 is the North–South Economic Corridor, divided into two routes: R3A connecting Thailand–Lao PDR–China from Kunming–Jinghong–Mohan (Yunnan, PRC) to Bo Ten–Luang Namtha–Huay Xai (Lao PDR), crossing the Mekong into Thailand at Chiang Khong through to Chiang Rai. R3B connects Thailand–Kyaing Tong (Myanmar)–Kunming (PRC), diverges from R3A at Jinghong to Daluo (PRC) into Myanmar at Mengla–Kyaing Tong–Tachileik to Mae Sai in Chiang Rai and joins R3A at Mueang District, Chiang Rai. The final route is R10 in the Southern Coastal Sub-corridor linking Thailand–Cambodia–Vietnam, from Trat into Cambodia at Hat Lek, through Koh Kong–Sre Ambel–Sihanoukville (Cambodia) to Ca Mao in South Vietnam (Department of Highways 2013, p. 122).

among the commercial centres in the major border area (sister-city agreements) that were linked by transportation. Other aspects included the development of an economic zone by establishing an industrial estate and the development of a logistics and agricultural zone to enhance contract farming between Thailand and the neighbouring countries. The government provided financial assistance and loans for road construction linking sister cities in Myanmar, Cambodia, and Laos. Later, the Cross Border Transport Agreement (CBTA) instated the strengthening of trade and investment expansion among the GMS countries. This agreement stipulated important measures such as the one-stop service for customs and visa application, goods importation, and provision or allowance of more lenient standards for the conditions of goods and services.

From 2003 the North's border trade was largely expanded, especially with Myanmar and China. In 2005, the proportion of trade between the North and Laos was only 20 per cent of Thai–Laos border trade. The total value of border trade between the North, Myanmar, Laos, and southern China was 3,886 million baht in 1996, and it grew to 24,359 million baht in 2006 and 85,231 million baht in 2012.[214] Thailand had been accumulating trade surplus, from only 2,952 million baht to 16,534 million baht and 68,277 million baht in the same period.[215] The largest proportion of border trade was with Myanmar: 62.8 per cent of all border trade of the North in 2003, and slightly decreased to 60.2 per cent in 2012.[216]

There are several factors that accelerated the border trade between the North and Myanmar. Firstly, the Thai–Myanmar border is a very long distance stretching from Chiang Rai to the Central Region. Secondly, financial transactions such as the various forms of money transfer through commercial banks have been developed along with the financial deregulation of Thailand and Myanmar allowing such transactions through other institutions. If border trade at Sankhla Buri checkpoint (located in the West–Central), with the high value of natural

---

[214] Bank of Thailand, Northern Branch.
[215] Ibid.
[216] Ibid.

gas imports of more than 30,000 million baht per year was excluded, the Mae Sot checkpoint in Tak Province would have the highest volume of border trade.[217]

In 2006 border trade between Thailand and Myanmar at various customs checkpoints in the North, Central Region, and the South was as follows: Sankhla Buri in Kanchanaburi Province had the total trade value of 77,896 million baht or 74 per cent of all border trade with Myanmar; Mae Sot in Tak Province had the trade value of 12,249 million baht or 11.6 per cent of Ranong checkpoint which had 9.4 per cent of border trade; Mae Sai in Chiang Rai (2.4 per cent); Chiang Saen in Chiang Rai (1.1 per cent); Mae Sariang in Mae Hong Son (less than 1 per cent); Prachuap Khiri Khan (less than 1 per cent); Mae Hong Son (less than 1 per cent); and Chiang Dao (less than 1 per cent).[218] From 2002 to 2012 the North's border trade had increased ten folds.[219] Most of the exports to Myanmar and Laos were consumer goods such as foodstuff, construction materials, and fuel oil.[220] The expansion of border trade contributed to changes in the Northern Region's economy.

The impacts of border trade on the North's economy were far and wide. This led to growth of economic, industrial, commercial related businesses, and tourism expansion; movement of both domestic and foreign labour; income and employment; urban growth both in terms of the economy and physical changes; as well as the border people's economic livelihoods. This section will address only some of these issues.[221]

Border trade at Mae Sot checkpoint (the checkpoint with the highest volume of border trade in the North, Tak Province, and Myawaddy) continued to increase. In 2004 the trade value at Mae Sot was 13,980 million baht and it grew to 29,782 million baht in 2010. Major

---

[217] Akarapong (2007, pp. 94–95).

[218] Tsuneishi (2008, p. 39).

[219] Bank of Thailand, Northern Branch.

[220] Ibid.

[221] Studies concerning the impact of the border trade changes on the Northern economy can be found in Tsuneishi (2007 and 2008), Akarapong (2007), and International Institute for Trade and Development (2014).

exports included sodium glutamate, iron, diesel oil, motorcycles, garments, television sets, vegetable oil, etc. Imports into Thailand consisted of processed wood, furniture, fresh and dried fish, and other agricultural produce.[222] In 2010 the value of exports at Mae Sot checkpoint was 28,673 million baht whereas imports were only valued at 1,103 million baht, representing a huge trade surplus of 27,564 million baht.[223] Expansion of border trade with high level of trade surplus had considerable impact on the continuing economic expansion and opportunity.

One study found that in 2006, there were 140 Thai exporters passing through Mae Sot District checkpoint. They were from various provinces: 20 from Tak (with 29.15 per cent share of the border trade), 84 from Bangkok (25.32 per cent), two from Ranong (6.65 per cent), five from Chiang Mai and Chiang Rai (4.77 per cent), 29 from other provinces (3.27 per cent), and the rest unspecified (30.94 per cent). On the other hand, importers in Thailand were mainly merchants including businessmen from Tak who controlled one-quarter of all import values. This reflects the ability of the local businessmen to have control over imports.[224] Moreover, the expansion of border trade in the North included Chiang Rai and the nearby provinces. Economic transactions involved large amounts of investment from Chinese businessmen for building entertainment complexes and industrial parks around the Golden Triangle .

Border trade expansion affected the North's economy, particularly at Mae Sot District. Mae Sot's economy grew along with the influx of Myanmar labour which sought employment in various economic sectors, especially in trade and services. Increasing income for Mae Sot translated into a change of the status of the local government from "Mae Sot *Tambon* Municipality" to "Mae Sot *Mueang* Municipality" (on 9 November 2001) and finally to "Mae Sot *Nakhon* Municipality" (on 28 January 2010). Its population had increased from 106,413 in 2000 to 121,062 in 2010.[225] The population growth of the *nakhon*

---

[222] Tsuneishi (2008, pp. 27–28).
[223] <www.danmaesot.com>.
[224] Akarapong (2007, p. 101).
[225] 2010 Population Census.

municipality and other municipalities in Mae Sot, from the influx of Myanmar labour, also affected the population structure of Tak Province in general. Non-Thai population increased from 6.7 per cent in 2000 to 13.6 per cent in 2010.[226] The proportion of Buddhists slightly decreased from 95.1 per cent to 94.0 per cent whereas the proportion of Christians increased from 2.9 per cent to 4.4 per cent in the same period.[227] The population of Mae Sot District in 2010 was 121,062: 54,098 of whom lived within the municipality boundary while 66,964 people lived outside the boundary. The population of Mae Sot District accounted for 22.8 per cent of Tak Province's population while the population of Mae Sot Nakhon Municipality constituted 36.8 per cent of the municipal population in Tak Province.[228]

The growth of border trade at Mae Sot checkpoint led to the expansion of the manufacturing and services sector, such as hotels. Investments in industrial plants were made with a plan to develop an industrial estate in a 2,500 *rai* plot to accommodate such investments (there were 300 industrial plants in Mae Sot district in 2006). It was expected that once the industrial estate was completed, all the plants would be relocated there.[229] In 2014 the Thai government introduced a policy to establish a special economic zone in the Mae Sot District through the recommendation of the Industrial Estate Authority of Thailand (IEAT) to set up a *"Nakhon* Mae Sot Special Border Economic Zone"*. Preparations were also made for the revision of the law to empower the operation of public utilities in the industrial estate as well as incentives for the investors. It was aimed that by 2015 more than 4,000 *rai* in the industrial estate would be sold, creating income of more than 5,200 million baht. Establishment of ten more industrial estates were also in the pipeline.[230]

---

[226] Ibid.
[227] Ibid.
[228] Ibid.
[229] Tsuneishi (2008, p. 25).
[230] *Thairathonline*, 22 October 2014, <www.thailand.co.th/content/458360>.

Border trade growth had positive effects on the service sector as well. In the early 2010s, hotels and other types of accommodation were increasingly being built, resulting in income generation and employment. Migrant workers from Myanmar were crucial in the industrial development of the Mae Sot District. Its proximity to the Myanmar border and two to three folds higher wages than in Myanmar were pull factors for Myanmar labourers to work in Mae Sot's manufacturing and service industries. In 2014 it was estimated that there were more than 0.10 million Myanmar workers in Mae Sot District.[231] The actual numbers could be higher since this figure covered only registered Myanmar labour, most of whom worked in garment and textiles, electronics, pottery and ceramic factories, and agricultural products processing. All of these manufactures were labour intensive[232] and led to linkages with other economic sectors such as manufacturing and services sector as well as urban growth that characterized provincial economic growth in the North.

The 2000s saw a significant economic transition of Chiang Saen District, especially the Chiang Saen checkpoint in Chiang Rai Province (also a river port). Chiang Saen Port, linking the trade between Thailand, China, Laos, and Myanmar, had considerable impacts on border trade. Trade values between Thailand and southern China through Chiang Saen checkpoint grew from 215 million baht in 1996 to 4,162 million baht in 2003 and 4,946 million baht in 2012. Thailand's trade surplus during the same period rose from a mere 60.8 million baht to 1,987 million baht and 3,724 million baht, reflecting export growth over imports.[233] When trade with Laos and Myanmar was taken into consideration, Thailand's international trade in 2011 had a total value of 11,000 million baht, with imports of 1,000 million baht and exports of 10,000 million baht.[234] In 2006 the proportion of trade value between Thailand and China at Chiang Saen checkpoint was 75.9 per

---

[231] <www.chaoprayanews.com> (accessed 31 December 2014).
[232] <www.prachatai.com/journal/2013/01/44794>.
[233] Akarapong (2007, p. 113); <www.chiangsaencustoms.com>.
[234] International Institute for Trade and Development (2014, p. 120).

cent, followed by Myanmar with 18 per cent and only 6.1 per cent with Laos.[235]

Rapid trade expansion in the 2000s, partly due to the Thailand–China Free Trade Agreement signed in 2003, resulted in significant increase of trade between the two countries at Chiang Saen checkpoint. In the mid-2000s, more than half of the major Thai exports to China were dried longans and Para rubber. On the other hand, Chinese imports were largely agricultural produce such as vegetables, apples, pears, and garlics. Chiang Saen Port facilitates trade with Jinghong Port and Guan Lei Port in China's Yunnan Province.[236] Border trade expansion at Chiang Saen checkpoint prompted the revision of customs regulations and procedures, construction of a new port, improvement of port capacity to accommodate large vessels, and expansion of warehouses for the expected growth in transportation, particularly the capacity to support and link with trade using the R3A route that would increase trade opportunities from China to Thailand.

Chiang Saen Port links waterway transportation between Thailand and China. It starts from Chiang Saen District to Ban Pung Port in Myanmar and Si Lei Port in China. Freighters from southern China have to traverse 264 km to Chiang Saen Port. Although waterway transportation (via the Mekong) takes longer than land transportation, the obvious advantage is much lower cost, particularly for bulky products. One study found that transportation from China to Chiang Saen (over 1,834 km) via the Mekong River took about twice as long but the cost was only US$271 per tonne compared to land transportion: the R3B route through Myanmar (1,867 km) cost US$470 per tonne and the R3A route through Laos (1,906 km) cost US$392 per tonne.[237]

---

[235] Tsuneishi (2008, p. 20).
[236] Ibid.
[237] Ruth, cited by International Institute for Trade and Development (2014, p. 121).

Border trade and cross border trade are thus essential to the North's economy. Not only were there various supports for trade by building economic infrastructure, such as roads and ports, trade deregulation, and investments in the GMS, there were also high levels of economic expansion of its trading partners. Throughout the previous decade, the economy of Yunnan Province, including the overall economy of China, had more than 10 per cent of annual economic growth rate whereas Myanmar's economy grew more than 6–7 per cent annually. Border trade, therefore, was a major factor of economic growth in the North that also affected its urban areas, construction industry and service expansion, and tourism.

Conclusion

Before the railway reached Chiang Mai in 1921, the mountainous terrain was the major obstacle to the North's economic development. Waterway transportation, especially from Bangkok to Chiang Mai, was very time-consuming and costly since the trip was going against the currents. Most of the North's trade was with Yunnan Province in China and Moulmein in Burma due to convenience and lower transportation cost. Trade within the Northern Region was rather limited. Its economy was mainly subsistence with rice cultivation for household consumption. Chiang Mai had been the North's economic, commercial, and administrative centre. Its role was heightened after centralization under the Bangkok government that had replaced the former administrative system of Northern princes. Expansion of teak exports depended on waterway transportation to Bangkok via Ping, Wang, Yom, Nan, and Chao Phraya rivers for processing and exporting. The Salween and the Mekong rivers were also essential for transportation to Myanmar and Vietnam, respectively. Most of the North's manufactures were local industry producing items for household consumption such as silk, textiles, silverwares, gem mining, umbrellas, mats, ceramics, etc.

Timber business was vital to the economic development of the North. Income from exporting teak constituted a major part of the Thai export earnings. Investments in the teak industry in the early twentieth century was contributed by foreign companies, mostly British, with 80 per cent of the total investment. The growth of teak exports inevitably led to bankruptcy of small timber companies in the North. Most of the timber industry workers were Khmu and Shan.

Major consequences of railway construction were the North's changing trade routes from China and Burma to Bangkok. Areas under rice cultivation also expanded. Rice mills began to grow along the rail line both in the upper North and the lower North. Agricultural technology in the upper North mainly involved the irrigation ditch system developed by the communities, leading to more regular rice cultivation and higher rice yields than in other parts of the country. Abundant forests in the North led to the expansion of related local industries such as furniture, polished wood, basketry, etc. Railways also brought a large variety of goods from Europe, India, and China. The local industry started to decline because of cheaper goods that flooded the market.

After the Second World War, population pressure and the construction of roads linking Bangkok to the Northern provinces led to a decline in waterway transportation, higher diversification of agricultural produce as well as expanding arable land. Upland crops that increased in production were maize, sugarcane, and soybean, mostly for exports.

The North's manufacturing industry had grown. From 1987, the upper North's major manufactures were electronics and handicrafts whereas the lower North's were agro-industry and food-related such as rice milling, processed foods, sugar, and beverages. Local handicraft, once the traditional home industry of the North, had declined because of manufactured goods that continued to flood the market.

Tourism has also been essential to the North's economic development, especially Chiang Mai which is a centre for cultural and natural tourism as well as a centre of handicrafts. Indeed, Chiang Mai is a world class tourist destination. Income from tourism affected the urban growth and the service sector in Chiang Mai, particularly in the increase number of hotels and resorts. This expansion, in turn, meant overall physical changes in Chiang Mai.

Border trade in the North had accelerated since the 2000s. The major contributing factors were the economic quadrangle project, economic cooperation in trade and investment among the GMS countries, and the ACMECS. Border trade, particularly with Myanmar, affected the North's economic development that led to economic, commercial, and investment expansion in the manufacturing and service sectors, foreign labour movement, as well as urban growth in the North.

5

THE SOUTH

Background

The Southern Region's society and culture are quite different from that of the other regions. The South has the highest number of Muslims. Ethnic problems are prevalent. Interventions by imperialist Britain also created political problems at the multi-national level. The region has its own history and culture which is related to neighbouring Malaya. It is the smallest of Thailand's regions, making up just 14 per cent of the country's land area (after 1909). It contains the thinnest point between Myanmar and the Gulf of Thailand, with the Ta Nao Si mountain range running along its length.

The Siamese settled in Nakhon Si Thammarat in the thirteenth century. At the time, the city was the region's commercial hub with links to Malaya. Nakhon Si Thammarat was later established as an independent state. The centres in the east side of the Southern Region (as it is today), which comprised Pattani, Narathiwat, Yala and parts of Songkhla, were once important cities belonging to the ruler of Malaya. They traded with Kelantan, Terengganu, and Melaka, which were commercial centres in Muslim Southeast Asia. Pattani became prosperous and was home to multiple ethic groups. The Thai state started to expand its reach into the state of Pattani and there were a number of skirmishes around the seventeenth century. In 1786, Pattani was under Bangkok's rule, but nevertheless had a degree of autonomy as a tributary state. The Muslim population held numerous anti-Siamese state protests in Bangkok and Pattani. The Siamese government tried to restore order by appointing a provincial commissioner to rule Pattani under the *thesaphiban* system. In 1909, the Anglo-Siamese Treaty legitimized "the incorporation of Pattani into Siamese nation at the same time as it created, on the province of Satun, henceforward separated from Sultanate of Kedah which has passed into the hands of the British".[1]

The Muslims in the four Southern provinces — Pattani, Yala, Narathiwat and Satun — had close historical, ethnic, religious and cultural links to Malaya. Communications between them were easy because Malaysian was the local language. The people in these provinces became Thai due to political reasons. During the reign of King Rama II, Pattani consisted of seven small cities: Pattani, Nong Chik, Yala, Bang Nara, Raman, Ra-ngae (Tanyong Mat), and Sai Buri. They were ruled by the city of Songkhla, whose governor was directly appointed by Bangkok. Eventually the seven cities would be reduced to just three: Pattani, Yala, and Bang Nara (later Narathiwat). Afterwards, in 1901–2, there were protests and civil disobedience against the *thesapiban* system. Finally, the area was divided into four cities: Pattani, Yala, Bang Nara, and Sai Buri. Sai Buri would eventually become an *amphoe* of Pattani in 1932.[2]

Because of frequent unrest, the Siamese government in Bangkok had always been trying to gain full control of the Muslim communities in the South, particularly the four southernmost provinces, in the areas of administration and education. During the reign of King Rama V, there were government centralization efforts. The Thai language, culture, and education based on the "Bangkok's" example was asserted with the goal of fully uniting the Thai state. This started in 1917 and became increasingly intensified through nationalism. In the 1940s, the effort to merge the Southern Muslim provinces was still continuing.

---

[1] Torres (2004, pp. 161–71).
[2] Nantawan (2002, p. 451).

There was resistance from an anti-Thai group called the "Malayan Nationalist Movement", or MALAYU, which was supported by the "Pan Malayan Movement". These groups were formed during the Second World War by the Muslim Malayans as a result of nationalist ideologies that grew amidst colonized rule. The groups gave their support to the Malay and Muslim leaders in the South in order to free their country from Britain and the Thai state. Due to the ethnic and religious "identity" that the group represented, the liberalization movement caused the Southern Region to become one of the most politically sensitive in the country.[3]

The geography of the South had an effect on its economic development. The southward-projecting peninsula saw heavy rainfall throughout the year. Some said that "the Southern region has just one season". Its fertile land was the source of agricultural produce, particularly from fisheries and fruit farming, which had long been the main source of food for the population. The region was also a producer of rubber for exports. The income of the Southerners had always been dependent on agriculture.

The South has a very large basin which is the Songkhla River basin. It is 5.3 million *rai* in size and covers some *amphoes* in Songkhla, Narathiwat, and Patthalung. Full of various marine life, the fertile basin is suitable for rice farming and is a source of other natural resources. The area is an important centre of economic development for the region and for Thailand — supporting the people's traditional way of life, subsistence and commercial production.

THE SOUTH UP UNTIL 1941

Before the Second World War, the Southern Region had little trade with Bangkok (particularly before the railroad was built in the 1920s). Because the region was closer to Singapore and Penang, goods could be shipped to these destinations directly without going through the capital. The geography and resources of the South were factors that

---

[3] Torres (2004, pp. 161–71); <http://prachatai.com/journal/2005/01/2464>. For the issue concerning the nationalist movement aiming to partition Southern Thailand, see a detailed analysis in Thanet (2012).

made the economic structure of the region similar to Malaya, that is, suitable for tin mining and rubber production. The construction of the railroad connected the South's economy to Bangkok, and soon the connection started to gradually replace the region's commercial relationship with Singapore, even though the integration was not as tight as the economic link between Bangkok and the North and Northeast. The economic development of the South was highly dependent on exports, especially tin and rubber. The growth of commerce was a result of capital accumulation, the growth of the city and the increase in investor groups, local businessmen and merchants.

Population and Settlement

The 1904 Population Census reveals that the population of the Southern Region was 1.35 million. The largest *monthon*, Nakhon Si Thammarat, had the highest population of 645,000, consisting of 9,033 Chinese and 242,000 Malays. The *monthon* of Phuket was home to 178,000 people, where 32,408 were Chinese and 34,903 were Malays. Kelantan had a population of 300,000 million people, while Terengganu had 114,000.[4] There were 129,000 people in the *monthon* of Chumphon, with 3,129 Chinese and 1,986 Malays.

The 1909 Population Census shows the population distribution in the South as shown in Table 5.1.

TABLE 5.1
Population of the Southern Region, 1909

Monthon	Population
Nakhon Si Thammarat	502,317
Pattani	215,638
Chumphon	166,154
Phuket	227,052
Total	1,111,161

Source: 1909 Population Census.

---

[4] 1904 Population Census cited by Grabowsky (1996, p. 78).

The population of the South in 1909 was 1.11 million. Approximately 45 per cent, or 502,000 lived in the *monthon* of Nakhon Si Thammarat. The next largest *monthons* in terms of population were Phuket (227,000) and Pattani (251,000) (see Table 5.1). The population of the region rose from 1.25 million in 1919 to 1.84 million in 1937. That year, the three most populous provinces of the region were Nakhon Si Thammarat (386,000), Songkhla (300,000) and Pattani (193,000). The population of the South in 1909 was 12.7 per cent of the entire population of Thailand.[5]

The Southern Region has been made up of several ethnic groups. In 1929, Malays and Indians (particularly of Malay ethnicity) made up 22.1 per cent of the region's population. A majority, 272,494 to be precise, lived in the *monthon* of Pattani. Nakhon Si Thammarat had the second largest population of the group at 56,442 people (see Table 5.2). Most Malays were Muslims, making up 54 per cent of the Islamic population of the country.

The Malays were the largest non-Buddhist minority group. Most of them were Muslims and descendants of the Malays who had settled in the country many centuries ago. The most important occupations of the Malays in Thailand were rice farming and saltwater fisheries. In 1909, Thailand lost some of its land to Britain, namely Kelantan, Terengganu, Kedah, Perlis, Raman, Satun remained under Thai rule and was part of the *monthon* of Phuket.[6]

Although the Chinese made up just 5.44 per cent of the working population of the South, their roles needed emphasis. The Chinese played an important role in commercial development, both in the agricultural and non-agricultural sectors. They worked in rubber

[5]   1937 Population Census.
[6]   Grabowsky (1996, p. 53).

TABLE 5.2
Population of the Southern Region by Nationality, 1929

Nationality	Monthon		
	Nakhon Si Thammarat	Pattani	Phuket
Siamese	821,475	55,628	224,412
Chinese	30,708	7,000	15,961
Malays and Indians	56,442	272,494	1,069
Cambodians and Vietnamese	73	–	–
Chan and Burmese	21	1	417
Westerner	91	11	156
Japanese	28	14	11
Others	337	–	15

Source: *Statistical Yearbook of the Kingdom of Siam* (1931–33).

plantations and tin mines and became merchants and middlemen, etc. In 1937, the Chinese made up a significant portion of workers in the provinces where the economy was expanding. In Phuket, there were 3,797 ethnic Chinese, or 23.1 per cent of all workers in the province. In Chumphon, the figure was 3,456 (7 per cent), Yala 6,142 (14.5 per cent), Songkhla 13,518 (9.6 per cent), and Phangnga 2,690 (14.2 per cent).[7]

In 1937, workers in the agricultural sector, namely rice farming, forestry, fisheries, rubber, etc. made up 91 per cent of all workers in the region. Industry made up just 3.2 per cent, while services (retail, public, vocational work, housework and clerks) employed only 5.8 per cent of the workforce (see Table 5.3).

---

[7] 1937 Population Census.

TABLE 5.3
Population of the Southern Region by Economic Sector, 1937

Province	Agriculture and Fishery	Forestry	Trade	Manufacturing	Mining	Transportation	Public Service	Professional Work	Domestic Work and Personal Service	Clerical Service	Total
Krabi	24,419	235	541	182	28	66	226	153	449	77	26,117
Chumphon	44,324	103	1,750	589	571	336	277	345	420	131	48,786
Trang	52,590	175	1,842	783	454	370	257	378	449	252	57,444
Nakhon Si Thammarat	157,276	167	5,521	2,150	1,059	804	583	920	709	276	171,469
Narathiwat	67,085	176	2,704	1,270	302	579	317	261	809	124	73,626
Pattani	93,188	126	3,535	1,499	23	547	375	117	628	179	100,501
Phangnga	15,223	211	1,266	389	4,129	271	351	232	647	136	100,501
Patthalung	56,035	37	976	276	3	176	153	247	175	73	58,151
Phuket	8,768	93	1,865	749	2,601	629	423	394	720	205	16,447
Yala	37,348	37	1,300	565	1,251	188	395	204	675	136	42,099
Ranong	6,443	77	611	222	1,843	108	307	130	167	74	9,982
Songkhla	126,378	186	5,388	2,626	1,197	1,404	1,011	821	1,460	361	140,833
Satun	18,036	351	592	151	22	112	156	143	158	83	19,804
Surat Thani	70,960	345	3,201	1,671	931	589	416	518	583	177	79,391
The South	778,073	2,319	31,092	13,122	14,414	6,179	5,247	4,863	8,049	2,284	836,130

Note: Workers over the age of ten.

Source: 1937 Population Census.

Growth of Cities

The South comprised of outer provincial cities and cities in the tributary state. Cities that were important to the region's economy and government were Nakhon Si Thammarat and Phuket. Nakhon Si Thammarat (known as Ligor by Westerners and Lakhon by the Siamese) had the status of a tributary state of Siam from the time of King Taksin. Prior to 1904, the kingdom of Nakhon Si Thammarat extended its administration to Pattani, Narathiwat and Yala. It also acquired two cities into its control: Patthalung and Songkhla. Nakhon Si Thammarat and Songkhla had the status of chief town from the time of King Rama I. Nakhon Si Thammarat governed Sai Buri and Kelantan, while Songkhla had Terengganu and Pattani[8] under its rule. Bishop Palegoix recorded the following about Nakhon Si Thammarat in and around 1847:

> The city resides on a beautiful plain with forests. It is surrounded by a brick wall and a deep city moat. Beautiful temples were the sight to be seen. The population, including the Chinese, totaled 12,000 people. At Pak Nam there are large ports that were strong enough to allow commercial ships to dock in order to trade. Important products of the state were rice, tin, gold, pepper, rattan, olibanum, ivory, etc. Large row-able sail boats of Nakhon were very beautiful. The crew were expert sailors who used white canvass sails instead of reed-woven fabrics like those found on Malayan ships. The gold jewelry craftsmen of the city were skilled at making jewelry of their own unique design, which involved plating gold onto metal bowls or other silver utensils, then carving their designs onto the black surface.[9]

Nakhon Si Thammarat's trade was linked to Singapore and Bangkok. As a port city, ships on various routes docked there. In 1909,[10] "The Siam Steam Navigation Company, an off-shoot of the Danish East Asiatic Company run regularly down the east coast of the peninsular, between Bangkok and Singapore. They call at Nakhon Si Thammarat and Songkhla twice weekly in each direction." The value of the trade of *monthon* of Nakhon Si Thammarat is as shown in Table 5.4.[11]

---

[8] Bowring, vol. 2 (2007, pp. 66–71).
[9] Pallegoix (reprinted 2006, p. 40).
[10] BCR, *Monthon Nakonsri Tammarat and Pattani* (1909).
[11] Ibid.

TABLE 5.4
Value of the Trade of *monthon* **of Nakhon Si Thammarat, 1907–9**

Year	Pounds
1907	196,129
1908	279,413
1909	268,583

Source: BCR, *Monthon Nakonsri Tammarat and Pattani* (1909).

The number of Malay and Chinese sailing ships calling at the ports of the *monthon* is considerable. The value of goods exported through the port in 1907, 1908, and 1909 were 25,062 pounds, 136,000 pounds, and 112,256 pounds, respectively. The exported goods consisted of rice (milled and unmilled), tin and tin ores, hides, pigs, cattle and buffaloes.[12] Rice made up a majority of the export, totalling 70–75 per cent of the value of all exported goods in 1909. Other important products for exports were silk, cotton products, oil, and iron products. The British Consular Report noted in 1909 that:

> Nakonsri Tammarat, however, shows a very great increase in the export of rice, due to the erection early in the year 1908 of a large mill in Pak Phanang, eight miles away. …. In 1906, the export of rice rose to 115,112 pounds, more than five times as much as the value of that exported in the preceding year. In 1908, the figure fell to 82,470 pounds partly owing to a bad crop.[13] …. Nakonsri Tammarat is more fertile than that of Songkhla, and it is likely that the export of rice will continue to increase. At the Senggora [Songkhla] port, where a small rice mill has been working for many years past, the export is pretty constant, being somewhere about 30,000 pounds in value for all three years.[14]

---

[12] Ibid.
[13] Ibid.
[14] Ibid.

As an important province for rice exports, Nakhon Si Thammarat played an important role in the commercial development of the Southern Region as well as the growth of rice mills, Chinese immigrant workers, wholesale and retail trade, and capital accumulation.

Phuket

Phuket had been the most important port city of the *monthon* and the Southern Region. Its port was bigger than those in Trang, Phangnga, Ta Kua Pa and Ranong, all of which were small and inadequate for large volume exports. Tin made up more than half of all of the *monthon's* exports.[15] Phuket was also an important port city in Southeast Asia. It had long been a tributary state of Siam.[16] The signing of the Bowring Treaty between Siam and Great Britain, made Phuket into an increasingly important producer of tin up until the beginning of the twentieth century. More than 90 per cent of the country's tin came from *monthon* Phuket. In 1912, the province of Phuket produced 59,605 *hab* of tin, or 60 per cent of the output of the *monthon* itself.[17]

Between 1909 and 1914, the province of Phuket produced 56 per cent of the tin in the entire Southern Region. The percentage of tin production, by province, is as shown in Table 5.5.[18]

In 1921, 8,643 tonnes of tin, worth 0.986 million pounds, were exported. *Monthon* Phuket contributed 87 per cent of the export. Of the rest, 8 per cent came from Nakhon Si Thammarat and 4 per cent from Pattani.[19] Almost all of the exports went to Penang. There were more than 30 tin mining companies, most of which were British. Two

---

[15] BCR, *Monthon Phuket* (1914).

[16] Phuket had continually been the vassal state of many realms since the middle of the thirteenth century: Tambralinga, Srivijaya, Sri Dharmaraja, Sukhothai, and Ayutthaya. Until the early Rattanakosin before 1892, Phuket was strictly controlled by the Bangkok government as its tributary state. Especially in 1880–89, Bangkok administered Phuket as the centre of tin mining on the western seaboard of the Malay Peninsula (Wyatt 2013, p. 349).

[17] *Directory for Bangkok and Siam 1914* (1914, p. 202).

[18] Falkus (1996, p. 89) calculated from the British Parliamentary Papers, Diplomatic and Consular Reports (Siam).

[19] BCR, *Senggora* (1921).

TABLE 5.5
Percentage of Tin Production by Province

Province	1869–74	1889–94	1909–14
Phuket	70.8	64.2	55.9
Trang	–	1.0	3.3
Ranong	4.1	8.4	10.1
Ta Kua Pa	13.9	16.0	7.8
Phangnga	3.3	4.1	12.3
Pattani	–	0.8	4.0
Nakhon Si Thammarat	–	1.2	3.8
Chumphon	–	–	1.9
Others	7.9	5.3	0.9
Total	100.0	100.0	100.0

Source: Falkus (1996, p. 89) calculated from the British Parliamentary Papers, Diplomatic and Consular Reports (Siam).

shipping lines stopped via Phuket: the Eastern Shipping Company and the Strait Steamship. Both companies had ships capable of transporting about 400 tonnes. They sailed between Penang and Phuket every week, and also sailed on other routes to Tavoy, Ta Kua Pa, Ranong, Trang, Satun, Krabi, and Phangnga.[20]

The population of Phuket increased very quickly. In 1870, the population of the city comprised of 25,000 Chinese, 300 Siamese, 200 British-Malayan, 200 British, 200 Indians, and other Europeans.[21] Dr R.B. Bradley visited Phuket in 1870 and wrote the following description:

> The Chinese soon flocked in numbers to Phuket …. Pra Palat (senior officials) furnished them with funds to commence work and the place prospered and grew apace …. and now what was a paddy field is covered with brick houses and numerous population …. Most of the buildings have been built by the raja [governor].[22]

---

[20] BCR, *Monthon Phuket* (1914).
[21] Bradley cited by Mackay (2012, p. 310).
[22] Ibid., p. 318.

In 1890, over 50,000 Chinese immigrant workers moved into the city. The Chinese population that year was more than the Siamese and Malays put together, which was estimated to be about 1,000–2,000 people. (The British Foreign Office concluded that in 1885, the Chinese population in Phuket may have been 45,000, and there were possibly 1,000 Thais.) In 1890, when King Rama V visited the city, "685 shop-houses were constructed in town, 318 were built from bricks and 367 of wood".[23]

In 1909, then Crown Prince Vajiravudh visited Phuket and witnessed its development and prosperity — new houses, buildings and theatres, breweries, ice factories, numerous horse carriages, cars on city roads. He recorded that "Apart from Bangkok, no other city in Siam could possibly match Phuket's development."[24]

The population of Phuket decreased when Europeans started using the bucket dredging method, a labour-saving technology, to replace open-pit and other traditional mining methods from 1907 onwards. It was brought by Tongkah Harbour Tin Dredging Company.[25] The number of Chinese

---

[23] Mackay (2012, p. 319).

[24] Ibid., p. 335.

[25] One source noted in 1926: "There are now many methods of mining in use in the industry, but the most important individually of these, namely bucket-dredging was not introduced into Siam until 1907, when the Tongkah Harbour Company began dredging operations in the Harbour of Tongkah [Phuket island] for the purpose of winning tin. These operations were so successful that additions were made to their own plant by this Company, and other Companies followed their lead, such as the Ranong Tin Dredging Company, the Siamese Tin Syndicate, the Ratrut Basin Company, and Ronpibun Tin N.L. At one time, in 1919–20, the amount of tin won by dredging was greater than by other methods, namely 75,000 piculs [*hab*] against 68,500 piculs: but this proportion has not been maintained, and in 1923–24 the figures were 44,000 piculs by bucket dredging, and 84,000 piculs by other methods, such as open cast mining, shaft mining, and hydraulic pressure. Attempts are now being made in certain centres to introduce suction-cutters in the place of buckets into the dredging used, as being less expensive to maintain, but these have not yet passed the experimental stage, in Siam at least" (N.A. Department of Railways 2/10).

immigrant workers, which used to peak at 50,000, was reduced to 25,000 in the 1920s.[26] The growth of tin exports not only affected the number of Chinese workers, but also the number of Chinese investors. More taxes could be collected. One study noted that

> Tongkah bay is port of Poket [Phuket]. A good road leads to a town which is 1.5 miles distant from the harbor master office and this is about two miles from the junk anchorage. .... These [Chinese] men during the south-east monsoon [the rainy season], finds plenty of employment [at] the tin mines but during the northeast monsoon number of them are idle being out of employment owing to the scarcity of water for washing the tin ... Gambling predominates more than in Bangkok, and is the principle cause of so much trouble in the island.[27]

The increase in exports reflected the growth of the city of Phuket. In 1914, the value of imports totalled 298,000 pounds. Almost half of the imports were materials to be used for ore mining by tin dredging companies that had obtained government concessions. Of the 756,000 pounds worth of exports from Phuket, more than 750,000 pounds were from tin ores.[28] Chinese businessmen, also known as "*taw kae*", the mine owners, also ran other businesses on the side such as gambling, shops and opium houses. These businesses became important sources of income for the city. After the Chinese workers made money from the mines, more than half would be spent on opium smoking, and another portion spent on gambling and prostitution. These incomes therefore were important to the growth of the city.[29] The Hokkien Chinese made up a majority of the Chinese population. Most mine owners and middlemen were Hokkiens. The group had influence over the western coast of the Southern Region, from Ranong down to Trang.[30]

---

[26] Mackay (2012, p. 367).
[27] Bradley cited by ibid., p. 310.
[28] BCR, *Monthon Phuket* (1914).
[29] Mackay (2012, p. 312).
[30] Skinner (1957).

The import of opium into the *monthon* was also on the rise, partly due to the increase in the number of mine workers in Phuket.[31] The growth of the city resulted in a shortage of rice to feed Chinese mine workers. Phuket ended up having to buy rice from other areas. The 1914 British Consular Report concluded that: "The continued increase of the quantity of rice imported is due to the neglect of the agricultural possibilities of the *monthon* for the larger profits of mining. Most of the rice imported comes from Penang, Ranong and Takua Pa, are largely supplied by Tavoy."[32]

Phuket became increasingly important economically and politically. During the change in governance to the *thesapiban* system, *Phraya* Ratsadanupradit Mahisara Phakdi (Khaw Sim Bee Na Ranong),[33] the governor of Trang, was appointed high commissioner of the *monthon* of Phuket. He brought prosperity to Phuket through various aspects of city development such as building roads and utilities. He also played an important role in the drafting of mining laws, and spearheaded the growing of rubber trees in Phuket and other parts of the Southern Region.

The growth of tin mining resulted in physical and economic changes in the city of Phuket. Because the growth of Phuket was significant for Thai economic development, in 1892 the government established the Department of Mining to administer tin mining. The government of Bangkok and the local government rushed the construction of roads and utilities, the improvement of shipping ports, the establishment of the postal and telegraph services, and the construction of the city hall, hospitals, banks, and schools. An airport was also built to accommodate air shipments from Don Muang Airport in the 1930s.

---

[31] BCR, *Monthon Phuket* (1914).

[32] BCR, *Senggora* (1921).

[33] *Phraya* Ratsadanupradit was born in Ranong Province and went into the civil service in 1882. He was granted the title of *Luang* Borirak Lohavisai and held the position of Deputy Governor of Ranong. Later he was promoted to *Phra* Atsadongkhot Thitraksa, Governor of Kraburi in 1885. In 1890 he was promoted to *Phraya* Ratsadanupradit Mahisara Phakdi, Governor of Trang. He was one of the most prominent provincial civil servants in that period and was a favourite of King Rama V and King Rama VI.

The Economy of the South

Before 1855, trade in the South was largely monopolized by the government. Major exports were tin, bird's nests, animal hides and other wild products. Most of the exports went to Singapore. After the signing of the Bowring Treaty in 1855, exports began to increase, with tin and rubber (after 1922) leading the expansion. Tin export growth boosted its size to 70–85 per cent of the total value of goods exported from the South.[34] It became the second or third most important source of export income for the country after rice. Royalty fees collected from tin was an important part of the taxes collected by the government, as shown in Table 5.6.[35]

TABLE 5.6
Royalty Fees Collected from Tin, 1899–1928

Year	Income of Royalty (thousand baht)
1899	626.0
1904	1,020.8
1910	1,185.8
1912	2,670.0
1918–24 (on average)	3,250.0
1924–28 (on average)	3,653.7

Source: N.A. Department of Royal Railways 2/10; *Directory for Bangkok and Siam 1914* (1914, p. 207); Ministry of Commerce and Communications (1930, p. 118).

Rubber was an important economic crop. However, before the Second World War, its growth was minimal and made up just a small fraction of exports. In 1932–34, rubber amounted to only 2 per cent of

---

[34] BCR, *Monthon Phuket* (various years).
[35] N.A. Department of Royal Railways 2/10; *Directory for Bangkok and Siam 1914* (1914, p. 207); Ministry of Commerce and Communications (1930, p. 118).

the region's export value.[36] The economy in most parts of the region was still subsistence in nature.

Before the Second World War, the economy of the South had little trade connection with Bangkok (especially before the construction of the railroad). The region's primary industries were similar to that of Malaya, namely tin mining and rubber production. Its close vicinity to Penang and Singapore meant that the South could directly transport goods to these destinations without having to ship via Bangkok. In 1900, the value of exports from the region to Bangkok was 400,000 dollars (or 10 per cent of the region's exports). The value of imports from Bangkok was 1.5 million dollars (40 per cent of total imports). The average value of exports to Singapore was three million dollars, while the value of imports from Singapore was 2.5 million dollars.[37]

The Royal State Railway of Thailand constructed the railroad linking Bangkok to Malaya at Pedang Besar in 1918. Rice from Patthalung, Songkhla and Bangkok and pork began to be shipped to Malaya. The railroad allowed the Southern Region's rice imports to come primarily from Bangkok instead of Burma. The construction of railroads within the region itself in the 1920s also allowed goods to be shipped to Bangkok.[38] It linked the South's and Bangkok's economy, and affected the growth of the Southern cities, investor groups, businessmen, and local merchants.

Tin Industry

As previously mentioned, most tin mines were located on the western side of the Southern Region, with a majority on the island of Phuket. In the nineteenth century, the resources used for tin mining were capital, labour and business operations, with most of the business operators

---

[36] Chatthip (reprinted 1999, p. 66).
[37] The Foreign Trade and Navigation of the Kingdom of Siam and Straits Settlement Government Gazettes cited by Kakizaki (2007, p. 14).
[38] Chatthip (reprinted 1999, p. 65).

being Chinese. There were no tin smelting plants in Thailand.[39] Tin ore was cleaned, shipped and sold to Penang and Singapore. Many Chinese mines utilized gravel pumping (pumping water into the mines and collecting ore from the sludge) instead of manual labour. In 1903, J.H. Heal, the director general of the Department of Mines stated that: "[G]enerally speaking, all the mining is in the hands of the Chinese; the labour is Chinese, and the smelting is done locally by Chinese methods ... the number of Siamese and Malays engaged in tin mining is very small, while practically the whole of mining on the island of Phuket is carried on at the present time by Hokkien Chinese".[40]

The Chinese played a major role in tin mining. The economy of the South was somewhat independent from the Bangkok government. The appointed governor was often a Chinese with interests in tin mining and was awarded a government concession to the tin mines. These Chinese governors would allow fellow Chinese to run mining businesses. The business interests of such governors often involved opium trade, shipping, and gambling that in turn involved other Chinese businesses with ties to him. Khaw Sim Bee, the governor of Trang between 1890 and 1900, who was later appointed high commissioner of the *monthon* of Phuket, had a wide network of trade connections with the Chinese in Phuket and other areas of the South. In the 1890s, his family was the owner of the Koh Guan Shipping Company based in Penang, and had other trading companies with stakes in tin mining and other businesses.[41]

---

[39] There was no tin smelter in the South because of its prohibitively high cost of operation. Sending tin ores to be smelted at Penang could have been less expensive than having a smelter in the South. The British-American Mining Company once offered to establish a tin ore smelter with an initial investment of half a million pounds. The Thai government was offered one-third of its share in 1933 with the stipulation that the government would have to find a site for the smelter and the waterways. The Company would be in charge of the financial matters, the control, and the operation as a monopoly. But the Thai government thought that the offer was in conflict with the country's diplomatic relations. To grant permission for the smelter would be against the treaty that called for freedom in vocation and equality. So the offer was duly rejected (N.A. M. of Finance 0301.1.37/77 (1933–34)).

[40] Heal cited in Breakspear (1994, p. 182).

[41] Falkus (1996, p. 148).

Prior to 1870, tin production skyrocketed because of the rising demand in the world market for canned foods and beverages. It expanded rapidly in the United States, Europe and the British colonies. The growth in the supply of tin was a result of the industrial revolution that took place in the nineteenth century. The metal was then used for ship building, railroad tracks, bridge construction, kitchen utensils, roofing, etc. In Europe, the need for tinning increased the demand for tin by 700 per cent between 1821 and 1875. That increase in demand boosted tin production in Southern Thailand, particularly after 1853 when Britain abolished high import taxes to protect industries in Cornwall. Britain's import of tin from Thailand rose from 4,000 tonnes in 1850 to 85,000 tonnes in 1870.[42] Between 1870 and 1910, the tin production business ran into difficulties and stagnation. Export growth was slow (see Table 5.7), partly because Malaya had grown into a world leader in tin production. Between 1906 and 1910, Malaya's share of the market was 44.9 per cent while Thailand's was 3.7 per cent.[43]

TABLE 5.7
Thailand's Tin Exports, 1871–1940

Year	Tonnes	Export Price (baht/tonne)	Export Value (million baht)
1871	2,500	747	1.87
1890	4,424	631	2.79
1900	3,900	1,499	5.85
1910	4,184	1,353	5.66
1920	6,201	1,893	11.74
1930	11,060	1,524	16.85
1940	12,978	2,887	37.47

Source: Sompop (1989, p. 149).

---

[42] Mackay (2012, p. 312).
[43] Falkus (1996, p. 79).

Factors that slowed down the growth of tin exports were: first, the technique used for tin mining was labour-intensive and not based on technology or machinery. Production efficiency was low while cost per unit was high. The labour-intensive technique was part of the simple, traditional mining technology used extensively by the Chinese. Back then, tin mining was still run as a family business. The Chinese migrant workforce was available for work in the mines, and the mines were still rich in ore. Therefore, there was no need to improve production technology and increase efficiency. As a result, output levels could not be expanded much. Second, worker employment was contractual and not full time. Most of the workers in the mines were Chinese immigrants who were available on a temporary or seasonal basis. Therefore, "labour shortage" problems arose when production needed to be increased. Wages rose as a result, and they formed an important part of the production cost. This, and the inability of the mines to operate with consistency, hindered the expansion of tin production. Third, the Bangkok government at the time did not give mining concessions to western countries for fear of colonization. Thailand was wary of the influence of the West. The incoming "foreign capital" was deemed a threat to Thai sovereignty. It was therefore impossible to "invest" in a mining business with advanced technology. Fourth, before the 1890s, the government of the *monthon* of Phuket was independent from the Bangkok government. The Bangkok government only appointed a representative to oversee its interests, but did not exercise stringent control. Also, the Chinese who held political positions and had control of the *monthon*'s budgets were not interested in improving the "tin economy". As long as he did not pose a threat to the central government, the ruler would be left to his own devices despite neglecting the development of his *monthon*. Fifth, transportation was the main focus of the government's policies, not mining business. In the 1890s, no roads nor railways nor bridges were constructed to link to tin production sites, especially in Phuket. Therefore, tin mining was only concentrated in Phuket and the neighbouring provinces.

Inadequate roads affected the development of the mining industry. The construction of roads in the region to connect tin mining provinces went on at a slow pace. Existing roads were virtually unusable in the rainy season. In 1914, roads were still insufficient and yet there were no plans to construct new ones. A report by the Department of Land Transport stated in 1914 that:

> At this time the island of Phuket needs to use the sea port in Trang as a means to connect to other regions in the kingdom. Seasonal winds have made commute via small boats difficult. Large ships that traverse between Trang and Phuket do not have set travel times. It would be very desirable if Phuket were to have a means of transport to the mainland that does not use the seas. In fact, such a means is feasible. It is possible to construct a road leading from Kanchanadit in the *monthon* of Surat Thani to Ta Kua Pa, then from there running along the shore line to a port in the strait. It was convenient to travel from that port to Phuket during every season. These routes have not yet been surveyed by the authorities.[44]

After 1910, the situation with tin mining in the South improved. This was partly due to rising costs in the Malayan tin mines and the scarcity of tin against growing world demand. The value of Thailand's tin exports rose very quickly from 2.65 million baht in 1900 to 11.7 million baht, 16.87 million baht and 37.4 million baht in 1920, 1930, and 1940, respectively (see Table 5.7). The increase in export value shows that both the volume and price of tin were on an upward trend. During the first half of the twentieth century, the expansion of Thailand's tin exports was higher than that of Malaya and the world average. Between 1911–16 and 1926–40, the annual growth rate of tin output increased by 3.2 per cent while the figure was 1 per cent and 1.7 per cent for Malaya and the world, respectively. This resulted in Thailand's market share of tin in the world market growing from 5.5 per cent to 8.8 per cent.[45]

---

[44] N.A. M. of Finance 0301.1.16/6 (1914–18).
[45] Sompop (1989, p. 149).

Important factors that affected the growth of tin after 1910 were: first, the expansion of the railway from Bangkok to provinces in the South helped to increase tin mining investment opportunities. Second, more modern technology was introduced in the mines. In 1907, the Tongkha Harbour Company from Australia was the first to utilize bucket dredging which increased tin output and reduced costs significantly.[46] Third, government policies between 1914 and 1940 provided greater support for foreign investment. As a result, foreign investments in tin businesses continued to increase, especially during 1914–40. The number of mining dredgers increased from 25 in 1928 to 30 and 40 in 1929 and 1936, respectively. Foreign capital from western countries in the tin industry totalled 50 million baht (about 4.5 million pounds) in 1928, and rose to 110 million baht (ten million pounds) in 1940.[47] Britain was the largest foreign investor in Thailand between 1927 and 1938, contributing about 58–70 per cent of the total foreign investment.[48]

Bucket dredging rapidly increased tin production capacity and soon overtook traditional mining. Tin produced by dredging rose from 467 *hab* in 1907 to 72,000 *hab*, 132,000 *hab* and 231,000 *hab* in 1924, 1929 and 1937, respectively. These were 32.9 per cent, 51.1 per cent and 63.3 per cent of the total output, respectively (see Table 5.8). In 1937, the output of western companies was 1.7 times that of Chinese companies that did not use dredging technology. Mine workers at both types of mines were still primarily Chinese, making up 45.6 per cent of the total labour force. In 1937, there were 7,551 Chinese workers and 8,960 Thai workers.[49]

---

[46] Ibid., p. 150.
[47] Ibid., p. 151.
[48] Falkus (1996, p. 123).
[49] Skinner (1957).

TABLE 5.8
Tin Production Output by Mining Method, 1907–37

(hab)

Year	Bucket Dredging	Other Methods	Total	Dredging as Per Cent of Total
1907	467	71,971	72,438	0.65
1912	67,569	77,678	145,247	46.5
1924	72,727	112,811	185,538	39.2
1928	81,369	117,471	198,840	40.9
1929	132,755	124,117	256,872	51.7
1930	163,166	116,342	279,508	58.4
1931	166,163	98,929	265,592	62.6
1932	142,265	84,279	226,544	62.8
1933	149,499	98,274	247,773	60.3
1934	144,885	109,922	254,807	56.9
1935	135,581	102,386	237,967	57.0
1936	193,002	116,867	307,869	62.7
1937	231,461	134,479	365,940	63.3

Source: *Directory for Bangkok and Siam 1914* (1914, p. 204); *Statistical Yearbook of the Kingdom of Siam* (1937).

The use of dredgers helped to expand Phuket's tin output. They were soon adopted in other provinces in the Southern Region.[50] Between 1932 and 1938, tin production increased the most in Nakhon Si Thammarat, Surat Thani, Yala and Trang (see Table 5.9).

[50] Apart from tin, lignite was mined in small quantities at Surat Thani Province. Wolfram was also smelted during the First World War.

TABLE 5.9
Tin Production by Southern Provinces, 1912–38

(*hab*)

Province	1912	1932	1936	1937	1938
Phuket	59,605	41,806	54,934	58,491	63,843
Ranong	13,403	39,054	39,652	58,408	48,935
Phangnga	14,846	42,400	54,468	53,755	40,154
Ta Kua Pa	8,588	44,119	53,073	62,676	51,879
Trang	3,457	1,930	6,429	6,057	8,730
Songkhla	451	15,560	19,803	25,465	20,832
Nakhon Si Thammarat	1,113	10,335	19,615	23,731	24,703
Surat Thani	2,351	6,671	13,892	12,674	15,134
Chumphon	741	5,392	11,650	13,525	8,106
Yala	505	17,080	29,374	41,197	47,820
Pattani	5,552	6,274	3,688	4,596	3,998

Source: *Directory for Bangkok and Siam 1914* (1914, p. 202); *Statistical Yearbook of the Kingdom of Siam* (various years).

Captain Edward Miles' Tongkah Harbour Company started its tin mining business in 1907 and was tremendously successful. In the first year, the Company made 4,462 pound sterling in profits.[51] In 1913, it was able to pay 67,000 pounds in dividends. The Company was registered in Tasmania, Australia, with a starting capital of 150,000 pounds funded by Henry Jones, his associate A.W Palfreymenan and the Khaw Sim Bee family as the majority shareholder. Paid-in capital was 17,500 pounds, 50 per cent of which came from Chinese merchants in Penang. In 1916, the Company bought its first dredger from the William Simon and Company in Scotland. Profit growth allowed Tongkah Harbour to

---

[51] Falkus (1989, pp. 151–52).

purchase five more dredgers.[52] Following the success of the Company, western investment in mining began to rise. New mining sites were surveyed on the western coast, namely in Ranong. In 1913, three new tin dredging companies were registered in Melbourne, Australia by Captain Miles. The companies were Deebook Dredging, Kathu Deebook Dredging and Bangnon Valley Dredging. Some time later, Miles also set up companies to operate on the east coast which were Ronpiboon and Ronpiboon Extended Companies. In 1912, the Siamese Tin Syndicate was established with a starting capital of 120,000 pounds. It utilized bucket dredging in Ranong, Phangnga, Ta Kua Pa and Bang Non. In 1913, it had two dredgers. Soon there were six which were worth 1.4 million baht (108,000 pounds) altogether. After that, there were 20 dredgers in 1919 and 30 in 1930. The Company was able to pay a dividend of 10 per cent on the first payout.[53]

The Great Depression in the 1930s caused significant changes to the tin mining business. The price of tin dropped after 1929 (a time when many companies were established and funding gathered from various sources). In 1931, many companies became bankrupt, both western and Chinese-owned. These companies were soon acquired by holding companies for their tin business such as the Anglo Oriental Company and Tongkah Harbour.

The Depression affected the tin mining business in Nakhon Si Thammarat and Pattani, but less so than in Phuket. Many companies closed down. Mine workers became jobless, especially those from western companies. Chinese mines were still operating normally such as the Chinese Syndiate in Penang. The government at the time, led by Prince Kamphaengphet, the Minister of Commerce and Communications, asked that the jobless workers be employed and put to work on roads. He also asked that the tin mining provinces survey the number of people put out of work by the recession.[54]

---

[52] Ibid., p. 151.
[53] Falkus (1996, p. 152).
[54] N.A. R.7. M. of Interior 1/75 (1930).

A memorandum regarding jobless mine workers in Phuket in 1930 indicated that the Chinese Syndicate Company "still employed European employees. Skilled workers were asked to halve their work time to five hours per day. If work was not enough for every worker, those put out of work first would be those without families. Workers with families were always employed."[55] The Chinese Syndicate Company in 1930 had the following policy regarding unemployment aid:

Unskilled workers shall be paid 35 *satang* per day in currency or in rice, and would be allowed to do other work such as fishing or gathering (wild fruits) to sustain themselves until the mines operate again, which is estimated to be in two months, or until the worker could find employment elsewhere. Apart from the daily wage, the spouse and child of the worker will also receive rice. An adult shall receive 1.5 buckets per month, while children's share is based on their age and size. The company has 461 workers in Ranong. The East Asiatic Company also provides assistance to its mine workers by giving away one bucket of rice per month per person, plus an additional wage of 25 *satang* per day. They are paid one baht per day on work days.[56]

A report by the Ministry of Interior stated that in 1930:

[T]here were jobless workers in only two provinces: Phuket (97 Thais, 111 Chinese, 18 Indians) and Ta Khua Pa (30 Thais, 85 Chinese). Combined, there were 127 unemployed Thais, 196 Chinese, 18 Indians, for a total of 341 people. In Phangnga, Trang, and Ta Khua Pa, while some people were put out of work, they managed to find work elsewhere, hence the nonexistence of unemployment.[57] The economic depression forced some Chinese workers to find employment elsewhere. Some emigrated back to China or went to Malaya.[58]

---

[55] Ibid.
[56] Ibid.
[57] Ibid.
[58] As shown in the following statistics: "June 1930, in-coming passengers: 247 males and 56 females, totalling 303 persons; out-going passengers: 251 males and 68 females, totalling 319 persons. July 1930, in-coming passengers: 206 males and 35 females, totalling 241 persons; out-going passengers: 291 males and 42 females, totalling 333 persons. August 1930, in-coming passengers: 229 males and 33 females, totalling

In 1931, Thailand joined the League for International Agreements on Tin Mining and had its contract extended in 1933. In 1936, the country received a larger quota. In 1940, the tin mining business boomed again with 45 dredgers. That same year, Phuket became the world's largest producer of tin at 44,500 tonnes.[59]

During the Second World War, the export of tin was continuously in decline, from 15,269 tonnes in 1941 down to just 96 tonnes in 1945. The value of exports went from 44.4 million baht to merely 150,000 baht, resulting in a decrease in the income from loyalty fees that the government received from tin mining which fell below 11.1 million baht in 1941 and 1.54 million baht in 1945.[60]

Western investments in tin mining showed the following differences when compared to investments in the Northern teak forestry, especially in the 1920s: (1) teak investment was mainly carried out by major trading companies while tin mining was normally carried out by specialized tin dredging companies; (2) tin mining required a large investment and advanced technology, particularly in bucket dredging, while teak required just traditional techniques; (3) the *chaos* of Chiang Mai and Lampang were willing to offer teak concessions to the British, but in tin mining the British had to face competition from the local Chinese businessmen.[61]

Rubber Economy

Rubber was first planted in the Southern Region around 1901. The person credited for bringing rubber to the region was Khaw Sim Bee, the governor of Trang Province. During a visit to the island of Sumatra, he brought rubber seeds and had them planted in 36 *rai* of land.[62] After

---

262 persons; out-going passengers: 209 males and 81 females, totalling 250 persons. For these three months there were 682 male and 124 female immigrants, totalling 806 Chinese immigrants, on the other hand, there were 751 male and 151 female emigrants, totalling 902 Chinese emigrants" (N.A. R.7. M. of Interior 1/75 (1930)).

[59] Mackay (2012, p. 355).
[60] *Report of the Financial Advisor 1941–1950* (1951).
[61] Falkus (1989, pp. 146–47).
[62] Mackay (2012, p. 358).

seeing fruitful results, he asked the government in Bangkok to change the law to allow the clearing of forest land for rubber cultivation and to grant ownership of that land to the farmers.[63] After the First World War, rubber production grew rapidly, increasing exports to 49,000 long tonnes in 1941 (the number included Chantaburi's exports).[64] In 1938, rubber became one of the major exported products, making up 12.9 per cent of Thailand's export value.[65]

Significant factors that resulted in the expansion of rubber exports were as follows. First, the high price of rubber, especially before 1930, which was the result of growing demand from abroad — particularly the expansion of automotive, chemical, electrical, tank production and military armament industries in developed countries in the mid-1920s. The growth of the automotive industry, particularly in the United States, had tremendous impacts on the country's rubber imports. By the end of the 1920s, about 75–80 per cent of the world's demand for rubber was for the automobile industry. At the time, the United States produced 85 per cent of the world's motorcars and used 60 per cent of the total rubber consumption.[66] The price of rubber rose from 12.52 baht/kg in the 1900s to 15.73 baht/kg in 1911–12.[67] Second, the construction of the Southern rail line and roads in some areas of the South led to the clearing of forests to grow rubber. These rubber plantations brought about the

---

[63] *Phraya* Ratsadanupradit could not read but was fluent in nine languages: Thai, Melayu, English, Hindi, and five Chinese dialects. While accompanying King Rama V to Europe, Malaya, and Indonesia, he had gathered a vast amount of knowledge and expertise. In agriculture, he put in a lot of effort to change subsistence production to a commercial one especially rubber that later spread to other provinces. He searched for information on neighbouring countries' market, focusing on the Malaya frontier for regular dissemination to the villagers so that they could broaden their production or switch to agriculture. He ordered the village heads to persuade the villagers to stake their claim on arable land for rice cultivation, to collaborate in building small dams, and to pitch in (*long khaek*) in rice cultivation that all enabled on-time rice production (Suthanm 1994, p. 125).

[64] Donner (1978, p. 486).

[65] *Statistical Yearbook of the Kingdom of Siam* (1939).

[66] Sompop (1989, p. 108).

[67] Ibid., p. 107.

establishment of towns. In 1926 Ebbe Kornerup, a Danish national, impressed with the changing of Southern forests into rubber planted areas, recorded the following:

> Southern Siam has now been opened up by roads and railways ....
> One rubber plantation succeeds another .... The old towns that a few
> years ago lay sound asleep surrounded by all possible romance have
> suddenly put forth new shoots and flowers. An entirely new tradition
> of wheels, motors and machinery has been created. The country is
> unrecognizable.[68]

Third, the influx of Chinese migrant workers and the relocation of capital, workers and businesses from Malaya away from tin mining into rubber production in the 1930s. Rubber planters were Thais, Malays and Chinese. Chinese businesses had virtual control of all rubber trade. These Chinese investors used Penang and Singapore as bases for the storage and export of rubber since the end of the First World War.[69]

The Chinese played an important role in the development of the rubber industry. They established two rubber plantation companies in 1917: The Jeng Jeng Plantation and the Wae Chang Yen Plantation with a registered capital of over six million baht. Both companies reclaimed over 50,000 *rai* of land in the South for rubber cultivation in Songkhla and its peripherals. Both companies hired Hakka Chinese workers who previously were labourers for the Southern railway line as well as those from the British and Dutch colonies.[70] The *monthon* of Phuket was the major exporter of rubber. In 1923, it exported 75 per cent of the country's rubber. Another 20 per cent came from the *monthon* of Pattani. Rubber cultivation started to extend into other parts of the South, starting from Trang in the *monthon*

---

[68] Kornerup cited in Mackay (2012, p. 360).
[69] See Phuwadon (1992).
[70] Kitti (2009, p. 94).

of Phuket into other *monthons* such as Pattani and Nakhon Si Thammarat. The growth in Nakhon Si Thammarat was particularly high. In 1923, the *monthon* exported only 1,066 long tonnes of rubber worth 67,250 pounds. But in 1930, it had a market share of 81.9 per cent of the country's rubber export, up from just 0.9 per cent in 1921.[71]

Rubber plantation records of each *monthon* show that in 1929, there were 679,000 *rai* of harvested and unharvested rubber. Pattani had the most planted area at 412,000 *rai*, with Nakhon Si Thammarat in second place at 166,000 *rai* (see Table 5.10). The growth of rubber exports was due to the increase in price as a result of production curbs in the Great Britain colonies.[72] Thailand had no restrictions on rubber production because it was a minor producer, causing its production to grow. To solve the issue of price fluctuations, Thailand joined the "International Rubber Regulation Agreement" in 1934 to put control on rubber production according to world demands. Rubber prices rose as a result. Soon afterwards, there was an expansion of rubber planted areas and production, but all was halted during the Second World War.

TABLE 5.10
Number of Rubber Trees, 1929–30

Monthon	In Tapping (*rai*)	Immature (*rai*)	Total No. of Trees (*rai*)
Nakhon Si Thammarat	85,495	80,899	166,394
Pattani	139,041	273,291	412,332
Phuket	30,725	60,177	90,902
Chantaburi	2,781	7,541	10,295
Total	258,042	421,881	679,923

Source: Ministry of Commerce and Communications (1930, p. 218).

---

[71] Sompop (1989, p. 110).
[72] *Report of the Financial Advisor 1941–1950* (1951).

In 1941, the rubber industry saw a very high growth due to priority purchasing by England and Japan which totalled 49 million kg and was worth 58.5 million baht. Most exports went to Malaya, Japan and China. The onset of the Second World War brought a decline in rubber demand. Prices and production plummeted. Exports that once reached 58.5 million baht before the war dwindled to just 945,00 baht in 1944, as shown in Table 5.11.[73] Rubber production virtually ceased in 1945, but after the war, exports quickly regained traction.[74]

Rubber cultivation in the Southern Region was different from that of Malaya. In Malaya, the British government granted concessions of empty land to private firms, particularly those from Britain, to operate large rubber plantations. Labour was brought in from India and China. Production management and operations were efficient, and yields per unit of cultivated land were high. In Thailand, the government did not provide substantial support, so most farms were smaller in size and run by families. The average size of holdings was no more than 15 *rai*.[75] Chinese immigrants had, on average, more holding land than Thai

TABLE 5.11
Export Amount and Value of Rubber, 1941–44

Year	Export Amount (million kg)	Value (million baht)
1941	49,308	58.5
1942	11.9	10.0
1943	4.9	3.0
1944	1.61	0.945

Source: *Report of the Financial Advisor 1941–1950* (1951).

---

[73] Ibid.
[74] Ibid.
[75] Ingram (1971, p. 103).

farmers.[76] As noted by Ingram: "[I]mmigrant Chinese own over half the holdings of over 50 *rai* but only 7 percent of those under 50 *rai*, and that Chinese-owned holdings under 50 *rai* averaged nearly 25 *rai*, compared to only 14 *rai* for Thai owned ones. For the most part the Thai rubber grower is a very small operator."[77] Furthermore, in 1925, the government of Malaya, in partnership with the private industries, established the Rubber Research Institute of Malaya with the purpose of improving production efficiency. Research was carried out to find better breeds of rubber plant. Quality control was implemented. Cost savings were improved and packaging was introduced. The Malaya government supported large-scale plantations and allowed European companies to operate rubber farms in more than 400,000 *rai* of land, compared to only 3,000–5,000 *rai* in Thailand, most of which were operated by small-scale farmers. Having better economy of scale, better research and development and access to new breeds of rubber plant, larger plantations were more productive. Rubber output in Malaya was apparently two to three times higher than in Thailand.[78]

Thailand used simple technology and outdated rubber breeds. Yields per *rai* were low. Larger Thai rubber producers also ran into a major problem: labour shortage. As a result, harvests could not be carried out in full capacity (they were also limited by insufficient funds). For example, in 1934, the rubber growing area around the Songkhla lake had a labour shortage of 7,239 workers. Patthalung was 395 people short, and Songkhla needed 6,844 more workers.[79] During the same year, more than 10,000 farm owners were unable to harvest their rubber due to labour shortage and other reasons. Of these, 5,567 were from the area around the Songkhla lake, 5,242 from Songkhla, and 325 from Patthalung.[80]

---

[76] Skinner stated that: "There were approximately 70,000 rubber plantation workers at the end of the 1930s. Most of the Chinese were Hakka, but some were Teochew and Hokkien. The Chinese's rubber plantation in the 1930s usually had less than 3,000 long tonnes of rubber trees but the plantation's average size was still much larger than those of the Thais or the Muslims. Owners of small rubber plantation usually sold their raw rubber sheets to rubber traders who had large rubber sheet smoking operation. The Chinese who owned large rubber plantation generally smoked the rubber sheets themselves. Rubber traders, buying either raw rubber sheets or smoked sheets, would grade them by their quality and repacked them for exports. These traders were mainly Hokkien" (Skinner 1957, p. 221).

[77] Ingram (1971, p. 103).

[78] Stifel (1973, p. 123).

[79] Kitti (2009, p. 103).

[80] Ibid.

Rice

The signing of the Bowring Treaty in 1855 had little effect on the commercial rice economy. Rice producers in the South were mostly subsistence farmers. The region contributed very little in terms of rice exports. Even with the construction of the railway in the 1920s, commercial rice product was still fairly low compared to the Northeast and Northern Regions. Important rice growing areas were primarily on the eastern side of the region. Notable rice farming provinces included Nakhon Si Thammarat and Songkhla. Between 1907 and 1909, the value of rice exports from Nakhon Si Thammarat was proportionately significant compared to the export of other goods (see Table 5.12).

TABLE 5.12
Value of Principal Articles Exports from the *monthon* of
Nakhon Si Thammarat, 1907–9

(pounds)

Year	1907		1908		1909	
Category	Songkhla	Nakhon Si Thammarat	Songkhla	Nakhon Si Thammarat	Songkhla	Nakhon Si Thammarat
Rice and padi	37,701	22,361	30,439	115,112	28,756	82,470
Tin and tin ore	214	1,809	2,551	20,169	1,750	20,798
Cattle and buffaloes	8,453	–	8,088	–	2,655	–
Hides	2,679	–	882	810	3,515	436
Pigs	30,490	–	3,768	–	15,210	1,043
Torches	–	–	–	–	–	6,705
Others	52	75	75	134	3,811	800
Total	74,589	25,062	45,797	136,225	55,727	112,252
Grand Total	99,651		182,022		167,979	
Rice as a percentage of the *monthon*'s exports	60.2		79.9		66.2	

Source: BCR, *Monthon Nakonsri Tammarat and Pattani* (1909).

The value of rice exports from the *monthon* of Nakhon Si Thammarat (consisting of the provinces of Nakhon Si Thammarat and Songkhla) increased during the years 1907–9. Nakhon Si Thammarat, in particular, increased its exports from 22,300 pounds to 110,000 pounds and decreased to the equivalent of 82,470 pounds (*sic*). During the same period, rice made up 60–80 per cent of the total export value (see Table 5.12). In 1927, the *monthon* of Nakhon Si Thammarat occupied a total of 840,000 *rai* of rice cultivated area, or a quarter of the South's. The province of Nakhon Si Thammarat had the most rice cultivated area at 328,000 *rai*, followed by Songkhla at 162,000 *rai*. The total amount of rice cultivated area in the South made up only 7.4 per cent of Thailand's total.[81]

In 1929, the South's rice exports were merely 10 per cent of the country's total.[82] Table 5.13 shows the rice production in each *monthon*.[83]

Zimmerman indicated in 1930–31 that plantation methods in the South were technologically behind all other regions. People grew rice merely to feed their families. Although rice could be grown twice per year, the output was not as high as it should have been. In some areas such as *tambon* Tha Taphao, Chumphon people relied on ocean fishing instead.[84]

The income of rural Southern families was low at 126 baht per family on average in 1930. He also found that rice contributed just 38 baht or 31 per cent of the income. The rest of the family's income were from animal farming (10 per cent), fishing (4 per cent) and others (56 per cent).[85]

---

[81] Calculated from *The Record* (1931), rice yields per *rai* in various provinces of *monthon* Nakhon Si Thammarat were rather high in comparison to other *monthons*: 5.23–7.29 *hap* per *rai* in 1923–28. Such yields ranked second after *monthon* Phayap with 5.57–6.65 *hap* per *rai* in the same period. *Monthon* Pattani, on the other hand, had low yields of 3.85–5.00 *hap* per *rai* and ranked 12th in the country from a total of 14 *monthons* (*The Record*, 1931).

[82] N.A. Department of Royal Railways 2/16.

[83] Ibid.

[84] Zimmerman (1999).

[85] Ibid., pp. 129 and 135.

TABLE 5.13
Rice Production by *monthon* in 1929

Monthon	Hab	Value (baht)
Nakhon Si Thammarat	70,947	501,039
Phuket	53	266
Pattani	340	2,532

Source: N.A. Department of Royal Railways 2/16.

Rice Mills

The growth of rice exports had an impact on rice mills. In 1929, mills in the South could only be found in the *monthon* of Nakhon Si Thammarat (they were not yet built in Phuket and Pattani). That year, there were only 34 mills in the South. Seven were established before 1919, six were built between 1919 and 1925 and 21 between 1926 and 1929 (six of the mills had no date of establishment).[86] These rice mills were distributed geologically as follows: 13 in Nakhon Si Thammarat (eight in *amphoe* Pak Phanang, five in *amphoe mueang* Nakhon Si Thammarat); four in the province of Songkhla; four in the province of Chumphon (all in *amphoe* Taphao); 11 in Surat Thaini (six in *amphoe* Ban Don, three in *amphoe mueang* Chaiya, one in *amphoe* Kanhanadit, and one in *amphoe* Ban Na) and one in Patthalung (*amphoe* Khu Ha Sawan). Almost all of the mills were owned by the Chinese. All were small and were either motor or steam powered. The mills in Pak Phanang had the most powerful engines, with a majority having more than 50 horse power. In other *amphoes*, the engines were mostly less than 30 horse power.[87] This shows that Pak Phanang was the most important *amphoe* in the South for the rice mill industry.

In 1937, there were only 611 workers employed in the Southern rice mills — a very small number.[88] Most workers were on the eastern side

---

[86] N.A. 2.41/2 Personal File (1929).
[87] Ibid.
[88] 1937 Population Census.

of the region, and were distributed among the provinces as follows: 324 in Nakhon Si Thammarat, 107 in Surat Thani, two in Yala, 13 in Pattrani, 32 in Chumphon, 11 in Trang, 11 in Patthalung, 106 in Songkhla and five in Satun. The Second World War had considerable impacts on rice farming and milling. Export controls were enforced. When Japan invaded Thailand in 1941, an export ban was imposed because rice was considered a military supply. Rice production decreased. As a war ally with Thailand, Japan mandated rice purchases to feed its army in Malaya. The Kaisha and Mitsubishi companies were given the task of mass purchasing rice from *amphoe* Pak Phanang and *amphoe mueang* Songkhla. Later, to solve the problem of Japan's forced under-pricing of rice, the Thai government established the Khao Thai Pak Tai Company to maintain the price of milled and unmilled rice at suitable levels. It persuaded various mills to join the Company. The following number of mills joined in: 14 from the Pak Phanang basin, 20 from the Songkhla basin, 15 from Patthalung and three from Songkhla.[89] The Khao Thai Company Ltd. was the largest shareholder. The government passed on a law forcing all rice milling businesses to be rented by the Company, but all operations such as rice trading and purchasing were still carried out by owners of the individual mills. The Khao Thai Pak Tai Company was disbanded in 1946.[90]

Fisheries

Geographical characteristics of the South are such that it has a long coastline extending along the peninsula. The region is ideal for coastline fisheries. Almost all provinces border the sea. Between 1910 and 1925, the government invited experts from the United States, namely Hugh McCormick Smith et al., to survey the South's marine life species in the rivers and sea (considered to be the nation's natural resources) and to make a feasibility study of a fishing industry and to establish a ministry of fisheries.[91] The survey was completed in 1925. McCormick's report on "A Survey of the Resources of Siam with a Review of Foreign Trade

---

[89] Kitti (2009, p. 103).
[90] Ibid.
[91] N.A. Department of Royal Railways 2/10.

and Commerce of the Country during the Reign of King Rama VI (1910–1925)" stated that "The fisheries of Siam are, therefore, of great importance to the country, and rank second only to agriculture, both in extent and value, among its basic industries ...."[92]

"[W]ell-informed estimates the value of the annual output of water products at not less than 25 million ticals [baht] not including the casual catches of large quantities of fish shrimps and molluscs by farmers and individual fishermen".[93]

In summary, the report made by the expert team stated that the export of dry salt fish was between 187,000 and 294,000 *hab* during 1911–24, with a value between 1.58 million and 3.45 million baht.[94] As noted by the report:

> The export of Salt Fish, already referred to in the note on Fisheries, has long been a profitable industry in Siam. Although the quantity exported has decreased slightly in the last ten years, the value has increased from about Tcs. 8/- a picul to nearly Tcs. 14/- a picul and thus the loss in quantity, which dropped from 294,000 piculs in 1910–11 to 187,000 piculs in 1923–24, has been more than made good by the advance in value, from Tcs. 1,580,000 in the first-named year to Tcs. 2,532,000 in the last-named. The record year for value was 1921–22, when it stood at Tsc. 3,455,000.[95]

In 1923, the export of dry salt fish from the *monthon* of Nakhon Si Thammarat was 4,141 tonnes, valued at 71,312 pounds, which was a decrease from the value of 120,000 pounds in 1922.[96]

This was in accordance with a report by the Board of Commercial Development. The export of salt mackerel from the port of Bangkok (most of which came from the South) was 100,000 *hab* per year, valued at 700,000 baht between 1907 and 1911. The number was reduced to 40,964 *hab* per year, equivalent to 349,000 baht per year between 1912 and 1916. Later, from 1917–21, exports went up to 72,280 *hab* per year,

---

[92] Ibid.
[93] Ibid.
[94] Ibid.
[95] Ibid.
[96] BCR, *Monthon Nakonsri Tammarat and Pattani* (1924).

totalling 745,000 baht. During the years 1920–24, there had been the exports of mackerels and powdered salt fish (and other salt fish) from the Southern Region's port.[97]

Mackerel trade boomed between 1925 and 1926 with exports reaching between 346,000 and 298,000 *hab*, and export values totalling between 2.5 million and 2.7 million baht. The average price per *hab* of exported fish was 6.11 baht, 8.53 baht, 10.30 baht, and 8.53 baht during 1907–11, 1912–16, 1917–21 and 1922–24, respectively. They were exported to Singapore, Hong Kong, and China.[98] The export of salt fish (apart from mackerel) between 1907 and 1911 equalled 123,000 *hab* per year, or 763,000 baht. The average price was 6.19 baht per *hab*. Between 1912 and 1916, exports were 161,000 *hab* and valued at 1.143 million baht, with an average price of 7.10 baht per *hab*. Between 1920 and 1924, exports increased yet again both in volume and value at 296,000 *hab* and 2.84 million baht (part of the increase was due to the inclusion of salt mackerel from the South). In 1925 and 1926, the export statistics for mackerel and other fishes (the numbers were recorded separately) were 135,000 *hab* at 1.08 million baht, with an average price of 8 baht per *hab*. The exports were sent to Singapore and Hong Kong.[99]

The 1934 economic report by *Phra* Sarasasana Palakhandh indicated that:

> Most fishermen in the Southern seas were made up of Thais, Muslims and some Chinese, with Chinese merchants buying each fish haul. The Songkhla lake had large-scale fishing activities. People from Pattani (Muslims) migrated into Laem Sai to fish from the 4th to the 11th lunar months of each year. Fresh fish was sold to Penang and transported via trucks. More dried shrimps were sent from Songkhla to Bangkok than from any other province. (Fishing was also prevalent in Prachuab Kirikhan, including *amphoe* Hua Hin, and in Chumphon, particularly in *amphoe* Tha Taphao and *amphoe* Lang Suan.) Fishermen earned 0.75–1.00 baht per day, higher than ordinary labourers who made 0.50 baht per day.

---

[97] N.A. Department of Royal Railways 2/1.
[98] Ibid.
[99] N.A. Department of Royal Railways 2/16.

Chumphon was the most important saltwater fishing province in Thailand. Many shallow and deep water fishing pontoons were deployed. The most notable fish was mackerel which was sold fresh to Bangkok through shipping ports, with a small portion going through the railway. Due to the inconvenience of transportation, salt fish was sent to Singapore.[100] ... Fishing was also practiced in *amphoe* Ban Don, Surat Thani, especially barramundi and pomfret fishing. Fresh fish was sold to Bangkok twice a week. Dried, salt fish was sent to the Singapore market. Surat Thani was abundant in Indian mackerel, while mackerel was more scarce. Fishermen in this province were made up of the locals and Muslims from Pattani. Some were also from Petchaburi. Apart from fish, another abundant animal was cockle which was a popular catch for the locals.[101]

Fisheries in the South were primarily subsistence rather than commercial, though some trades did exist within each community. The abundance of the sea benefited all related economic activities such as the makers of pontoon, fish traps, nets and other fishing tools; boat fishermen; producers of salt fish, shrimp paste, pickled products, and other seafoods. The industry created jobs in fishing, restaurants, and dried goods shops. The 1937 Population Census shows the number of workers engaged in the marine fisheries industry in some Southern provinces as shown in Table 5.14.[102]

TABLE 5.14
Number of Workers Engaged in Marine Fisheries Industry by Province, 1937

Province	Marine Fisheries	Restaurants
Surat Thani	957	796
Pattani	4,143	507
Narathiwat	786	468
Chumphon	1,559	382
Nakhon Si Thammarat	1,871	608
Phuket	430	322

Source: 1937 Population Census.

---

[100] N.A.(2) Office of the Prime Minister 0201.22/8 (1934).
[101] Ibid.
[102] 1937 Population Census.

Coconuts

The export of coconut meat from the Southern Region to Penang and Singapore existed for a long time. Coconut farming was mainly for domestic consumption. In the nineteenth century, when compared to neighbouring countries such as Malaya and the Philippines, Thailand exported very few coconuts. Important products derived from coconuts were coconut milk, soap and lubricants. The spathe could be made into mattresses, brushes, ropes, dried coconuts etc. Coconut was grown in many provinces, with Surat Thani as the biggest producer. In 1928–29, there were 5.18 million coconut trees (both bearing and not yet bearing), or 68.2 per cent of the country's total. The number of coconut fruits produced was 58.1 per cent of the national total (see Table 5.15).

TABLE 5.15
Number of Palms Registered in the
Principal Coconut Growing *monthon*, 1928–29

Monthon	in Bearing	No. of Trees Not Yet Bearing	Total No. of Trees	No. of Coconuts
Phuket	293,608	2,273,498	576,106	10,013,080
Nakhon Si Thammarat	1,391,386	1,555,472	2,946,858	48,495,430
Pattani	859,838	799,989	1,659,827	30,011,505
Total	2,544,832	2,628,959	5,182,791	88,520,015
National Total	4,690,529	2,894,534	7,585,063	152,342,395
Percentage of National Total	54.2	90.8	68.2	58.1

Source: Ministry of Commerce and Communications (1930, p. 219).

As stated in the 1934 economic report by *Phra* Sarasasana Palakhandh,

More coconuts were planted in this province [Surat Thani] than in any other place in Siam. There were more than one million coconut trees. When prices were favourable, about a million coconuts were exported each week. But right now [in the depression], only 700,000 were exported. *Amphoe* Samui had the most number of coconut trees. Dried coconut products should be supported, and foreign markets surveyed.[103]

In summary, the economic development of the South before the Second World War had always been connected to the exports of tin and rubber. The South had a trading relationship with Malaya and Singapore. The revenue from tin and rubber had always been an important part of the export income. The expansion of tin and rubber production prompted the immigration of Chinese workers. The Chinese and the Westerners invested in the region (especially in tin production). The growth of the tin industry helped to boost the growth of Phuket. The Chinese made up a significant part of the population of the city of Phuket, an important tin production and export site in Thailand.

THE SOUTHERN REGION AFTER THE SECOND WORLD WAR

After the Second World War, the Southern economy was increasingly associated with Bangkok whereas previously it had a close relationship with Malaya and Singapore. One reason was the construction of highways linking the South to the capital. Although the process of economic diversification has taken place in the South in the last 60 years or so, the economy of the South has still been highly dependent on agriculture, both in terms of income and employment generation. This reflects the high agricultural value added of rubber, palm oil, and fisheries.

---

[103] N.A. (2) Office of the Prime Minister 0201.22/8 (1934).

The geo-economic characteristics of the eastern and western sides of the region differ drastically. The East has an economy based on agriculture and manufacturing, while the West is highly dependent on tourism. The region has some world-famous tourist destinations. The tourism industry became increasingly important and had an impact on the economy of the west coast in terms of income, economic growth, physical features of the city and tourism destinations.

Population and Employment

After the Second World War, the population of the Southern Region increased rapidly from 2.16 million in 1947 to 4.27 million in 1970 and 8.84 million in 2010 — a four-fold increase in 63 years. Compared to other regions, the South was the least populous. The annual growth rate of the population was high at 3.0 per cent between 1950 and 1960 (compared to 2.2 per cent between 1940 and 1950) and was 2.7 per cent both between 1960 and 1970 and between 1970 and 1980.[104] The natural population growth rate was 3.2 per cent per annum between 1964 and 1967 and 3.0 per cent per annum between 1974 and 1976.[105] In 1979, three Southern provinces were the first to have a population of over one million: Nakhon Si Thammarat, Songkhla and Surat Thani. Three areas were ranked in the top ten urban areas with the highest population in Thailand: Had Yai (97,839), Songkhla (74,728) and Nakhon Si Thammarat (65,190).[106]

The annual population growth rate in the South in the past 20 years had been decreasing from 1.49 per cent between 1990 and 2000 to 0.89 per cent between 2000 and 2010.[107] During the latter period, the annual growth rate in most provinces were positive, but some had negative growth such as Nakhon Si Thammarat (−0.47 per cent) and Patthalung (−0.42 per cent).[108] Most of the population worked in the agricultural sector followed by the service sector. In 2009, the region had a labour force of 5.09 million. Most were in agriculture at 45 per cent, followed by the service sector at 41 per cent, with industry having the least number of workers at 14 per cent (see Table 5.16).

---

[104] ESCAP (1982, p. 14).
[105] Ibid., p. 15.
[106] Population Census (various years).
[107] 2010 Population Census.
[108] 2000 and 2010 Population Censuses.

TABLE 5.16
Number of Employed Workers in the Southern Region by Economic Sector, 2009

Sector	Southern Region		Gulf of Thailand Side[1]		Andaman Side[2]		Deep South[3]	
	Employed Workers	Per Cent	Employed Workers	Per Cent	Employed Workers	Per Cent	Employed Workers	Per Cent
Agriculture	2,286,820	44.9	1,082,049	50.0	448,495	44.5	7,562,276	39.3
Industry	724,359	14.2	277,802	12.8	114,766	11.4	331,791	17.2
Service	2,085,810	40.9	803,891	37.2	444,241	44.1	837,678	43.5
Total	5,096,989	100.0	2,163,742	100.0	1,007,502	100.0	1,925,745	100.0

Notes: [1] The Gulf of Thailand side provinces consisted of Surat Thani, Chumphon, Nakhon Si Thammarat and Patthalung.
[2] The Andaman side provinces consisted of Phuket, Phangnga, Krabi, Trang and Ranong.
[3] The deep Southern provinces consisted of Songkhla, Satun, Pattani, Yala and Narathiwat.

Source: Office of the National Economic and Social Development Board (2011).

The Gulf of Thailand side of the region had the highest employment at 2.16 million workers or 42.4 per cent of the labour force. The number of employed workers near the Malaysia border and on the west coast was at 37.8 per cent and 19.7 per cent respectively (see Table 5.16). The ratio of employed workers in each sector was proportional to its economic significance. Agriculture constituted the highest portion of GRP at one-third of the total output in 2002–7. It also employed the most number of workers. In other regions, although agriculture employed a higher percentage of the population, it contributed the least to the GRP. In 2009, agriculture in the Northeast contributed only 21.5 per cent, the North 25.9 per cent, the Central Region 7.69 per cent, the Central-West 18.5 per cent and the Central-Eastern Region 5.9 per cent.[109] The value of the agricultural output of the South was higher in comparison to non-agricultural output. This meant that its agricultural products had higher value. Rubber and palm oil, the main contributors to the economy, had high prices in comparison to the main agricultural products from other regions such as rice.

Muslim Inhabitants

Since the past up to the present, Muslim settlements have often been concentrated in groups, for example, villages. Each has its own mosque as a centre for religious activities such as daily prayers. The way of life of the Muslims in the South is closely linked to small-boat coastal fishing (with a capacity for just 12 kg of fish). An example is the fishing village of Rusamilae near the Pattani bay which is rich in marine life. "Kolae" boats are a traditional fishing vessel. They are a means of fishing as well as a status symbol and a valuable asset.[110] These cultural factors contribute to the conflict between state-supported commercial fishing and traditional fishing, which will be explained next.

---

[109] Gross Regional Product (2009).
[110] Nantawan (2002, p. 456).

In 2010, Muslims in the Southern Region made up 28.6 per cent of the entire population (most of which reside in the four southernmost provinces of Pattani, Narathiwat, Yala and Satun, and made up 80 per cent of the population of those provinces combined). More than twice the population of Muslims live in rural areas than in urban areas.[111] This shows that they tended to make a living from agriculture and fishing outside of the city. The ratio of Muslims living in remote rural areas was higher than the Thais and Chinese-Thais. Aside from fishing, the Muslims also made a living selling food, fish and other marine products in fresh markets. They had rice, rubber, palm and fruit farms. The Thais and Chinese-Thais, on the other hand, tended to live in the city and commercial areas. They often ran their own businesses, both big and small, from retail, export, gold trading and department stores. However, the new generation of Muslims who were higher educated preferred to own and run modern businesses, such as housing and apartment rental. Many worked for the government and state enterprises.[112]

Fisheries had always been an important source of income for the Southern Muslims, though recently its importance had somewhat declined. For example, between 2005 and 2009, the income from fisheries was 24–30 per cent of Pattani's GPP and 19–26 per cent of Satun's GPP.[113]

Pattani had one of the largest shipping ports in the South. Between 1993 and 1995, more than 4,000 fishing boats docked there. About 200,000 tonnes of fish were caught yearly. In 1993, the value of fishing was two billion baht, and it rose to almost four billion baht in 1995.[114] The growth of the fishing economy forced Pattani to improve its infrastructure and related industries such as ice factories, ground fish factories, cold storage rooms and other factories.[115]

---

[111] 2010 Population Census.
[112] See Nantawan (2002, p. 459).
[113] Gross Regional and Provincial Product (various years).
[114] Nantawan (2002, p. 456).
[115] Ibid., p. 459.

Migration and City Growth

The emigration from the South was at a low level partly because of the higher income in agriculture and the abundance of resources in the region, such as those from the sea that was enough to substain a livelihood. In 1970 only 10 per cent of the population, or 464,000, was not born locally. Between 1965 and 1970, in the provinces with high immigration rates such as Ranong (28.0 per cent), Phuket (16.2 per cent), Yala (27.3 per cent), and Phangnga (16.8 per cent), 50 per cent of immigrants relocated internally in the Southern Region, with another 14 per cent coming in from the Central Region (including Bangkok). However, the immigration rates of the top migrant destinations, namely Phuket and Ranong, were on average only slightly higher than the national average.[116]

Between 2005 and 2010, there were 756,000 migrants in the region, or 8.5 per cent of the population.[117] Overall, the growth of the urban population of the South was low, with an annual growth rate of only 3.2 per cent and 4.3 per cent between 1960 and 1970 and between 1970 and 1980, respectively.[118] However, some urban areas saw very high growth rates. At one time, the population of the urban areas of Songkhla increased very rapidly. Between 1970 and 1980, municipal Songkhla grew 5.79 per cent per annum and municipal Hat Yai grew 7.20 per cent per annum, sending the population of the former up from 41,193 to 72,326[119] and the population of the latter from 47,953 to 96,091.[120] In 1980, the population of Hat Yai and Songkhla combined was nearly 200,000. Hat Yai and Songkhla were the 3rd and 8th most populous cities in the country, respectively.[121] In 2000, the number of people living in all municipal areas of Songkhla combined was 407,000. This number rose to 800,000 in 2010, a 100 per cent increase in just ten years.[122] It was considered to be a province with one of the highest municipal populations in the country.

---

[116] Donner (1978, pp. 473–74).
[117] 2010 Population Census.
[118] ESCAP (1982, p. 25).
[119] Ibid., p. 26.
[120] Ibid., p. 25.
[121] Population Census (various years).
[122] 2010 Population Census.

Songkhla had been rich in important natural resources, namely marine resources and rubber. This led to various industrial developments, particularly the food and beverages industry and other industries related to rubber.[123] Songkhla had been the most important port city on the Gulf of Thailand side of the region, second only to the port of Bangkok. The Songkhla Port had been the centre of transportation in the Gulf of Thailand for all Southern provinces. Many coastal trading boats and international cargo ships docked at the port to transport goods. The port has also been a transportation hub of the South, linking the seaport with the railway, highway (national and provincial) and commercial airports. The port itself has connected to nearby provinces and all other provinces in the country. Songkhla has also been the educational centre of the region, the site of the Prince of Songkhla University located at *amphoe* Hat Yai.

The Thai government had been trying to improve the port to accommodate the growth of commerce and industry in Songkhla. It hired Transportation Consultation Inc. to carry out a feasibility study on the investments and developments involved in improving the port. The study shows that, in 1962, a small improvement project with an investment of 30 million baht would yield a ratio of benefit of 1:1.74. A large project requiring 450 million baht would result in a 1:1.38 ratio. However, even though the larger project produced a smaller ratio of benefit, in the long term it was the more worthwhile investment.[124] A report by Transportation Consultation Inc. in 1962 concluded that:

---

[123] 2007 Industrial Situation Report, Songkhla Province.

[124] The project to improve large ports was to construct a two-kilometre windbreaker from Laem Sai to Ko Nu and another two-kilometre windbreaker from Laem Hin on the mainland to Ko Nu as well. Then the enclosed area and its opening would be dredged so that ships of ten-metre draught, or 15,000 gross tonnes could pass at all times. The project to improve small ports was for small ships of 5.6-metre draught or 1,000 gross tonnes to pass through at any time. Both projects would require a budget of 30 million baht and would involve the construction of 670-metre windbreakers near Laem Sai and cut through the end of the beach at Laem Sai into Songkhla Lagoon for the entrance. This would enable utilization of the Lagoon's thalweg for navigation and for berthing the ships. At the same time the existing windbreakers and the piers would also be upgraded (N.A. M. of Industry 0201.2/62 (1964)).

When compared to Si Racha port improvements [in Chonburi Province in the Central Region], the large improvement project at the Songkhla port was much cheaper. The Si Racha project was estimated to cost 900 million baht, but its 'hinterland' [a far away place] did not compare to Songkhla's. It was deemed appropriate to start with Songkhla's smaller improvement project to benefit domestic cargo ships and those from nearby countries. They could dock in a nearby freshwater lake that has a trench deep enough to comfortably accommodate ships as large as 1,000 gross tonnage... The large project should also commence in synchronization with the small one. The existing breakwater would continue to benefit the large project.[125]

After that, the Songkhla Port was continually improved and developed to support the growth of sea-based shipping. In 1984, the share of Songkhla's industrial output made up just 15 per cent of the GPP. In 1995, this quickly rose to 22 per cent and continued to reach 28–30 per cent between 2005 and 2008. The province had the highest percentage of industrial production in the Southern Region.[126] In 2007, Songkhla had 1,965 registered factories (535 of which were rice mills). Most of the factories were small. About 80 per cent of them had an investment capital of less than ten million baht. About 28 per cent were operating in *amphoe* Hat Yai (with 10.8 per cent in *amphoe mueang* Songkhla). The rest were distributed among all the other districts of Songkhla.[127]

The Economy of the South

Up until the 1960s, the economies of the eastern and western sides of the region were significantly different. The east side had connections to Bangkok, via the Gulf of Thailand. For west side provinces such as Ranong, Phangnga, Phuket, Krabi, Trang and Satun, most trades were done with Malaysia through Penang.[128] After the construction and development of highways in the region, trade with Bangkok increased,

---

[125] N.A. M. of Industry 0201.2/63 (1964).
[126] Gross Regional and Provincial Product (various years).
[127] 2007 Manufacturing Report, Songkhla Province.
[128] Silcock (1970, p. 161).

particularly in fruits.[129] Although shipments from the South to Bangkok could be done through the railway and shipping lanes, they were not sufficient to accommodate the growth of trade. In 1960, 1,752 km of highways existed in the Southern Region.[130] A report on the proposal to develop Thailand's highways described the importance of highways to the economy of the South in 1962 as follows:

> The South was a region rich in tin and rubber. These products were the second and third largest source of income for the country... Hua Hin had developed into a fruit production area, with pineapple and cantaloupe as its main products... The proposed highway construction will help to stimulate production growth... The areas between Hua Hin and Chumphon which lie parallel to the eastern coast practiced fisheries and had fish as their main product... The amount of fish caught exceeded the local needs, but with inadequate roads, fishermen could not send their products to Bangkok and other markets. The improvement of roads will stimulate trade between Bangkok and the South... The construction of highways linking cities and villages between Nakhon Si Thammarat and Trang would promote production on the east and west coasts because they would facilitate the shipment of goods in the region to shipping ports.[131]

The development of agricultural economy in the South was different from other regions. Tin and rubber combined made up more than 36 per cent of the total exports (in the 1960s). After that period, there was a decrease in the South's agricultural production partly due to the decrease in the price of rubber and other factors. In 1969, tin and rubber made up 29.4 per cent of the region's production. Between 1957 and 1969, within the agricultural sector, fisheries saw the highest growth from 18.6 per cent in 1960 to 31.1 per cent in 1969. This was followed by the growth of forestry from 13.9 per cent to 15.4 per cent in the

---

[129] Ibid.
[130] N.A. M. of Transport 0202.8.10/20 (1962–63).
[131] Ibid.

same period.[132] The region's non-agricultural economy, however, grew at a slow rate, causing its output share in GRP to decline. For example, the manufacturing industry fell from 8.4 per cent to 5.5 per cent. Transport and communications decreased from 13.3 per cent to 9.8 per cent during the same period. As a result, the economy of the South were certainly not diversifying the regional economic structure as should have been.[133]

In 1970, agriculture made up 40 per cent of GRP, while non-agricultural sector, which were industry and services, made up 60 per cent combined. In the agricultural sector, rubber, coconut, seafood and palm oil were the leading products that together made up 63 per cent of the sector's output. Forestry contributed 7.8 per cent of the GRP, with trade at 38.8 per cent, followed by services at 15.2 per cent, and manufacturing at 12.3 per cent.[134]

The situation in the 1970s was such that the South's economy was still staggering. The economy was not diverse and was highly dependent on rubber, forestry and fisheries. The fundamental problems that hindered economic diversification were insufficient economic infrastructure. For example, in 1978, there were not enough roads, with only 7,813 km of state and provincial highways combined. The Northeast, in comparison, had 27,076 km, the North 12,898 km, and the Central Region 13,696 km.[135] Insufficient roads certainly had an impact on the shipment of goods to external markets in exchange for cash. Furthermore, the South also suffered from irrigation problems that affected agriculture. However, these problems were primarily a lack of proper flood control measures and water drainage issues, especially as the region was prone to heavy rainfall. Irrigation (to bring in water) was less of a problem here

---

[132] In comparison to other regions, the South's economy in the 1960s was expanding rather slowly (except the Northeast). Income per capita increased from 2,417 baht to 3,448 baht, representing a change of 42.7 per cent. At the same time the Central Region (including the lower North) had a 94.2 per cent expansion while the upper North expanded at 55.2 per cent (Donner 1978, p. 475).

[133] Ibid., p. 476.

[134] Ibid., p. 474.

[135] Medhi (1986, pp. 5–16).

than in other regions. In 1978, the total irrigated land in the South was 1.4 million *rai*, or 8.2 per cent of all irrigated land in the country. The Central Region, which benefited the most from irrigation, contained 64 per cent of the irrigated land, followed by the North at 17 per cent and the Northeast at 10 per cent.[136]

Another important fundamental problem of the South's economy was the inefficiency of the shipping ports. This had been a long running problem since older times. Almost every province in the region had a shipping port, but they were not adequately developed by the state. A major problem at many ports was the relatively shallow sea which prohibited large ships from docking. Goods had to be offloaded from such ships into smaller boats to be brought into the port. Even facilitative resources for this type of goods transfer were lacking. The ports in the region had undergone continual developments since 1969, but these were not enough. A report from the Director-General of the Marine Department in 1964 stated the following regarding Songkhla Port:

> The channel that is the entryway to the port of Songkhla was a natural channel that had not been modified. It was shallow and a major obstacle for ships to dock at the Songkhla lake. At the lowest tide, the entrance was merely 0.61 meters deep (2 feet). Trade vessels of all sizes, as well as fishing boats, could not pass through the channel to dock. They had to wait to dock at the highest tide. Ships that could dock at this port had to be no larger than 200 gross tonnage in size and had to have some of the cargo removed to clear a 2.71 meter (9 foot) deep channel before docking. Larger ships had to remain outside of the sand bar next to Kho Nu and Kho Maew and had their goods transported via small boats. These conditions resulted in high shipping price.[137]

The fact that the Southern ports were inadequate to support large cargo ships made shipping cost per unit expensive. This hindered economic

---

[136] Ibid., pp. 5–14.
[137] N.A. M. of Industry 0201.2/62 (1964).

development in various sectors. Although the South's economy began to diversify into both the agricultural and non-agricultural sectors, the share of agriculture in the GRP continued to decrease. This was because of the continued increase in both volume and price of rubber and palm oil. The share of agriculture in the GRP was 37.1 per cent in 1981 and it decreased to 34.4 per cent in 2010. Industry constituted 21.7 per cent and services 43.8 per cent in 2010. (see Table 5.17).

The agricultural sector has been more important to the Southern Region's growth than any other sector. Between 2002 and 2007, the region was the only one where agriculture made up one-third of the GRP. This was at a time when agriculture made up only 9 per cent of the nation's GDP.[138] The primary agricultural products of the South were rubber, palm oil and fish. Their combined annual growth was 3 per cent in the same period. Agriculture made up the highest percentage of GRP in this region than in any other region. As a result, the sector also constituted a high percentage of the region's household income. Between 1994 and 2002, agriculture made up 61–63 per cent of the household income, while in all other regions it contributed less than the non-agricultural sector.[139] In short, workers in the South earned the most from agriculture. For example, in 2002, a worker's income from agriculture in the South was 49,443 baht, followed by 37,720 baht in the Central Region, 17,417 baht in the North and 11,863 baht in the Northeast.[140] In 2007, the GRP of the region was primarily made up of output from the eastern side and the five southernmost provinces which together made up 74 per cent. However, income per capita in the West of the region was higher than in the East owing primarily to the income from tourism in addition to agriculture.

---

[138] Gross Regional and Provincial Product (2003).
[139] Agricultural Statistics of Thailand (various years).
[140] Gross Regional and Provincial Product (2002).

TABLE 5.17
Gross Regional Product of the Southern Region, 1981–2010

(million baht)

Sector	1981	1990	2000	2010
Agriculture	27,771 (37.1)	66,241 (34.7)	133,988 (28.3)	363,885 (34.4)
Industry	14,792 (19.7)	46,732 (24.5)	102,004 (21.6)	229,844 (21.7)
Service	32,229 (43.0)	77,644 (40.7)	237,075 (50.1)	462,802 (43.8)
Gross Regional Product (GRP)	74,729 (100.0)	190,617 (100.0)	473,068 (100.0)	1,056,530 (100.0)
Average income per capita (baht)	12,401	26,058	57,228	118,184

Source: Gross Regional Product (various years).

Agricultural land usage in the South was completely different from other regions. In 1965, land dedicated to rubber plantations and other perennial plants totalled 8.12 million *rai*, or 61 per cent of the region's agricultural land. Rice and crop farms together occupied only 28.5 per cent.[141] Rubber and perennial plants grown in the South made up 78.8 per cent of the country's total. Another distinguishing geo-economic characteristic of the region was the existence of ponds and lakes making up the Songkhla lake basin, which was advantageous for various uses. In 2003, rubber farm land in the South was 83.8 per cent of the country's total,[142] while the region had only 11.0 per cent of the rice land for planting. This was low compared to other regions. In 2003, rice farmland occupied 69 per cent in the Northeast, 53 per cent in the North and 40 per cent in the Central Region.[143]

---

[141] Donner (1978, p. 477).
[142] *Statistical Yearbook of Thailand* (2010).
[143] *Statistical Yearbook of Thailand* (2003).

Rubber Economy

After the Second World War, rubber production rapidly picked up pace, in part due to demand caused by the Korean War and the expansion of the world market. In the 1950s, the value of rubber exports was second only to rice. Its price rose very quickly. Between 1927 and 1939, the price of rubber fluctuated between 0.13 and 0.66 baht per kg. During most times it was not higher than 0.60 baht per kg. During the Second World War, the price remained at 0.40 baht per kg, rose to 5–7 baht in 1948, then to 14.88–17.29 baht between 1950 and 1951. Although it fluctuated during 1950–71, it rarely fell below 7 baht per kg. Rubber prices continued to outperform the price of rice. In some years it rose as high as 23 times the price of rice (such as in 1950). Between 1950 and 1959, it was ten times the price of rice at most times. It then decreased in the 1960s where it was between five and 15 times the price of rice.[144] The increase in the price of rubber resulted in a rapid allocation of resources and workforce in the South toward rubber plantations. It became the monoculture industrial crop that was important to the economic development of the region. Rubber production, an important source of income and employment, grew from 1.5 million *rai* in 1949 to 2.09 million *rai* in 1955, an increase of 39.3 per cent.[145] In 1953, rubber occupied 57.9 per cent of the agricultural land in the four Muslim provinces, followed by 17 per cent in Songkhla and 9.4 per cent in Trang. The six provinces combined contained 84.3 per cent of the rubber farmland (a slight decrease compared to 1938 when the percentage was 88.5 per cent).[146] Rubber planters included Thais, Chinese and Muslims. During the 1950s, the industry employed 150,000 people — from farm workers and tappers to factory workers. Of these, 91,000 were farm workers and 50,000–60,000 were hired labourers for tapping, factory workers and trade workers.[147]

In his speech in 1970 at the Siam Society, Dr Laurence Stifel concluded that:

---

[144] Calculated from Stifel (1973, pp. 131–34).
[145] Kitti (2009, pp. 92–93).
[146] Stifel (1973, p. 124).
[147] Ingram (1971, p. 104).

The Chinese plantations are clean and orderly, the Thai plantations are rather overgrown and dirty, and the Muslim plantations are more appropriately called rubber jungles rather than rubber plantations.[148]

Changes in the price of rubber and tin inevitably affected the livelihood of the Southern farmers and workers. For example, when rubber prices plummeted in the 1960s, not only was the GRP affected, but the increase in income per capita of the region also declined to the lowest in the country. Between 1960 and 1970, the growth of the South's per capita income (1962 prices) at 42.7 per cent was the lowest when compared to other regions. The Central Region grew by 94.2 per cent, the North 55.2 per cent, and the Northeast 48.3 per cent (see Table 5.18).

TABLE 5.18
Per Capita Income of Each Region, 1960–70

(1962 prices)

Region	1960 (baht)	1970 (baht)	Difference (baht)	Growth (%)
Central	3,528	6,310	3,324	94.2
South	2,417	3,448	1,031	42.7
North	1,554	2,412	858	55.2
Northeast	1,121	1,663	542	48.3
Thailand	2,135	3,464	1,329	62.2

Source: Donner (1978, p. 475).

In 1972, Thailand was the third largest exporter of rubber after Malaysia and Indonesia. Thailand's share of the export market was 11 per cent, and the country produced 12 per cent of Asia's output. Rubber planted area increased by more than 5.6 million *rai* or 150 per cent in 1972 compared to 1962. The average yield continued to increase from 275 kg to 325 kg and 540 kg per hectare in 1975 and 1985, respectively.[149]

---

[148] Uthis cited in Stifel (1973, p. 123).
[149] Falvey (2000, pp. 192–93).

In the 1990s, more than 60 per cent of all rubber planted areas were concentrated in Songkhla, Surat Thani, and Nakhon Si Thammarat.[150] Most of the rubber was exported, with only 10 per cent used domestically. More than half of the rubber were exported as smoked sheets, 30 per cent as bars and 10 per cent as concentrated latex.[151] In the 1990s, there were 820,000 rubber producing families, most of which were small producers with about 15 *rai* of land. Only 10 per cent of the producers had more than 250 *rai*. As many as five million workers were employed by the industry (including rubber tappers).[152]

The expansion of rubber exports was due in part to the government's policy to provide incentives for rubber growers. New rubber varieties were introduced to increase yield and supporting systems were provided. The Rubber Authority of Thailand was established in 1960 to promote the plantation of good rubber varieties and other perennial plants instead of traditional varieties, and to provide the varieties to farmers who had never grown rubber before. They also provided grants and education to the farmers to help them raise the quality of their products to meet world-class standards using the appropriate technology. A Rubber Research Centre was established in Hat Yai, however during its initial phase between 1961 and 1965, its operation output was not satisfactory. Southern farmers were given new rubber species by the grant, and replaced old rubber trees in 149,000 *rai* and 165,000 *rai* of planted areas, mostly in Songkhla (30,819 *rai*), Narathiwat (26,680 *rai*), Yala (14,559 *rai*) and Trang (12,012 *rai*).[153] After that, rubber replacements greatly expanded. For example, between 1961 and 1996 in the Songkhla lake basin, 1.09 million *rai* of rubber were replaced, or 49.45 per cent of the rubber planted areas in the basin. While in Patthalung, farmers replaced 303,000 *rai*, or 54.5 per cent. Songkhla managed to replace 787,000 *rai*, or 47.75 per cent.[154] In 1965, production increased to 170,000 tonnes, and eventually to more than two million tonnes in 1996–97. The average increase

---

[150] Torres (2004, p. 98).

[151] Ibid., p. 98.

[152] Ibid., p. 4

[153] Silcock (1970, p. 75).

[154] Kitti (2009, p. 143).

in yield per hectare was from 350 kg between 1960 and 1970 to 1.3 tonne in 1996.[155]

Rubber planting had increasingly extended from the South to other regions from the 1990s. Rubber planted areas in the Northeast grew from 270,000 *rai* in 1998 to 550,000 *rai* in 2003. In the Central Region, it shrunk from 1.04 million *rai* to 980,000 *rai* during the same period.[156] In 2010, the amount of productive rubber planted areas in the South was 11.8 million *rai*, or 66 per cent of the country's total. The region produced 79.5 per cent of the country's output. The provinces with the most rubber planted areas were Surat Thani (1.7 million *rai*), Songkhla (1.2 million *rai*), Nakhon Si Thammarat (1.2 million *rai*) and Trang (1.1 million *rai*). Between 2007 and 2010, 736,000 *rai* of rubber area was added to the South. The value of exported rubber from the region in 2010 was 236,000 million baht.[157] The rapid expansion of area and export value was caused by demand from China, an important rubber market. Thailand exported 16.5 per cent, 23.1 per cent and 34.1 per cent of its rubber to China between 1997 and 2001, 2002 and 2006, and 2007 and 2012, respectively.[158]

Palm Oil

Palm was a new economic crop of the South whose value saw very high growth. In the last 20 years, productive palm farmland grew from just 1.04 million *rai* in 1996 to 2.02 million and 3.44 million *rai* in 2003 and 2013, respectively. Between 2010 and 2012, more than 85 per cent of all palm-oil producing farmland was in the South. Palm oil production in the region increased from 1.65 million tonnes in 2003 to 9.64 tonnes in 2012. During its first phase, palm farming was concentrated in Chumphon. It later spread to other provinces of the South. In 2012, important oil-producing farmland were in Krabi (930,000 *rai*), Surat Thani (960,000 *rai*) and Chumphon (720,000 *rai*). Yields per *rai* had always been on the increase, from 2,545.5 kg per *rai* in 2003 to 2,920 kg per

---

[155] Torres (2004, p. 98).
[156] *Statistical Yearbook of Thailand* (2010).
[157] NESDB (2011, p. 16).
[158] Rubber Thai Information Centre, <http://rubberwarroom.com/index.php>.

rai in 2012. The average yield per *rai* of the South was higher than any other region.[159] In 1995, Thailand was able to produce 2.3 million tonnes of palm oil and was the 5th largest producer after Malaysia (60 million tonnes), Indonesia (27 million tonnes), Nigeria (10 million tonnes) and Brazil (4 million tonnes). Thailand used 90 per cent of its palm oil domestically. The Thai government had always supported the farming of palm as an economic crop. Provinces that produced high yields of palm oil were Krabi (3,209 kg per *rai*), Chumphon (2,898 kg per *rai*), Ranong (3,050 kg per *rai*) and Surat Thani (3,084 kg per *rai*).[160]

Fisheries

Being a peninsula with an eastern and western coast, the Southern Region was geographically suitable for freshwater, brackish water, coastal and ocean fisheries. Coastal and ocean fisheries had always been important to the region's economy. After the Second World War, the fishing industry expanded very rapidly between 1960 and 1970, growing in value from 136.3 million baht in 1960 to 1,214 million baht in 1970 (1962 prices). Its share in regional agricultural product of the South increased from 4.2 per cent to 20.7 per cent. The rapid growth was due to ocean fisheries which grew exponentially by 845 per cent between 1960 and 1969.[161]

Ocean fisheries had a high growth rate because of the increasing use of motored boats (beginning in the 1950s), the increase in the population of the region and country, and the growth of exports due to world demands. The value of the South's fisheries output rose from 4,098 million baht in 1981 to 18,254 million baht and 21,662 million baht in 1999 and 2009, respectively (see Table 5.19). The South's value of fisheries constitutes 50–60 per cent of the country's total, owing much to the expansion of ocean fisheries. Aside from generating an income from exports and employing many workers in the region, the expansion of fisheries also led to fish farming in the coastal areas, also known as coastal fisheries.

---

[159] Agricultural Statistics of Thailand (various years).
[160] Ibid.
[161] Donner (1978, p. 507).

TABLE 5.19
Value of Fishing Production by Region, 1981–2009

(million baht)

Region	1981	1991	1999	2009
Bangkok and Vicinity	2,712	5,712	16,905	16,305
North	641	666	2,171	3,492
Northeast	963	1,234	3,369	4,427
Central	2,309	8,823	18,252	21,662
South	4,098	26,704	62,765	58,581
Thailand	10,723	43,139	103,462	104,467
The South as Per Cent of Thailand	38.2	61.9	60.6	56.1

Source: Gross Regional Product (various years).

In 2003, there were 3,000 coastal fishery businesses using 21,736 *rai* of area for the purpose.[162] The fish industry paved the way for the rise of other related industries such as ice making, cold storage, processing plants and boat making. Today, 64 per cent of ocean fish are caught and transported via the Southern harbours. Fish farming is mostly for domestic consumption.

In 2008, fisheries were still an important and high potential sector of the Southern Region's economy, as stated in the following report by NESDB:

> Fisheries had a very high potential... more than 65% of the country's farmed shrimps were produced in the Southern region. In 2008, the amount of ocean fish loaded at harbors in the South totaled 950,464 tonnes, or 67%. Areas with the most salt-water catches were around the deep south (529,167 tonnes), or 56% of the total ocean fish produced in the South, with Songkhla as the port with the most salt-water fish at 243,513 tonnes.

---

[162] 2003 Agricultural Census, the Southern Region.

Next were the Andaman coast at 27%, and the Gulf of Thailand coast at 17%. The South was also a coastal fish and shrimp farming site. In 2008, the southernmost border provinces had the highest fish farming potential. The area produced 75% of farmed Asian sea bass and 25% of farmed grouper. The provinces on the Gulf of Thailand coast had the highest shrimp farming potential and produced more than 98% of farmed Pacific white shrimp.[163]

The high growth rate of fisheries was due to the increase in cross-border fishing — a result of Thailand's neighbours granting Thai fishing boats access to their waters. Other factors were the investment partnership with landowners along the shoreline and the increase in coastal fish farming, particularly giant tiger prawn farming.[164] The growth of fisheries brought about the degradation of ocean resources due to the use of inappropriate tools such as push nets, trawl nets and bombs. Other factors also contributed to the deterioration of the sea such as waste water from factories, pollution from communities, shrimp farming and the destruction of mangrove forests, coral reefs and sea grass which were natural breeding grounds for marine life.[165] In the 1990s, the growing giant tiger prawn farming needed very high investment capital. A shrimp pond three *rai* in size required no less than 300,000 baht in investment, but could yield profits many times over.[166] The government promoted tiger prawn farming by stating in the 7th National Economic and Social Development Plan (1992–96) that the goal was to produce 300,000 tonnes of shrimps in 1996, twice the output of 1992.[167] In 1992, Thailand was the world's biggest exporter of giant tiger prawns. Between 1996 and 1999, the South was able to produce between 170,000 and 220,000 tonnes per year, or 60 per cent of the national output. Then, in the 2000s, tiger prawn farming began to decline due to low prices, stringent import restriction of importing countries, environmental and soil problems

---

[163] NESDB (2011).

[164] *Statistical Yearbook of Thailand* (2010).

[165] NESDB (2011).

[166] Sangob (2003, p. 78).

[167] For issues concerning investments, problems, and the impacts of tiger prawn culture, see Sangob (2003, pp. 75–83).

and the deteriorating mangrove forests. In 2009, the South was able to produce only 1,700 tonnes of shrimps, more than half of which came from Nakhon Si Thammrat (particularly the Pak Phanang watershed) and Trang.[168]

The expansion of commercial fishing affected traditional fishing. The number of sea animals declined until not enough could be caught and fishermen were forced to sail further out at sea. Their income continually decreased, and they were forced to change or take on second jobs.[169] Traditional fishing was an important occupation in the South in which three out of four families took part. In 1998, there were more than 50,000 fishing families in the region with more than 100,000 fishermen. The encroachment of commercial fishing put immense stress on the economy of the community and caused conflicts between various groups. The Muslim fishermen, who made up 80 per cent of the traditional fishermen, were particularly affected. They usually did not have a very high income due to the subsistence nature of their production method. The pressure from commercial fishing caused social relationships to change. Thai businessmen of Chinese descent saw fisheries as a trade and a large investment, and started to trespass into traditional fishing grounds. The government supported such enterprises in hopes of generating revenue and expanding the economy. Many traditional fishermen started to use motorized boats to survive and began to find other jobs to compensate for their dwindling income. Many groups were formed to negotiate with the state to protect the interests of traditional fishing. Conflicts regarding coastal resources stem from the basis that the government and private corporations viewed the resources as public property and encouraged their exploitation for economic gains. The Muslim communities, however, saw them as their homes and sources of livelihood for many generations, and as such should belong to the community.[170]

---

[168] Falvey (2000, p. 237); Agricultural Statistics of Thailand (2009).
[169] See Sangob (2003, pp. 182–266).
[170] See Nantawan (2002, pp. 445–76) and Srisak (2000, p. 490).

Manufacturing Industry

In 1980, tin mining was the 4th largest income generating industry in Thailand, but in 1985, it fell to 9th place and continued its downtrend. Tin production statistics in selected years are as follows: in 1970, 21,800 tonnes; in 1985, 16,900 tonnes; and in 1990, 14,700 tonnes. The main problem with tin was the rising mining cost due to the ore's increasing scarcity. The smuggling of tin into the country (an import ban was imposed in the 1970s because of the opening of the smelting plants in the South) and also political issues during the decade caused the people's movement to protest the industry. The Temco Company had exceeded its mining concession period during the administration of Field Marshall Thanom Kittikachorn and Field Marshall Prapas Charusathien, and its mining permit was revoked. But the real issue was with the plummeting tin prices. In 1985, the attempt to set up an international quota by the International Tin Council failed because many countries did not honour the quota and major manufacturers (including Brazil) withdrew from the agreement. In 1984, there were 600 tin dredging companies in Thailand. In 1990, only 35 remained.[171]

Most industries in the Southern Region involved natural resources such as the food, fruits, wood and other agricultural processing industries (such as rubber and rubber products). In 1970, there were 434 industrial businesses that employed more than ten workers. Most of them were in Nakhon Si Thammarat (71), Surat Thani (33) and Songkhla (69).[172] These figures may actually be lower than in reality because there were many other businesses with less than ten employees. In 1984, the South had just 2,607 factories and employed the least number of workers among Thailand's regions. The region constituted only 6.4 per cent of the total number of factories nationwide. Most factories were small (employing one to nine people). Bangkok had the highest percentage of factories at 47.4 per cent, followed by the Central Region at 25.6 per cent, the North at 8.2 per cent and the Northeast at 12.3 per cent (see Table 5.20).

---

[171] International Tin Research Institute (ITRI), "Historical Trend in Tin Production", p. 3, available at <https://www.itri.co.uk/index.php?option=com_mtree&task=att_download&link_id=49601&cf_id=24>; *Mineral Statistics of Thailand* (various years).

[172] Industrial Census cited by Donner (1978, p. 530).

TABLE 5.20
Distribution of Registered Factories by
Number of Employees and Region, 1984

Employment	Greater Bangkok	Central	North	Northeast	South	Total
1–9	63.7	61.9	61.4	68.5	66.4	63.8
10–49	31.1	26.5	31.2	27	27.7	29.2
50–99	3.0	5.0	4.2	2.5	3.2	3.8
100–199	1.1	3.3	1.6	1.3	1.8	1.6
200 or more	1.0	3.3	1.6	0.7	0.9	1.6
Total	100.0	100.0	100.0	100.0	100.0	100.0
No. of factories	19,355	10,470	3,328	5,024	2,607	40,784

Note: Excluding rice mills.
Source: Nipon (1995, p. 124).

A report by the Bank of Thailand painted the following picture of the industry's impact on the economy of the Southern Region:

> The industry sector did not have a significant impact on the economy of the Southern region... Between 1981-1993, industry contributed to only 10% of the region's output. This was because most factories in the region were small and required small investments. If categorized according to TSIC (Thailand Standard Industrial Classification), the food and beverages industry sector had the most factories at about 60%. Of those, 83% were rice mills, or 50% of all factories in the region. Larger industries with large investments were mostly agricultural such as rubber sheets, rubber bars, concentrated latex and frozen seafood. They mostly involved simple processing that added relatively little value.[173]

The expansion of the industrial sector grew at an average pace of 7.5 per cent in 1985 to 12.9 per cent in 1989 and 8.7 per cent per annum between 1990 and 1995. Factories in the region were spread out based on geography and sources of raw materials. Almost 85 per cent of all

---

[173] RYT9 Economic News, 15 October 2000, available at <http://www.ryt9.com/s/ryt9/261321>.

factories were on the eastern side which was the site of rice, rubber and coconut farms, and an important fishing area. Important factories included rubber, seafood and vegetable oils. The west side contained only 15 per cent of the region's factories. Industries in this area included rubber, charcoal, saw mills and powdered fish.[174] Factories in the South, aside from being small in size, were also less advanced. Most utilized only basic agricultural production techniques. The Gulf of Thailand side of the region contained 30 factories, followed by the deep South at 28, and the Andaman side at 20. Most rubber processing plants were in the deep South (14 factories), while most palm oil processing plants could be found on the Gulf of Thailand side, followed by the Andaman side and the deep South.

Industrial processing plants were concentrated mainly in the three provinces on the eastern coast, namely Songkhla, Nakhon Si Thammarat and Surat Thani. These three provinces were instances of an uneven distribution of industry in the South. In 1995, the three provinces combined produced 47 per cent of the output value of the region. In 2005, the industrial output of Songkhla made up 29–30 per cent of the GPP. The same figure for Nakhon Si Thammarat was 25–26 per cent and for Surat Thani was 17–20 per cent.[175] Between 2004 and 2009, the investment value of the factories in the three provinces combined constituted 60–70 per cent of industrial investments in the whole of the region, and they employed 65–70 per cent of all workers. In 2004, investments made in the industrial sector in the three provinces totalled 114,000 million baht, with 47,731 million baht in Songkhla, 43,043 million baht in Nakhon Si Thammarat, and 19,406 million baht in Surat Thani.[176] Although the GRP of the east side was higher than the west, the provinces with the highest per capita income were in the latter such as Phuket, Trang and Ranong. This was due to the growth of tourism. In 2007, Phuket's per capita income was 212,000 baht, with Krabi at 115,000 baht and Phangnga at

---

[174] Ibid.
[175] Gross Regional and Provincial Product (various years).
[176] *Statistical Yearbook of Thailand* (2006).

114,000 baht. These were higher than the national average which was only 92,700 baht.[177] These high per capita figures reflect the growth of tourism which had an impact on the income of the provinces on the Andaman coast.

Between 2001 and 2009, the region's industrial production as a whole saw little expansion. It grew just 1.3 per cent per year, especially from 2005 onwards. The value of the industrial sector continued to shrink each year. Investments in the South's industries, especially food and beverages and rubber, did not increase by much. This was while other sectors with relatively low investments continued to expand well such as non-metal ore products, wood and wooden products (which together grew 13 per cent per year), industrial machinery and equipment (which grew 16.3 per cent per year) and clothing (which grew 13.3 per cent per year).[178] In 2012, there were 33,538 factories in the South, employing 232,000 workers.[179]

The government was aware of the limited role of industry in the economic development of the South and the obstacles standing in the way of economic development such as the lack of skilled labour, insufficient economic infrastructure, political and Communist issues (up until the 1980s) and the unrest in the four deep South provinces. Many successive governments tried to speed up industrial development. NESDB had started a developmental study of the Southern coasts from 1975 and launched in the National Economic Development Plan. The year 1989 marked the beginning of the Plan. The areas of focus were Surat Thani, Phangnga, Phuket, Krabi and Nakhon Si Thammarat. The Plan comprised the development of deep sea ports and oil industry development with oil shipment ports on both coasts of the region. They would link to land-based transportation. The Plan called for the construction of highways connecting Krabi and the Gulf of Thailand (at Khanom), a railway linking Surat Thani (Khirirathaniyom) with Phangnga (Tha Nun), the development of the oil industry, the securing of water sources and the

---

[177] Gross Regional and Provincial Product (various years).
[178] NESDB (2011).
[179] 2012 Manufacturing Census.

development of industrial estates, etc. After that, in the 2010s, additional feasibility studies were carried out to determine the area's suitability for the petrochemicals and energy industries, etc. Importance was given to new land allocation for industry in order to accommodate low-pollution industries. These new areas would be linked by new transportation routes to the Laem Chabang and Mab Ta Phut ports. An economic bridge between the Andaman and Gulf of Thailand sides would be developed to support industrial expansion.[180] Nevertheless, many projects were unsuccessful due to the lack of clarity in the policies and policy enforcement. Some also encountered protests by the local citizens. Some were terminated such as the construction of an underground gas pipeline from Malaysia (The Marine Terminal Project).

Although the manufacturing industry had been in operation for some time, but its overall expansion was weak. This was particularly true for the South's main industries which were food and beverages and rubber processing. The industry remained low in the GRP, contributing only 24.5 per cent in 2010. That percentage was close to the period between 1987 and 2000. The said figure was 24.5 per cent in 1990 and 21.6 per cent in 2000, showing a slow adoption of the industry in the region's economic structure.[181]

Although the manufacturing industry had a low contribution to the region's GRP, the South's resources nevertheless had high potential for industrial use and for the region's economic development. Palm oil, for example, was an important raw material for oleochemicals, which required input from petrochemicals and agriculture. Other products could be developed into alternative energy sources in order to reduce the use of crude oil and to preserve the environment. Such products were biodiesel and bioplastic, foods (such as vegetable oil) and rubber. They could in turn be linked to the automotive parts industry such as tyres, tubes, rubber seals and other rubber products, as well as furniture. Products from fisheries and agriculture such as rice and fruits could be processed or frozen to make ready-to-eat and halal foods.[182]

---

[180] NESDB (2011, p. 4).
[181] Gross Regional and Provincial Product (various years).
[182] PTT Public Company (2010).

Hotels and Tourism

Tourism generated an enormous income for the South's economy. Important world-class tourism destinations in the region are Phuket and Samui island. The tourism boom in the South started in the 1980s. Its growth caused the economic structure of the provinces with tourist destinations to shift towards more services-led growth. This led to the expansion of other related industries such as hotels, guest houses, beverages, souvenirs and construction, and created more jobs. It also physically changed the tourist destinations.

In 2007, the GPP of Phuket in the hotels and restaurants sector was 33,559 million baht, or 45 per cent of its total GPP.[183] In comparison, the figure was 26.1 per cent in 1995, 40.4 per cent in 2001 and 31.7 per cent in 2010. Another province with a relatively high percentage of provincial income from hotels and restaurants was Surat Thani at 10 per cent, particularly after 2000.[184] In 2004, the number of accommodations in the region, which included hotels, guest houses, bungalows, resorts, apartments and motels etc. was 2,655, totalling 108,000 rooms. Hotels and accommodations in the South made up 36.9 per cent and 29.7 per cent of the country's total, respectively.[185]

Tourism continued to grow, boosting the economy of the Andaman side. NESDB reported that:

> In the year 2006, the number of tourists coming into the region was 17.1 million. The industry generated 147,000 million baht, or 21 per cent of the country's total income from tourism. Areas with the most tourists and the highest income were the Andaman side followed by the Gulf of Thailand side and the deep South. Between 2007 and 2008, the number of tourists rose to 19 and 21 million, generating about 170,000 and 190,000 million baht, respectively.[186]

---

[183] Gross Regional and Provincial Product (various years).
[184] Ibid.
[185] *Statistical Yearbook of Thailand* (various years).
[186] NESDB (2011).

Phuket

Tourism had been the main factor in the economic development of Phuket. Though a small province with a growing population of just 166,000, 249,000 and 552,000 in 1990, 2000 and 2010, respectively, it had nevertheless been an important city in the region and in Thailand. Before 1977, the province's economy was dependent on tin mining. But after the decline of tin, its economy became dependent on tourism. The tourism boon from the beginning of the 1970s altered the production structure and employment in Phuket. The area grew rapidly due to the influx of tourists. After the economic crisis of 1997, the weaker baht attracted foreign visitors. Phuket was a destination for foreign and domestic tourists alike. Each year, millions of Thais visited the province on average.[187] At the beginning of the 2010s, Phuket received six million tourists annually on average, and the trend continued upwards. In 2000, there were only about 20,000 rooms for visitor accommodation in Phuket, but in 2010, there were 44,000. Table 5.21 illustrates the rapid growth in the number of rooms.[188]

TABLE 5.21
Growth of Hotels and Rooms in Phuket, 2000–10

Year	No. of Hotels	No. of Rooms
2000	344	20,596
2004	579	32,076
2006	570	34,297
2008	636	37,884
2010	678	44,330

Source: Tourism Authority of Thailand.

---

[187] Tourism Authority of Thailand.
[188] Ibid.

There are many modern deluxe hotels in Phuket such as Club Med in Kata; Holiday Inn in Pa Tong; the Meridien, Karon, Chedi an Amanpuri in Surin; and Laguna Resort in Bang Tao. The economic structure of Phuket is completely different from that of other Southern Regions. The GPP from the hotels and restaurants sector made up 40–50 per cent of the total, showing the importance of tourism in the city's development. In 2004, hotels and restaurants constituted 46.9 per cent. The figure was reduced to 38.7 per cent in 2008. This was while the percentage of hotels and restaurants in the GRP of the South as a whole was only 5.7 per cent (see Table 5.22).

TABLE 5.22
Gross Provincial Product of Phuket and the Southern Region, 2004–8

(per cent)

Sector	Phuket			The South
	2004	2006	2008	2008
Total (million baht)	54,962	57,089	61,395	913,383
Agriculture	2.9	4.2	3.7	27.9
Fishery	2.9	4.4	3.5	5.7
Mining	0.0	0.0	0.0	2.4
Industrial production	3.7	4.2	5.0	12.8
Utilities	2.5	2.6	2.6	2.7
Construction	4.5	5.1	5.0	3.5
Retail and wholesale	8.2	10.7	10.6	11.0
Hotels and restaurants	46.9	38.5	38.7	5.7
Transportation and communications	12.0	14.5	14.3	6.3
Financial intermediation	2.6	3.6	4.3	3.8
Real estate and rentals	2.5	3.0	2.9	3.9
Public administration	2.1	2.3	2.5	5.5
Social welfare and public health services	1.8	1.7	1.8	1.8
Education	1.4	2.7	2.5	5.8
Community, social and private services	2.3	2.4	2.1	1.1
Private household services	0.08	0.1	0.1	0.06
Total	(100.0)	(100.0)	(100.0)	(100.0)

Source: Gross Regional and Provincial Product (various years).

Although Phuket had a lower GPP than some provinces in the South, its per capita income had always been among the highest. Phuket's income per person was 129,000 baht in 1995, and it rose to 180,000 baht and 221,000 baht in 2006 and 2009, respectively. Between 1995 and 2010, more than one out of five employed workers worked in the hotels and restaurants sector. Between 2004 and 2010, the number of workers in the sector was 46,397 — 17,581 males and 28,816 females — or 28.8 per cent of all workers employed.[189] The percentage of skilled labour working as professionals, technicians, managers was around 14–16 per cent between 2002 and 2010. This percentage was entirely different from that of the Southern Region as a whole which was around 8–9 per cent.[190] The growth of tourism and Phuket fostered the employment of skilled workers in various fields.

Phuket has been a tourist attraction as a well as a desired destination for temporary and permanent residency and work in various economic sectors. In 2010, the population of the province was 525,709. There were 431,019 Thais, 72,377 Asians (58,590 of which were Burmese), 2,782 people from the Americas (about 2,241 were Americans), 17,617 Europeans, 1,472 Australians and New Zealanders and 314 Africans.[191] In 2010, there were 3,188 businesses in Phuket. Of these, 199 had a partnership of some form with foreign investors. Foreign investment had a stake of 10–14 per cent in 114 of these businesses, upwards of 56 per cent in another 59 businesses, and 10 per cent in the remaining 26 businesses.[192] Phuket was quickly filled with construction sites in and outside of the municipality. Table 5.23 lists the growth statistics of new construction areas which were dedicated to structures such as homes, condominiums, hotels and commercial buildings.[193]

---

[189] Labor Force Survey of Phuket Province (2004–10).
[190] Ibid.
[191] National Statistical Office (2010).
[192] 2012 Business and Manufacturing Census, Phuket Province.
[193] National Statistical Office, <www.nso.go.th>.

TABLE 5.23
Growth Statistics of New Construction Area in Phuket, 2006–10

Year	Municipal Area (square metres)	Outside of the Municipal Area (square metres)
2006	509,765	1,748,925
2008	533,619	1,736,888
2009	1,112,492	522,361
2010	1,416,671	819,805

Source: National Statistical Office.

The boom in the construction sector was indicative of an expanding economy that was the result of tourism bringing about growth in Phuket and its surrounding area. Lands that were once fields, farms and forests had been urbanized. Hotels, condominiums, residences and commercial buildings were constructed. Land prices skyrocketed. The growth in construction created many jobs due to its labour-intensive characteristic. Between 2007 and 2010, there were about 11,000–16,200 workers in the construction sector, or 8–10 per cent of all workers. Some of the workers were Myanmarese.[194]

The income from tourism had an impact on the economic growth of Phuket. The province's per capita income was the highest in the South, up to 1.6 to 1.7 times (in 2006 and 2008, respectively)[195] that of Surat Thani which had the highest GPP in the region.

---

[194] Labor Force Survey of Phuket Province (various years).
[195] Gross Regional and Provincial Product (2006 and 2008).

Tourism had the effect of transforming villages into urbanized areas. Pa Tong is one of the most famous tourist destinations in the region and in Thailand, with some of the highest growth. It resides on the Andaman coast of Phuket. Before 1970, it was just a small fishing village with coconut trees, fruit trees, swamps and farmland. In the 1970s, tourists started to visit the area. Bungalows were built, and a road leading from the mountains down to the village was constructed in 1976. Electricity was made available in 1979. In 1980, the northern part of Pa Tong bay had neither accommodations nor restaurants. There were no apartments on the beach or up in the mountains. Land prices along the coast was less than 50,000 baht per *rai*. After the Phuket international airport was built in 1976, airlines, both domestic and international, brought an influx of tourists onto the island. This boosted the growth of Pa Tong, and the construction of hotels, guest houses, bars and discotheques quickly picked up pace.[196]

The growth of tourism caused the price of land to skyrocket. In 2010, land price in Pa Tong rose to 80 million baht per *rai*, or 1,500-fold increase in 30 years. It meant that the average increase in price was 50 per cent per year every year from 1980.[197] From the 1980s, Phuket saw a rapid growth in tourism, particularly from foreign tourists. There are many modern deluxe hotels on the island such as Club Med in Kata; Holiday Inn in Pa Tong; the Meridien, Karon, Chedi an Amanpuri in Surin; and Laguna Resort in Bang Tao.[198]

Most tourist attractions in the South are related to the sea, with beautiful beaches and islands as highlights. Other popular tourist destinations in the South include Krabi (Phi Phi island), Surat Thani (Samui island) and Phangnga (Kao Lak). The number of tourists visiting the four destinations rose rapidly. In 2011, people visiting the four sites constituted 80 per cent of all travellers to the South, which numbered 11.68 million.[199]

---

[196] Mackay (2012, pp. 410–11).
[197] Ibid., p. 410.
[198] Ibid., p. 411.
[199] Tourism Authority of Thailand.

These coastal cities generated a revenue of 201,000 baht, or 91.6 per cent of income from tourism in the region.[200]

Conclusion

The Southern Region has long had an economic and trade relationship with Penang and Singapore. It was settled by people of various ethnicities, cultures and traditions. It had the highest percentage of Muslims in Thailand, which set it apart from other regions. The Muslims continued to practise their traditions. Tin had, for a long time, been a product of the region. Its production peaked after the 1850s and the South had some of the most important tin production sites in the country. During its first phases of development, the *monthon* of Phuket was a significant tin producer which contributed 80–90 per cent of the country's output during the First World War. After that, tin production expanded into other provinces in the region.

Tin mines were largely owned by the Chinese. Some Westerners had also set up tin dredging companies at the beginning of the twentieth century. Most workers were Chinese. Major investments came from the West. Westerners brought in dredgers to use in tin mining, an investment-intensive technology that saved on labour. The South sent its tin to Singapore and Penang for smelting. Tin dredging boosted the economy of Phuket. The Chinese made up a substantial portion of the population, which saw a significant increase from the influx of Chinese immigrant workers. The booming economy prompted the rise of commercial buildings, movie theatres, houses, gambling dens, shops, opium production and other services.

---

[200] In 2011 the number of tourists visiting the South ranked second following Bangkok. The number included both Thai and foreign tourists who travelled to more than one province in each trip, 43 per cent of whom were foreigners, generating more than 71 per cent of tourism revenues from the total amount of 307,239 million baht in 2011. <http://www.ksmecare.com/Article/82/29615>.

Geographical factors had an effect on the development of the South. The region had closer economic ties to Penang and Singapore than to Bangkok due to the ease of transportation via the ocean. Although the railway was constructed in the early twentieth century linking the region to Bangkok, it had little effect on the international economic and trade ties. Nevertheless, the railway did improve trade relations between the two sides of the region and with Bangkok. Apart from tin, the South also started to export rubber starting from the 1920s.

The signing of the Bowring Treaty in 1855 had little effect on commercial rice production in the South. Rice production was mainly for household consumption. The geography of the South was suitable for fisheries.

Fisheries were an important part of the economy in terms of employment, a source of food, a promoter of trade and restaurants, and a provider of products for exports. Most of the fishing activity was to feed the fishermen's family rather than for commerce. Most fishermen were Thais and Muslims, and some were Chinese. Fish was exported to Penang and Singapore.

Until the mid-1960s, there was a marked difference between the economies of the two sides of the region, the east and the west. The east was linked to Bangkok, with trade going through the Gulf of Thailand, while the west, comprising Ranong, Phangnga, Phuket, Krabi, Trang and Satun, traded primarily with Malaysia through the port city of Penang. When a network of national highways was constructed and improved, commercial relations with Bangkok increased as a whole, especially in trading fruits. Though the increase in population had put pressure on the South, its economy did not diversify as much as in other regions, with tin and rubber continuing to be the main products in its economy until the 1970s.

Agriculture had always been important to the South's economic development. Rubber was an important source of income and employment. Almost all rubber was exported, making Thailand one of the largest exporters of the product. Most rubber was grown in Songkhla, Surat Thani and Nakhon Si Thammarat. The South's economy had always been dependent on agriculture, which constituted a major portion of its GRP. Even today, more than one-third of the region's GRP is made up of agricultural output. Agriculture made up more than half of the average household income.

Fisheries were also an important sector in the South's economy that had seen great expansion. From 1987, the region contributed to 60 per cent of the country's fisheries output. Fishing could be found in virtually every Southern province.

The industrial role in the economic development of the South is limited. Even today, most factories are small, using relatively little capital investment, and has low added value. Major industries include the food and beverages and basic food processing industries. Most factories are located in three eastern provinces: Songkhla, Nakhon Si Thammarat and Surat Thani.

Tourism has been a very important industry in the South's western region since the 1980s. With Phuket being a world-class tourist destination, income from this industry was significant for the city's development. The economic structure of the city shifted towards the services based on professional occupations. The city's landscape also changed with the rise of hotels, resorts and other structures related to tourism. Phuket's income has been primarily from tourism and services which has contributed to a major portion of the GPP. The employment structure of Phuket was completely different from those of other Southern provinces.

6

THE NORTHEAST

Background

For a long time (before 1760), the Northeastern Region, also known as Isan, had been under the rule of the Kingdom of Lan Xang. After 1779, the whole of Northeast and Laos came under Bangkok's rule and in 1893, western Laos was taken over by the French. Then, in 1903, some parts of the Northeast fell under French colonial rule as well.[1] The centralization during the reign of King Rama V (which strengthened the unification between the central government and the national treasury) and the construction of the railroad linking Bangkok to Khorat allowed the educational system and culture of the region to be under the control of Bangkok.

The Northeast was a tributary state. Major *mueangs* in the region sent levies to Bangkok to fund exports and construction projects such as the construction of royal palaces. The growth of the Bangkok elites could in fact be attributed to levies from the Northeast.[2] These levies reflected the economic expansion of the country even before the signing of the Bowring Treaty in 1855. A majority of the levies,

---

[1]   Suwit and Dararat (1998, pp. 6–16).
[2]   See Koizumi (1992); Boonrawd (1975).

particularly those paid in gold, came from the Northeast. This shows that the region was able to pay its taxes in kind, rather than "money" or "labour", which meant that the region was, to a certain degree, affluent.[3]

The Northeast has arid weather because it is located in a rain shadow behind mountain ranges that separate it from other regions. The mountain ranges block the southwestern storms. As a result, the agricultural economy of the region became dependent solely on the South China Sea cyclones.[4] The main river in the region is the Mekong which flows through a host of nations such as China, Laos, Vietnam, Cambodia and Thailand. Also present are the Mun, Chi and Songkhram rivers. The Northeast is sometimes called the Khorat Plateau. The mountain ranges that form the boundary between itself and other parts of Thailand are the Petchabun, the Dong Phya Yen and the Khao San Kamphaeng. The Phanom Dong Rak range separates the region from Cambodia.

The soil in the Northeast is generally not suitable for rice farming. Therefore, farmers produce little excess rice. Many areas in the region have a rather arid climate. Some areas had been settled by migrant Laotians who had crossed the Mekong River from Laos. The culture of the people in the Northeast is very similar to the people of Laos. Some parts of the region, especially those that border Cambodia, are also home to many Cambodians.

Many people in the Northeast therefore were descendants of the "Laotians" who had immigrated to Thailand. In 1904, there were about half a million[5] Laotians (or Thais of Laotian descent) among the one million inhabitants of the region. The rest were a combination of Siamese, Chinese, Khmers and Suais. The Laotian population was distributed throughout the Northeast. They came from many Laotian subgroups, including Wiang (from Vientiane), Phu Tai, Phuan, Khao and Song. There were also the Thai Khorat subgroup, who were neither Lao nor Thai, but had migrated from Cambodia from the fourteenth century during the reign of King Ramathibodi. There are also Cambodians (or Thais of Cambodian descent) and Kuys living in the Northeast, most of whom are in Surin, Buri Ram and Si Sa Ket close to the Phanom Dong Rak mountain range and the Cambodian border.

---

[3]   Koizumi (1992); Boonrawd (1975).
[4]   Pendleton (1962 reprinted 1976, p. 118).
[5]   Carter (reprinted 1988, p. 52).

THE NORTHEAST UP UNTIL 1941

The Northeast had been lagging behind other regions economically. One important problem was its large number of inhabitants. Despite the population size, it had no commercially significant products. The North had teak, the Central Region grew rice, the South mined tin and grew rubber. Rice, teak and tin were the most important elements of the country's exports, together making up around 90 per cent of the export value in 1910.

A survey of the resources of Siam by the Ministry of Commerce and Communications Board of Commercial Development in 1910–25, stated that:

> The North-Eastern provinces have hitherto remained in a rather backward state as far as the export of their produce is concerned, though there has doubtless always been a certain amount of trade with French Indo-China. Generally it may be said that there still only produce enough of most commodities for their own immediate needs, but with the advent of the railway these circles [*monthons*] are now beginning to export padi in considerable quantities to Bangkok.[6]

This same survey also indicated that the natural resources in other regions were more abundant compared to the Northeast, be they mixed deciduous or dry dipterocarp forests in the North; fruits such as durians, mangosteens, grapefruits and other citrus, and freshwater fish and ocean fish in the Central Region; and freshwater fish and ocean fish in the South. There does not appear to be a record of the natural resources found in the Northeast (except for the abundance of pigs, bullocks and buffalos) compared to what is known in other regions.[7]

Population and Settlement

Before the 1909 Population Census, the population estimates for the Northeast were highly varied. Larry Sternstein estimated that the region had a population of 1.71 million in 1850, which gradually increased to

---

[6] *The Record* (1926, p. 266).
[7] Ibid., pp. 283–84.

1.79 million, 2.04 million and 2.20 million in 1860, 1880 and 1890, respectively.[8] The 1909 Population Census shows the population to be 2.74 million, or one-third of the kingdom's population.

In 1919, the population of the Northeast was 3.09 million and it grew to 3.88 million and 4.92 million in 1929 and 1937, respectively (see Table 6.1). The three most populous provinces in 1937 were Ubon Ratchathani (744,836), Nakhon Ratchasima (593,503) and Khon Kaen (475,516).[9] Settlements in the region comprised many ethnic groups (though there was never a thorough survey). The 1904 Population Census only covered two-thirds of the country's population (in just 12 *monthons*). The *monthon* of Nakhon Ratchasima was the only one in Northeast that was surveyed. It had a population of 402,000 people which was made up of 356,272 Siamese, 2,431 Chinese, 41,038 Khmers, 2,259 Mons, and 65 Karens.[10]

TABLE 6.1
Population of the Northeast, 1850–1937

Year	Population ('000)	Total Population ('000)	Per Cent of Total Population
1850	1,716	5,200	33.0
1860	1,799	5,540	32.4
1870	1,906	5,775	33.0
1880	2,046	6,200	33.0
1890	2,201	6,670	32.9
1900	2,416	7,320	33.0
1910	2,741	8,305	33.0
1919	3,092	9,207	33.5
1929	3,887	11,506	33.7
1937	4,952	14,464	34.2

Source: Sternstein cited in Sompop (1989, p. 36); Wilson (1983, p. 33).

---

[8] Sternstein cited by Sompop (1989, p. 36).
[9] Wilson (1983, p. 33).
[10] Grabowsky (1996, pp. 77–84).

Nakhon Ratchasima, also known as Khorat, had been the region's centre. In the 1850s, the population of the town of Khorat was 7,000.[11] A gateway to the other regions, it naturally became a trading hub, with most of the trading done through the Chinese.[12] During the age of colonization where Thailand's neighbours fell under the rule of Britain and France in the nineteenth century, Nakhon Ratchasima was strategically important to the nation's security. The construction of the railway linking it to Bangkok in 1900 was primarily for political and national security reasons. A high commissioner was appointed in accordance with the government centralization during the reign of King Rama V in Nong Khai, Nakhon Ratchasima and Champasak.[13] Hence Nakhon Ratchasima was not just economically significant, but was also an important centre for the administration of the Northeastern Region.

The province was the centre of sericulture and silk exports. Other products included pork, antlers, leather and other wild products. Rice, fruits and grains were all produced for household consumption. Nakhon Ratchasima began to gain further economic significance after the construction of the railway linking it to Bangkok. In 1890, it became a worker's hub for thousands of "Northeasterners" or "Laotians" who work annually in the Central Region's rice farms in areas such as Rangsit. Because of the arid climate and the dependence on rainfall for rice farming in their own land, a number of Northeastern rice farmers had migrated to work as hired farm labourers in rice fields in the Central Plain. Northeastern workers became extremely important to the rice economy and population growth of Thanyaburi, an important rice growing area up until the beginning of the twentieth century.[14]

H. Warington Smyth estimated the total value of trade in the Khorat Plateau in 1893 to be 120,000 pounds (1.5 million baht). Imports and exports into and from the region were about equivalent. Most of the trading was with Bangkok. Goods were shipped to Bangkok via Saraburi by

---

[11] Bowring (2007, p. 67).
[12] Sees Ingram (1971); Antonio (1904 reprinted 1997); Smyth (1898 reprinted 1994).
[13] Tej (1977, pp. 61–63).
[14] Suntharee (1987, p. 94).

boats, then transported across mountain ranges by caravans. Of the 60,000 pounds worth of imports, 50,000 were from textiles. Imported goods were handled as follows: one-third was sold in Nakhon Ratchasima, one-third was sent eastwards to Ubon Ratchathani, and one-third was sold along the route from Nong Khai northwards.[15] Smyth also estimated that the population of the town of Nakhon Ratchasima was about 5,000 in 1896, while W.A. Graham reported in 1924 that the population was at 12,000, comprising Siamese, Lao and Khmers. In 1928, W. Credner indicated that it was a bustling city with about 40,000 inhabitants. A traveller's journal written in the late 1920s shows that Nakhon Ratchasima had visible fortresses and was a "Lao city" at heart. Its distinct characteristics included Chinese communities and fortresses manned by soldiers.[16]

Ubon Ratchathani was another city of importance. It sat on the easternmost border of the Northeast on the bank of the Mun River. It had a vast land area which included Yasothon and Amnat Charoen. It covered the plains and important rivers in the region which were the Mekong, Mun and Chi rivers, all of which were essential for the growth of the region. In 1890, the population of the town of Ubon Ratchathani, as estimated by Smyth, was 4,000. Graham thought the number of people in the town was 7,000 in 1926.[17] The poor condition of the transport routes before the construction of the railway up to Ubon Ratchathani (at Warin Chamrab, before 1930) was the limiting factor for the trade and commercial development of the province and for the southern area of the region, as reported by the French Consular Report Ubon Ratchathani:

> In 1925, Ubon Ratchathani was a trading hub. It served as a gateway between Siam and Indochina. An old Isan realm, it comprised the *monthon* of Ubon Ratchathani and Roi Et. It occupied an area of 50,000 square kilometers, stretching from the Phu Phan mountain range to Phanom Dong Rak. It sat atop a plateau. The Mun, with various tributaries joining it, flowed through the middle of the plateau. Although Ubon Ratchathani

---

[15] Ingram (1971, p. 117).
[16] Donner (1978, p. 585).
[17] Ibid.

contained many rivers that could have been suitable for boat harbours, the riverways, however, contained many small islands and the current was too strong for the purpose. To travel to other cities (or to the outside world), one needed to start at Nakhon Ratchasima. From there, traveling by land is a distance of more than 350 km to Bangkok. Alternatively, before the age of the railroad, one could travel by boat in the Mun river during the rainy season, though it would be a rather treacherous undertaking. As a result of these obstacles, Ubon Ratchathani was considered the capital of a closed realm. The people of Ubon Ratchathani—at one time one of the most densely populated areas in Siam—depended largely on themselves for their livelihood and led a slow life.[18]

Once the railroad from Bangkok to the Northeast was completed in 1930, Bulletin e'conomique de l'Indochine noted:

> [I]t helped to reduce travel time... and many *tambon* and villages along
> its route prospered as a result. For example, land prices in *amphoe* Warin
> Chamrab increased. Chinese merchants started to offer to buy rice from
> the Northeast to sell elsewhere. When the train station in Si Sa Ket
> opened for operation, the city became an important centre of industry
> and trade, with rice mills, saw mills, electricity plants, glass factories,
> movie theatres and car repair shops sprang up. More importantly, cities
> situated along the railway from Si Sa Ket to Khorat through Surin saw
> an expansion in trade. Goods were transported to Bangkok for exports
> to Singapore and China, while imported goods came in from Europe, the
> United States and Japan.[19]

Rice was the basis for the Northeast's economy in terms of landholding, output and employment. In 1937, out of the 2.42 million workers in the region, 2.35 million worked in the agricultural sector (including fisheries and forestry), equivalent to 97 per cent of the workforce. The remaining workers worked in the industry and services, for example, manufacturing, mechanics, commerce, transport, and professional works. These made up only 3 per cent of the total employed workers (see Table 6.2).

---

[18] French Consular Report cited in Faculty of Letters (2011, p. 312).
[19] Bulletin e'conomique de l'Indochine cited in Faculty of Letters (2011, p. 314).

TABLE 6.2
Northeast's Employment by Economic Sector, 1937

Province	Agriculture and Fishery	Forestry	Commerce	Manufacturing	Mining	Transportation	Public Service	Professional Work	Domestic Work and Personal Service	Clerical Work	Total
Khon Kaen	231,385	175	3,519	1,058	–	1,092	414	738	770	137	239,288
Chaiyaphum	111,196	53	1,733	190	–	11	162	432	189	81	114,047
Nakhon Phanom	121,724	34	1,292	388	–	150	303	460	319	106	124,776
Nakhon Ratchsima	268,086	527	7,781	2,092	–	1,078	3,677	1,129	10,941	448	285,918
Buri ram	114,164	161	1,693	734	1	195	237	332	535	60	118,152
Maha Sarakham	268,136	50	1,133	450	–	90	436	1,245	224	131	271,895
Roi Et	206,306	414	1,700	334	–	92	550	918	375	157	211,266
Loei	56,561	–	139	116	–	21	172	238	66	70	57,383
Si Sa Ket	182,831	59	1,042	551	–	135	222	699	138	82	185,759
Sakon Nakhon	105,789	28	622	273	1	18	216	450	138	84	107,619
Surin	163385	87	1,714	337	1	247	256	558	299	85	166,969
Nong Khai	56,603	6	1,063	399	1	142	232	336	263	85	59,103
Udon Thani	118820	13	1,049	399	–	733	1,101	555	329	133	123,132
Ubon Ratchathani	349,747⁻	112	6,110	1,323	–	349	1,063	1,832	605	224	361,365
The Northeast	2,354,733	1,719	30,590	8,644	4	4,353	9,041	9,922	15,191	1,883	2,426,672

Note: Persons older than ten years of age.
Source: 1937 Population Census.

Agriculture

The signing of the Bowring Treaty in 1855 had virtually no effect on the Northeast. The region's economy was fundamentally subsistence in nature. Farmers grew rice and vegetables to feed their families and made products for their own use such as clothing and other consumables. Cash was infrequently used. Trade was limited only to transactions between villages and families. The rotation of workers and agricultural production resources in a subsistence system was limited due to low demand. Trading among families and communities was frequent. This type of subsistence economy went on until 1932.[20]

Geography and transportation had an effect on the expansion of a market economy. Before the construction of the Bangkok–Nakhon Ratchasima railway in 1900, travelling from Bangkok to the Northeast was very difficult, much more so than from the North. The Northeast was cut off from the other regions by mountain ranges. There were no waterways that could connect it to Bangkok. Every river in this region flows eastwards into the Mekong down to Saigon. Few rivers could be traversed by boat, and most dried up during the dry season. In 1895, it often took eight to nine weeks[21] to travel from Bangkok to Khorat because of the lack of roads and waterways. The cost of transportation between Bangkok and the Northeast, or within Northeast itself, was very high. This limited the expansion of markets. The high transportation cost made commercial production unprofitable.

Some villagers in the Northeast tried to produce high value products such as silk (as well as products that had high value despite high cost such as wild products, cows and buffalos). These goods could fetch a profit if they could be sold in Bangkok and other regions. The government supported silk farms and the production of silk textiles for commercial and export purposes. The Sericulture Department was established in 1901. It hired Toyama, a silk expert from Japan, to aid in experimental silk farming using Japanese methods and cross-breeding Japanese and

---

[20] Chatthip (reprinted 1999).
[21] Smyth (1898 reprinted 1994).

Thai silkworms to create better breeds. The Ministry's personnel were trained in sericulture. Silk farming in the Northeast became highly popular. It was taught in schools and textile-producing locals were given production guidance. A laboratory and demonstration centre was established in Nakhon Ratchasima. The centre brought in modern weaving machines and taught the locals without charge how to use them. As many young women graduated from sericulture schools, the government purchased and distributed these new weaving machines to them.[22] As a result, large volumes of silk were produced and exported, bringing in enormous revenues for the country. But in 1914, an outbreak of Pebrine disease and the increase in rice cultivated areas (which rose 80 per cent in 1907–29)[23] caused the slowdown and eventual cessation of sericulture in the region.[24]

Important silk-producing areas in Thailand were Khorat and Battambang, the latter of which at the time was part of Thailand. A 1884 report by the British Consulate stated the following:

> The great centres of the production of silk in Siam are Korat, 130 miles to north-east of this city, and Battambong, 200 miles to the south-east as the crow flies.... The production is, however, small in comparison with that of Cambodia, and Annam, and the export is consequently unimportant, consisting entirely of so-called Korat silk. It is taken to the latter place in small quantities from the neighbouring Laos and Cambodian provinces, such as Bua Chum, Phimai, Suwanaphum, Si Sa Ket, Khukan, Sangkha, and Surin, and there sold, or more generally bartered for cotton and other goods to Chinese traders, who resell it at Bangkok to the exporters. A number of these traders are, however, settled in other small localities, where they have greater facility in purchasing the silk from the producers, and amongst these Pakrio, which is about half-way to Korat by way of Saraburee [Saraburi], is the most important centre.[25]

---

[22] Ingram (1971, p. 117).
[23] Kakizaki (2007, p. 28).
[24] Sutham (1994, p. 130).
[25] BCR, *Monthon Nhakonratchsima* (1884).

Most of Thailand's exported raw silk came from Nakhon Ratchasima, the volume of which often fluctuated. In 1870, most of the raw silk was exported to India, Singapore, Cochinchina, Shanghai and Burma via Chiang Mai.[26] However, due to the rising transportation costs, many families decided to produce only enough for family and community consumption. Many decided to grow rice, cotton and farm silk for their own use.

The construction of the railway to Nakhon Ratchasima was completed in 1900, Buri Ram in 1925, Surin in 1926, and Ubon Ratchathani in 1930. Commercial production began to expand because transportation between the region and Bangkok now took only one day. In 1925, about 102,000 tonnes of rice were exported, or 10 per cent of the national total. This rose to 270,000 tonnes, or 21 per cent of Thailand's rice exports in 1935.[27] The amount of goods such as sugarcane, oranges, beef, pork, tamarind, leather and antlers coming out of Nakhon Ratchasima in 1889 (before the reach of the railway) altogether was only about 150–200 tonnes per month, or 1,800–2,400 tonnes annually. But after the reach of the railway, the figure rose to 18,873 tonnes in 1905 and continued to increase to 73,927 tonnes in 1918.[28] The expansion of rice trade allowed the villagers to afford goods from Bangkok such as clothing, tiles, betel, and red lime powder.[29] In 1935, 370,000 tonnes of goods were shipped from the Northeast to Bangkok, including 91,943 pigs. At the same time, the region imported 47,678 tonnes of goods and 245 animals. In 1935, the values of goods exported from and imported into the region were 24.23 million baht and 12.48 million baht,

---

[26] Dilok (reprinted 2000, p. 162). Export volume of silk was 776 *hap* in 1870 but it dropped to 108 *hap* in 1875 and jumped to 1,094 *hap* in 1884. Statistics for 1900–5 are not available but export values were 0.180 million baht, 73,353 baht, and 0.164 million baht in the same period. After 1900, export values increased from 0.253 million baht in 1900 to 0.287 million baht in 1903 and 0.391 million baht in 1905 (ibid., pp. 161–62).

[27] Sompop (1989, p. 79).

[28] Chumpol cited by Suwit (2005, p. 334).

[29] Ibid., p. 339.

respectively. Important exported goods included rice (18.06 million baht), forest products such as wood (2.26 million baht) and pigs (1.68 million baht). Rice made up a majority, or 75 per cent, of the goods sold to Bangkok. Important imported goods were textiles (6.03 million baht), soap (1.01 million baht) and machinery and metals (0.96 million baht).[30]

This corresponded with a report from the French embassy in Ubon Ratchathani, which mentioned that the construction of the Bangkok–Ubon Ratchathani railway had the following effects on the trading economy at the beginning of the 1930s:

> The Siamese Laotian realm [southern Northeast] began to see an economic future after the construction of the railway. Si Sa Ket, Surin, and even Buri Ram and Khorat, important cities since the olden times, would not have seen such growth if not for the railway. Each kilometer of the railway cleared up what was once a dense forest. Many rail lines were constructed and junctions created, allowing for new possibilities for the Siamese Laotian region. Train cars filled to the brim with goods made their way to Bangkok, a centre of western goods. Exported goods included rice, leather, silk, spice, salt and valuable wood. They were exchanged for money to be used for purchasing imported textiles from England, machinery from Germany, processing factories from America, matches from Poland, toys and imitation silk from Japan, egg noodles, dried mushroom, and thousands of other kinds of food from China, dried fish from Cambodia and fruits from Malaya etc. These products had become familiar everyday items for the Siamese. Si Sa Ket today is Ubon Ratchathani tomorrow. It will become a centre for goods from Laos and France, to be exported to Penang and Singapore.[31]

The railway helped to boost the expansion of rice farmland from 3.9 million *rai* in 1920–24 to over 12 million *rai* in the 1940s. However, yields per *rai* began to decrease from 4.30 *hab* in 1921–25 to 3.22 *hab* and 2.47 *hab* in 1931–34 and 1941–45, respectively.[32]

---

[30] Kakizaki (2007, p. 33).
[31] Bulletin e'conomique de l'Indochine cited by the Faculty of Letters (2011, p. 314).
[32] Ingram (1971, p. 50).

The stagnation in crop yields was due to alkaline soil, lack of agricultural technology, and the absence of irrigation systems. Zimmerman's rural economic survey in 1930 shows that Northeastern households made the lowest income among the regions at 83 baht.[33] He also indicated that landholding problems in the Northeast were rather few. This was because most farmers, approximately 82 per cent of them, owned their farmland. Only 18 per cent rented land. The average size of landholdings of the region was 5.83 *rai*. The average amount of additionally-rented land was just 3.9 *rai*.[34] The low income shows that farmers owned relatively little land and reflected subsistence production. Up until the early 1940s, crops other than rice such as sugarcane, coconut, tobacco and corn were of little importance in terms of land usage and employment.

Despite the ability to export rice after the advent of the railway, rice farming expansion was still slow. Sticky rice had long been a favourite staple of the people of the Northeast. Most of the sticky rice produced is for family consumption. Transportation had always been a fundamental problem for the region. The rail connected only certain provinces, and its construction was slow compared to other regions. The Bangkok–Nakhon Ratchasima route, opened for service in 1900, took 8.5 years to build despite a five-year construction plan. Many workers died building the rail line due to malaria. As many as 8,000 Chinese and 38 Europeans were among the deceased.[35] Although the railway was built up to Ubon Ratchathani (Warin Chamrab station), the train could not cross the Mun River.

One characteristic of a subsistence economy was the limited growth of hired labour both in and outside of the agricultural sector, though this did not pertain to Northeastern workers working in the Central Region. Workers in Thanyaburi constituted a small fraction of the total Northeastern labour force. In the past, Northeastern workers seldom chose to work outside of the agricultural sector. The labour force in the

---

[33] Zimmerman (reprinted 1999, p. 48).
[34] Ibid., p. 18.
[35] Cited by Whyte (2012, p. 16).

government's civil construction projects, such as railway construction or road repair, were often immigrant Chinese or Vietnamese (such as in Nakhon Phanom). Prince Damrong recorded that although the State Railway paid Thai workers as much as 0.75 baht per day, there was still a labour shortage because they preferred to do tree cutting and charcoal-making.[36] The shortage of workers had been prevalent in Northeast before the Second World War, indicative of a small population and the subsistence nature of the region's livelihood. Some farmers resorted to hiring more helpers at peak times when their own workers were insufficient. However, most chose to rely on a traditional labour rotation custom called *"long khaek"* that was often used during worker shortages.[37]

The subsistence economy, the distinguishing characteristic of the rural Northeast, gave villages in the region immunity against the economic depression in the 1930s. Compared to the Central Region, the Northeast was less affected. This was because production in the Central Region used more capital and labour than in the Northeast, particularly in the farming areas in the Rangsit plain. Problems that had an impact on the Northeast were mostly nature-related, such as droughts and floods. The fluctuations of the price of rice and other agricultural goods had little effect due to the subsistence nature of the region's production.[38]

---

[36] Damrong (1913, p. 121).

[37] Chatthip (reprinted 1999, p. 27).

[38] N.A. M. of Agriculture 15.2/25 (1929). Subsistence economy restricted the growth of market economy, household income, as well as expansion into other economic sectors such as services. Cattle, buffalos, and carts were essential factors of production in the fields and transportation mode inside the village as well as between the village and town. In 1929, the Northeast had the highest number of cattle, buffalos, and carts in comparison to other *monthons* and regions in the country. *Monthon* Nakhon Ratchasima had 1.35 million heads of cattle (36.3 per cent of the country's), 0.895 million heads of buffalo (26.7 per cent), and 0.157 million carts (37.4 per cent). *Monthon* Udon had 0.585 heads of cattle, 0.415 million heads of buffalo, and 37,091 carts (1929 Population Census).

Manufacturing Industry

The Northeast had no industrial base even when large volumes of crafts were produced for domestic consumption. Only rice mills saw a gradual growth along with commercial rice production. In 1929, the region had a total of 33 rice mills, with 13 in Khorat, five in Ubon Ratchathani, five in Khukhan, four in Surin, two in Buri Ram, one in Roi Et and three in Khon Kaen. Most of these mills were operated by the Chinese.[39] They were concentrated in the south of the region where railroad access was available, with virtually no presence in central or northern Northeast.[40] Most of the mills opened for operation in 1926–29. They were small, with machines no larger than 35 horsepower. They milled rice for the province and nearby *monthon*, a sign of slow and uneven economic growth. Thai and Chinese workers worked in the mills.[41] In 1929, the salary paid by the rice mills at *amphoe* Phon, Khon Kaen was 50 baht/month for an engineer and 100 baht/month for the mill manager.[42] In 1937, only 1,676 workers worked in the rice and saw mills in Northeast, with 856 in the former and 820 in the latter (see Table 6.3).

In the 1940s, apart from rice mills, sugar factories were also established in *amphoe* Kumphwapi, Udon Thani. After that, factories were constructed in Nakhon Ratchasima and Buri Ram. In 1941, a brewery owned by the Excise Department, Ministry of Finance, was set up in Chaiyaphum using a capital of 1.21 million baht. It produced rice whiskey and mixed alcoholic beverages, with a capacity of 1,200 litres per day.[43] In 1937, the service sector, which comprised commerce, transportation, public services, professional works, housework and personal services, and clerical service was very small. It employed only 2.5 per cent of the region's workforce. Even in provinces with high non-agricultural employment, services still created low-level labour employment. The number of workers employed in the service sector in some selected provinces is given in Table 6.4. Nakhon Ratchasima totalled 15,207 (or 5.4 per cent of workers), in Khon Kaen 6,670 (2.7 per cent) and in Udon Thani 3,900 (3.1 per cent) (see Table 6.4).

---

[39] N.A. Personal File 2.41/2 (1929).
[40] Chatthip (reprinted 1999, p. 68).
[41] N.A. Personal File 2.41/2 (1929).
[42] N.A. M. of Agriculture 15.2/25 (1929).
[43] N.A. M. of Finance 0301.2.2/3 (1957).

TABLE 6.3
Number of Employed Workers in Rice Mills and Sawmills in the Northeast, 1937

Province	Rice Mills	Sawmills
Khon Kaen	249	87
Chaiyaphum	–	7
Nakhon Ratchasima	196	330
Nakhon Phanom	16	23
Buri Ram	98	275
Maha Sarakham	19	6
Roi Et	13	5
Loei	2	–
Si Sa Ket	27	5
Sakon Nakhon	–	–
Surin	31	5
Nong Khai	3	8
Udon Thani	48	23
Ubon Ratchathani	154	46
Total	856	820

Source: 1937 Population Census.

TABLE 6.4
Number of Employed Workers in the Service Sector in Udon Thani, Khon Kaen and Nakhon Ratchasima, 1937

Subsector	Udon Thani	Khon Kaen	Nakhon Ratchasima
Commerce	1,049	3,519	7,781
Transportation	733	1,092	1,078
Public service	1,101	414	3,677
Professional work	555	738	1,129
Domestic work and personal service	329	770	1,094
Clerical work	133	137	448
Total	3,900	6,670	15,027

Source: 1937 Population Census.

In 1942, a survey of Thai-owned retail stores (under state economic nationalism at the time) in the Northeast shows a total of 3,709 stores. Nakhon Ratchasima had the highest number of stores at 644, followed by Khon Kaen at 508 and Roi Et at 470 (see Table 6.5). Although the figure was incomplete due to the exclusion of Chinese-owned stores which was an important group of businesses, nevertheless, it did show Nakhon Ratchasima and Khon Kaen as important regional retail areas during the Second World War.

TABLE 6.5
Thai-owned Stores and Shops in the Northeast, 1942

Province	Grocery Store	Clothing	Traditional Crafts	Repair Shops	Total
Nakhon Ratchasima	478	152	7	7	644
Nong Khai	28	87	11	3	129
Buri Ram	54	53	–	1	108
Loei	15	16	1	2	34
Si Sa Ket	1	3	49	1	74
Surin	154	62	–	–	216
Sakon Nakhon	–	174	20	–	194
Khon Kaen	246	190	70	2	508
Chaiyaphum	144	1	1	3	149
Nakhon Phanom	3	26	15	1	45
Maha Sarakham	85	280	86	7	458
Ubon Ratchathani	263	214	61	1	302
Udon Thani	131	75	21	5	232
Roi Et	37	106	–	3	146

Source: N.A. (3) Office of the Prime Minister, 0201.45/1 (1942–43).

In summary, the Northeast had a large population but lacked the resources to stimulate commercial production, particularly national-level production like the teak in the North, rice in the Central Region, and tin and rubber in the South. The region's low agricultural productivity, in addition to high transportation costs, had for a long time made the region's economy a subsistence one. This limited the growth of markets and the region's economy, both in and outside of the agricultural sector.

THE NORTHEAST AFTER THE SECOND WORLD WAR

Even after the Second World War, the Northeast still lagged behind other regions in terms of economic advancement. Its per capita income was the lowest among Thailand's regions. One of the region's fundamental problems was its high alkaline and low quality soil. In many areas, the soil's composition was so sandy that it was unable to retain water, causing longer dry seasons and extreme heat. Low agricultural productivity resulted in poverty, forcing its workers to find work elsewhere. The region also faced unrest due to the threat of Communist insurgents. Other problems included poor transportation in some areas (up until the mid-1980s) and unequal access to public services such as education and public health. Despite the government's efforts to speed up economic development from the 1960s, progress was only seen in certain areas. Many other parts of the Northeast still faced numerous problems, the most important being the farmers' income and low agricultural productivity, lack of adequate irrigation, low educational levels and lack of skilled labour.

Population

After the Second World War, the population of the Northeast rose rapidly from 3.1 million people in 1947 to 15.6 million and 18.9 million in 1980 and 2010, respectively (see Table 6.7). The annual population growth rate was 2 per cent, 2.9 per cent and 2.5 per cent in 1950–60, 1960–70 and 1970–80,[44] respectively. After 1980, the annual population growth rate declined rapidly to 0.9 per cent in 1990–2000. A negative growth rate of −1.02 per cent per annum was seen in 2000–10[45] (see Table 6.6).

---

[44] ESCAP (1982, p. 14).
[45] 2000 and 2010 Population Censuses.

TABLE 6.6
Population and Population Density of the Northeast, 1947–2010

Year	Population ('000)	Annual Growth Rates (%)	Population (density per square km)	Percentage of Thailand's Population
1947	3,157	–	38.6	35.6
1960	8,992	2.7	53.3	34.2
1970	12,025	2.9	71.0	35.0
1980	15,698	2.5	93.0	35.0
1990	19,038	2.3	112.7	34.9
2000	20,832	0.9	123.0	34.2
2010	18,966	–1.02	111.4	33.9

Source: Population Census (various years).

In comparison to the other regions, the Northeast had the highest natural growth rate.[46] Despite this fact, the region still experienced a high emigration rate.[47]

Most of the population growth was seen in rural Northeast. In 1960–80, as much as 96 per cent of the population lived in rural areas. The region had a higher percentage of rural population than any other region.[48] The population density of the rural areas increased very rapidly. In 1947, the density was 29.3 persons per square km. This rose to 51 persons in 1960 and 68 persons in 1970.[49] From 1947–2010, the Northeast was

---

[46] The annual rate of natural increase was 3.2 per cent in 1964–67 and 3.4 per cent in 1971–76. The annual natural increase rate in the North was 3.1 per cent and 1.8 per cent; 2.9 per cent and 2.4 per cent in the Central Region; and 3.2 per cent and 3.0 per cent in the South during the same periods (ESCAP 1982, p. 15).

[47] The rate of emigration per 1,000 population in the Northeast was –1.33 in 1955–60 and –1.41 in 1965–70, resulting in a population decrease of 0.2 million from emigration (ESCAP 1982, pp. 14–15) and it continued to lose hundreds of thousands in the ensuing years (Population Census, various years).

[48] The proportion in the North was 92.5–94.0 per cent; 60.9–72.6 per cent in the Central Region; and 87.4 per cent in the South during 1960–80. Although the proportion of rural population (those living outside municipal areas) in the Northeast slowly decreased to 76 per cent in 2000, such proportion was still the highest in the country (Population Census, various years).

[49] ESCAP (1982, p. 15); Suwit and Dararat (1998, p. 78).

home to the majority of the nation's population, and the percentage was relatively steady at 34–35 per cent. The three most populous provinces in 1990–2010 were Nakhon Ratchasima, Khon Kaen and Udon Thani. In 2000–10, all provinces with the exception of two saw an annual negative population growth. The two provinces, Ubon Ratchathani and Khon Kaen, grew at 0.26 per cent and 0.01 per cent annually, respectively.[50] Negative growth meant a high level of population emigration.

The Growth of Cities

Nakhon Ratchasima, the region's economic centre, saw a very rapid growth from the 1960s. In 1960, the number of people living in the city and its municipality was 50,000. The population of the entire province was then 1.09 million making it the third largest province in the country. Nakhon Ratchasima was also a rail transportation hub with links to southern Northeast (Buri Ram, Surin, Si Sa Ket and Ubon Ratchathani), central Northeast and northern Northeast (Khon Kaen, Udon Thani, and Nong Khai). In 1960, the province was also a crop farming centre with 284,000 *rai* of crop farmland, up from just 73,000 *rai* in 1950 (a 400 per cent increase in nine years). Almost half of the expansion of farmland was in 1956–59. In 1950, 23 per cent of the total area planted in Nakhon Ratchasima was used for crops such as sugarcane, beans and corn. Crops made up 70–80 per cent (by weight in tonnes) of the region's total agricultural output.[51] The growth of upland crops helped to boost other sectors such as commerce and finance, setting up Nakhon Ratchasima as a prominent city in the region.

The fact that Nakhon Ratchasima was home to a US military base during the Vietnam War, and that its development had received a boost since the first National Economic Development Plan, gave the province various benefits as the region's "commercial centre". The Friendship Highway linking the city to Saraburi, Ayutthaya and Bangkok aided the growth of crop farming and other trades. Other roads (such as the Chokchai–Detudom highway) connected Nakhon Ratchasima with other provinces such as Surin and Ubon Ratchathani, allowing for the

[50] Population Census (various years).
[51] USOM (1960, p. 28).

growth of commercial services, banking, utilities and other businesses fundamental to the economy. At the beginning of the 1990s, under General Chatchai Choonhavan's government (1988–91), the province saw continuous development. This was partly due to the fact that the Premier was the province's representative in parliament from 1975. The fact that many members of parliament were also from various election districts in Nakhon Ratchasima also contributed significantly to its development.

During Chatichai's government, five representatives were from Nakhon Ratchasima. One of them held the rank of Deputy Minister of Transport and was involved in many large-scale governmental projects. Suranaree University of Technology was established, the first autonomous university to be situated outside of Bangkok. The growth of the province's economy in general, particularly in the non-agricultural sector, was high, and was a factor in the city's expansion. The industrial sector's growth was 19.6 per cent in 1980 and it increased to 21.9 per cent and 27.3 per cent in 1985 and 1990, respectively. Wholesale and retail trade increased by 18.8 per cent, 18.3 per cent, and 17.3 per cent during the same period.[52]

Although most of the Northeast's population resided in rural areas, the annual growth of urban areas (including the entire population of the municipalities) in 1960–70 was 3.6 per cent, a high percentage compared to other regions. The Northern Region's city growth was 1.8 per cent, the Central Region's (excluding Bangkok) was 2.4 per cent and the South's was 2.6 per cent annually.[53]

The growth of cities in the Northeast coincided with the role of US military bases in Thailand during the Vietnam War. At the beginning of the 1960s, many cities, particularly those that were host to the bases, experienced rapid growth. In 1960, there were five such cities: Nakhon Ratchasima, Udon Thani, Nakhon Phanom, Ubon Ratchathani and Khon Kaen. The population of each city's municipality grew rapidly between

---

[52] Ueda (2000, p. 156).
[53] ESCAP (1982, p. 25).

1947 and 1980. The number of people in municipal Nakhon Ratchasima grew from 22,340 to 88,876 (3.97 times). In Khon Kaen, the figure rose from 14,346 to 94,019 (6.55 times). Udon Thani's population grew from 13,076 to 81,060 (6.2 times), while Ubon Ratchathani's increased from 7,390 to 50,788 (6.9 times) (see Table 6.7). In 1979, Nakhon Ratchasima, Khon Kaen and Udon Thani were ranked 4th, 5th and 7th largest cities in Thailand, respectively.

TABLE 6.7
Growth of the Urban Population (in Some Municipalities)
in the Northeast, 1947–80

Municipality	1947	1960	1970	1980
Nakhon Ratchasima	22,340	42,218	66,071	88,876
Khon Kaen	14,346	19,548	29,431	94,019
Udon Thani	13,076	30,884	56,218	81,060
Ubon Ratchathani	7,390	27,222	40,650	50,788

Source: Population Census (various years).

The presence of US military bases affected the economic and city growth in the region. In 1965–72, high-level American military expenditures made up 10.6 per cent of the GRP of the Northeast.[54] They included personnel salaries, construction costs, and wages for the Thai workers working in the bases. American military spending in construction in the region was US$10.6 million, US$50.6 million, US$37.5 million, US$2.6 million and US$1.4 million in 1963–65, 1966, 1967, 1968 and 1969 respectively, totalling US$107.2 million between 1963 and 1969. The recipient provinces were Nakhon Ratchasima with 41.3 per cent of the amount, Ubon Ratchathani with 17.1 per cent, Udon Thani with 26.5 per cent, and Nakhon Phanom with 15.0 per cent.[55]

---

[54] Boonkong (1974, p. 117).
[55] Ibid.

The military expenditures gave rise to the hiring of Thai workers. In 1972, 34,638 Thai workers, both skilled and unskilled, worked in American bases nationwide. About 40 per cent were residents of the Northeast, where most of the workers came from rural areas. The spending by military personnel themselves notably encouraged the growth of bars, night clubs and massage parlours. Workers in these industries in Udon Thani numbered more than 5,000. Military spending resulted in the expansion of the city due to an influx of migrants from rural areas.[56] From 1965, the economic growth of cities caused an expansion in businesses such as hired transportation (passenger tricycles and minibuses), hotels, restaurants, wholesale and retail stores, clothing stores, barbers etc. which naturally caused an increase in income and employment.

In the 1990s, large cities still saw significant growth, especially Nakhon Ratchasima, Udon Thani and Khon Kaen. This was partly because these three cities were linked to the modern, four-lane Friendship Highway that ran between Nakhon Ratchasima, Khon Kaen and Nong Khai. The growth was also due to the expansion of upland crops, commerce, services and industry. In 1991, the Northeast was home to several top ten largest cities in the country, namely Nakhon Ratchasima in third place (202,000), Khon Kaen in sixth place (131,000), Ubon Ratchathani in eighth place (98,950 people) and Udon Thani in tenth place (78,489).[57]

Another factor that contributed to the growth of the urban population was the development policies implemented in the region. During the rule of Field Marshal Sarit Thanarat, Khon Kaen was developed with the goal of becoming "the centre of the Northeast region". It was to be the hub of agriculture and education. Khon Kaen University was established in 1964 along with several educational institutions. The city plan and utilities were systematically developed. The location of Khon Kaen was advantageous to the growth of the city because it was another centre of the region that was linked to Nakhon Ratchasima, Udon Thani, Nong Khai, and Loei.[58]

---

[56] Ibid., p. 113.
[57] Department of Provincial Administration.
[58] Donner (1978, p. 586).

The economic structure of the Northeast was increasingly shifting from agriculture to industry and services. One outstanding characteristic of the region is the high ratio of unpaid family workers, which was higher than in any other region. In 1980, such workers made up 60.9 per cent of all workers, with the North at 50.0 per cent, the Central Region at 50.7 per cent, the South 39.0 per cent and Bangkok at 14 per cent.[59] Even up until 2010, the percentage of such workers was still high at 26.2 per cent (the North 25.5 per cent, the Central Region 16.6 per cent, the South 20.9 per cent and Bangkok 8.7 per cent). The Northeast had a lower share of professional technicians and vocational workers than all other regions. In 2010, they made up 8.3 per cent of the entire region's labour force (down from 9.9 per cent in 2002), while the figures were 8.8 per cent for the North, 12.6 per cent for the Central Region and 9.38 per cent for the South. This reflects a shortage of skilled labour.[60]

Migration

After the Second World War, the Northeast was the region with the highest migration, both internally and externally. From 1947–54, there were 5.6 million migrants in Thailand, equivalent to one-quarter of the population. Out of this figure, 1.9 million were migrants relocating within the Northeast.[61] Pressure in terms of high population and low agricultural productivity, especially for rice, was the driving force for emigration in search of better economic opportunities. Forests were cleared to make way for arable land in the Northeast such as Udon Thani, which ranked among the provinces with the highest immigration rate. Sugarcane farmland expanded rapidly and peaked in 1947–57. Field crops' farmland (sugarcane, mango, coconut) in Udon Thani increased from 32,000 *rai* to 260,000 *rai*. The rate of increase was greater than that of rice both in proportion and

---

[59] Labor Force Survey, Second Round (1980).
[60] Labor Force Survey (various years).
[61] USOM (1960, p. 4).

farmland area. In total, the increase in crop and rice farmland was 40 per cent from 1950–57. Sugarcane occupied the largest percentage of crop farmland at 44 per cent, followed by peanuts (10 per cent), maize (9 per cent) and bananas (8 per cent). In 1958 and 1959, sugarcane production reached 6.6 and 8 metric tonnes respectively, or 89.4 per cent and 90.7 per cent of all crop production. The exponential growth of sugarcane output was a result of the forest clearing for new farmland by migrants who decided on permanent residency in Udon Thani.

In 1960, the Northeast's emigrants outnumbered immigrants by 186,000 people. The high emigration rate mainly originated from provinces that relied primarily on rice for its economy. These provinces experienced drought and lacked fertile soil for farming. Emigrants moved away from these densely populated provinces to less densely populated areas such as Nong Khai and Udon Thani. From 1965–70, apart from internal migration, the emigration rate was still high. One out of three emigrants in Thailand came from the Northeast.[62] Provinces in the region with the highest rate of emigration per 1,000 people in 1965–70, from the most to the least, were Roi Et (–57.6 people), Maha Sarakham (–57.5), Khon Kaen (–44.8) and Kalasin (–32.7). Provinces with a positive net immigration rate (more people coming in than moving out), from the most to the least, were Nong Khai (+110.2 people), Loei (+53.5), Udon Thani (+27.3) and Sakon Nakhon (+17.6). Apart from domestic migration, some Northeasterners, numbering tens of thousands per year, also relocated abroad to the Middle East for work.

Emigration from the Northeast continued to increase even after 1987 due to limited farmland. The emigration rate remained at a high level from 1990–97. There were 356,000, 280,000 and 252,000 persons leaving the region in 1990–92, 1992–94, and 1995–97, respectively.[63]

Following the economic crisis of 1997, immigration into the Northeast soared, causing a net positive migration rate. There were 1.46 million

---

[62] ESCAP (1982, p. 39).
[63] Economic Research and Training Centre (2002).

immigrants in comparison to 617,000 immigrants seen in 1995–97 before the economic crisis.[64] The crisis had caused the shutdown of many factories and businesses, particularly in Bangkok. As a result, many Northeasterners had to return home. The National Statistical Office's estimate shows that about 800,000–1,000,000 labourers returned home, and the in-migrants outnumbered out-migrants.[65] Northeast's migrants had long been the largest group of Bangkok-bound immigrants. In 2000, there were over 700,000 such workers in the city, amounting to nearly one-third of all immigrants. Workers from this region could be found in every region, and always made up the largest group of immigrants.[66]

The Economy of the Northeast

The economic development of the Northeast at the start of the 1960s was not independent of the political changes in Indochina, the role of the United States in the Vietnam War, and the financial aid given by the US to Thailand under cooperation with and support for Sarit Thanarat's government (1958–63). From 1950–58, the US engaged in the war and joined the effort to thwart Communist expansion in Southeast Asia, fighting against the Viet Cong. The role of the US gained significance in 1961 and 1962. Many military bases were set up in the Northeast region, which was viewed as sensitive to Communist expansion. A major problem at the time was the political unrest in Laos which was a result of this advancement of Communism. Sarit ordered the mobilization of the Thai military to face off against Laos at the Northeast region's border.

The construction of the Friendship Highway had commenced from the 1950s during the rule of Phibun's government. It was open for use during Sarit Thanarat's government and its primary purpose was to oppose the Communist expansion as part of a Cold War strategy. The construction of new highways in 1962 (after the Friendship Highway was open in 1958) was approved by the House of Representatives. An important

---

[64] Migration Survey (various years).
[65] Ibid.
[66] 2000 Population Census.

part of the construction plan was to establish a route between Nakhon Ratchasima and Ubon Ratchathani, link it to Roi Et and eventually to the existing Friendship Highway, effectively connecting Khon Kaen, Udon Thani and Nong Khai together. The purpose was to have the roads reach the American bases in Nakhon Ratchasima, Ubon Ratchathani and Khon Kaen with funding provided by the US government for its construction, creating an alliance to defend against any Laotian offensives. The construction of standardized modern highways was to facilitate any military movement into Communist-threatened areas. Although the highways built in the Cold War era under the rule of Sarit was for defence against Communist Laos and Vietnam, they nevertheless triggered significant changes to the economy of the Northeast.[67]

The development plan of the Northeastern Region was inextricably linked to the political situation of Indochina, Thailand's national security and the Communist threat. The plan had an impact on the region's economy and society. The Sarit government devised the plan for the Northeast along with the first National Economic Development Plan. Projects were initiated in many sectors. Examples in the agriculture and cooperatives sectors included the development of irrigation systems, upland crops research and promotion, promotion of rice farming, promotion of freshwater fishery, the development of rural cooperatives, establishing loans for agriculture, etc. Some examples in the industry and energy sectors were the survey of underground water as sources for public water supply, ore and raw materials survey, energy needs and sources survey, region-wide transportation, promotion of home industries, and promotion of manufacturing industries. The transportation sector saw the construction and repair of national highways and the building and expansion of airports, etc. Examples of local developments included the improvement of community development methodology, construction and repair of 50 provincial and rural highways totalling 2,000 km, improvement and expansion of electricity lines, etc. Other areas of improvement included health and education. The budget for the development of the Northeast in 1962–66 came from the

---

[67] Thak (2007, p. 239).

national treasury, aids and loans, totalling 6,716.8 million baht. Funding from aids and loans made up 82 per cent of the entire development budget. The budget for transportation was the highest at 3,379.5 million baht.[68]

The province of Khon Kaen was chosen as the Northeast's development centre. The reason was that "it had the railway and transportation hub for Kalasin, Sakon Nakhon, Udon Thani and Loei. Agricultural products from the said provinces must pass through Khon Kaen before being sent to Bangkok..."[69] Also, Khon Kaen had a large enough population to act as a centre. It also had the Phong River that could be used as a source of hydropower to be sold to nearby provinces.[70] The government was able to speed up the city planning process, land reclamation for public utility projects, and the construction of public utilities in Khon Kaen to accommodate the economic growth of the Northeast. Land was allocated to industry, commerce and business, government buildings and transportation infrastructure.

The Northeast's development plan not only affected the economic growth of the region in the areas of agriculture, industry and services, it also had an impact on the growth of provinces, especially the province of Khon Kaen which saw an increase in population and an expansion of its economy as a whole. Another factor that made Khon Kaen an important city in the region was the establishment of Khon Kaen University in 1964. It was promoted as the centre of education and regional development, which facilitated the development of the city's and region's economy. The fact that a US military base was situated in the province during the Vietnam War also helped to stimulate Khon Kaen's economic growth.

The GRP of the region rose from 10,082 million baht in 1960 to 20,001 million baht in 1970 (almost twofold in ten years). It continued to increase to 514,000 million baht in 2000. The per capita income increased from 1,046 baht in 1960 to 1,782 baht, 6,294 baht, 13,606 baht and 24,186 baht in 1970, 1980, 1990 and 2000, respectively. During 1960–2000,

---

[68] N.A. M. of Transport 0202.2.10.3.1 (1961–66).
[69] Khon Kaen City Plan (1982, p. 17).
[70] Ibid., p. 16.

the economy of the Northeast gradually shifted from agriculture towards industry and services. In 1960, agricultural production made up 57.6 per cent of the GRP; in 2000 it constituted only 17.7 per cent whereas industry and services together made up 82.3 per cent (see Table 6.8).

TABLE 6.8
Economic Structure of the Northeastern Region, 1960–2010

Year	Agriculture	Industry	Service	Total
Gross Regional Product (million baht)				
1960	5,803 (57.6)	1,174 (11.8)	3,104 (30.8)	10,082 (100.0)
1970	8,761 (43.8)	3,828 (19.1)	7,411 (37.1)	20,001 (100.0)
1990	71,522 (27.4)	49,436 (18.9)	140,389 (53.7)	361,347 (100.0)
2000	90 649 (17.7)	107,928 (20.9)	316,146 (61.4)	514,717 (100.0)
2010	227,615 (21.8)	291,931 (27.8)	527,269 (50.3)	1,046,815 (100.0)
Employment ('000 persons)				
1960	4,658 (93.5)	64 (1.2)	266 (5.3)	4,989 (100.0)
1970	5,748 (91.8)	102 (1.6)	411 (6.6)	6,262 (100.0)
1990	9,777 (85.6)	226 (1.9)	168 (11.9)	11,411 (100.0)
2000	9,196 (76.2)	565 (4.7)	2,308 (19.1)	12,070 (100.0)
2010	7,869 (70.4)	783 (7.0)	2,516 (22.6)	11,171 (100.0)

Source: Population Census (various years); Labor Force Survey (various years).

The source of the Northeast's GRP was primarily from four provinces: Nakhon Ratchasima, Khon Kaen, Ubon Ratchathani and Udon Thani. In 1981, the output of these provinces made up one-third of the GRP. Nakhon Ratchasima constituted 11.9 per cent, Khon Kaen 8.1 per cent, Udon Thani 7.7 per cent and Ubon Ratchathani 6.7 per cent. In 2009, their contribution rose to 42 per cent with Nakhon Ratchasima at 15 per cent, Khon Kaen 13 per cent, Ubon Ratchathani 7 per cent and Udon Thani 7 per cent.[71]

The per capita income of the Northeast was significantly lower than all other regions. For example, in 1980, its income per head was 6,294 baht. In the Central Region, the figure was 20,647 baht, the North 10,511 baht, the South 14,052 baht and Bangkok 45,300 baht.[72] In 2009, the same figure for the Northeast was 45,766 baht, 4.98 times[73] less than that of the Central Region, 1.53 times less than the North's, 2.04 times less than the South's, and 4.98 times less than Bangkok's. The Northeast's income per head had always been the lowest in the country. In 1996–2008, ten provinces in the region were ranked as having the least income in the country.[74] In 2009, nine provinces had per capita income of less than 40,000 baht, namely Nakhon Phanom, Sakon Nakhorn, Yasothon, Buri Ram, Surin, Maha Sarakham, Si Sa Ket, Nong Bua Lamphu and Amnat Charoen. No other province in Thailand had an income of less than 40,000 baht per person.[75]

The income per head also differs between each province in the Northeast. In 1981, the per capita income of Khon Kaen was 7,526 baht per person, but in 2009 it eventually rose to 76,385 baht (10.14 times). In Si Sa Ket, the same figures were 4,847 baht and 34,426 baht (7.08 times) during the same period. This shows a difference in the income of the people in Khon Kaen who earned 1.55 times and then 2.25 times the income of the people in Si Sa Ket.[76]

---

[71] Gross Regional and Provincial Product (various years).
[72] Gross Regional and Provincial Product (1980).
[73] Gross Regional and Provincial Product (various years).
[74] Ibid.
[75] Gross Regional and Provincial Product (2009).
[76] Gross Regional and Provincial Product (various years).

The decrease in the share of agricultural production did not mean a rapid decrease in the share of the population in the agricultural sector. This was an important factor that made for a low per capita income in comparison to other regions (agricultural production constituted a mere 17.7 per cent of the GRP in 2000, but the sector employed more than nine million people, or 76.2 per cent of the region's labour force). Provinces with a higher share of agricultural output tended to generate lower income per person (because yields per *rai* were low). Table 6.9 shows that provinces with agricultural output at 25.1–30.5 per cent (with low yields per *rai*) included Yasothon, Roi Et, Mukdahan, Surin and Buri Ram. Provinces with a low agricultural share, such as Khon Kaen and Nakhon Ratchasima had higher per capita income. Agricultural productivity was therefore an important factor in determining the income of the people in the Northeast.

TABLE 6.9
Per Capita Income and Agricultural Productivity of
Some Provinces in the Northeast, 1989 and 2003

Province	1989			2003		
	Per Capita Income (baht)	Rice Yield (kg/*rai*)	Agriculture as a Percentage of GPP (%)	Per Capita Income (baht)	Rice Yield (kg/*rai*)	Agriculture as a Percentage of GPP (%)
Yasothon	10,238	258	27.3	22,942	304	21.5
Roi Et	10,449	256	31.5	25,458	359	19.2
Mukdahan	11,189	253	30.5	27,698	359	22.6
Surin	12,306	249	25.1	22,422	380	21.5
Buri Ram	10,692	241	25.4	22,925	336	23.0
Khon Kaen	24,746	240	20.4	45,860	343	12.1
Nakhon Ratchasima	15,151	226	20.0	41,321	317	16.6
Ubon Ratchathani	11,458	226	26.9	28,425	274	15.8
Udon Thani	12,117	219	31.0	31,359	338	18.1

Source: Gross Provincial Product (various years).

Rice and Other Types of Agriculture

In 1950, almost 98 per cent of agricultural land was owner-occupied (compared to the national average of 87 per cent). Most were smallholder rice farmers, with approximately 24 *rai* of land per family. The region's economy as a whole was stagnant. The economy of many areas was subsistence. Both trade with outside parties and the level of the commercial economy was low. Income from agriculture was low in comparison to other regions. The income per agricultural household (including the value of goods produced for consumption within the family) was 3,873 baht, which was lower than the national average of 5,660 baht. The per capita income of the region was 588 baht, lower than the national average of 959 baht (see Table 6.10).

TABLE 6.10
Household's Incomes from Various Sources, Northeast and Thailand, 1953

(baht)

	Northeast	Thailand
Cash from sale of farm products	954	2,147
Cash from non-farm activities	1,139	1,756
Value of own production consumed by producing farm family	1,780	1,755
Total real income	3,875	5,660
Real income per capita	588	959

Source: USOM (1960, p. 18) based on the 1953 Economic Farm Survey.

The economic situation in the Northeast in 1950 was such that there was a general underemployment of workers according to a 1960 report by the United States Operations Mission (USOM):

> The average northeast family member actively contributing to the cultivation of the family farm worked about 83 days a year on the farm and put in an additional 43 days in non-agricultural work (wage labour and home occupations, like weaving), leaving 239 idle days per year. The picture that emerges from these statistics is clearly one of a subsistence economy. Despite the predominance of rice cultivation, only 58% of the farms surveyed derived any cash income from the sale of rice. Such sales comprised only 31% of total sales of farm products per farm family; other field crops contributed 9%, tree crops 11%, livestock and livestock products 49%.[77]

---

[77] USOM (1960, p. 18).

In 1950, farmers used cattle and buffaloes on 91 per cent of the region's farmland with less than 1 per cent of farmland utilizing agricultural machinery and about 8 per cent of farmers solely relied on their own labour.[78] At the beginning of the 1950s, many Northeastern farmers began to adopt commercial agriculture. They started to farm cattle, buffaloes and swines for sale domestically and outside of the country. In 1950, "The Northeast was the only area of the country that sold more livestock than it bought. About one-quarter of the farm families in the area derived cash income from sales of livestock."[79] In 1958, there were 2.9 million buffaloes, 2.3 million cattle and 1.03 million swines in the region, equivalent to 47.0 per cent, 46.7 per cent and 26.2 per cent of the livestock in the country.[80]

The high population growth rate after the Second World War,[81] in addition to limited farmland, caused a general decline in agricultural productivity. In many areas production was below subsistence level, as was the case in Si Sa Ket and Roi Et. This was partly due to a sharper increase in the population in rural areas than in urban areas. The rice yield per *rai* of the Northeast was the lowest in comparison to other regions in 1957–58 and 1958–59, which was at 140 kg per *rai* during both periods.[82] This was in comparison to the national average of 175 kg and 198 kg per *rai* for the same periods. In 1960, rice production in Nakhon Ratchasima was only at 109 kg per *rai*.[83] This resulted in the province being a net buyer of rice in 1957–60. [84]

The Rice Division of Nakhon Ratchasima reported that the "total rice demand in the *changwad* in 1959 was about 230,000 tons or about 115,000 tons more than production".[85] The low agricultural productivity put pressure on farmers to seek income from non-agricultural sources and drove the emigration of workers to find jobs outside of the province.

---

[78] 1953 Economic Farm Survey.
[79] USOM (1960, p. 20).
[80] Ibid., p. 21.
[81] ESCAP (1982, p. 15); Suwit and Dararat (1998, p. 78).
[82] N.A. M. of Finance (1) 1.3.3.2/4 (1960).
[83] Ibid.
[84] Ibid.
[85] Ibid.

They gradually switched from being temporary, seasonal migrants to permanent ones.[86] In Khon Kaen, although the rice productivity was higher than in Nakhon Ratchasima, during years with low yields the province too, found it necessary to import rice for consumption.[87]

After 1950, a number of highways were constructed in the Northeast. Some important ones included the Friendship Highway (linking Saraburi to Nakhon Ratchasima), Nakhon Ratchasima–Ubon Ratchathani, Loei–Chumphae–Khon Kaen, and Udon Thani–Nakhon Phanom. In 1976, the region had a total of 7,019 km of national and provincial highways and 16,028 km of rural highways. In comparison, in 1962, there were only 3,090 km of roads, 207 of which were paved.[88] Highways had limited coverage, were narrow, and were unusable in the rainy season.

Although the construction of highways was part of an anti-Communist strategy, it did succeed in opening up opportunities for the rural population to expand their farmlands. This led to higher agricultural output and an increase in area available for rice and crop farming such as corn, cassava, kenaf and sugarcane. The new roads were beneficial to the expansion of agricultural output and other economic gains. One report proposed for the development of the Udon Thani–Nakhon Phanom highway in the early 1960s is worth quoting at length:

> The area traversed by the Udorn–Nakorn Panom highway is quite densely populated. The main occupation of the people is agriculture. Instead of producing on a large scale for outside markets, the people tend to produce on a large scale for home consumption. Without adequate transportation, there is no incentive for them to enlarge their farming units. The level of business activity is low, and each village (or even each household) has to maintain a certain degree of self-sufficiency because of the difficulty and the high cost of transportation to and from other areas. Since the existing highway is the only means of communication with the rest of the country, some villages are isolated during the rainy season. Consequently, stocks of food and other supplies have to be stored. Despite the foregoing difficulties, tobacco, maize, kenaf and cattle are produced in this area.

[86] Ibid.
[87] Ibid.
[88] Department of Highways, Ministry of Transport (2013).

An improved highway connection between the provinces of Udorn, Sakon Kakorn and Nakorn Panom is of vital importance to the economic development of this area. Since an improved road would reduce operating costs for vehicles using it, we could expect an increase in traffic and a reduction in freight rates. This would stimulate business activities between the three provinces and between this area and other areas. The people would be encouraged to produce more for outside markets.[89]

In 1963–78, the cultivated area rose from 26.3 million *rai* to 40.5 million *rai*. The number of holdings increased from 12.2 million to 16.6 million (36 per cent) (see Table 6.11). The clearing of land for agriculture became widespread, helped by the use of machinery, particularly tractors. Using machines instead of livestock for the purpose allowed much more land to be reclaimed. In 1963, agricultural land in the Northeast made up 39 per cent of the agricultural land nationwide. The figure rose to 44.2 per cent and 46.8 per cent in 1978 and 2013, respectively.[90]

TABLE 6.11
Total Area Under Holdings, Number of Holdings,
the Northeast, 1963, 1978, and 2003

	Area under Holdings (million *rai*)			Change	
Year	1963	1978	2003	1963–78 (%)	1978–2003 (%)
Total	26.3	40.5	50.7	53.4	25.2
Rice	18.1	27.8	35.4	53.5	27.3
Upland crops and so on	8.2	12.4	16.3	53.6	31.4
No. of Holdings ('000 persons)					
Year	1963	1978	2003	1963–78 (%)	1978–2003 (%)
	12,220	16,601	10,652	36.0	−35.8

Source: World Bank (1983, p. 44); Agricultural Census (various years).

---

[89] N.A. M. of Transport 0202.8.10/20 (1962–63).
[90] 1978 Agricultural Census.

Rice

Rice farming saw very high growth. Rice farmland increased from 6.7 million *rai* in 1950 to 20.9 million *rai* in 1970, 30.7 million *rai* in 1989 and 32.1 million *rai* in 1997, showing a slower growth rate towards the end.[91] The slowdown was attributed to the increasing use of farmland for planting other upland crops for higher profits. Although its expansion was reduced, the share of rice farming was still high in comparison to other crops. In 1950, rice farmland made up 96.1 per cent of all farmland. The figure was reduced to 80.7 per cent in 1970 and 71.3 per cent in 1989. In 1989, the size of rice farmland in the Northeast was 51.30 per cent of all rice farmland in the country.[92]

Although rice output was greatly boosted after 1950 — from 1.8 million tonnes in 1950 to 7.1 million tonnes in 1989 and 10.1 million tonnes in 2003 — rice yields per *rai* on average were lower than in other regions with the exception of the South. The yield per *rai* in the Northeast in 1989 was 329 kg (while the average in the same year in the North, South and Central Region was 411 kg, 288 kg and 387 kg, respectively).[93] The figures show a production imbalance; the Northeast had generally the most rice farmland but yielded very low. As a result, labour productivity, measured by dividing the total rice produced by the number of workers (yields per head), was shown to be low. To summarize, rice yields per head in the Northeast rose from 1.10 tonnes to 1.29 tonnes and 1.79 tonnes in 1968–73, 1988–92 and 2003–7, respectively. However, the average productivity of the country was 1.45 tonnes, 1.69 tonnes and 2.87 tonnes per head.[94] The reasons behind the low agricultural labour productivity were that the region practised rain-fed or seasonal rice farming (once per year) and had limited access to chemical fertilizers and machinery despite a rapid adoption of agricultural machinery during the past two decades. The region also used a local rice breed for the most part, one that yielded less rice than other faster yielding breeds.[95]

---

[91] Agricultural Census (various years).
[92] Suwit and Dararat (1998, p. 92).
[93] Agricultural Statistics of Thailand (various years).
[94] Somporn (2010, p. 18).
[95] For this issue, see Somporn (2010); Suwit (2003).

The type of rice farmed in the Northeast was different from that in other regions (with the exception of the upper Northern Region). In 1970, the people primarily grew sticky rice. It occupied two-thirds of the region's rice farmland (sticky rice farmland area was 13.3 million *rai*, while the total rice farmland was 20 million *rai*). The sticky rice constituted no less than 78 per cent of the total rice production of the region. The total rice output (sticky rice and white rice combined) was 4.4 million tonnes.[96] Sticky rice farming could be found in every province in the Northeast, particularly north of the Mun River. Sticky rice requires a shorter time to grow at only 120–135 days. Sticky rice growing area in the region expanded by 22 per cent in 1959–70, while white rice area grew by 54 per cent. This caused sticky rice farmland to drop from 72 per cent to 67 per cent of all rice farmland in the same period. The expansion of rice was partly due to support from the government for commercial rice farming. In 1970, sticky rice productivity per *rai* was higher than white rice.[97] Almost all of the sticky rice produced was for domestic consumption, and most of that was in the Northeast itself.[98]

In 1973–77, there were 10.36 million *rai* of sticky rice farmland which increased to 11.18 million *rai* in 1988–92 and declined to 9.59 million *rai* in 2003–7. Most of the sticky rice in the region was grown on land traditionally used for yearly rice farming. However, output did not decline because the breed used was non-photosensitive, thus giving higher yields. It replaced the local traditional rice in some areas. Production went up from 2.08 million to 2.75 million and 2.93 million tonnes, and the yield per *rai* increased from 203 kg to 246 kg

---

[96] Donner (1978, p. 602).

[97] Ibid.

[98] Sticky rice from the Northeast was sent to Bangkok for exports and for domestic consumption (about 24 per cent of the total sticky rice production). Around 13 per cent of milled sticky rice (after milling at Bangkok) was exported to Laos while the rest was sold domestically. Export market for sticky rice was small amounting to 0.12 million tonnes in 1967, 0.095 million tonnes in 1969, and 0.13 million tonnes in 1970. Major importers included Japan (32 per cent), Laos (28 per cent), and Malaysia (15 per cent). The rest of the production was exported all over the world (Donner 1978, p. 602).

and 305 kg in 1973–77, 1988–92 and 2003–7 respectively.[99] Farmers then began to switch to white rice because of the higher price, particularly Jasmine Rice 105 (Hom Mali rice) which has been very popular in the past two decades. In 2007, there were 15.97 million *rai* of Jasmine rice farmland, or 82.39 per cent of the nation's rice farmland. Its total output was 5.12 million tonnes, accounting for 78 per cent of Thailand's Jasmine rice output.[100] Also in recent decades, Jasmine rice (or Hom Mali rice) which was mostly produced and exported from the southern provinces of the Northeast generated export income of about 57,000 million baht a year and made up 35 per cent of the total Thai rice export in 2010–15.[101]

Although lesser farmland was allocated to sticky rice, some farmers decided on growing both white rice and sticky rice at the same time.[102] About 28.5 per cent of farming families in the Northeast grew rice for domestic consumption — a proportionately high quantity. In 2003, 5.55 million *rai* of farmland was dedicated to growing rice for self-subsistence. They yielded 1.57 million tonnes of output. Sticky rice made up 47.2 per cent of the total in-season farming output, and 25 per cent of off-season output.[103]

Upland Crops

Before the Second World War, upland crops were of little significance to the Northeast, whether in terms of landholdings, output or employment. However, after 1950, upland crops farming grew very rapidly. These crops included maize, sugarcane, cassava, kenaf and soybeans (see Table 6.12).

---

[99] Somporn (2010, p. 11).
[100] Ibid., p. 12.
[101] Porphant (2016, p. 13).
[102] 2003 Agricultural Census.
[103] 2003 Agricultural Statistics of Thailand.

TABLE 6.12
Upland Crops Planted in the Northeast, 1950–2005

('000 *rai*)

	1950–52	1958–60	1965–67	1980–81	1989–90	2003–5
Maize	125	424	419	2,267	2,107	1,638
Sugarcane	113	266	187	294	668	2,407
Cassava	–	21	77	4,637	5,947	3,658
Kenaf	43	420	2,290	1,005	756	102
Rubber	–	–	–	–	–	510

Source: Pasuk and Baker (1995, p. 54); Agricultural Statistics of Thailand (various years).

In 1950–52, there were 43,000 *rai* of kenaf farmland. This grew to 420,000 *rai* and 2.2 million *rai* in 1958–60 and 1965–67, respectively (see Table 6.12). In 1965–67, kenaf farmland in the Northeast constituted 90–95 per cent of the country's total. It was the second most numerous type of farmland after rice. Up until 1975, kenaf was primarily grown in the region's centre such as Khon Kaen and Maha Sarakham and in the South such as Ubon Ratchathani and Chaiyaphum. These areas together made up 80 per cent of all kenaf farmland in the Northeast. Kenaf farming skyrocketed at the beginning of the 1960s due to high world demand and crop losses in India and Bangladesh, the two major producers of the plant in that decade.[104] In 1974–75, the following were important provinces in terms of kenaf farming (with more than 100,000 *rai* each): Nakhon Ratchasima (495,000 *rai*), Khon Kaen (321,000 *rai*), Ubon Ratchathani (256,000 *rai*) and Buri Ram (154,000 *rai*).[105] After the 1970s, there was a continuous decline in kenaf cultivation. Its low and fluctuating price, along with the complexity involved in growing it, led farmers to abandon the plant in favour of other crops that gave better yields such as cassava, corn (as animal feed), and sugarcane. In

[104] Donner (1978, p. 603).
[105] Suwit and Dararat (1998, p. 99).

2003–5, only 120,000 *rai* of kenaf cultivated area was left.[106] Apart from cassava, other upland crops also began to see high expansion rates such as sugarcane, maize, and sweet corn. However, rubber turned out to experience the highest growth rate. In 2003–5 there were 510,000 *rai* of rubber growing area in the Northeast, up almost twofold from 276,000 *rai* in 1998.[107]

Cassava was first planted in the region in *amphoe* Phimai, Nakhon Ratchasima in 1961. It quickly gained popularity in other provinces, starting from Udon Thani and Nong Khai. The Northeast became the centre of cassava farming since the 1980s. In 1997, the region grew the crop on 4.7 million *rai* of planted areas. This was 60 per cent of the country's total (25 per cent was in the Central Region and 15 per cent in the North).[108] Most of the cassava was exported, taking advantage of the EU's import quota. The Northeast was suitable for the crop because of infertile soil and unpredictable rainfall. Cassava planting needed little care or management. Farmers could conveniently take out loans, and the produced goods were purchased using future contracts by local middlemen.[109] The rapid expansion of cassava production caused soil fertility to quickly degrade. The Thai government tried to reduce this type of farming to preserve the environment.

Landholding

Land clearing to expand arable land resulted in an almost unchanged arable land per capita. From 1961–85 arable land per capita in the Northeast did not decrease, on the contrary, it tended to stabilize. In 1961 arable land per capita in the upper Northeast was 4.0 *rai*, rising to 5.28 *rai* in 1975, and slightly declined to 4.88 *rai* in 1984. In the lower Northeast, it was 4.47 *rai*, 5.49 *rai*, and 5.41 *rai* per capita during the same period.[110]

---

[106] Agricultural Statistics of Thailand (2005).

[107] Ibid. (1999 and 2005).

[108] Falvey (2000, p. 184).

[109] Ibid., p. 183.

[110] Ammar (1987, p. 13).

Arable land per capita had the tendency to rise and remain stable before 1985, reflecting the ability of the agricultural sector to attract and sustain its employment. The proportion of agricultural workers in the Northeast remained high. Moreover, in the years that agricultural produce could fetch soaring prices, employment in the agricultural sector would be high as well. The agricultural sector, thus, was crucial to provincial economic growth until the beginning of the 1980s despite the slowly decreasing role of agricultural produce in GRP as well as the proportion of agricultural workers. From the end of the 1980s, the importance of the agricultural sector was clearly declining. The proportion of agriculture in GRP decreased from 27.4 per cent in 1990 to 17.7 per cent in 2000, but employment in the agricultural sector remained high with a slight decrease to 76.2 per cent. After that, however, both the GRP and employment in the agricultural sector continued to decline.[111]

In 2003 there were 2.64 million household heads in the Northeast, representing 45.6 per cent of all agricultural holdings in the country, or 10.7 million people engaging in agriculture. Among them, 94 per cent grew various crops and/or tended livestock, 0.19 per cent were engaged in freshwater aquaculture, and 5.6 per cent grew crops as well as tended livestock and engaged in freshwater aquaculture.[112] The top three provinces with the highest number of agricultural holdings, accounting for 24 per cent of the region's agricultural holdings, were Nakhon Ratchasima (0.252 million), Ubon Ratchathani (0.204 million), and Khon Kaen (0.2 million). Provinces with 0.1–0.2 million holdings were Kalasin, Chaiyaphum, Buri Ram, Maha Sarakham, Roi Et, Si Sa Ket, Sakhon Nakhon, Surin, and Udon Thani.[113]

In 2003, about 59.8 per cent of the Northeast's agricultural holdings had 10–39 *rai*, followed by 15.6 per cent with landholdings smaller than 6 *rai*. Land holdings with more than 140 *rai* were every few (0.3 per cent). From 1998 to 2003 agricultural holdings rose to 64,037 (2.5 per cent), most

---

[111] 2011 Labor Force Survey.
[112] 2003 Agricultural Census.
[113] Ibid.

of them with a small plot of less than 6 *rai* (totalling 99,166 or 31.4 per cent). Those who had 10–39 *rai* were decreasing,[114] indicating the effect of population growth on the increase of small landholdings and higher land fragmentation. The number of farms rose to 2.1 million in 1990, 2.6 million in 2000, and 2.7 million in 2009. On the other hand, the average farm size slightly shrank to 22 *rai*, 22.2 *rai*, and 21.3 *rai* during the same period.[115]

Although agricultural land holdings appear to have few problems, at the macro-scale problems were severe: a lack of title documents, land leasing, and loss of land eventually led to landlessness and land quality. Professor Medhi Krongkaew found that the smaller the income of agricultural household, the higher the proportion of land renting. He also discovered that in 1975–76 and 1979–80, the poorest rural people in the Northeast had lost their land or had increasingly changed their status from landlords to tenants: from 6.9 per cent to 9.1 per cent of the poorest agricultural households.[116] The 2003 Agricultural Census reports that: "There were 8 per cent landless farmers [in the Northeast] during the past five years [1998–2003] ... There was a trend for the increase in the proportion of landless farmers."[117]

Land renting could be problematic for agricultural productivity because tenants usually had less incentive to increase productivity than farmers working on their own land. Farmers with secure title documents also had more incentive to labour on their own farms and could increase their productivity per *rai* through loans from formal financial institutions that could be used to buy factors of production to help boost their output more than farmers with less secure title documents. In 2003 the proportion of households engaging in agricultural activities on their own land was 79.0 per cent, a decrease from 89.0 per cent in 1998. On the other hand, those working on non-owned land rose to 8.0 per cent from 3.8 per cent during the same period. There were 63.3 per

---

[114] Ibid.
[115] Office of Agricultural Economics, <http://oae.go.th>.
[116] Medhi (1986, pp. 5–42).
[117] 2003 Agricultural Census.

cent of the households with title documents (for their own land) such as title deeds (*chanot thidin*) NS 5, NS 3, NS 3K, NS 3khor while the other 36.7 per cent had less secure title documents such as *SPK 4-01/NK/STK/KSN*.[118] Such less secure title documents were a hindrance to productivity growth.

Changes in the Agricultural Sector and Their Impact

Rapid changes in agriculture had a profound effect on the Northeastern way of life. Capitalist production had expanded and replaced subsistence production. In 1953 the proportion of production for consumption was as high as 80 per cent of all rice production: the smaller the holdings, the more rice would be grown for household consumption. Farmers with holdings of less than 6 *rai* who cultivated rice for their own consumption accounted for 98 per cent of the total value of rice production. Such proportion dropped to 91 per cent for holdings of 6–15 *rai*, 75 per cent for 30–60 *rai* plots, and 64 per cent for plots of 60 *rai* and larger (see Table 6.13).

TABLE 6.13
Value of Rice Grown for Household Consumption and Income from Selling Rice in the Northeast, by Farm Sizes, 1953

Farm Size	Rice Yield for Household Consumption (baht)	Income from Selling Rice (baht)	Value of Rice Yield for Household Consumption Per Total Paddy Production (%)
Less than 6 *rai*	665	13	98.1
6–15 *rai*	1,039	102	91.0
15–30 *rai*	1,198	218	84.6
30–60 *rai*	1,324	435	75.3
More than 60 *rai*	1,647	922	64.1

Source: 1953 Economic Farm Survey.

---

[118] Ibid.

In 1962–63, the proportion of rice, especially glutinous rice, for rural household consumption in the Northeast was as high as 75.9 per cent.[119] After the Green Revolution in the 1960s, the proportion of rice grown for household consumption began to decrease, and many households started to grow rice commercially. Nevertheless, such decrease was less than in other regions partly because the expansion of market economy in the Northeast took place much later than in other regions. Many villages could not sell their products due to limited transportation stemming from seasonal road conditions. Besides, farmers in many areas still grew traditional varieties of rice. A study of 24 Northeast villages found that from 1932 to 1983 farmers planted as many as 15 traditional varieties.[120] The names of these traditional varieties were coined by the villagers themselves. High-yielding or non-photosensitive varieties were adopted belatedly partly due to their confidence in the traditional varieties long produced from local wisdom along with their own developed new varieties that made them reluctant to accept new varieties. Furthermore, irrigated areas in the Northeast were limited leading to lower productivity from traditional varieties. Once the high-yielding varieties of rice that could be harvested in a shorter period of time became popular in the Northeast, farmers began to produce them commercially while cultivation for household consumption declined. Expansion of commercial rice cultivation also reduced communal labour since expedited cultivation could be achieved much more efficiently by hired labourers.

One survey of village economy covering some 1,574 households in 12 villages in ten Northeastern provinces found that more than half (57.4 per cent) of all households hired agricultural workers.[121] Agricultural technology was increasingly adopted at a rapid pace: the number of households using tractors rose from 2,152 in 1978 to 22,776 in 1997, tillers increased from 13,196 to 0.288 million, water pumps increased

---

[119] Silcock (1967, p. 237).
[120] Suwit (2003, p. 290).
[121] Ibid., p. 305.

from 45,352 to 0.402 million, rice thrashers increased from 1,216 to 7,646.[122] Massive expansion of agricultural technology especially after 1987 signified the diffusion of labour-saving technology to replace increasingly costly workers. To further complicate the situation, population birth rate had continually decreased while the younger generation migrated from the villages to seek higher pay in manufacturing plants and the urban service sector.

Commercial agricultural growth resulted in increasing utilization of fertilizers and insecticides. Expenses for wage labour, fertilizers, and insecticides accounted for half of the total production cost.[123] Economic growth affected not only production costs that continued to increase, but also consumption expenses as consumption demand had spread among farmers, especially those living near urban areas or in rural areas with easy access to information from radio and television. While total expenses kept increasing, the price of agricultural produce did not increase accordingly. As a result, agricultural households became heavily indebted.[124] The 2003 Agricultural Census shows that most of their debts ranged from 20,001 to 50,000 baht, representing 60 per cent of agricultural households in the Northeast with debt.[125]

Low income in the agricultural sector together with indebtedness, drought, and restricted job opportunities in this sector pushed the younger generation in the village to seek income outside agriculture. Non-agricultural income, therefore, constituted a high proportion of the total income of agricultural households. In 1978 the average total income of Northern agricultural households was 15,210 baht whereas the average income from non-agricultural activities was 9,032 baht, or

---

[122] Ibid., p. 287.

[123] Ibid., p. 342.

[124] Ibid., p. 354. In 2003, around 65 per cent of agricultural households were in debts (approximately 1.7 million households): 1.37 million households had agricultural debts, 0.125 million households had non-agriculture debts, and 0.241 million households had debts for both. Major sources of loans were the Bank for Agriculture and Agricultural Cooperatives and the village fund (2003 Agricultural Census).

[125] 2003 Agricultural Census.

59.4 per cent of the total income.[126] Such proportion rose very quickly. In 2009–10 cash income from the non-agricultural sector accounted for 81 per cent of all cash income — a very large proportion in comparison to other regions. In 2009–10, the proportion was 52 per cent in the North, 57 per cent in the Central, and 38 per cent in the South.[127] Non-agricultural income was, therefore, a determiner of stability in household income in the Northeast. This situation differed from the past when the stability of the farmer's total income depended upon the supply factor, mainly the harvest. But for the past three decades it was the growth of the total household income that relied upon the external demand factor, mainly the growth of the urban economic sector.

The expanded cultivation of other field crops had increasingly replaced rice. In the beginning it led to higher incomes but at the same time it greatly affected land quality. For instance, sugarcane and cassava, and later eucalyptus (in the 1990s) all greatly reduced land productivity. Field crop expansion also led to the increasing number of hired farm labourers that continued to replace household labour, thus disrupting village life. Rural tradition and culture such as household collaboration in rice production was continually undermined.[128]

The increasing number of household members becoming hired farm labourers in the Northeast was a distinctive characteristic of economic change from an agricultural economy to a market economy. In 2003 there were 1.39 million households whose members were hired in farm activities, amounting to 2.11 million household members (averaging 1.6 household members being hired per household). Hired farm labour in the Northeast accounted for 49.9 per cent of all hired farm labour in the country, which was the highest proportion, followed by the North (27.9 per cent), the Central (13.5 per cent), and the South (8.7 per cent), respectively.[129] These hired farm labour worked in the Northeast and in other regions as well. The four provinces with the largest number

---

[126] World Bank (1983, p. 116).
[127] Basic Agricultural Economic Data for the Year 2010.
[128] See Chatthip and Pornpilai (1998, pp. 57–122).
[129] 2003 Agricultural Census.

of hired farm labour were Nakhon Ratchasima (0.254 million), Khon Kaen (0.175 million), Chaiyaphum (0.166 million), and Udon Thani (0.144 million).[130] These figures reflected low agricultural productivity as well as low income combined pushed these workers to become hired labourers. Thus, it could be argued that hired farm labour from the Northeast had an important role in Thailand's agricultural economic development in every region.

Ever since the Northeast began to develop its economy in the 1960s, its natural resource has continued to be degraded. The Northeastern forests had alarmingly shrunk from 45.91 per cent in 1971 to 12.43 per cent in 1998. In 1971, before natural resources began their tremendous degradation, Northeastern forests covering 78,153 square km could produce 817,479 cubic metres of wood that could be processed into 128,141 cubic metres of boards (by saw mills) as well as 43,653 cubic metres of charcoal for household usage.[131] Furthermore, the forest had been a source of food and medicine with great biodiversity as well as a habitat for a large variety of animals.

Deforestation was caused by many factors. The major factor was the economic development of the agricultural sector that focused on profit-making commercial monoculture driven by the construction of roads linking Northeastern villages which, in turn, had encouraged land expansion and reclamation. Tractors and other agricultural machinery had a great effect upon arable land expansion. Illegal logging coupled with timber concessions also caused widespread deforestation. Many hills in the Northeast were denuded. Previously fertile forests in many areas became "vacant land" from encroachment and were subsequently wiped out.

The government's development projects involving construction of dams and reservoirs also caused deforestation. Dams constructed in the Northeast during the 1960s with massive investment included the Sirindhorn, Lam Phra Phloeng, Nam Un, and Chulabhorn. Later, numerous weirs and reservoirs were built. Such irrigation projects

---

[130] Ibid.
[131] Donner (1978, p. 615).

could supply water to two million *rai* or 5.41 per cent of the agricultural land,[132] but did very little to increase the output. Dam construction technology was not appropriate for the Northeast's topography because "... the sandy loam soil structure could not absorb water for a long period of time with the almost impermeable hardpan resulting in low water containment coupled with the saline soil problem all over the Northeast ..."[133] Benefits were much lower than the expected target. Moreover, construction of dams, particularly the Pak Mun Dam, devastated natural fertility as well as the farmers' self-reliance. In fact, farmers in the past had the wisdom of superior water management and environmental protection; they utilized the dikes around the rice fields along with weirs and shallow wells as small reservoirs. Dam construction caused the obstruction of water outlets resulting in the extinction of many fish species, degraded biodiversity, and decreased natural fishery output.[134] An impact study of the construction of Rasi Salai Dam (construction began in 1992) in Si Sa Ket Province indicated that as many as 7,856 households had lost their rice fields, 46,937 *rai* of rice fields in nine subdistricts were flooded, rice output dropped, while major household income mainly from agriculture decreased by 11,520 baht per annum, which was equivalent to 546 million baht per annum. Furthermore, Rasi Salai Dam construction resulted in the loss of pasture and forested areas rich in biodiversity.[135]

Dam construction across the Mekong in China and Laos also resulted in the loss of various natural resources and environmental problems. The Mekong greatly influenced livelihoods involving natural and resource base of the Northeast (including China and neighbouring countries of Laos, Cambodia, and Vietnam). The Mekong flows through several districts in the seven Northeastern provinces: Ubon Ratchathani, Amnat Charoen, Nakhon Phanom, Bueng Kan, Nong Khai, Mukdahan,

---

[132] Sanun (2013*b*, p. 90).
[133] Ibid.
[134] *Thang Isan* (2012, p. 38).
[135] Sanun (2013*a*, p. 28).

and Loei. People living along the river banks were engaged in either fishery or agriculture, and some were employed in tourism. Interviews of farmers in Chiang Khan, Loei Province reported catching a total of 136 species of aquatic animals in the Mekong: 115 species of fishes, three species of crabs, four species of prawns, and seven species of mollusk.[136] The Chinese government had planned to construct more than 20 dams across the Mekong. By 2012, four dams were completed. Dam construction in China and Laos has had a major impact on the ecosystem of the entire river by disrupting its natural flow. The impact has devastated food sources, breeding grounds, and fishery resources. It had caused extinction of some aquatic animal species and eroded the river banks.[137] Village-level research pointed out that the consequence of dam construction in China and Laos was a continuing decrease in output and income.[138]

Overall, the national and regional economic development tended to grow at high levels after 1960, resulting in a decreasing proportion of the poor in the Northeast, but the number of the poor remained high. In 1960–63, the number of the poor in the Northeast accounted for 74 per cent of the region's population and sharply decreased to 44 per cent in 1975–76. In some areas farmers' income had not increased while poverty lingered.[139] Poor farmers in the Northeast were mostly those who cultivated rice for their own consumption and those in areas far from the urban areas and the markets. Among farmers who practised agriculture for the market economy, those who cultivated rice, cassava, and jute had low incomes and remained poor whereas maize farmers were a little better off.[140] In 2000, the Northeast still had the highest proportion of the poor compared to another regions:

---

[136] For full discussions, see Channarong (2004, pp. 39–49).

[137] Ibid., pp. 41–42.

[138] Ibid., p. 42.

[139] Muscat (1990, p. 287).

[140] Ibid.

36 per cent (7.2 million people) that decreased to 17.0 per cent (three million people) in 2013.[141]

For the past two decades one of the major changes was the expansion of contract farming initiated by private businesses such as raising chickens and hogs, and asparagus cultivation. Contract farming aims to minimize agricultural price fluctuation through the control of supply which resulted in sustained income and production to satisfy the market demand. Through the mechanism of price control, production costs could also be lowered with less fluctuation. However, contract farming could only fulfil a small portion of agricultural produce since it mainly focused on producing a few specialized items.

One research on contract farming in the Northeast focusing on Khon Kaen, Nong Khai and Nakhon Ratchasima in 2009 made the following findings. Firstly, investment per farm was rather high in comparison to income or revenue expected from the production. For instance, investment could range from 0.5 to one million baht. In some cases, costs could be as high as 84 to 92 per cent of the income with a long pay-back period, sometimes 20 years. Secondly, production costs involving electricity, wages, fertilizers, and pest control chemicals constituted the most important portion of the total cost. Some farmers were not able to lower costs, especially for fertilizers and chemicals. Thirdly, apart from high investment costs and operational costs that the farmers had to bear, they also had to face several major risks: (1) most farmers were oblivious of their own rights and did not possess a copy of the contract; (2) most farmers did not know how much income they really had due to the complexity of calculations; (3) the contracts did not clearly specify the party to bear the risk of floods, electricity, global warming, and uncontrollable accidents. Although some farmers could earn more income from contract farming compared to other agricultural activities or the minimum wage, the

---

[141] National Statistical Office, <www.nso.go.th>; Medhi (1986, pp. 5–21).

differences remained small. At the same time farmers had to be responsible for high levels of investment, especially fixed capital investment to the tune of a million baht. Such high investment in comparison to the low income level of agricultural households led to financial burdens (particularly long-term interest to be paid to financial institutions).

Major contract farming included raising chickens and hogs that required intensive management and care based on skills and expertise not only in raising the animals but also in general management. Many farmers lacked the necessary skills and expertise, resulting in production disasters and ended up with huge debts. Risk factors for farmers also included the following: first, farmers lacked knowledge in cost management of the farms; second, farmers might have to bear higher costs of production; third, farmers were not knowledgeable about contracts; and fourth, farmers could not collaborate as a group, and hence had no bargaining power against the buying companies.

The study also found that many farmers involved in contract farming for decades still could not say for certain that their livelihood had improved (some of them were highly in debts and wanted to switch to other occupations but were not able to do so since their capital investment was too high). The financial and market structure was such that there were few buying companies which therefore had monopoly power over the market at every stage. These companies could control factors of production such as the prices for seeds and breeding stocks, chemicals, fertilizers, and feeds, and the power to set product prices. In such a monopolized structure, farmers could hardly bargain for a better price or change the stipulations or conditions of their contracts.[142]

Farmers had to face problems of discrimination that might arise, such as the inability to acknowledge contract details while the buying companies were fully aware of them and could set the conditions. Even

---

[142] Kalapapruek et al. (2009).

if the contract were drawn in writing, farmers might fail to comprehend the complex details. In many cases, when the signing was done, the companies usually retained both copies of the contract, leaving the farmers without any evidence. To further aggravate the situation, the low socio-economic status of the farmers precluded them from setting up a joint bargaining group or to ask for fairness. They could not even organize themselves into a strong association of farmers. All of these factors led to discrimination and unfairness for farmers as partners of the buying companies.[143]

Manufacturing Industry

After the Second World War, manufactures in the Northeast were small enterprises. In the 1950s the government operated several manufacturing enterprises such as a distillery at Nakhon Ratchasima that was opened in 1948 with a capacity to produce 1,180 litres per day of rice whisky and blended whisky or 4.24 million litres employing 70 workers.[144] The government also owned tobacco factories, trading stations, and curing sheds in Nakhon Phanom and Nong Khai.[145] In 1954 wages for tobacco curing workers were as follows. At Tha Uthen in Nakhon Phanom, female workers and unskilled labourers were paid 90–100 baht per month. At Phon Phisai in Nong Khai, female workers were paid 4 baht per day; if they continued working for two years they would be paid 120 baht per month while the male workers were paid 5–6 baht per day, or 150–180 baht per month. Workers in a tobacco factory earned better wage rates: female workers at That Phanom in Nakhon Phanom were paid 123 baht per month while those working in *mueang* district of Nong Khai were paid 130 baht per month, their wages would increase if they worked more than one to two years.[146]

---

[143] Ibid.

[144] N.A. M. of Finance 0301.2.2/3 (1957).

[145] ILO (1954, p. 32).

[146] Ibid.

Rice milling, another major industrial enterprise in the Northeast, was characterized as a light and small-scale industry, labour intensive and low value added. Its production was mainly for local consumption. In 1964 there were 1,163 rice mills in the Northeast representing almost one-fifth of all rice mills in the country, with a daily capacity of not more than 5 *kwian* (1 *kwian* = 1,000 kg).[147] When compared to other regions, the Northeast had the smallest number of rice mills: the North had 1,500 mills, the South had 1,377 mills, and the Central had 2,026 mills. Daily capacity of rice mills in the Northeast in 1964 was 11,113 *kwian*, or one-seventh of the national capacity. In 1964, daily capacity of rice mills in other regions was 7,342 *kwian* in the North, 44,761 *kwian* in the Central, and 8,161 *kwian* in the South.[148]

There are no statistics for factories and various manufactures for the Northeast in 1957; they are available only for certain provinces. Nakhon Ratchasima, the Northeast's most developed province at the time, had 415 rice mills (excluding small rice mills at the village and subdistrict levels), 15 sawmills, three ice factories, 35 sugar mills, three pottery and cement factories, two beverage producers, one rock quarry, one distillery, one rubber products factory, one flour mill, one timber business, and one other manufacture[149] as well as one gunny-bag factory, one power plant, one waterworks, one printing house, 21 building construction plants, and 19 other construction plants, totalling 510 manufacturing enterprises (see Table 6.14). The 415 rice mills were the largest employers with more than 10,000 workers whereas the 35 sugar mills employed 1,410 workers, and the gunny-bag factory employed 1,000 workers.[150] Pak Thong Chai District, a major sugarcane producer, had 70 per cent of the provincial land under sugarcane (37,000 *rai* in 1959). The district was also the location for 35 sugar mills, 32 of which produced only brown sugar.

[147] Silcock (1970, p. 67).
[148] Ibid.
[149] USOM (1960, p. 35).
[150] Ibid., pp. 36–37.

TABLE 6.14
Number of Manufacturing Plants in Nakhon Ratchasima, Khon Kaen, and Udon Thani, 1960

Manufactures	Nakhon Ratchasima	Khon Kaen	Udon Thani
Pottery, cement	3	7	1
Quarry	1	11	2
Ice	7	3	–
Beverages	2	–	–
Rubber products	1	–	–
Flour mill	1	–	–
Distillery	1	–	–
Wood products	1	–	–
Rice mills	415	252	388
Saw mills	16	13	3
Gunny-bag factory	1	–	–
Power plant	13	8	4
Waterworks	1	2	–
Printing and publishing	6	9	–
Building construction	21	4	–
Other construction	9	12	1
Sugar mill	35	–	54
Tannery	–	1	–
Jewelry	–	13	–
Other	–	4	–

Source: Compiled from USOM (1960).

The gunny-bag factory in Nakhon Ratchasima was the major producer in the country. In 1959 it could produce 1.76 million bags, 1.5 million each in 1956 and 1957, and 1.9 million in 1958. In 1960 it could produce 2.3 million gunny-bags.[151] This factory bought jute from Bua Yai and *mueang* district in Chaiyaphum Province. About half of the gunny-bags were for rice packing. Out of one-fifth of the rest of the bags, 10 per cent were sold in Nakhon Ratchasima and the other 90 per cent were sold to Bangkok for sugar packing. The rice mills employed 1,000 workers, 800 of whom were females and semi-skilled workers who were paid 10 baht per day. The manufacturing sector (including construction and utilities) generated one-third of the total revenue from non-agricultural business.[152] At Khon Kaen, apart from rice mills and saw mills which were major manufactures, there was also a jute processing plant. At Udon Thani, apart from rice mills which were the province's major manufacture, there were also 54 sugar mills generating 26.4 per cent of the revenue from manufacturing and non-agricultural services. Such revenue was second only to rice mills (rice mills had a revenue of 35 per cent of the total non-agricultural earning).

Manufactures in the three provinces were small and light industrial plants, including the home industry with a small employment and contributing small value-added to the regional economy. Overall, Nakhon Ratchasima's manufacturing sector was more developed than Khon Kaen's. Udon Thani (with the exception of the sugar mills) was less developed than Nakhon Ratchasima and Khon Kaen.[153] Nakhon Ratchasima had a moderate level of revenue from non-agricultural sector but was higher than Khon Kaen and Udon Thani. Its revenue from the manufacturing sector (including the service sector) was 672.62 million baht or 685 baht per capita, making it a middle-income province with 4 per cent of the country's population.

---

[151] Ibid., p. 34.
[152] Ibid., pp. 35–37.
[153] Ibid., p. 34.

Its revenue from business tax in 1959 constituted 1 per cent of the country's tax.[154]

Revenues from sales in Khon Kaen were 452 million baht or 540 baht per capita. Khon Kaen's population was 1.15 per cent of Thailand's population. The collected business tax constituted only 1 per cent. Udon Thani had a per capita revenue of 300 baht.[155] The proportion of Nakhon Ratchasima's manufacturing revenue constituted one-third of non-agricultural revenues, 20 per cent of which were generated by rice mills. The proportion of manufacturing revenue in Khon Kaen was 28.7 per cent, 25.7 per cent of which were from rice mills. Udon Thani's manufacturing revenue was 69.8 per cent, 34.99 per cent of which were from rice mills and another 26.14 per cent from sugar mills.[156]

Although the manufacturing sector was small and could generate small revenues and employment, there were signs of expansion to accommodate accelerated growth in some provinces such as Nakhon Ratchasima. After the opening of the Friendship Highway in 1958, the number of vehicles rapidly rose. From 31 December 1957 to 26 April 1960, the number of buses increased from 170 to 270, private cars from 180 to 244, and trucks from 296 to 640. Gasoline sales also increased from 5.5 million litres to 10.6 million litres in 1957–59.[157]

In 1964 there were some 440 manufacturing plants in the Northeast, each employing more than ten people, totalling 21,592 workers. In 1970 the number of manufacturing plants rose to 541 with 21,194 employees. Such statistics do not reflect the actual number since they do not take into account the small-scale home businesses.[158] The 1970 Population Census reports some 78,332 workers in the Northeast's manufacturing sector, as shown in Table 6.15.

---

[154] Ibid., p. 35.
[155] Ibid., p. 58.
[156] Ibid., p. 45.
[157] Ibid., p. 27.
[158] Donner (1978, p. 640).

TABLE 6.15
Manufacturing Industry and Employment in the Northeast, 1970

Main Branch	Employed Workers	Major Provinces
Textiles	32,697	Nakhon Ratchasima, Khon Kaen
Food, beverages, and tobacco	14,964	Nakhon Ratchasima, Ubon Ratchathani, Khon Kaen
Wood and furniture	12,551	Khon Kaen, Nakhon Ratchasima, and Ubon Ratchathani
Non-metallic products	3,727	Surin, Khon Kaen, Nakhon Ratchasima, and Buri Ram
Printing and publishing	711	Nakhon Ratchasima
Chemicals	605	Khon Kaen
Other metal products	13,077	Khon Kaen, Nakhon Ratchasima, and Udon Thani

Source: Donner (1978, p. 640).

From 1947 to 1980 the number of workers in the manufacturing industry was only 1.3 per cent of the total labour force in the Northeast, and it shows a slight increase to 1.9 per cent in 1980.[159] More than 90 per cent of the factories in the Northeast produced food, beverages, tobacco, and textiles, employing approximately 40–50 per cent of the region's manufacturing workers. After the 1980s the numbers of factories, registered capital, and workers continued to grow considerably (see Table 6.16).

---

[159] 1980 Population Census.

TABLE 6.16
Number of Manufacturing Plants in the Northeast, 1980–2010

Category	1980	1990	2002	2005	2007	2010
No. of factories	12,943	40,490	41,976	41,220	41,920	42,408
Registered capital (million baht)	411.74	1,904.9	195,764	232,894	296,378	333,138
No. of employed workers	61,043	138,698	324,575	338,704	361,075	386,442

Source: *Statistical Yearbook of Thailand* (various years).

The growth of manufacturing factories in the Northeast was related to the expansion of agro-industry such as rice mills, sugar mills, and tapioca flour mills. It was necessary that these mills were located close to the sources of their raw materials as it was difficult for them to be transported over long distances. In 2000 there were 485 rice mills in the Northeast (269 large mills and 189 medium-sized mills) but the number decreased to 412 in 2008 (355 large mills and 57 medium-sized mills). The capacity of large mills was 13,240 tonnes in 2000 and this increased to 53,633 tonnes in 2008. The medium-sized mills had an average capacity of 1,591 tonnes that sharply dropped to 551 tonnes (see Table 6.17). This was probably due to the growth of medium-sized mills into large mills.[160]

In 1996–2006 the number of manufacturing establishments increased from 33,258 to 215,295, more than 95 per cent of which were small factories with one to five workers. In 1996 there were 17,398 textile and leather factories (52.3 per cent), followed by 8,125 food, beverages, and tobacco factories (24.4 per cent). In 2006 beverages and tobacco production dominated the manufacturing sector with 73,983 factories (34.3 per cent), followed by 30,596 textile and leather factories (14.2 per cent). Wood products manufacture jumped from 1,806 to 29,682 factories, representing a 16.4-fold increase in ten years (see Table 6.18). These figures illustrate the dominance of agro-industry in the rural area that needed to be located near sources of raw materials and the labour pool.

---

[160] Somporn (2010, p. 88).

TABLE 6.17
Number of Rice Mills and Production Capacity in the Northeast, 2008

Province	No. of Rice Mills	Total Production Capacity (tonne/day)	Average Capacity (tonne/day/mill)
Nakhon Ratchasima	58	7,178	123.7
Buri Ram	32	3,701	115.6
Surin	53	10,631	200.5
Si Sa Ket	31	3,784	122.0
Ubon Ratchathani	52	8,265	158.9
Yasothon	19	2,676	140.8
Chaiyaphum	11	473	43.0
Khon Kaen	28	2,849	109.5
Udon Thani	27	2,997	111.0
Loei	2	66	33.0
Nong Khai	8	726	90.7
Maha Sarakham	8	1,001	125.1
Roi Et	22	5,098	231.7
Kalasin	19	1,421	74.7
Sakhon Nakhon	17	677	39.8
Nakhon Phanom	7	500	71.4
Mukdahan	7	385	55.0
Nong Bua Lam Phu	4	490	122.5
Amnat Charoen	9	1,268	140.6
Northeastern Region	412	54,184	131.5

Source: Somporn (2010, p. 103).

TABLE 6.18
Number of Manufacturing Establishments in the Northeast, 1996 and 2006

Manufacturing Type	1996	2006
Food, beverages, tobacco	8,125	73,983
Textile, leather	17,398	30,569
Wood products	1,806	29,682
Paper and printing	434	872
Chemicals and petroleum	297	914
Metal products	1,027	1,098
Basic metals	150	111
Metal and machinery	3,419	8,003
Others	472	8,339
Total	33,258	215,295

Source: 1997 and 2007 Industrial Censuses, Northeastern Region.

During 1996–2006 the number of manufacturing establishments with 11 workers or more increased very rapidly, from 1,941 to 5,970, representing a 207.6 per cent increase while the number of workers increased by 142.7 per cent (if establishments with more than one employee in 2006 were taken into account, there would have been 0.215 million establishments). On the other hand, the average number of workers per establishment dropped from 63 to 50 (a 20.9 per cent decrease), as a result of human labour being substituted by machinery[161] (see Table 6.19).

---

[161] If all establishments with more than one employee were taken into account, there would be 0.215 million manufacturing establishments in the Northeast in 2006. Most of these establishments were small enterprises (about 98.2 per cent) employing one to five people. Food and beverages industry was the largest group (34.4 per cent), followed by textiles (30.1 per cent). There was a total of 0.6 million workers, 0.4 million of whom were regularly employed (79 per cent) while 21 per cent were employed seasonally. Manufactures with high seasonal employment were tobacco products (92 per cent of all employment), followed by non-metal products (37.7 per cent), wood and products of wood and cork (except furniture), manufacture of articles of straw and plaiting materials (30.2 per cent) (2007 Industrial Census, Northeastern Region).

TABLE 6.19
Manufacturing Establishments in the Northeast, 1996 and 2006

Category	1996[1]	2006[2]	Per Cent Change
No. of establishments	1,941	5,970	207.6
No. of persons engaged ('000)	125.7	305.0	142.7
Average employees per establishment	64.8	51.1	21.1
No. of employees ('000)	122.4	297.7	143.1
Average employees per establishment	63.1	49.9	20.9
Remuneration (million baht)	6,571.8	19,497.1	196.7
Average remuneration per person per year (baht)	53,658.3	65,487.6	22.0

Notes: [1] Establishment with more than 10 employees.
           [2] Establishment with more than 11 employees.
Source: 1997 and 2007 Industrial Censuses, Northeastern Region.

The distinctive feature of manufacturing in the Northeast was that most of the industrial workers were unpaid family members. In 2006 these workers constituted 43.2 per cent of the total manufacturing workforce. If classified by the level of skills in the production process, there would be 64.1 per cent of skilled labour and 35.9 per cent of unskilled labour. Such a high proportion of skilled labour was partly due to the upgrading and technological development of production that required higher skilled labour.[162]

Manufacturing plants in the Northeast had a high concentration in Nakhon Ratchasima, Khon Kaen, Udon Thani, and Ubon Ratchathani,

---

[162] The average enterprise value-added and the average per capita value-added in the Northeast were the lowest in the country in 1996 and 2006 (except 2007 when the Northeast's per capita value-added was slightly higher than the North's). In 2007 the average value-added per enterprise was 0.329 million baht in the Northeast, 0.456 million baht in the North, 14.1 million baht in the Central, 2.26 million baht in the South, 3.8 million baht in Bangkok, and 23.05 million baht in the vicinity of Bangkok. In the same year, the average value-added per worker in the Northeast was 0.11 million baht, 0.107 million baht in the North, 0.58 million baht in the Central, 0.346 million baht in the South, 0.378 million baht in Bangkok, and 0.482 baht in Bangkok and its vicinity (2007 Industrial Census, Northeastern Region).

indicating spatial inequality within the region. In 1987–2008, the proportion of manufacturing plants in the four provinces ranged from 46.2 to 48.3 per cent of the regional plants. Investments in the four provinces totalled 71 per cent of regional investment. In 2008 these four provinces had a total employment of 0.21 million workers or 57.8 per cent of the regional employment (see Table 6.20). The figures in Table 6.20 indicate large provincial differences in the concentration of manufacturing plants: 7,299 in Nakhon Ratchasima with 0.117 million employees whereas some provinces i.e. Nakhon Phanom, Mukdahan, and Yasothon had a total of 1,667 plants with 7,325 workers.

TABLE 6.20
Number of Manufacturing Plants in the Northeast, 2008

Province	No. of Plants	Capital Investment (million baht)	No. of Employed Workers		
			Male	Female	Total
Nakhon Ratchasima	7,299	112.1	64,628	52,496	117,124
Buri Ram	1,551	6.9	7,672	6,632	14,204
Surin	1,117	10.4	6,275	3,267	9,542
Si Sa Ket	1,902	3.0	5,053	1,480	6,533
Ubon Ratchathani	4,069	19.0	11,657	5,705	16,762
Yasothon	902	1.8	2,893	1,403	4,296
Chaiyaphum	1,660	13.6	12,205	33,056	45,261
Amnat Charoen	310	1.7	1,575	802	2,377
Nong Bua Lamphu	1,209	16.8	3,587	693	4,280
Khon Kaen	4,808	73.8	27,729	26,282	54,011
Udon Thani	4,006	13.9	15,079	7,893	22,972
Loei	1,005	2.4	3,883	923	4,806
Nong Khai	1,169	2.7	4,424	1,670	6,094
Maha Sarakham	2,398	6.8	7,775	6,094	13,860
Roi Et	3,226	6.1	7,095	3,686	10,754
Kalasin	2,011	6.7	16,741	1,680	18,421
Sakhon Nakhon	2,296	2.5	6,468	1,145	6,613
Nakhon Phanom	340	1.8	2,375	1,444	3,819
Mukdahan	425	4.7	2,057	1,029	3,086
The Northeast	41,705	307.5	207,474	157,356	364,824

Source: *Statistical Yearbook of Thailand* (2010).

Services

The beginning of the 1960s saw only a small service sector in the Northeast. However, growth took place in three provinces: Nakhon Ratchasima, Khon Kaen, and Udon Thani, as illustrated in Table 6.21.

TABLE 6.21
Number of Commercial and Service Establishments in
Nakhon Ratchasima, Khon Kaen, and Udon Thani, 1960

Category	Nakhon Ratchasima	Khon Kaen	Udon Thani
Tailoring	385	285	264
Garage	9	12	4
Machine shop	4	3	1
Other	250	90	18
Shops: wholesale and retail	3,515	2,833	1,092
Photography	24	16	10
Advertising	4	3	–
Rental (excluding real estate)	7	10	1
Warehousing	3	–	–
Hotels, boarding houses	44	29	1
Restaurants	403	322	71
Transport	122	149	64
Hospitals	1	1	–
Entertainment	10	6	2
Agents, brokers	20	36	–
Banking	5	5	3
Total	4,806	3,800	1,531

Source: Complied from USOM (1960).

There were a total of 10,137 business and service establishments in Nakhon Ratchasima, Khon Kaen, and Udon Thani. Nakhon Ratchasima had the highest number of establishments: 47 per cent. The service sector generated approximately two-thirds of the revenue from all non-agricultural sectors in Nakhon Ratchasima and Khon Kaen. The proportion for Udon Thani was lower because the sugar mills dominated 26 per cent of its non-agricultural sector.[163]

The service sector was an important employment source and had an increasing share in the GRP. The 1970 Population Census reports the distribution of employees in the various services as follows: 47,300 in transportation and warehousing and 0.388 million in commerce and services (there were 210,410 working in the service sector: 81,820 in public administration, 54,321 in education, 7,931 in health services, and 27,265 in restaurants, hotels, cinemas, and tourism).[164]

The Northeast's service sector grew partly because of the contracting agricultural sector from the latter part of the 1980s, as a result of the inability to expand arable land. The service sector, thus, became the new source of employment for agricultural workers. Expansion of the manufacturing sector also played an important role in the growth of the service sector. In 2010 there were 0.4 million commercial and service establishments employing almost a million people, 0.344 million of whom were employees in various enterprises (36.8 per cent of all workers), the rest were non-paid workers in small enterprises with 1–15 employees. These small enterprises comprised the largest proportion, or 99.2 per cent of all establishments, employing 0.796 million people or 85.1 per cent of all workers. All these commercial and service establishments contributed 178 billion baht to the economy of the Northeast (see Table 6.22).

---

[163] USOM (1960, p. 58).
[164] Donner (1978, pp. 644–45).

TABLE 6.22
Commercial and Service Establishments in the Northeast by Size, 2010

| Establishment Size | No. of Establishments | No. of Workers | Employees | | Value-Added ('000 baht) |
			No.	Remuneration ('000 baht)	
1–15	399,779	796,041	236,178	11,868.5	127,221.6
16–25	1,719	35,193	26,892	1,606.2	7,355.0
26–30	205	5,719	4,553	311.0	1,311.9
31–50	579	22,613	18,327	1,438.3	13,099.6
51–200	689	62,630	45,605	3,641.7	23,827.3
More than 200	48	13,320	13,299	1,616.5	5,194.3
Total	493,019	935,516	344,854	20,482.4	178,009.9

Source: 2010 Business and Trade Survey, Northeastern Region.

Tourism in the Northeast has continued to increase in importance because of distinctive ruins and numerous historical attractions such as *Prasat* Phanom Rung, *Prasat* Hin Phimai, and *Khao Phra Wihan*. Easy access to neighbouring countries, such as Laos and Cambodia, also helped. Moreover, there are cultural tourist attractions in several provinces such as the Elephant Round-up in Surin, *Ngan Bun Bung Fai* in Yasothon, Procession of the Buddhist Lent Candles in Ubon Ratchathani, *Ngan Bung Fai Phaya Nak* in Nong Khai, and other tourist attractions along the Mekong. Natural attractions include Khao Yai National Park, Phu Luang, Phu Ruea, and Phu Kradueng. Cultural tourism is also important. Although tourism in the Northeast had not generated revenues and employment to the same extent as the South or the North, the number of tourists continued to grow leading to the construction of more hotels. In 2009 there were 22.2 million tourists visiting the Northeast, generating 33,876.9 million baht in revenue. Hotels and other accommodations in the Northeast also grew. In 1994 there were 415 hotels and other accommodations with 18,162 rooms that continued to increase. In 2006 there were 727 hotels with 32,307 rooms.[165]

Highways and the Integration of the Northeast's Economy

As mentioned earlier, up until the Second World War there was no road connecting Bangkok to the Northeast. Travelling from the Northeast to Bangkok was by rail or carts. Indeed, railways enabled the Northeast's economy to be linked with Bangkok. It also stimulated the expansion of trade between the two regions. Some of the goods from the Northeast such as pork were regularly exported to Bangkok and they gained a fair share of the Bangkok market very quickly. By 1906 it had more than 80 per cent of the Bangkok pork market, increasing from 39 per cent in 1901.[166]

---

[165] *Statistical Yearbook of Thailand* (various years).
[166] Kakizaki (2007, p. 24).

The expansion of highways after the Second World War was the factor that accelerated commercial production to replace subsistence production because the villagers could now have easy access to markets by the new roads. Highways also led to lower transportation costs per unit while carrying large volumes. Road transportation thus quickly replaced rail transportation due to increased efficiency both in speed and capacity. The immediate effect of the opening of the Friendship Highway in 1958 was the decrease in the number of passengers, goods, and livestocks that went by rail, reducing the revenue of the State Railway of Thailand to almost 11 million baht compared to 1957, "[A]lthough general trade recession was also blamed for the drop in revenue".[167] Roads also affected transportation costs, enabled all season accessibility to villages, increased the number of trucks and other transport vehicles, saved travelling time, as well as lowered the losses through perishability of agricultural produce since roads could be used at all times. Speedy movements to destinations coupled with lower costs resulted in market expansion. Apart from upland crops, road expansion also led to increased cultivation of vegetables, fruits, beans, etc., enabling farmers to earn higher revenues (net income) while consumers enjoyed lower prices. Increased revenues led to increased demand for fabricated goods from Bangkok. In the 1960s, industrialization was geared towards import-substitution. Goods from Bangkok began to dominate markets in the Northeast. Locally-made goods, including consumer goods for daily life, began to fade away. Garments, radio sets, bicycles, and other durable goods such as plates, bowls, and plastic buckets flooded the Northeast market. In 1968 one-third of households in the Northeast had their own looms and one-tenth had mat-making tools. By 1975 only a small percentage still owned looms and wove their own mats.[168] Such changes were widespread in the lower Northeast which is closer to Bangkok while the upper Northeast had a slower decline.

---

[167] USOM (1960, p. 6).
[168] Nipon (1983, pp. 5 (2)–37) and the World Bank (1983).

Despite the expansion of factories in the Northeast, a study conducted by Somluckrat Wattanavitukul (1989) found that even though the rural population could earn higher real income, the demand for goods and services at the regional or the rural level was lower than expected. Most households bought fabricated goods from Bangkok and its vicinity. Increased household income, in fact, had significantly stimulated production activities in the service sector rather than the manufacturing sector.[169]

The Northeast's economy had been increasingly integrated to Bangkok's while experiencing the expansion in agriculture, manufactures, and services as a result of the expanded road network connecting the villages. Provincial commercial banks expanded to facilitate economic growth. In 1957 there were only 12 branches of commercial banks in the region, ten of which were concentrated in only four provinces: three each in Nakhon Ratchasima and Udon Thani, and two each in Khon Kaen and Ubon Ratchathani. The other two branches were in Surin and Nong Khai while nine other provinces did not have any commercial banks at all.[170] However, in 1961 — the beginning of the National Economic Development Plan — the number of commercial bank branches had grown to 40 and continued to grow to 135 in 1976 and 402 in 1993, with most of them clustering in the above four provinces. During the same period, deposits and loans also grew rapidly. Deposits increased from seven billion baht in 1976 to 34 billion baht in 1984 and 115 billion baht in 1992 while loans grew from 2.3 billion baht to 30 billion baht and 103 billion baht, during the same period.[171]

Growth of commercial bank branches, deposits, and loans in the Northeast had funnelled surpluses to Bangkok and thus supported the industrial and service sector development in Bangkok more than in the rural areas.[172] This was particularly true during the expansion of the agricultural sector in the region in the 1970s when more loans and technology were needed to encourage higher production. But the loans were much smaller than what they should have been, as with

---

[169] Somluckrat cited by Nipon (1995, p. 129).
[170] Suwit and Dararat (1998, p. 120).
[171] Ibid., p. 121.
[172] Ammar (1975, p. 41).

other regions in Thailand. Not more than 3 per cent of all loans were allocated to the Northeast's agricultural sector. Most of the retail and wholesale trade, manufacturing, as well as exports and imports were concentrated in Bangkok, accounting for 65–70 per cent of the total loan.[173] Such figures clearly show that commercial banks overlooked the social rate of return of the agricultural sector as the largest employment provider. They also emphasized strategies for imbalanced growth amongst the various economic sectors.

Road expansion in the Northeast not only stimulated the movement of resources in the forms of goods and capital to Bangkok, but also migration of the villagers which was part of the regional economic merging. Prior to 1977, rural migration to Bangkok was dominated by migrants from the Central Region. From 1977, the situation changed. Migrants from the Northeast overtook their Central Region counterparts and have remained the largest group of migrants, indicating the declining role of distance while economic and other factors have gained dominance. Road expansion, therefore, effectively linked Bangkok — the country's economic region with high productivity and high levels of income in the manufacturing and service sectors — to the Northeast with a high concentration of people in the agricultural sector that had low productivity and low levels of income. Labour migration from the Northeast, thus, was the significant factor contributing to the urban growth of Bangkok.

Border Trade

Trade along the Northeast border had increased significantly. Trade, especially with Laos, was important to the Northeast, which also borders Cambodia. Several Northeastern provinces are located along the Mekong, the natural border between Thailand and Laos. These provinces are Loei, Nong Khai, Ubon Ratchathani, Nakhon Phanom, Mukdahan, Bueng Kan, and Amnat Charoen. Border trade through

---

[173] Rungsun (1976, p. 249).

checkpoints had been in existence for a long time partly because of limited domestic transportation in the past. Such geographic limitation facilitated trade between the Northeast and the neighbouring countries, particularly Laos, while the value of trade with Cambodia was less than with Laos.

The 1960 report by USOM indicated that border trade at Nong Khai, particularly at the *mueang* Nong Khai Municipality customs checkpoint was the most vital compared to other checkpoints since it was the break-of-bulk point for Vientiane, the capital city of Laos.[174] Other checkpoints for exports and imports at Nong Khai included Si Chiang Mai, Tha Bo, and Bueng Kan (which at that time was a district in Nong Khai). The total value of exports to Laos at checkpoints in Nong Khai was 268.5 million baht in 1958 and 183.3 million baht in 1959. Imports from Laos to Thailand were 31.17 million baht in 1958 and 15.14 million baht in 1959. Eighty per cent of such exports and imports were handled at *mueang* Nong Khai Municipality Checkpoint.[175] However, trade with Laos diminished after its change to the socialist system of government in 1975.

It was not until 1988 that border trade was revitalized when General Chatichai Choonhavan's government introduced the policy to "change the battlefields into market places". The Thai–Lao Friendship Bridge was constructed and officially opened in 1994 resulting in the expansion of trade and tourism, especially the increase of foreign tourists. Nong Khai was suddenly a major tourist destination for both domestic and international tourists as well as tourists crossing to other Indochina countries.[176]

Similar to the North, the 1990s was pivotal to trade development in the Northeast, particularly between the region and Laos under "The Greater Mekong Subregion (GMS) Economic Cooperation Program" involving six countries: Thailand, Myanmar, Laos, Cambodia, Vietnam, and China. This cooperation programme was initiated by the Asian Development

---

[174] USOM (1960, p. 67).
[175] Ibid., p. 68.
[176] Chuthatip and Wu (2004, p. 149).

Bank. One of its important plans was the development of the East–West Economic Corridor (EWEC) by constructing 1,500-km of highways linking the six countries from Myanmar's Andaman Coast to Danang Port in central Vietnam, passing through Khon Kaen and Sawannakhet. Another plan was the Southern Economic Corridor linking Thailand, Cambodia and Vietnam. After the completion of these routes, transport volumes and economic activities with connections to other activities along the border were expected to increase. Furthermore, the Program also encouraged the introduction of policies and measures to enhance the movement of goods under the cooperation of various countries in the region. The Northeast was expected to benefit from the Program with its enormous capital investment to strengthen trade and increase investment.[177]

Border trade continued to grow, especially with Laos. For instance, three years after the GMS agreement the value of Thai–Lao border trade (in the Northeast) in 1995 was 9.87 billion baht, representing a 28.3 per cent increase from 7.69 billion baht in 1994 (or an increase of 40 per cent when compared to 1993). In 1994–95 border trade of the Northeast increased at almost every checkpoint (e.g. 5.6 per cent at Nong Khai checkpoint, 11.3 per cent at Mukdahan, 2.6 per cent at Chong Mek, 70.3 per cent at Nakhon Phanom, and 49.5 per cent at Chiang Khan[178]).

In 2004 the value of border trade at the Northeast's checkpoints amounted to 22.2 billion baht, a 2.72-fold increase from 1994, representing 94.38 per cent of all the Thai–Lao border trade. The value of Thai exports to Laos was 18.0 billion baht whereas imports were 4,599 million baht, a 13,414 million baht trade surplus. Nong Khai had the highest proportion of border trade (41.83 per cent), followed by Mukdahan (24.66 per cent), Ubon Ratchathani (14.8 per cent), Nakhon Phanom (8.18 per cent), and Loei (5.53 per cent).[179] In 2004

---

[177] See World Bank (2005, pp. 132–33).
[178] Bank of Thailand, Northeastern Office (2005).
[179] Ibid.

the Thai–Lao border trade of major exports from the Northeast consisted of petroleum products (17.6 per cent); consumer goods (16.5 per cent); cars, motorcycles, and spare parts (8.6 per cent); construction materials (7.1 per cent); and electrical appliances (6.6 per cent). On the other hand imports to Thailand consisted of processed wood and wood products (72.7 per cent); vehicles and parts for tractors, dump trucks, and (used) pick-up trucks (9.5 per cent); and agricultural produce (field crops) (8.5 per cent). In 2008 the value of border trade between Thailand and Cambodia was 51.0 billion baht with a trade surplus of 44.6 billion baht for Thailand. On the other hand, the value of border trade with Laos was 75.2 billion baht with a 36.7 billion baht trade surplus for Thailand.[180]

Expansion of border trade between the Northeast and Laos was a significant turning point for the Northeast's economy that had continued to grow, especially since the early 2000s. Economic growth in the Northeast for the past decade, a direct consequence of the border trade, led to increases in the prices of land and construction in provinces along the Mekong. However, construction of condominiums and housing estates in many Northeastern provinces continued to expand. At the same time, the service sector also expanded with new shopping centres and hospitals in Udon Thani and Khon Kaen, resulting from an increase in revenue from expanding border trade as well as entrepreneurs preparing for the ASEAN Economic Community (AEC). Indeed, the growth in border trade had widespread impacts.

A fieldwork study conducted by Professor Suvit Teerasaswat on the impacts of the Second Thai–Lao Friendship Bridge linking Mukdahan and Sawannakhet (opened in 2007) found the construction of eight new hotels during the bridge's construction, representing a 44 per cent increase. Hotel guests in Mukdahan increased by 82.61 per cent compared to the period before the bridge's opening. Hotel guests increased by 66.67 per cent whereas apartment occupancy increased by 21.05 per cent. Lao tourists to Thailand increased by 320 per cent but Thai tourists

---

[180] Bank of Thailand, <www.bot.or.th>.

to Laos increased only slightly, by 8.33 per cent.[181] Construction areas in Mukdahan, reflecting the expansion of the construction, service, and tourism sectors, increased from the period prior to the construction of the bridge by 120–156 per cent. Prices of land in the *Mueang* Municipality increased by 699 per cent.[182]

Loans for the construction of the Second Mekong International Bridge (SMIB) were granted by the Japan International Cooperation Agency (JICA) with the expectation that after its completion, two cities — Mukdahan and Sawannakhet — would be connected through transportation, government, and transport networks such as the East–West Economic Corridor. Such network would enable Thai–Laos trade to grow through Mukdahan and Sawannakhet. Competition between the two cities was also expected. Moreover, there were other projects in which both the Thai and Lao governments have cooperated with support from the Asian Development Bank (ADB), targeting the creation of strategies for the development of manufacturing and border trade. Construction of an economic zone and goods distribution centre in Sawannakhet and an industrial estate in Mukdahan were undertaken.[183] In 2014, the Thai government headed by General Prayuth Chan-ocha decided to establish a special economic zone in Mukdahan.

Changes resulting from border trade after the bridge construction led to Mukdahan's physical changes. The city had expanded in multiple directions, especially in the East–West direction. Urbanization had continued along with road construction and improvement between Khon Kaen and Mukdahan through Kalasin. Khon Kaen's growth also influenced the expansion of Mukdahan towards the suburbs. Roadside economic activities began to grow as well.[184]

The immediate effect of SMIB was increased trade in terms of volume and value in both countries. In 2006 the value of trade at Mukdahan checkpoint, the Northeast's second largest border trade checkpoint, was

---

[181] Suwit (2009, p. 7).
[182] Ibid., p. 9.
[183] Laine (2004, p. 348).
[184] Ibid., p. 352.

less than five billion baht, but it quickly rose to more than 23 billion baht in 2007 and jumped to around 50 billion baht in 2008. Mukdahan had a 12.5 per cent share in the Northeast's border trade in 2006 that increased to 30 per cent in 2007 and almost 35 per cent in 2008.[185] Border trade between the Northeast and Laos continued its influence in the economic and commercial development of the region, as well as catalysing the region's economic and urban growth, distributing economic opportunity to various areas, lowering migration from the Northeast to other parts of the country, and creating the balance between its economic growth and the rest of the country.

Prior to the commencement of the AEC in 2015 there had been signs of brisk border trade especially after the opening of the third bridge across the Mekong in 2011. Border trade at Nakhon Phanom during the first seven months of 2012 was very strong, with an export value of 3.537 billion baht through Nakhon Phanom checkpoint, representing a 16.0 per cent increase compared to the same period of the previous year whereas the import value was 1.5417 billion baht or an increase of 20.9 per cent.[186] It had been expected that after the AEC became effective, border trade would grow further and the Northeast would reap the benefits from business expansion in logistics, warehousing (such as the case of agricultural produce requiring silo and refrigerated facilities to preserve its quality for a certain period of time), tourism, touring coaches and vans, hotels, retail trade, real estate, etc.

The growth of the Northeast's border trade was an important factor in enhancing Khon Kaen's role as the regional commercial centre and to support the AEC through the GMS. Khon Kaen is the logistic hub of the North–South and East–West Economic Corridors. Khon Kaen benefits from the Ayeyawady–Chao Phraya–Mekong Economic Cooperation Strategy (ACMECS) both in trade and economic investment through the allocated investments in economic infrastructure such as the industrial estates. Under the GMS and ACMECS, Khon Kaen and the surrounding

---

[185] Ibid., p. 355.
[186] <http://www.ksmecare.com/Article/82/27983/>.

provinces of Maha Sarakham and Roi Et were chosen to be the industrialization cluster (2005–8) with the aim to boost Khon Kaen as the regional logistic hub that would benefit from these agreements.[187]

The past decade has experienced many changes in the Northeast's economy with the border trade boom and the expectation that the Northeast, especially important provinces such as Nakhon Ratchasima, Khon Kaen, and Udon Thani, would be strategic points in the economic development with neighbouring countries. The Northeast has attracted lots of interests from private sector investors, thus rapidly pushing land prices upward. The Bank of Thailand's financial report stated that:

> Land speculation values in the Northeast had accelerated from mid-2012 to mid-April 2013, with numerous real estate construction projects from Bangkok and the local ones focusing particularly on the proposed high speed train routes in Nakhon Ratchasima, Khon Kaen, and Udon Thani — the three largest economies in the Region. As a result, the Northeast had several construction projects in 2013–2015 amounting to 10,000 units of dwelling.[188]

Conclusion

The Northeast has long been home to one-third of the country's population but it lacks the resource base necessary to increase economic value added and industrial base. At the dawn of the twentieth century, teak from the North, tin from the South, and rice from the Central Region constituted approximately 90 per cent of the country's total exports. Transportation problems had seriously affected the Northeast's economic development in comparison to other regions. Prior to the construction of railways to Nakhon Ratchasima in 1900, land transportation was by carts

---

[187] Tsuneishi (2007, p. 24).
[188] Bank of Thailand, Northeastern Office (2013, p. 51).

only and could require months at a time. Moreover, land routes were fraught with dangerous wildlife and malaria. Such transportation conditions encouraged the Northeast's economy to remain mainly subsistence in nature.

Nakhon Ratchasima has long been an important city and the commercial centre of the Northeast. The reach of the railway in 1900 led to the integration of the Northeast's economy with Bangkok's, resulting in increasing commercial growth. Apart from rice, salt and pork, natural products were also sent to Bangkok. Railways also enabled labour migration from the Northeast to work as hired farm labourers in rice fields in the Central Plain. Rice mills, sawmills, and various businesses also expanded. The Northeast was an agricultural region. Its only significant manufacture was the small rice mills for regional consumption that expanded along with commercial rice production.

The Northeast's population rapidly grew after the Second World War with high population growth rates, mostly in the rural areas. Despite high natural increase, intraregional and interregional migrations also took place. Northeastern labour widely dispersed all over the country. Emigration from the Northeast reflects the movement away from low agricultural productivity areas with low income levels in an effort to seek higher paying jobs.

The basic problems in the Northeast are unproductive saline soil, drought, and lack of irrigation that had long been retarding agricultural productivity and income. Per capita income of the Northeastern provinces ranked among the lowest in the country. In fact, the region had the highest proportion of the poor. The major factor for economic changes in the Northeast was the construction of highways in the region to connect with other provinces in the 1950s and 1960s. These highways were instrumental in the merging of the Northeast's economy with Bangkok and the national economy at large. They also enabled commercial production that replaced subsistence production and led to market expansion, production of rice and upland crops for exports, and rural to urban migration.

The establishment of U.S. bases during the Vietnam War in the 1960s greatly affected the Northeast's economic changes, especially urban and economic growth in the provinces hosting those bases, including Nakhon Ratchasima, Khon Kaen, Udon Thani, and Ubon Ratchathani. Urban population quickly grew due to immigrants seeking jobs and responding to the expansion of trade and services. Manufacturing plants in the Northeast mainly concentrated in four provinces: Nakhon Ratchasima, Khon Kaen, Udon Thani, and Ubon Ratchathani. Most manufactures were food and beverages followed by textiles. The plants were small, exploiting non-paid family members. Border trade growth resulted in significant economic changes, especially trade and services that, in turn, led to increase in income and employment.[189]

Trade, investment, and tourism all contributed toward regional economic growth, urban growth, and the distribution of economic progress to the whole region.

---

[189] Laine (2014, p. 355).

7

CONCLUSION

This study has provided a regional perspective on Thai economic history. Such a perspective is necessary in order to avoid an undue emphasis on Bangkok.

Of course, the long-term predominance of Bangkok in so many spheres has affected all parts of the country since the early nineteenth century. However, it is necessary to emphasize: (a) the continuous and autonomous development of the regions, even during periods of Bangkok's greatest primacy; (b) the relative lessening of Bangkok's primacy, which took place from the 1980s, and which saw considerable urbanization and economic diversification in the various regions; and (c) a growing integration of Bangkok's economy with that of the regions.

During the nineteenth century several factors influenced Thai regional development. One was the existence of natural resources. This could be seen most clearly in the South, where, for example, tin was mined predominantly by the Chinese — controlled and operated by enterprises, processed in Penang or Singapore, and exported to foreign markets. Later, the South developed rubber and other plantation commodities.

In other regions, too, specialization resulted in centres of commercial activity, sometimes geared towards foreign markets. Already before 1900, textiles from Chiang Mai and Phrae, gems from Kanchanaburi, and a variety of forest products throughout the country, found their way to domestic and foreign markets, including notable land border trades with Burma and Malaya. Later, such border trades expanded and widened.

A notable feature of Thai economic history has always been the unusually large proportion of the population engaged in agriculture (mainly rice farming), with consequent high proportions of Thais living in rural areas. A natural result of this has been very limited urbanization outside Bangkok until very recent decades. Such a pattern was well established before the First World War, and continued until the 1980s. The large agricultural populations that characterized all regions have influenced social and economic development. Only since the 1980s have there been marked changes, with regional urban centres such as Hat Yai, Chiang Mai, Nakhon Ratchasima, Udon Thani, Rayong, and many others, exerting a profound local and non-local influence.

Thai regional economic development has been influenced by geographical factors to an extent that cannot be overestimated. Both transport and agricultural productivity have been dominated by geography. Thus the Chao Phraya River and its tributaries determined the establishment of rice-growing settlements and a concentration of the population in the Central Plain from the early nineteenth century. The teak trade and trade in other commodities were likewise shaped by the river systems. At the same time the annual flooding of the rivers provided natural irrigation and determined agricultural productivity and rural income. Thus, in areas where rivers were less important and land was less fertile, relative poverty became entrenched. This has been an enduring feature of the Northeast, by contrast to the more prosperous regions of the South and the Central Plain. Thailand's long coastlines and the provinces bordering the Mekong also developed economies closely related to these geographical circumstances.

Transport developments have been fundamental to regional developments. Railways linked a number of regional centres to Bangkok between the late nineteenth century and the 1920s, while river and canal improvements and the construction of bridges were also important. But it was roads above all that provided the arteries of communication that promoted trade within regions, trade between regions, long-distance trade with Bangkok, and also trade across international borders.

Beyond that, we must emphasize the large variations within Thai regions, as well as between them. Such variations have arisen in many ways. One recent factor is tourism. Phuket, Chon Buri (notably Pattaya), Chiang Mai, and other tourist centres have created wealthy local economies in particular areas. Local politics has also produced regional variations, sometimes as a result of political influence. For example, Nakhon Ratchasima, among others, has benefited from the diversion of central funds to particular regions as a result of political machination. Above all, perhaps, variations within regions have resulted from the process of urbanization. Large cities in many provinces have sprung up in recent decades, and have resulted in major local growth hubs. A similar effect has come from the creation of special economic zones.

Overall, Thai regions have become of increasing economic significance in recent decades. The previous dominance of Bangkok has given way to a more balanced development between the centre and the periphery. It is possible to view this change from a long-term perspective, and to suggest that during the nineteenth century relations between Bangkok and the regions were semi-colonial. Thus taxes and other imposts were sent to the metropolis, and manufactures from the metropolis (sometimes imported goods such as textiles) undermined local production. But later the relationship has shifted fundamentally. Investments and enterprises in the regions often emanate from the centre, while reserves of cheap labour encourage Bangkok entrepreneurs (and foreigners) to establish themselves in the regions.

A regional perspective of Thai economic history must make brief reference to the recent years of political conflict in the country. The striking feature of this conflict is that it appears to have a very definite regional core, despite the nation-wide relevance of many issues.

While it is simplistic to see the conflict in stark regional and class terms (a rich Bangkok-centred elite versus a poor rural Northeast), a regional perspective does provide matters for reflection. Thus, the continuing large rural populations in certain regions (large because of low agricultural productivity, lack of alternate occupations, and limited education) have an obvious influence on an electoral system based on universal suffrage. To the extent that inequality is one of the major problems in present-day Thai society, it is a problem that can be usefully viewed through the lens of regional economic history.

SELECTED BIBLIOGRAPHY

DOCUMENTS FROM BANGKOK NATIONAL ARCHIVES

Citations to the archives begin with "N.A.". The citation "N.A. R.5. M. of the Capital 14/4 (1899)" refers to the Fifth Reign and the Ministry of the Capital involved and the accompanying number classified to a specific series and file. The citation "N.A. M. of Finance 0301.1.1/139 (1931)" refers to the date and file number for the archive of the Ministry of Finance.

PUBLICATIONS IN THAI LANGUAGE

Adisorn Muakpimai. "Port Authority and Thai Economy: An Analysis in Structure and Change from Thonburi Period up to the Concord the Bowring Treaty, 1767–1855" [กรมท่ากับระบบเศรษฐกิจไทย:วิเคราะห์การเปลี่ยนแปลงตั้งแต่ สมัยธนบุรีถึงการทำสนธิสัญญาเบาริง พ.ศ. 2310–2398]. M.A. thesis, Thammasat University, 1988.

Alfa Research Company. *Basic Figures of Thailand, 2010–11* [ตัวเลขต้องรู้ของเมือง ไทย 2553–2554]. Bangkok: A.N.T. Office Express, 2011.

Akarapong Unthong. *The Potential and Opportunities of the Thailand's Export Goods in Greater Mekong Subregion Market* [โครงการศึกษาศักยภาพและโอกาสของสินค้าส่งออกไทยในตลาดกลุ่มอนุภูมิภาคแม่น้ำโขง]. Social Research Institute, Chiang Mai University, 2007.

Ammar Siamwalla. "Basis Structure of the Thai Economy" [พื้นฐานทางเศรษฐกิจ ของไทย]. Teaching Material for the course of Thai civilization, Thammasat University, 1973.

Ammar Siamwalla and Chermsak Pintong. "The Future of Thai Agriculture" [ภาพเศรษฐกิจการเกษตร ไทยในทศวรรษหน้า]. In *Direction of Thai Rural Development: Past, Present and Future* [ทิศทาง เศรษฐกิจไทยในทศวรรษหน้า]. Paper read at Annual Symposium, Faculty of Economics, Thammasat University, 13–14 February 1986.

Ammar Siamwalla and Viroj na Ranong. *The Knowledge on Rice* [ประมวล ความรู้เรื่องข้าว]. Bangkok: Thailand Development Research Institute, 1990.

383

Amphan Saothongyai. "Agricultural Productivity: Raised-Bed Production in Kok Khlang, Don Khlang, Damneonsaduek District, Ratchburi Province" [ผลิตภาพของ ระบบการผลิตทางการเกษตร: กรณีศึกษาการปลูกพืชบนร่องสวนในหมู่บ้านโคกก ลาง ตำบลดอน คลัง อำเภอดำเนินสะดวก จังหวัดราชบุรี]. M.A. thesis, Faculty of Agriculture, 2000.

Anonymous. "Before *niyom Thai*" [ก่อนจะถึงนิยมไทย]. *Silapawattanatham* 7, no. 1 (1985*a*): 71–78.

———. "Thai Nationalist Economy after the 1932 Revolution" [เศรษฐกิจนิยมไทย ยุคหลังเปลี่ยนแปลงการปกครอง พ.ศ. 2475]. *Silapawattanatham* 7, no. 1 (1985*b*): 79–90.

Apichai Puntasen. *Thai Rural Development* [พัฒนาชนบทไทย: สมุทัยและ มรรค]. Bangkok: Amarin Printing and Publishing, 1996.

Atchana Wattanukit. "Thai Industrial Development" [พัฒนาอุตสาหกรรม: ความสามารถ ของใคร]. In *If Thailand Became NICs: What Do Thai People Get?* [หากไทยเป็น NIC: คนไทยจะได้อะไร]. Paper read at Annual Symposium, Faculty of Economics, Thammasat University, February 1989.

Boonrawd Kaewkhanha. "The Collection of Suay During the Early Ratanakosin Period (1782–1868)" [การเก็บส่วยในสมัยรัตนโกสินทร์ตอนต้น (พ.ศ. 2325–2411)]. M.A. thesis, Chulalongkorn University, 1975.

Bowring, Sir John. *The Kingdom and People of Siam* [ราชอาณาจักรและราษฎรสยาม (Vol. 2)], translated by Chanvit Kasetsiri and Kanthika Sriudom. Bangkok: The Foundation of Science and Humanities Textbook Project, 2007.

Chai Ruengsilp. *The History of Thailand: Social Aspects, B.E. 2352–2453* [ประวัติศาสตร์ ไทย สมัย พ.ศ. 2352–2453 ด้า นสังคม]. Bangkok: Amarin Publishing Office, 1976.

———. *The History of Thailand: Economic Aspects, B.E. 2352–2453* [ประวัติศาสตร์ไทย สมัย พ.ศ. 2352–2453: ด้านเศรษฐกิจ]. Bangkok: Thai Wattana Panich Press, 1979.

Channarong Wongla. "Mae Khong River: River for Life" [แม่น้ำโขงสายน้ำแห่งชีวิต]. *Thang Isan* 2, no. 22 (2004): 6–33.

Chatthip Nartsupha and Pornpilai Lertvicha. *The Thai Village Culture* [วัฒนธรรมหมู่ บ้านไทย]. Bangkok: Sangsan Press, 1998.

Chatthip Nartsupha and Sompop Manarangsan, eds. *The Economic History of Thailand up to 1941* [ประวัติศาสตร์เศรษฐกิจไทยจนถึง พ.ศ. 2484]. Bangkok: Thammasat University Press, 1984.

Chermsak Phintong. "Bangkok: Who Gains Benefit from Thai Agriculture Development" [กรุงเทพฯ: ผู้เก็บเกี่ยวผลประโยชน์จากการเกษตรของประเทศไทย]. In *Thailand is Bangkok?* [ประเทศไทยคือกรุงเทพฯ?]. Faculty of Economics, Thammasat University, February 1983.

Chira Hongladarom. "Population and the Growth of Bangkok" [ประชากรกับการ ขยายตัวของกรุงเทพฯ]. In *Thailand is Bangkok?* [ประเทศไทยคือกรุงเทพฯ?]. Paper read at Annual Symposium, Faculty of Economics, Thammasat University, February 1983.

Chollada Wattanasiri. "The Privy Purse and the Business Investment, 1890–1932" [พระคลังข้างที่กับการลงทุนเศรษฐกิจในประเทศ พ.ศ. 2435–2475]. M.A. thesis, Silapakorn University, 1986.

Chulalongkorn University. *The Composition of Physical Growth of Bangkok* [องค์ประกอบทางกายภาพกรุงรัตนโกสินทร์]. Bangkok: Chulalongkorn University Press, 1991.

Damrong Rajanuparb. *Thesapiban* [เทศาภิบาล] 13, no. 1 (1913).

Dow Mongkolsmai. "Irrigation in Thailand: A State of Knowledge" [การศึกษาว่า ด้วยการชลประทานพรมแดนแห่งความรู้]. *Thammasat Economic Journal* 2, no. 1 (1984): 6–41.

Faculty of Letters, Silapakorn University. "Primary Source of French Document in the Reign of King Prajadhipok" [เอกสารชั้นต้นฝรั่งเศสกับรัชสมัยพระบาทสมเด็จ พระปกเกล้าเจ้าอยู่หัว]. Research submitted to King Prajadhipok Museum, 2011.

Faculty of Economics, Thammasat University. "Thailand is Bangkok?". *Annual Symposium* [สัมมนาวิชาการประจำปี], 17–18 February 1983.

International Institute for Trade and Development. "International Land Trade of the Northern Region" [การค้าระหว่างประเทศทางบกด้านเหนือ]. Bangkok: Seltaka Press, 2014.

Jiraporn Stapanawattana. *Village Economy in Lower Northern Region* [เศรษฐกิจชุมชน หมู่บ้านภาคเหนือตอนล่าง]. Bangkok: Sangsan Press, 2003.

Johnston, D.B. *Rural Society and the Rice Economy in Thailand, 1880–1930* [สังคม ชนบทและภาคเศรษฐกิจข้าวของไทย พ.ศ. 2423–2473], translated by Pornpirom Iamtham et al. Bangkok: Thammasat University Press, 1987.

Kakizaki, Ichiro. "Railways and the Economic Integration of Thailand before World War II" [รถไฟกับ การรวมตัวทางเศรษฐกิจของไทยในสมัย ก่อนสงครามโลกครั้งที่ 2]. *Journal of Historical Society* 29 (2007): 1–45.

Kalapapruek Phiewthongngam et al. *Contract Farming: Returns, Risks and the Justice* [เกษตรพันธะสัญญา: ผลตอบแทน ความเสี่ยง และ ความเป็นธรรม]. Bangkok: Thai Health Promotion Foundation, 2009.

Kitti Tunthai. *A Century of People at Songkhla Lake* [หนึ่งศตวรรษเศรษฐกิจของ คน ลุ่มทะเลสาบสงขลา]. Bangkok: The Thailand Research Fund, 2009.

Krirkkiat Phipatseritham. "Land Reform". In *Agricultural Economics* [ศรษฐกิจ การเกษตร], edited by Rungsun Thanapornphan. Bangkok: Kled Thai Press, 1974.

———. "Thai Political Economy of Rural Society". In *Political Economy of Thailand*. Chapter in Textbook [เอกสารการสอนชุดวิชา เศรษฐกิจกับ การเมืองไทย]. School of Political Science, Sukhothai Thammathirat Open University, 2006.

Mayuree Nokyoongthong. "The Economic Problems of Thailand during the Reign of King Rama VII. (1925–35)" [ปัญหาเศรษฐกิจ ไทยในรัชสมัยพระบาทสมเด็จ พระ ปกเกล้าเจ้าอยู่หัว พ.ศ. 2468–2477]. M.A. thesis, Chulalongkorn University, 1977.

Medhi Krongkaew. "Direction of Thai Rural Development: Past, Present and Future" [ทิศทางการพัฒนาชนบทไทย: อดีต ปัจจุบัน และอนาคต]. In *The Direction of Thai Economy in the Next Decade* [ทิศทางเศรษฐกิจไทยในทศวรรษหน้า]. Paper read at Annual Symposium, Faculty of Economics, Thammasat University, 13–14 February 1986.

Mingsan Kaosaad. *Thai Tourism from Policy to Grass Root* [การท่องเที่ยวไทย จาก นโยบายสู่รากหญ้า]. Chiang Mai: Linking Design Work, 2011.

Muscat, Robert J. *Thailand and the United States: Development, Security, and Foreign Aid* [สหรัฐอเมริกากับการพัฒนาเศรษฐกิจและความมั่นคงในประเทศไทย], translated and edited by Praipol Koomsup. Bangkok: Thammasat University Press, 1990.

Nantawan Phuswang. "The Southern Region in the Mixture of Culture: Thai, Chinese and Mayalu". In *Geography and Thai Way of Life* [ภาคใต้ในระบบ วัฒนธรรมผสมผสาน: ไทย จีน มลายู" ในภูมิศาสตร์กับวิถีชีวิตไทย]. Seminar Paper. Princess Maha Chakri Sirindhorn Anthropology Centre, Bangkok, 2002.

Narongchai Akrasanee et al. *Off-Farm Income Employment in Rural Thailand.* Summary Report. [การจ้างงานของกิจการนอกฟาร์มในชนบทไทย บทสรุป]. Bangkok: The Industrial Management, 1983.

Nidhi Eoseewong. *Pen and Sail: Literature and History in Early Bangkok* [ปาก ไก่และ ใบเรือ:ว่าด้วยการศึกษาประวัติศาสตร์วรรณกรรมต้นรัตนโกสินทร์]. Bangkok: Amarin Printing and Publishing, 2000.

Nipon Poapongskorn. "Land Acquisition in Thailand" [การถือครองที่ดินในประเทศไทย]. In *Agricultural Economics* [เศรษฐกิจการเกษตร], edited by Rungsun Thanapornphan. Bangkok: Kled Thai Press, 1974.

———. "Wages: A Story of the Poor?" [ค่าจ้าง:เรื่องของคนจน]. *Thammasat Journal* 10, no. 3 (1981): 76–95.

———. "Labor Market in Bangkok" [ตลาดแรงงานในกรุงเทพมหานคร]. In *Thailand is Bangkok?* [ประเทศไทยคือกรุงเทพฯ?]. Faculty of Economics, Thammasat University, 1983.

Orawan Bandikul. *Company in 1000 Years* [บริษัท 100 ปี]. Bangkok: Manager Media Group, 2004.

Paiboon Changrien. *The Public Administration of Bangkok* [การปกครองมหานคร]. Bangkok: Thai Wattana Panich, 1973.

Paitoon Sayswang. "An Economic History of the Chao Phya Delta". In *An Economic History of Thailand up to 1941* [ประวัติศาสตร์เศรษฐกิจของลุ่มแม่น้ำเจ้าพระยา" ในประวัติศาสตร์เศรษฐกิจไทย จนถึง พ.ศ. 2484], edited by Chatthip Nartsupha and Sompop Manarangsan. Bangkok: Thammasat University Press, 1984.

Pallegoix Jean-Baptise. *Description du Royaume Thai ou Siam* [เล่าเรื่องเมืองไทย], translated by Santi. T. Komolsutr. Bangkok: Progressive Publishing Office, 1962, reprinted 2006.

Panit Songprasert "Economic Development Policy under Field Marshall PhibunSongkhram, 1938–1944" [นโยบายการพัฒนาเศรษฐกิจสมัยรัฐบาลจอมพล ป.พิบูลสงคราม]. In *An Economic History of Thailand up to 1941* [ประวัติศา สตร์เศรษฐกิจไทย จนถึง พ.ศ. 2484], edited by Chatthip Nartsupha and Sompop Manarangsan. Bangkok: Thammasat University Press, 1984.

Pannee Bualek. *The Characteristics of Thai Capitalist during 1914–1939* [ลักษณะ [ของนายทุนไทยในช่วงระหว่าง พ.ศ. 2457–2482 บทเรียนจากความรุ่งโรจน์สู่โศกนาฏ กรรม]. Bangkok: Phantakit Press, 2002.

Photjana Luangaroon. "Commercial Shipping and the Thai Economy 1855–1925" [การเดินเรือพาณิชย์กับเศรษฐกิจไทย, พ.ศ. 2398–2468]. M.A. thesis, Silapakorn University, 1980.

Poonporn Poonthaachak. "Economic Change in Monthon Phayab after the Railway Construction during 1921–1941" [การเปลี่ยนแปลงทางเศรษฐกิจในมณฑลพายัพหลังการ ตัดเส้นทางรถไฟ สายเหนือ พ.ศ. 2464–2484]. M.A. thesis, Silapakorn University, 1987.

Porphant Ouyyanont. "Wages in the Thai Economic History" [ค่าแรงงานในประวัติ ศาสตร์เศรษฐกิจไทย]. *Thammasat Economic Journal* 14, no. 1 (1996): 48–86.

———. "Bangkok Economic History and the Development of Cheap Labour, 1855–1980" [ประวัติศาสตร์เศรษฐกิจกรุงเทพฯ กับพัฒนาการแรงงานราคาถูก ค.ศ. 1855–1980]. *Journal of the Historical Society* 19 (1997): 11–52.

———. *Village Economy in Central Thailand* [เศรษฐกิจชุมชนหมู่บ้านภาคกลาง]. Bangkok: Vitheethud, 2003.

———. "People's Party and the Thai Economy" [คณะราษฎรกับเศรษฐกิจไทย]. *Silpawattanatham* 34, no. 4 (2013a): 120–33.

Porphant Ouyyanont and Siriporn Sajjanand. "An Economic History of Wages and Labor Markets in Thailand, 1932–1995" [ประวัติศาสตร์เศรษฐกิจของค่าจ้างและ ตลาดแรงงานในประเทศไทย]. Research submitted to National Research Council of Thailand, 2001.

Pranee Tinakorn. "The Path of Industrialization in Thailand" [เส้นทางการพัฒนา อุตสาหกรรมในประเทศไทย]. In *Thai Economy: On the Road to Peace and Justice* [เศรษฐกิจไทย: บนเส้นทางแห่งสันติประชาธรรม], edited by Rungsun Thanapornphan and Nipon Poapongskorn. Bangkok: Thammasat University Press, 1988.

Pratueang Narintarangkul na Ayutthaya. "The Development of Economic Institution of Community at Highland Area" [ทิศทางทางการพัฒนาสถาบันเศรษฐกิจชุมชนบน พื้นที่สูง]. In *Community Enterprises* [วิสาหกิจชุมชน: กลไก เศรษฐกิจฐานราก], edited by Narong Petchprasert and Pittaya Wongkul. Bangkok: Chulalongkorn University Political Economy Centre, 2009.

PTT. Public Company. "Development Guide for the Southern Region based on the Regional Product to Promote Energy and Forward Linkage Industries" [แนวทางการพัฒนาภาคใต้โดยใช้ผลิตผลในพื้นที่เสริมสร้างอุตสาหกรรมพลังงานและ อุตสาหกรรมต่อเนื่องเป็นตัวนำร่อง]. *Research Report*, vol. 1 (2010).

Rattanaporn Setthakul. *One Century of Village Economy in Northern Thailand* [หนึ่งศตวรรษเศรษฐกิจชุมชนหมู่บ้านภาคเหนือ]. Bangkok: Sangsan Press, 2003.

Royal Chronicle King Rama IV, vol. 2. [พระราชพงศาวดาร รัชกาลที่ 4 เล่ม 2]. Bangkok: Kurusapa Press, 1961.

Rungsun Thanapornphan. "Thai Commercial Bank" [ธนาคารพาณิชย์: ปลิงดูดเลือด สังคมไทย]. In *Society and Economy of Thailand* [สังคมกับเศรษฐกิจไทย], edited by Rungsun Thanapornphan. Bangkok: Thammasat University Press, 1976.

————. *The Economics of the Rice Premium: A State of Knowledge* [เศรษฐศาสตร์ว่าด้วย พรีเมียมข้าว]. Bangkok: Thammasat University Press, 1987.

Sangob Songmuang. *Village Economy in Southern Thailand in the Past Five Decades* [เศรษฐกิจชุมชนหมู่บ้านภาคใต้ในรอบห้าทศวรรษที่ผ่านมา]. Bangkok: Vitheethud, 2003.

Sanun Chuskul. "The Truth at Rasri Salai" [ความจริงที่ราษีไศล" "ป่าทม" มดลูกของแม่ น้ำอีสานกับเขื่อนแห่งโครงการโขงชีมูล]. *Thang Isan* 11, no. 1 (2013a).

————. "Mun River and Dam Development" [เมื่อแม่น้ำมูนถูกพัฒนาด้วยเขื่อน]. *Thang Isan* 11, no. 4 (2013b).   .

Sarassawadee Ongsakul. *History of Lan Na* [ประวัติศาสตร์ล้านนา]. Bangkok: Amarin Printing and Publishing, 2008.

Sayomporn Tongsari. "The Impact of the Building of Roads in Bangkok During the Reign of King Rama V (1868–1910): A Study in the Area within the City Walls, the Northern and the Southern Parts of the City" [ผลกระทบจากการตัด ถนนในกรุงเทพฯในรัชสมัยพระบาทสมเด็จพระจุลจอมเกล้าเจ้าอยู่หัว (พ.ศ. 2411–2453): ศึกษาเฉพาะการตัดถนนในกำแพงพระนครด้านเหนือและด้านใต้พระนคร]. M.A. thesis, Silapakorn University, 1983.

Sirilaksana Khoman. "The Evaluation of Economic Policy under Prem Government: The Case of Export Promotion" [ประเมินนโยบายเศรษฐกิจ8ปีเปรม: นโยบายส่งเสริม การส่งออก]. Seminar Paper, Faculty of Economics, Thammasat University, 1988.

Skinner, G.W. *Chinese Society in Thailand: An Analytical History* [สังคมจีนใน ประเทศไทย:ประวัติศาสตร์เชิงวิเคราะห์], edited and translated by Chanvit Kasetsiri et al. The Foundation of Social Science and Humanities Textbook Project, 1986.

Slairat Dolarom. "The Development of Teak Industry in Thailand, 1896–1960" [พัฒนาการของการทำป่าไม้สักในประเทศไทย พ.ศ. 2396–2503]. M.A. thesis, Silapakorn University, 1985.

Somboon Sriripachai. *Migrants from Rural Areas to Bangkok: A State of Knowledge* [ผู้ย้ายถิ่นจากชนบทสู่กรุงเทพฯ: บทสำรวจสถานภาพแห่งความรู้]. Thai Khadi Research Institute, Thammasat University, 1985.

Sompop Manarungsan. *Economic Development of Thailand Before and After the Political Reform in 1892* [แนวโน้มพัฒนาการเศรษฐกิจไทยก่อนและหลังการ ปฏิรูปกครองในรัชสมัยพระบาทสมเด็จพระจุลจอมเกล้าเจ้าอยู่หัว]. Bangkok: Chulalongkorn University Printing House, 1993.

Somporn Isvilanonda. "Income Differentials and Inequality of Agricultural Households" [ความแตกต่างของรายได้และการกระจายรายได้ที่ไม่เท่าเทียมกันของครัวเรือนเกษตร]. *Kasetsart Economic Journal* 8, no. 1 (2001): 29–42.

————. *Thai Rice: Structural Change in Production and Distribution* [ข้าวไทย: การ เปลี่ยนแปลงในโครงสร้างการผลิตและช่องทางการกระจาย]. Bangkok: The Knowledge Network Institute of Thailand and The Thailand Research Fund, 2010.

Srisakra Valibhotama. "The Society of the Chao Phraya Delta: Development and Change" [สังคมลุ่มแม่น้ำเจ้าพระยา: พัฒนาการและการเปลี่ยนแปลง]. Paper read at *The Chaophraya Delta: Historical Development, Dynamics and Challenges of Thailand's Rice Bowl*. Kasetsart University, Bangkok, 12–15 December 2000.

Suntharee Asavai. *The History of Rangsit Canal: The Development of Land and the Social Impacts 1888–1914* [ประวัติคลองรังสิต: การพัฒนาที่ดินและ ผล กระทบต่อสังคม พ.ศ. 2431–2457]. Bangkok: Thammasat University Press, 1987.

———. *The Economic Crisis After World War I* [วิกฤตการณ์ทางเศรษฐกิจหลังสงคราม โลกครั้งที่ 1]. Bangkok: Thammasat University Press, 1990.

———. "The Great Depression and its Impacts on Thai Farmers in 1927–36" [ภาวะ เศรษฐกิจตกต่ำครั้งใหญ่และผลกระทบที่มีต่อชาวนาสยามในทศวรรษ2470]. *Thammasat Economic Journal* 11, no. 3 (1993): 71–110.

Suthanm Areekul. "Agricultural Knowledge from Foreign Countries and the Development of Thai Agricultural Development" [ความรู้เกษตรศาสตร์จากต่าง ประเทศกับการพัฒนาการเกษตรไทย]. In *The Role of Foreign Countries in the Creation of Knowledge in Thailand* [บทบาทต่างประเทศในการสร้างองค์ความรู้ ที่เกี่ยวข้องกับประเทศไทย]. Conference Paper, The Thailand Research Fund, 1994.

Suvinai Poranavalai. "The Economics of Becoming NICs: Development Strategy of Thailand" [ศรษฐศาสตร์การเป็น NICsยุทธศาสตร์การพัฒนาประเทศไทย]. *Thammasat Economic Journal* 7, no. 2 (1989): 5–76.

Suwit Paitayapat. *The Evolution of Village Economy in Central Thailand*, 1851–1932 [วิวัฒนาการเศรษฐกิจชนบทในภาคกลางของประเทศไทยระหว่าง พ.ศ. 2394–2475]. Bangkok: Sangsan Press, 1983.

Suwit Theerasasawat. *Economic History of Northeastern Village Economy* [ประวัติศาสตร์เศรษฐกิจชุมชนหมู่บ้านอีสาน 2488–2544]. Bangkok: Sangsan Press, 2003.

———. *A History of Agricultural Technology* [ประวัติศาสตร์เทคโนโลยีการเกษตร]. Bangkok: Mathichon Press, 2005.

———. "The Impact on the Second Friendship Bridge: Mukdahan-Suvanaket" [ผลกระทบของสะพานมิตรภาพไทย – ลาว 2: มุกดาหาร – สุวรรณเขต]. *Humanities and Social Science* 26, no. 1 (2009): 1–16.

Suwit Theerasasawat and Dararat Mettarikanon. *A History of the Northeast after World War II to the Present* [ประวัติศาสตร์อีสานหลังสงครามโลกครั้งที่สองจนถึง ปัจจุบัน]. Faculty of Humanities and Social Sciences, Khon Kaen University, 1998.

Tanom Tana. "The Rice Mills Business in the Central Plain Thailand, 1858–1938" [กิจการโรงสีข้าวในที่ราบภาคกลางของประเทศไทย พ.ศ. 2401–2481]. M.A. thesis, Silapakorn University, 1984.

Tasaka Toshio and Nhishizawa Kikuo. *The History of Land Holding in Bangkok* [ประวัติการถือครองที่ดินกรุงเทพฯ], translated from Japanese language by Nipaporn Rattachatapattanakul. Tokyo: Hyoronnsha, 2003.

Thailand. Bank of Thailand. *CLMV Report: A Report on Economy, Trade and Investment in Indochina* [CLMV Report: รายงาน "เศรษฐกิจ การค้า และ การลงทุน ในคาบสมุทรอินโดจีน 2013]. Bangkok, 2013.

———. Bank of Thailand. Northeastern Office. *The Northeast and Economic Change in Agricultural Sector* [อีสานกับการเปลี่ยนแปลงของภาคเกษตร]. Khon Kaen, 2013.

————. Bank of Thailand. Northeastern Office. *A Report on Financial and Economic Situation, Northeastern Region* [รายงานเศรษฐกิจและการเงินภาคตะวันออกเฉียงเหนือ]. Various years.

Thailand. Board of Commercial Development, Ministry of Commerce. *The Record.* [จดหมายเหตุของสภาเผยแผ่พาณิชย์]. Various years.

————. Department of Community Development, Ministry of Interior. *Data on Kor Chor Kor 2 Kor. Basic Data of Village Level* [กชช. 2ค. ข้อมูลพื้นฐานระดับหมู่บ้าน]. Bangkok, various years.

————. Department of Fine Arts. *Royal Duties of King Prajadhipok* [พระราชประวัติและพระราชกรณียกิจในพระบาทสมเด็จพระปรมินทรมหาประชาธิปกพระปกเกล้าเจ้าอยู่หัว]. Bangkok: Amarin Printing and Publishing, 1994.

————. Department of Highways, Ministry of Transport. *100 Years Anniversary of Department of Highways* [100 ปี กรมทางหลวง ร้อยรวมแผ่นดิน]. Bangkok: G.M. Multi Media, 2013.

————. Department of Post and Telegraph. *Register, Part 2 the Population of Bangkok Classified by Roads and Lanes Since a Year of Sheep, by the Department of Post and Telegraph, Bangkok 1883* [สารบาญชีส่วนที่ 2 คือราษฎรในจังหวัด ถนน และตรอก สำหรับพนักงานกรมไปรษณีย์กรุงเทพมหานคร ตั้งแต่จำนวนปีมะแม เบญจศก จุลศักราช 1245]. Bangkok: Thepplu Publishing House, 1883*a*.

————. Department of Post and Telegraph. *Register, Part 3 Classified Directory of the Population of Changwat [Krungthep] Following Clustered Villages and Rivers Since the Year of the Sheep* [สารบาญชีส่วนที่ 3 คือราษฎรในจังหวัดหมู่บ้านและลำน้ำ สำหรับเจ้าพนักงานกรมละลำน้ำ สำหรับเจ้าพนักงานกรมต่จำนวนปีมะแม เบญจศก จุลศักราช 1245]. Bangkok: Bradley House Press, 1883*b*.

————. Department of Post and Telegraph. *Register, Part 4 Classified Directory of the Population of Changwat [Krungthep] Following Ditches and Irrigation Canals Since the Year of the Sheep* [สารบาญชีส่วนที่ 4 คือ ราษฎรในจังหวัด และคลอง ลำประโดง สำหรับเจ้า พนักงานก รมไปรษณีย์ กรุงเทพมหานคร ตั้งแต่จำนวนปีมะแมเบญจศก จุลศักราช 1245]. Bangkok: Bradley House Press, 1883*c*.

————. Department of Provincial Administration, Ministry of Interior. *1929 Population Census* [สำมะโนประชากรปี พ.ศ. 1929]. Bangkok, 1931.

————. Department of Provincial Administration, Ministry of Interior. *1937 Population Census* [สำมะโนครัวทั่วราชอาณาจักร พ.ศ. 2480]. Bangkok, 1941.

————. Division of Agricultural Economics, Ministry of Agriculture. *1953 Thailand Economic Farm Survey* [รายงานผลการสำรวจ ภาวะเศรษฐกิจของที่ถือครองทำการเกษตร พ.ศ. 2496]. Bangkok, 1955.

————. Marine Department. *A History of Marine Department and its Operation* [ประวัติกรมเจ้าท่าและรายงานกิจการของหน่วยขุดลอกร่องน้ำ]. Bangkok: Marine Department, 1996.

————. Ministry of Commerce. *Thai Trade* [ไทยค้า]. Bangkok: Daily Mail Printing House, 1939.

————. Ministry of Interior. *Thesapiban* (Provincial Administration) [เทศาภิบาล]. *Monthly Journal* 30, no. 2 (1913).

————. Ministry of Interior. *Thesapiban* (Provincial Administration) [เทศาภิบาล]. *Monthly Journal* 46, no. 4 (1929).

————. National Statistical Office. *The 1986 Hill Tribe Population Survey Report: Chiang Mai* [รายงานการสำรวจประชากรชาวเขา: พ.ศ. 2529. จังหวัดเชียงใหม่]. 1987.

————. National Statistical Office. *Agricultural Census* [สำมะโนการเกษตร]. Various years.

————. National Statistical Office. *The Business Trade and Service Survey* [การสำรวจธุรกิจทางการค้าและธุรกิจทางการบริการ]. Various regions, various years.

————. National Statistical Office. *Household Socio-Economic Survey* [การสำรวจภาวะเศรษฐกิจและสังคมของครัวเรือน]. Various regions, various years.

————. National Statistical Office. *1997 and 2007 Industrial Census.* [สำมะโนอุตสาหกรรม 2540, 2550]. Various regions.

————. National Statistical Office. *Labor Force Survey* [การสำรวจภาวะการณ์ทำงานของประชากร]. Various regions, various years.

————. National Statistical Office. *Migration Survey* [รายงานการสำรวจการย้ายถิ่นของประชากร]. Various years.

————. National Statistical Office. *Population and Housing Census* [สำมะโนประชากรและการเคหะ]. Various regions, various years.

————. National Statistical Office. *Statistical Yearbook of Thailand* [รายงานสถิติรายปี]. Various years.

————. Office of Agricultural Economics. "A Study on a Change of Income and Wealth Distribution of Farmer Households" [การเปลี่ยนแปลงการกระจายรายได้และทรัพย์สินของครัวเรือนเกษตร]. Research Report, 2005.

————. Office of Agricultural Economics, Ministry of Agriculture and Cooperatives. *Agricultural Statistics of Thailand* [สถิติการเกษตรของประเทศไทย]. Bangkok. Various years.

————. Office of City Planning, Ministry of Interior. *Khon Kaen City Plan* [ผังเมืองจังหวัดขอนแก่น]. 1982.

————. Office of National Economic and Social Development Board (NESDB). *A Report on the Development of Coastal Southern Area* [รายงานการศึกษาเรื่องการพัฒนาพื้นที่ชายฝั่งทะเลภาคใต้]. Bangkok, 2011*a*.

————. Office of National Economic and Social Development Board (NESDB). *Direction of Regional Development in 11th Economic and Social Development Plan (2012–2016)* [ทิศทางการพัฒนาภาคในระยะแผนพัฒนาฯฉบับที่ 11 พ.ศ. 2555–2559]. 2011*b*.

————. Office of National Economic and Social Development Board (NESDB). *Report on Ecotourism on the Path of Green Sustainability: The Case of Northeastern Region* [รายงานผลการศึกษา การท่องเที่ยวเชิงนิเวศอย่างยั่งยืนบนเส้นทางสีเขียว: กรณีศึกษาภาคตะวันออกเฉียงเหนือ]. Bangkok, 2013.

————. Office of National Economic and Social Development Board (NESDB). *Report on the Analysis of Poverty Situation and Inequality in Thailand, 2013* [รายงานการวิเคราะห์สถานการณ์ความยากจนและความเหลื่อมล้ำในประเทศไทยปี 2556]. 2015.

————. Office of National Economic and Social Development Board (NESDB). *Gross Regional and Provincial Product* [ผลิตภัณฑ์ภาคและจังหวัด]. Various years.

————. Office of National Economic and Social Development Board (NESDB). *National Income Account of Thailand* [บัญชีรายได้ประชาชาติของประเทศไทย]. Various years.

Thailand, Office of the Prime Minister. *A Collection of King Chulalongkorn's Manuscripts* [ประชุมพระราชหัตเลขา พระบาทสมเด็จพระจุลจอมเกล้าเจ้าอยู่หัว ที่ทรงบริหารราชการแผ่นดิน ภาคที่ 3 ส่วนที่ 1]. Bangkok, 1970.

Thailand. *Royal Thai Government Gazette* [ราชกิจจานุเบกษา]. 23 (1907).

Thanet Aphornsuvan. *Historical Development of Theory on Separatism in Southern Thailand* [ความเป็นมาของทฤษฎีแบ่งแยกดินแดนในภาคใต้ไทย]. Bangkok: The Foundation of Social Science and Humanities Textbook Project, 2005.

Thanet Khongprasert. "The Role of Fertiliser in Improving Agricultural Productivity" [บทบาทของปุ๋ยกับการเพิ่มผลิตผลผลิตทางการเกษตร]. In *Thai Agricultural Economy* [เศรษฐกิจการเกษตรไทย], edited by Rungsun Thanapornphan. Bangkok: Klet Thai, 1974.

Thaweesilp Subvattana. "Rice Production and Rice Trade in Central Thailand from the Reign of King Rama V to the Reign of King Rama VII" [การผลิตและการค้าข้าวในภาคกลาง ตั้งแต่สมัยพระบาทสมเด็จพระจุลจอมเกล้าเจ้าอยู่หัว รัชกาลที่ 5 จนถึงรัชสมัยพระบาทสมเด็จพระปกเกล้าเจ้าอยู่หัว รัชกาลที่ 7 (พ.ศ. 2411–2475)]. M.A. thesis, Chulalongkorn University, 1978.

Thaweesilp Suebvattana. "The Role of Privy Purse in Economic Investment in the Past, 1900–32" [บทบาทของกรมพระคลังข้างที่ต่อการลงทุนเศรษฐกิจในประเทศไทย พ.ศ. 2433–2475]. *Thammasat University Journal* 14, no. 2 (1985): 122–59.

Thepchu Thubthong. *Bangkok in the Past* [กรุงเทพ ฯ ในอดีต]. Bangkok: Aksornbundit Press, 1975.

Thippawal Srijantr and Francois Molle. "Change in Agrarian System in the Central Plains" [การเปลี่ยนแปลงของระบบเกษตรในเขตที่ราบลุ่มภาคกลาง]. Seminar paper for the Conference on Dynamics of Cultural and Local Community Economy. The Thailand Research Fund [พลวัตวัฒนธรรมและเศรษฐกิจชุมชนท้องถิ่น], 30–31 May 2000.

Wanee Choikiatkul. "The Role of the Service Sector in Reducing the Disparity of Development" [บทบาทของการผลิตสาขาบริการในการลดความเหลื่อมล้ำของการพัฒนา]. In *Thailand is Bangkok?* [ประเทศไทยคือกรุงเทพฯ?]. Paper read at Annual Symposium, Faculty of Economics, Thammasat University, 1983.

Wanpen Suraruek. *The Geography and the Sustainability of Thai Agriculture* [มุมมองทางภูมิศาสตร์กับความยั่งยืนของการเกษตรไทย]. Department of Geography, Chiang Mai University, 2004.

Waranya Rawan. "Agricultural Machinery and the Development of Thai Agriculture" [เครื่องทุ่นแรงกับการพัฒนาการเกษตรของไทย]. In *Thai Agricultural Economy* [เศรษฐกิจการเกษตรไทย], edited by Rungsun Thanapornphan. Bangkok: Klet Thai, 1974.

Wilaiwan Wannithikul. "Bangkok is Thailand: Industrial and Service Sectors" [ประเทศไทยคือกรุงเทพฯ: ภาคอุตสาหกรรมและบริการ]. In *Thailand is Bangkok?* [ประเทศไทยคือกรุงเทพฯ?]. Paper read at Annual Symposium, Faculty of Economics, Thammasat University, 1983.

Worachat Meechoobot. *Chaos in the North and their Love Story* [เจ้านายฝ่ายเหนือ และตำนานรักมะเมียะ]. Bangkok: Sangsan Book, 2013.

World Bank. *A Public Development Program for Thailand* [โครงการพัฒนาการของรัฐ สำหรับประเทศไทย ฉบับแปล]. Bangkok: National Economic Development Board, 1960.

Wyatt, David K. *Thailand: A Short History* [ประวัติศาสตร์ไทย: ฉบับสังเขป], edited and translated by Chanvit Kasetsiri. The Foundation of Social Science and Humanities Textbook Project, 2013.

WEBSITES

<https://www.itri.co.uk/index.php?option=com_mtree&task=att_download&link_id=49601&cf_id=24>. International Tin Research Institute (ITRI). "Historical Trend in Tin Production".

<http://www2.tat.or.th/stat/web/static_index.php>. Thailand. Tourism Authority of Thailand. "Tourism Statistics in Thailand".

<http://www.nso.go.th>. Thailand. National Statistical Office. Home Industry Survey. [การสำรวจการประกอบอุตสาหกรรมในครัวเรือน].

<http://www.rubberwarroom.com/index.php>. ศูนย์ข้อมูลยางพาราไทย.

<www.ipsr.mahidol.ac.th/ipsr/annualconference/conferenceiii/Articles/Download/Article02.pdf>. กาญจนา ตั้งชลทิพย์ (2012) กรุงเทพมหานคร: เมืองโตเดี่ยวตลอด กาลของประเทศไทย.

<www.chaoproayanews.com>. สำนักข่าวเจ้าพระยา, 31 December 2014.

<www.oae.go.th>. Thailand, Office of Agricultural Economics, Ministry of Agriculture and Cooperatives. "Socio Economic Situation and Agricultural Labor" [ภาวะ เศรษฐกิจ สังคมครัวเรือนและแรงงานเกษตรปี 2549–2550].

<www.prachatai.com/journal/2013/01/44794>. "ทุนนิยาม: แม่สอด" ด่านแรกของคนงาน ข้ามชาติในภาคอุตสาหกรรม".

PUBLICATIONS IN ENGLISH LANGUAGE

Ammar Siamwalla. "Foreign Trade and Domestic Economy in Siam". Bangkok, mimeo, n.d.

————. "Stability, Growth and Distribution in the Thai Economy". In *Finance, Trade and Economic Development in Thailand*, edited by Prateep Sondysuvan. Bangkok: Sompong Press, 1975.

————. *Productivity and Competitiveness in Thai Agriculture*. TDRI Year End Conference, Bangkok, 1987.

Anan Ganjanaphan. "The Partial Commercialization of Rice Production in Northern Thailand (1900–1981)". PhD thesis, Cornell University, 1984.

Anderson, Dole. *Marketing and Development: The Thailand Experience*. US: MSU International Business and Economic Studies, 1970.

Andrews, James. *Siam: 2nd Rural Economic Survey, 1934–35*. Bangkok: The Bangkok Times Press, 1936.

Anonymous. *Siam Resources*, c. 1940.

Antonio, J. *The 1904 Traveller's Guide to Bangkok and Siam*. Bangkok: White Lotus, 1904, reprinted 1997.

Apichat Chamratrithirong. *National Migration Survey of Thailand*. Institute for Population and Social Studies, Mahidol University, 1995.

Asian Industry. "A Profile of the Bangkok Boom", May 1968, pp. 39–44.

Askew, Marc. "The Making of Modern Bangkok: State, Market and People in the Shaping of the Thai Metropolis". TDRI Year End Conference, Bangkok, 1993.

————. *Bangkok: Place, Practice and Representation*. New York and London: Routledge, 2002.

Baffie, Jean. "Ethnic Groups in the Central Plain of Thailand: The Setting of Mosaic". In *Thailand's Rice Bowl Perspectives on Agricultural and Social Change in the Chao Phraya Delta*, edited by Francois Molle and Thippawal Srijantr. Bangkok: White Lotus Press, 2003.

Bangkok Calendar, Annually. Various years.

Bangkok Times Weekly Mail [BTWM]. BTWM (18 June 1923); BTWM (15 December 1924); BTWM (3 July 1925); BTWM (3 December 1925); BTWM (2 September 1929); BTWM (9 September 1929); BTWM (30 September 1929); BTWM (7 October 1929); BTWM (25 November 1929); BTWM (6 January 1930); BTWM (27 January 1930); BTWM (19 May 1930); BTWM (24 November 1930); BTWM (2 March 1931); BTWM (14 December 1931); BTWM (23 March 1933).

Bangkok World Annual Review (1969).

Bank of Thailand. *An Economic Survey of Thailand, 1946–47*, n.d. (Available at Bank of Thailand Archives).

Bertrand, Trent J. *Thailand: Case Study of Agricultural Input and Output Pricing.* Washington, D.C.: World Bank, 1980.

Boomgaard, Peter. "Surviving the Slump: Developments in Real Income During the Depression of the 1930s in Indonesia, Particularly Java". In *Weathering the Storm: The Economies of Southeast Asia in the 1930s Depression*, edited by Peter Boomgaard and Ian Brown. Singapore: Institute of Southeast Asian Studies, 2000.

Boomgaard, Peter and Ian Brown, eds. *Weathering the Storm: The Economies of Southeast Asia in the 1930s Depression.* Singapore: Institute of Southeast Asian Studies, 2000.

Boonkong Hunchangsith. "Economic Impact of the US Military Presence in Thailand, 1960–72". PhD thesis, Department of Economics, Claremont Graduate School, 1974.

Bowring, John. *The Kingdom and People of Siam.* Two volumes. Singapore: Oxford University Press, reprinted 1977.

British Consular Report (BCR, *Bangkok*) for the years 1892, 1919.

———— (BCR, *Chieng Mai*) for the years 1891, 1895, 1896, 1897, 1898, 1899, 1910, 1913, 1922, 1925, 1930.

———— (BCR, *Monthon Nakonsri Tammarat and Pattani*) for the years 1909, 1924.

———— (BCR, *Monthon Nhakonratchsima*) for the years 1884, 1892, 1896.

———— (BCR, *Monthon Phuket*) for the year 1914.

———— (BCR, *Senggora*) for the year 1921.

———— *Report on the Commercial Situation in Siam in 1919.*

Carter, Cecil A. *The Kingdom of Siam, 1904.* Bangkok: The Siam Society, reprinted 1988.

Central Statistical Office. *First Report of the Economic and Demographic Survey 1954.*

Chaiyan Rajchagool. *The Rise and Fall of the Thai Absolute Monarchy: Foundations of the Modern Thai State from Feudalism to Peripheral Capitalism.* Bangkok: White Lotus, 1994.

Chatthip Nartsupha. *The Thai Village Economy in the Past*, translated by Chris Baker and Pasuk Phongpaichit. Chiang Mai: Silkworm Books, reprinted 1999.

Chatthip Nartsupha and Suthy Prasartset, eds. *The Political Economy of Siam 1851–1910.* Bangkok: The Social Science Association of Thailand, 1981.

Chatthip Nartsupha, Suthy Prasartset and Montri Chenvidyakarn, eds. *The Political Economy of Siam, 1910–1932.* Bangkok: The Social Science Association of Thailand, 1981.

Chuthatip Maneepong and Wu Chung-Tong. "Comparative Borderland Developments in Thailand". *ASEAN Economic Bulletin* 21, no. 2 (2004): 135–66.

Clarence-Smith, William G. "Hadhrami Arab Entrepreneurs in Indonesia and Malaysia: Facing the Challenge of the 1930s Recession". In *Weathering the Storm: The Economies of Southeast Asia in the 1930s Depression*, edited by Peter Boomgaard and Ian Brown. Singapore: Institute of Southeast Asian Studies, 2000.

Cohen, Erik. *Thai Tourism Hill Tribe, Islands and Open-Ended Prostitution*. Bangkok: White Lotus, 2001.

Crawfurd, John. *The Crawfurd Papers, A Collection of Official Records Relating to the Mission of Dr. John Crawfurd sent to Siam by the Government of India in the Year 1821*. Bangkok: Vajiranana National Library, Reprint Edition, 1915.

———. *Journal of an Embassy to the Courts of Siam and Cochin China*. Singapore: Oxford University Press, 1987.

Department of Ways. *Memorandum Concerning the Policy and Programme of Highways B.E. 2468*. Bangkok, 1925.

Development Oriented Research on Agrarian Systems (DORAS). *Agriculture and Irrigation Patterns in the Central Plain of Thailand: Preliminary Analysis and Prospects for Agricultural Development*. Bangkok: Kasetsart University, 1996.

Dilok Nabarath, Prince. *Siam's Rural Economy under King Chulalongkorn*. Bangkok: White Lotus, reprinted 2000.

Directory for Bangkok and Siam 1914. Bangkok: Bangkok Times Press, 1914.

Directory for Bangkok and Siam 1929. Bangkok: Bangkok Times Press, 1929.

Donner, Wolf. *The Five Faces of Thailand: An Economic Geography*. Queensland: University of Queensland Press, 1978.

Economic and Social Commission for Asia and the Pacific (ESCAP). *Population of Thailand*. Bangkok: Country Monograph, 1976.

———. *Migration, Urbanization and Development in Thailand*. Country Report. New York: United Nations, 1982.

Economic Research and Training Centre. "The Final Report on Social Protection for Thai Migrant Families (Phase I)". Faculty of Economics, Thammasat University, 2002.

Falkus, Malcolm. "The World Depression". Unpublished manuscript, 1975.

———. "Early British Business in Thailand". In *British Business in Asia Since 1860*, edited by R.P.T. Davenport-Hines and Geoffrey Jones. Cambridge: Cambridge University Press, 1989.

———. "The Economic History of Thailand". *Australian Economic History Review* XXXI (March 1991): 53–71. *Special Issue: Exploring Southeast Asia's Economic Past*, edited by G.D. Snooks, A.J.S. Reid, and J.J. Pincus.

———. "Bangkok: From Primate City to Primate Megalopolis". In *Megalopolis: The Giant City in History*, edited by Theo Barker and Anthony Sutcliffe. London: The Macmillan Press, 1993.

———. "Labour in Thai Mining: Some Historical Considerations". *Asian Studies Review* 20, no. 2 (1996): 71–95.

———. "Bangkok in the Nineteenth and Twentieth Centuries: The Dynamics and Limits of Port Primacy". In *Gateways of Asia: Port Cities of Asia in the 13th–20th Centuries,* edited by Frank Broeze. London and New York: Kegan Paul International, 1997.

Falvey, Lindsay. *Thai Agriculture: Golden Cradle of Millennia Bangkok*. Bangkok: Kasetsart University Press, 2000.

Far Eastern Economic Review (17 May 1990).

Feeny, David. *The Political Economy of Productivity: Thai Agricultural Development 1880–1975*. Vancouver and London: University of British Colombia Press, 1982.

Findlay, Ronald and Kevin H. O'Rourke. *Power and Plenty: Trade, War, and the World Economy in the Second Millennium*. Princeton: Princeton University Press, 2009.

Gisselequist, David. "A History of Contractual Relations in a Thai Rice Growing Village". PhD thesis, Yale University, 1976.

Grabowsky, Volker. "The Isan up to its Integration into the Siamese State". In *Regions and National Integration in Thailand, 1882–1992*, edited by Volker Grabowsky. Wiesbaden, 1995.

———. "The Thai Census of 1904: Translation and Analysis". *Journal of the Siam Society* 84, no. 1 (1996): 49–85.

Graham, Walter A. *Siam Vol. I*. London: Alexander Moring, 1924.

Heal, J.H. "Mines and Mining Administration". In *Twentieth Century Impression of Siam: Its History, People, and Resources*, edited by Arnold Wright and Oliver T. Breakspear. Bangkok: White Lotus, 1908, reprinted 1994.

Hewison, Kevin. "Industry prior to Industrialization: Thailand". *Journal of Contemporary Asia* 18, no. 4 (1988): 398–411.

Hubbard, Robert V. "Canal Construction in the Chao Phraya River Central Thailand". In *The History of Inland Waterway Development in Thailand*. Michigan: Department of Geography, University of Michigan, Ann Arbor, 1977.

The Impact. "Bangkok 1959: A Short 20 Years Ago", 10 February 1973, pp. 101–12.

Importers and Exporters Directory for Siam (1920).

Ingram, James C. "Thailand's Rice and the Allocation of Resources". In *The Economic Development of South-East Asia*, edited by C.D. Cowan. London: George Allen and Urwin, 1964.

———. *Economic Change in Thailand, 1850–1970*. California: Stanford University Press, 1971.

International Labour Organization (ILO). *Report to the Government of Thailand on a Survey of Labour Conditions in Thailand*. Geneva: ILO, 1954.

The Investor. Various years.

Kitahara, Atsushi. *Thai Rural Community Reconsidered: Historical Community Formation and Contemporary Development Movements*. The Political Economy Centre, Faculty of Economics, Chulalongkorn University, 1996.

———. "Lan Laem from 1980 to 1996: A Profile of Rice Growing Village in Nakhon Pathom Province". In *Thailand's Rice Bowl: Perspectives on Agricultural and Social Change in the Chao Phraya Delta*, edited by Francois Molle and Thippawal Srijantr. Bangkok: White Lotus, 2003.

Koizumi, Junko. "The Commutation of *Suai* from Northeast Siam in the Middle of the Nineteenth Century". *Journal of Southeast Asian Studies* 23, no. 2 (1992): 276–307.

Kornerup, Ebbe. *Friendly Siam: Thailand in the 1920s*. Bangkok: White Lotus, 1999.

Laine, Xuan Elsa. "Internationalization Process of Twin Mekong Border Cities". In *Transnational Dynamics in Southeast Asia: The Greater Mekong Subregion and Malacca Straits Economic Corridors*, edited by Nathalie Fau, Sirivanh Khonthapane and Christian Taillard. Singapore: Institute of Southeast Asian Studies, 2004.

Larsson, Tomas. *Land and Loyalty: Security and the Development of Property Rights in Thailand*. Singapore: NUS Press, 2012.

Lewis, Arthur W. "Economic Development with Unlimited Supplies of Labour". *The Manchester School* 32 (May 1954): 139–91.

Lowy, Stephen. *Century of Growth: The First 100 Years of Siam Commercial Bank*. Singapore: Editions Didier Millet, 2007.

Mackay, Colin. *A History of Phuket and the Surrounding Region*. Bangkok: White Lotus, 2012.

Maddison, Angus and Gé Prince. *Economic Growth in Indonesia, 1820–1940*. Dordrecht: Foris Publications, 1989.

Madge, Charles. *Village Communities in North-East Thailand*. New York: United Nations Technical Assistance Programme, 1958.

Meinkoth, Marian R. *Migration in Thailand with Particular Reference to the Northeast*. Bangkok: National Research Council of Thailand, 1962, reprinted 1971.

Molle, Francois and Thippawal Srijantr. *Agrarian Change and Land System in the Chao Phraya Delta*. DORAS Project, Kasetsart University, 1999.

Molle, Francois, Thippawal Srijantr, Lionel Latham and Phuanggladda Thepstitsilp. *The Impact of the Access to Irrigation Water on the Evolution of Farming Systems: A Case Study of Three Villages in the Chao Phraya Delta*. Bangkok: Kasetsart University, 2001.

Myint, H. "'The Classical Theory' of International Trade and the Underdeveloped Countries". *The Economic Journal* 68 (1958): 317–37.

Nipon Poapongsakorn. "Rural Industralization: Problems and Prospects". In *Thailand's Industrialization and its Consequences*, edited by Medhi Krongkaew. New York: St. Martin's Press, 1995.

———. *Thailand*. Southeast Asian Agriculture and Development Primer Series: SEARCA, 2007.

Oey Astra Meesook. *Income, Consumption and Poverty in Thailand, 1962/63 to 1975/76*. World Bank Staff Paper No. 364. Washington, 1979.

Paritta Chalermpow Koanantakool. "Urban Life and Urban People in Transition". *Who Gets, What and How? Challenge for the Future*. TDRI Year End Conference, 1993.

Pasuk Phongpaichit. *The New Wave of Japanese Investment in ASEAN*. Singapore: Institute of Southeast Asian Studies, 1990.

Pasuk Phongpaichit and Chris Baker. *Thailand: Economy and Politics.* Kuala Lumpur: Oxford University Press, 1995.

Pendleton, Robert L. *Thailand: Aspects of Landscape and Life*. New York: Duell, Sloan and Pearce, 1962, reprinted 1976.

Phuwadol Songprasert. "The Development of Chinese Capital in Southern Siam, 1868–1932". PhD thesis, Monash University, 1986.

Porphant Ouyyanont. "Bangkok's Population and the Ministry of the Capital in Early 20th Century Thai History". *Southeast Asian Studies* 35, no. 2 (1997): 240–60.

———. "Bangkok as a Magnet for Rural Labour: Changing Conditions, 1900–1970". *Southeast Asian Studies* 36, no. 1 (1998): 78–108.

———. "Physical and Economic Change in Bangkok, 1851–1925". *Southeast Asian Studies* 36, no. 4 (1999*a*): 437–74.

———. "Transformation of Bangkok and Concomitant Changes in Urban–Rural Interaction in Thailand in the 19th and 20th Centuries". *ASAFAS Special Paper* No. 1. Graduate School of Asian and African Area Studies, Kyoto University, 1999*b*.

———. "The Vietnam War and Tourism in Bangkok's Development, 1960–1970". *Southeast Asian Studies* 39, no. 2 (2001): 157–87.

———. "The Crown Property Bureau in Thailand and the Crisis of 1997". *Journal of Contemporary Asia* 38, no. 2 (2008): 166–89.

———. "Changes in the Village Economy in Thailand's Central Region During the Era of Industrialization". In *Comparative Perspectives on Moral Economy: Africa and Southeast Asia*, edited by S. Maghimbi, I.N. Kimambo, and K. Sugimura. Dar es Salaam: University of Dar es Salaam, 2011.

———. "Underdevelopment and Industrialisation in Pre-War Thailand". *Australian Economic History Review* 52, no. 1 (2012): 43–60.

———. "Bangkok Economy in 1937/38". In *Essays on Thailand's Economy and Society for Professor Chatthip Nartsupha at 72*, edited by Pasuk Phongpaichit and Chris Baker.. Bangkok: Sangsan Press, 2013.

———. "The Foundation of the Siam Commercial Bank and the Siam Cement Company: Historical Context and Alternative Historiographies". *SOJOURN: Journal of Social Issues in Southeast Asia* 30, no. 2 (2015): 495–96.

———. "Rural Thailand: Change and Continuity". *Trends in Southeast Asia*. Singapore: ISEAS – Yusof Ishak Institute, 2016.

Porphant Ouyyanont and Tsubouchi Yoshihiro. "The Population and Economic Activities of Bangkok in the 1883 Postal Census". *The 1883 Bangkok Postal Census and Nineteenth Century Bangkok Economic History*. Vol. 1, *ASAFAS Special Paper* No. 5. Graduate School of Asian and African Area Studies, Kyoto University, 2000*a*.

————. "Housing in Bangkok in the 1883 Postal Census". *The 1883 Bangkok Postal Census and Nineteenth Century Bangkok Economic History.* Vol. 2, *ASAFAS Special Paper* No. 7. Graduate School of Asian and African Area Studies, Kyoto University, 2000*b*.

————. "Aspects of the Place and Role of the Chinese in Late Nineteenth Century Bangkok". *Southeast Asian Studies* 39, no. 3 (2001): 384–97.

Public Record Office (PRO). *Siam Financial Position*, 1930 (FO. 371/14776).

Purcell, Victor. *The Chinese in Southeast Asia.* Kuala Lumpur: Oxford University Press, 1980.

Sarasin Viraphol. *Tribute and Profit: Sino–Siamese Trade, 1651–1853.* Cambridge, Massachusetts: Harvard East Asian Monographs, 1977.

Sarassawadee Ongsakul. *History of Lan Na*, translated by Chitraporn Tanratanakul. Chiang Mai: Silkworm Books, 2005.

Seksan Prasertkul. "The Formation of the Thai State and Economic Change 1855–1945". PhD thesis, Cornell University, 1989.

Silcock, Thomas H. "The Rice Premium and Agricultural Diversification". In *Thailand: Social and Economic Studies in Development*, edited by Thomas H. Silcock. Canberra: Australian National University Press, 1967.

————. *The Economic Development of Thai Agriculture.* Canberra: Australian National University Press, 1970.

Skinner, William G. *Chinese Society in Thailand: An Analytical History.* Ithaca: Cornell University Press, 1957.

Smyth, Herbert W. *Five Years in Siam, from 1891–1896.* Bangkok: White Lotus, 1898, reprinted 1994.

Somchai Jitsuchon. "A Framework for Revised Official Poverty Lines for Thailand". Paper presented to UNDP and NESDB on Review of Thailand's Official Poverty Line Project, 2004.

Somchai Ratanakomut. "Industrializing the Service Sector, with Special Reference Emphasis on Tourism". In *Thailand's Industrialization and its Consequences*, edited by Medhi Krongkaew. London: Macmillan Press, 1995.

Sompop Manarungsan. *Economic Development of Thailand 1850–1950: Response to the Challenge of the World Economy.* Bangkok: Institute of Asian Studies, Chulalongkorn University, 1989.

Somporn Isvilanonda and Mahabub Hossain. "Dynamics of Rice Farming in the Chao Phraya Delta: A Case Study of Three Villages in Suphan Buri Province". In *Thailand's Rice Bowl Perspectives on Agricultural and Social Change in the Chao Phraya Delta*, edited by Francois Molle and Thippwal Srijantr. Bangkok: White Lotus, 2003.

Sternstein, Larry. "Settlement in Thailand: Pattern of Development". PhD thesis, Australian National University, 1964.

————. "The Distribution of Thai Centres at Mid-Nineteenth Century". *Journal of Southeast Asian History* 7, no. 1 (1966): 66–72.

————. *Portrait of Bangkok.* Bangkok: Bangkok Metropolitan Administration, 1982.

Stifel, Laurence D. "The Growth of the Rubber Economy of Southern Thailand". *Journal of Southeast Asian Studies* 4, no. 1 (1973): 107–32.

Suehiro, Akira. *Capital Accumulation in Thailand, 1855–1985.* Chiang Mai: Silkworm Books, 1996.

Swan, William L. *Japan's Economic Relations with Thailand: The Rise to 'Top Trader'.* Bangkok: White Lotus, 2009.

Tej Bunnag. *The Provincial Administration of Siam 1892–1915.* Kuala Lumpur: Oxford University Press, 1977.

Terwiel, Barend J. *Through Travellers' Eyes: An Approach to Early Nineteenth Century Thai History.* Bangkok: Editions Duang Kamol, 1989.

Textor, Robert B. *From Peasant to Pedicab Driver: A Social Study of Northeastern Farmers Who Periodically Migrated to Bangkok and Became Pedicab Drivers.* Yale University Southeast Asia Studies, 1961.

Thai University Research Associates (TURA). *Urbanization in the Bangkok Central Region.* Bangkok: The Social Science Association of Thailand, 1976.

Thailand. Board of Commercial Development, Ministry of Commerce. "Monograph on Sugar in Siam". In *The Record.* Bangkok: Board of Commercial Development, 1922.

————. Board of Commercial Development, Ministry of Commerce and Communications. "A Survey of the Resources of Siam with a Review of the Foreign Trade and Commerce of the Country during the Reign of His Majesty Rama VI (1910–25)". In *The Record.* Bangkok: Board of Commercial Development, 1926.

Thailand. Department of Mineral Resource, Ministry of Industry. *Mineral Statistics of Thailand.* Various years.

Thailand. Ministry of Commerce and Communications. *Siam: Nature and Industry.* Bangkok: Bangkok Times Press, 1930.

Thailand. Office of the Financial Adviser, Ministry of Finance. *Report of Financial Advisor on the Budget of the Kingdom of Siam.* Various years.

Thailand. Office of the Prime Minister. *Foreign Records of the Bangkok Period up to 1932.* Bangkok, 1982.

Thailand. *Statistical Yearbook of the Kingdom of Siam* (Title Varied). Bangkok, various years.

Thailand Yearbook. Bangkok: Rung Ruang Publishing Office, various years.

Thak Chaloemtiarana. *Thailand: The Politics of Despotic Paternalism.* Cornell Southeast Asia Publication, 2007.

Thompson, Virginia. Labor Problems in Southeast Asia. New Haven: Yale University Press, 1947.

————. *Thailand: The New Siam.* New York: Macmillan, 1967.

Torres, Doryane K. et al. *Atlas of Thailand: Spatial Structures and Development*. Chiang Mai: Silkworm Books, 2004.

Tsuneishi, Takao. "Thailand's Economic Cooperation with Neighbouring Countries and Its Effects on Economic Development within Thailand". IDE Discussion Paper no. 115 (2007).

———. "Development of Border Economic Zones in Thailand: Expansion of Border Trade and Formation of Border Economic Zones". IDE Discussion Paper no. 153 (2008).

Ueda, Yoko. *Local Economy and Entrepreneurship in Thailand: A Case Study of Nakhon Ratchasima*. Kyoto: Kyoto University Press, 2000.

United States Operations Mission (USOM). *Economic Survey of the Korat–Nongkai Highway Area*. Bangkok: USOM Thailand, 1960.

Usher, D. "Wages, Land Rents and Land Prices and Interest Rates". Document from Thailand Information Centre, Chulalongkorn University, n.d.

van der Meer, Cornelis L.J. *Rural Development in Northern Thailand: An Interpretation and Analysis*. Groningen: Krips Repro Neppel, 1981.

Vella, Walter F. *Siam under Rama III, 1824–1851*. New York: J.J. Austin Incorporated Publishers Locust Valler, 1957.

Visid Prachuabmoh and Penporn Tirasawas. "Internal Migration in Thailand, 1947–1972". Research Paper no. 7. Institute of Population Studies, Chulalongkorn University, 1974.

Visit Achayanongit. "Inter-Relation between Friendship Highway and the Parallel Railway". Master thesis, Asian Institute of Technology, 1971.

Whyte, Brendan R. *The Railway Atlas of Thailand, Laos and Cambodia*. Bangkok: White Lotus, 2012.

Wilson, Constance M. *Thailand: A Handbook of Historical Statistics*. Boston: G.K. Hall & Co., 1983.

———. "Bangkok in 1883: An Economic and Social Profile". *Journal of the Siam Society* 77, no. 2 (1989): 49–58.

World Bank. *Growth and Employment in Rural Thailand*. Washington, D.C.: 1983.

———. *Thailand: Northeast Economic Development Report*. Washington, D.C.: 2005.

Wright, Arnold and Oliver T. Breakspear, eds. *Twentieth Century Impression of Siam: Its History, People, and Resources*. Bangkok: White Lotus, 1908, reprinted 1994.

Yoshihara, Kunio. *Japanese Investment in Southeast Asia*. Honolulu: University Press of Hawaii, 1978.

Zimmerman, Carle C. *Siam: Rural Economic Survey, 1930–31*. Bangkok: Bangkok Times Press, 1931.

———. *Siam: Rural Economic Survey, 1930–31*. Bangkok: White Lotus, reprinted 1999.

INDEX

Note: Page numbers followed with "n" refer to footnotes.

ABOUT THE AUTHOR

PORPHANT OUYYANONT is Associate Professor of Economics at Sukhothai Thammathirat Open University, Thailand. He obtained his doctorate in Economic History from the University of New England, Australia, and has published widely on Thai Economic History focusing on Bangkok, the village economy, and the Crown Property Bureau in Thailand. His Thai-language publications include *The Village Economy in the Central Region of Thailand* (2003), *The Thai Economy during the Reign of King Prajadhipok* (2015), and *A Regional Economic History of Thailand* (2015). He has been a visiting scholar at Kyoto University Center for Southeast Asian Studies in Japan and the ISEAS – Yusof Ishak Institute in Singapore (formerly the Institute of Southeast Asian Studies).

CPSIA information can be obtained
at www.ICGtesting.com
Printed in the USA
BVHW040821120919
558263BV00011B/70/P

9 789814 786126